Praise for *Cooperation and Social Justice*

"With clarity, compassion, and keen insight, Joseph Heath stands conventional assumptions on their head to offer new ways of understanding and responding to seemingly intractable problems of social justice. By turns provocative, intriguing, and inspiring (and sometimes all three at once), this book will challenge you to change the way you think about the leading policy issues of our day."
  Carolyn Hughes Tuohy, Professor Emeritus of Political Science, Munk School of Global Affairs and Public Policy, University of Toronto

"*Cooperation and Social Justice* comprises six brilliant essays on contemporary political controversies by one of the very best political philosophers. On topics such as immigration and border control, race relations in the United States, and egalitarianism, Joseph Heath skillfully isolates the important theoretical questions raised and forcefully and persuasively defends a position which is novel. His writing is accessible to serious readers in any field, a model for all of us thinking about contemporary politics. The opening essay on the scalability of cooperative solutions – a gem – raises the fundamental but neglected question of scale. Recommended for anyone interested in contemporary politics."
  Christopher Morris, Professor Emeritus of Philosophy, University of Maryland

"This excellent and wide-ranging book offers an insightful treatment of the importance of justice and maintaining social cooperation. Heath argues that much political philosophy fails to grapple with the complexities of cooperation and he provides provocative suggestions about the considerations that should guide the feasible pursuit of social justice in various domains. Even when it courts controversy, Heath's analysis is stimulating, informative, and challenging."
  Colin Macleod, Professor of Philosophy and Law, University of Victoria

"In his impressive and lucid book, Joseph Heath redirects our thinking about egalitarian justice. For such justice can only be achieved through social and political cooperation, and so we must deal with the many difficulties of achieving such cooperation in modern, complex societies. The insights we gain from this superb treatise are multiple, and they invite debate not just about realizing justice, but also about its very meaning."
  Rainer Forst, Professor of Political Theory and Philosophy, Goethe University Frankfurt/Main

"In this rigorous and iconoclastic book, Joseph Heath brings social scientific understanding to bear on a wide range of pressing topics in current politics and political philosophy from socialism to immigration. No reader will be persuaded by everything, but all will find their thinking productively challenged. Throughout, Heath treats the liberal order, the democratic state, and the market economy as complex institutions of large-scale societies rather than as mere applications of ordinary moral intuitions, and forces the reader to see how important that distinction really is."

Jacob T. Levy, Professor of Political Science,
McGill University

Cooperation and Social Justice

JOSEPH HEATH

UNIVERSITY OF TORONTO PRESS
Toronto Buffalo London

© University of Toronto Press 2022
Toronto Buffalo London
utorontopress.com

ISBN 978-1-4875-0857-9 (cloth)   ISBN 978-1-4875-3853-8 (EPUB)
ISBN 978-1-4875-2595-8 (paper)   ISBN 978-1-4875-3852-1 (PDF)

Library and Archives Canada Cataloguing in Publication

Title: Cooperation and social justice / Joseph Heath.
Names: Heath, Joseph, 1967–, author.
Description: Includes bibliographical references and index.
Identifiers: Canadiana (print) 20220211736 | Canadiana (ebook) 20220211752 |
    ISBN 9781487508579 (cloth) | ISBN 9781487525958 (paper) |
    ISBN 9781487538538 (EPUB) | ISBN 9781487538521 (PDF)
Subjects: LCSH: Social justice. | LCSH: Cooperation. | LCSH: Equality.
Classification: LCC HM671 .H43 2022 | DDC 303.3/72 – dc23

Cover image by June Clark.

We wish to acknowledge the land on which the University of Toronto Press operates. This land is the traditional territory of the Wendat, the Anishnaabeg, the Haudenosaunee, the Métis, and the Mississauga of the Credit First Nation.

This book has been published with the help of a grant from the Federation for the Humanities and Social Sciences, through the Awards to Scholarly Publications Program, using funds provided by the Social Sciences and Humanities Research Council of Canada.

University of Toronto Press acknowledges the financial support of the Government of Canada, the Canada Council for the Arts, and the Ontario Arts Council, an agency of the Government of Ontario, for its publishing activities.

 Canada Council for the Arts Conseil des Arts du Canada

For Alice, still

Contents

List of Figures   ix

Acknowledgments   xi

Introduction   3

1 On the Scalability of Cooperative Structures   12

2 Why Profit Is Not the Problem   65

3 Egalitarianism and Status Hierarchy   106

4 A Defence of Stigmatization   163

5 A Unified Theory of Border Control and Reasonable Accommodation   200

6 Two Dilemmas for US Race Relations   252

Bibliography   315

Index   339

Figures

1.1 Scalability profile of an institution   23
1.2 More vs. less scalable institution   24
1.3 Three institutional forms   38
1.4 Transition points between institutional forms   46
1.5 Developmental trajectory   57

Acknowledgments

Each of the chapters in this collection is concerned with an issue that I have spent a great deal of time, perhaps a little too much time, thinking about. This explains the major feature they all share, which is that they are substantially longer than the standard academic paper in philosophy. The reason is that, in each case, I had the idea for the paper long ago, but then one thing or another intervened, as a result of which it took me years before I got around to writing anything down. Each paper had a tendency to expand in the interim, as I made more and more mental notes of observations and arguments that merited inclusion. This tendency toward expansion unfortunately continued even after they were written, because being unpublishable in any of the standard journals on account of their length, each paper spent years being presented in various venues and discussed with different audiences.

Through the rather lengthy process involved in the production of these essays, I have accumulated a substantial number of intellectual debts, many of which exceed my powers of recall. I am confident that individual papers presented here benefited from audience response and commentary at conferences and invited lectures at Duke University, Stanford University (twice), Dartmouth College, George Mason University, University of York, McMaster University, Tilburg University, and McGill University. I can also recall some, but probably not all, specific individuals who provided feedback, and in many cases forced me to think harder about particular issues. I would therefore like to thank (in no particular order): Abraham Singer, Huub Brouwer, David Wong, Geoffrey Brennan, Daniel Silver, Martin O'Neill, Hasko von Kriegstein, Shruta Swarup, Joel Anderson, Stefan Gosepath, Andrew Potter, Pablo Gilabert, Wayne Norman, Rutger Claassen, Bruno Verbeek, Lisa Herzog, Waheed Hussain, Barrie Maguire, David Laitin, Jessica Flanigan,

Arthur Ripstein, Robin Hanson, Amy Allen, Max Pensky, Kevin Olson, and John Judis.

None of the chapters that appear in this volume have been published before. However, chapter 2 does include some lightly revised material that has appeared in two other chapters: "The Moral Status of Profit," in *Oxford Handbook of Ethics and Economics*, ed. Mark D. White (Oxford: Oxford University Press, 2019), 337–57; and "Public-Sector Management Is Complicated: Comment on Farrell," in *Nomos LX: Privatization*, ed. Jack Knight and Melissa Schwartzberg (New York: NYU Press, 2018), 200–22. As well, a popularized and radically shortened version of chapter 6 was published as "Why Are Racial Problems in the United States so Intractable?," *American Affairs* 5, no. 3 (2021): 157–84.

Thanks are owed to Len Husband at University of Toronto Press for having taken on the project and shepherding it through publication. I would also like to thank two more-than-ordinarily diligent readers for the press, whose comments improved the work in multiple ways. Finally, I would like to acknowledge financial support from the Social Sciences and Humanities Research Council of Canada, the Jackman Humanities Institute, as well as the Canada Council for the Arts.

COOPERATION AND SOCIAL JUSTICE

Introduction

One of the clearest points of demarcation between specialist discourses and everyday commentary and debate is that the former are often structured by what might be thought of as "explanatory inversions." These arise as a consequence of discoveries or theoretical insights that change, not our specific explanations of events, but rather our fundamental sense of what needs to be explained. A simple example would be the development of the principle of inertia in our understanding of physical motion. Common sense tells us that objects in motion have a tendency to come to rest, and so in order to keep them moving there must be a constant application of force (hence Aristotle's principle, "No motion without a mover"). Isaac Newton's first law of motion inverted this, by claiming that the tendency of objects in motion is to continue moving until something stops them. Common sense is wrong on this point, because we are fooled by a set of invisible forces – gravity, friction, air resistance – that act upon the objects we are most familiar with. If instead we accept Newton's suggestion, it is not just our understanding of the fundamental properties of matter that changes; our sense of what needs to be explained in physical systems changes. Most importantly, motion no longer needs to be explained, it is only changes in direction or velocity of motion that need to be explained. As a result, the entire approach to physical science is transformed, as scientists wind up focusing on questions that are quite different from those that common sense tells us are in need of response.

These explanatory inversions are perhaps the greatest source of miscommunication and misunderstanding between specialists and members of the general public. The challenge that they create is fairly obvious. It is possible to have productive disagreements and debate among people despite significant differences of opinion over many questions. But the conceptual divide created by an explanatory inversion can be quite difficult to talk across, because those who find themselves on either side of it are seldom even asking the same questions or trying to understand the same things. From the perspective of the public, the stance taken by specialists is often perceived as elitist, since those who have accepted the explanatory inversion usually become interested in talking only to others who "get it," or who understand what the correct questions and problems are. Furthermore, they often have become so comfortable with their way of framing the issues that they forget how unobvious it can be to others and so treat those who fail to grasp it as mentally infirm. At best they may recommend remedial education, which does little to diminish the charge of elitism.

The frictions that may result from the gap between the public and the specialist perspective are a well-known source of hostility toward the physical sciences (particularly evolutionary theory), but they have the potential to become even more explosive when they involve the social sciences. The latter are, of course, the subject of more scepticism across the board, particularly in their claim to have produced a useful or reproducible body of knowledge. Whatever one thinks about this broader question, however, the social sciences have also produced important explanatory inversions. Perhaps the clearest example involves the concept of social deviance in criminology. Common sense tells us that most people, most of the time, obey the law. Crime is an anomaly, and as such, stands in need of explanation. Common sense provides us with a wealth of explanations, which seek to identify the motives that impel people toward criminal acts. But if one stops to examine these motives, as social scientists began to do, the most striking thing about them is how ordinary and ubiquitous they are. For every angry person who commits an assault or greedy person who steals from others, there are hundreds of equally angry, equally greedy people who refrain from doing so. This is what prompted the realization, articulated in the late nineteenth century by Émile Durkheim, that it is not crime that cries out for explanation, but rather law-abidingness. Common sense is wrong on this point because we are all reasonably well-socialized adults, living in a well-ordered society, and so we take for granted the institutional arrangements that secure our compliance with the rules. But the underlying mechanisms are ones that we do not really understand, as a result of which it is difficult to explain why more people do not break the law more often (since it is so often in their interest to do so). Again, there is an explanatory inversion at work, because of the change in our understanding of what needs to be explained.

A similar explanatory inversion has taken place in our understanding of human cooperation. Common sense tells us that if a group of individuals have a shared interest in achieving some goal, it is natural that they will band together to perform the actions needed to realize that outcome. Thus it is natural to assume that, absent some external impediment, interest groups will be disposed to pursue their interests, corporations will pursue their corporate interests, classes will advance their class interests, nations will act in their national interests, and so on. One of the most significant achievements of twentieth-century social science was the realization that such cooperative action is actually more mysterious than it might initially appear. Groups often find themselves caught in what are now known as "collective action problems," where, despite having a common interest in achieving some outcome, no individual in the group has an adequate incentive to perform the actions needed to achieve that outcome, as a result of which the group as a whole will fail to act in its collective interest. And so, as Thomas Schelling put it, the default structure of social interaction lacks any mechanism that "attunes individual responses to some collective accomplishment."[1] It is not failures of cooperation that need to be explained, but rather successful collective action. Common sense is wrong on this point, because we all have the experience of being able to enter into cooperative relations with one another with relative ease. The analysis of collective action problems does not contradict this, it merely gives rise to an explanatory inversion. It suggests that the failure to advance collective goals is the default outcome, and cooperation is what cries out for explanation.

This insight was prefigured in earlier work. Thomas Hobbes's characterization of the state of nature, for example, contained a long list of collective accomplishments that individuals could not be expected to achieve if they just did whatever came most naturally to them. Economists had similarly noted a number of "public goods" that markets and private contracting failed to provide. What the story of the Prisoner's Dilemma, along with the game-theoretic model that accompanied it, did was to drive home the full generality of the problem.[2] Again, the point is not that cooperation is impossible – people obviously cooperate with one another all the time. The point is that, since non-cooperation is the default mode of social interaction, *failures* of cooperation require no special explanation, while successful cooperation is what needs to be explained. Merely pointing out that it is in our interest to cooperate does not discharge the explanatory burden.

Like most explanatory inversions, this insight about cooperation has driven a wedge between certain specialist and non-specialist discourses. Nowhere is this more apparent than in our thinking about social justice. The latter term is often used to draw a distinction between the "formal" type of justice ensured by courts and the more "substantive" conception of justice that deals with what individuals actually wind up receiving, in the form of income, status, health, leisure, and other "good things in life." The most important principle of justice in this domain is equality, and so the centrepiece of any account of social justice will be some conception of distributive justice.

The common sense way of thinking about distributive justice is to treat it like a "cutting the cake" division problem. You have some good, like a cake, and a bunch of people who all want as much as possible, and so the question becomes simply how to divide it among them. The problem with applying this view to society is that the goods that are subject to distribution by a conception of justice do not suddenly appear out of nowhere, the way that a cake does at a birthday party. They are the product of an ongoing system of cooperation. This cooperation is, in turn, difficult to achieve, often requiring a great deal of bargaining and compromise. As a result, it is difficult to apply principles of distributive justice to the outcome without knowing some of the backstory, about how that outcome came to be. It is equally difficult to say anything in a prescriptive vein about whether the outcome should be adjusted, without knowing a great deal more about how this will affect the underlying system of cooperation that produced those results. Trade-offs can easily arise if a particular scheme of redistribution can be expected to impair the effectiveness or stability of the system of cooperation.

An additional layer of complexity is added by the fact that systems of cooperation always have at their core a voluntary element. Although coercion can often be employed to extend the system of cooperation, there is no such thing as a perfect tyranny, or a social system that relies entirely upon coercion to secure compliance. At some level, people must be willing to play along in order for the social structure to be sustainable. A large part of their willingness to play along, however, will be based upon their acceptance of the justice of the overall arrangement, along with their specific place in it. So not only does the need to secure cooperation impose constraints on our conceptions of social justice; considerations of social justice also constrain our ability to institutionalize various schemes of cooperation.

As a result, even though it offends a certain political sensibility to say it, there is a gap between expert and public discourse on questions of social justice, because of the complex relationship between cooperation and principles of distributive justice. The chapters collected in this volume all explore issues that arise at this juncture. I take as my point of departure the basic framework of the most widely shared contemporary conception of justice among political philosophers, the view that is often referred to as liberal egalitarianism. This view can be traced back to arguments made by John Rawls in *A Theory of Justice*. And yet, even though Rawls described society as a "cooperative venture for mutual advantage," and "an ongoing scheme of fair cooperation over time," later theorists have varied considerably in their willingness to take seriously this aspect of Rawls's view.[3] His suggestion was that justice be thought of not in the image of divine law, as a set of cosmic principles that apply everywhere and at all times, but that it be seen rather as arising endogenously out of various schemes of cooperation, both constraining and enabling their formation. This is, in my opinion, his best and most important idea, and the papers in this collection all attempt to extend and apply it in one way or another.

If one could summarize my central conviction on this topic in one phrase, it would be that, although justice is desirable, cooperation is difficult. People have to be persuaded, cajoled, enticed, threatened, reminded, and rewarded in order to get them to do their part. Failures of cooperation are ubiquitous. Successful large-scale cooperation is the exception, not the rule. As a result, our capacity to achieve justice in this world is severely constrained by our limited capacity to organize successful systems of cooperation. This should not diminish our commitment to ideals of justice, or make us overly eager to accept compromise. What it should do, instead, is make us extremely alert to the opportunities that present themselves to improve the achieved level of justice of our society, because they do not arise all that often. It should also make us wary of wasting too much time speculating about utopian arrangements that could never be effectively institutionalized.

Each of the six papers collected here deals with a different normative question. In each, I wind up defending a position that differs from the one that would follow from a naive application of principles of social justice. This is not because I disagree with those principles – on the contrary, I start from the exact same egalitarian premises as those whose views I criticize. The difference is that I worry a great deal more than they do about the difficulty of achieving cooperative outcomes, and therefore I modulate the application of those principles in recognition of these difficulties. Thus the view that I defend, sometimes described as "left Hobbesian," insists on evaluating the justice or injustice of any social arrangement through the explanatory inversion that sees cooperation as a fragile accomplishment. The results may appear contrarian, which in a certain sense they are. I would like to think that they are not *merely* contrarian, but that they arise in a more principled fashion, as a consequence of the explanatory inversion brought about by a modern understanding of the relationship between cooperation and principles of social justice.

The basic structure of my analysis of cooperation is laid out most clearly in chapter 1, "On the Scalability of Cooperative Structures," which is both an extended commentary on G.A. Cohen's argument for socialism and an attempt to articulate a major constraint that human systems of cooperation are subject to. Having formulated an abstract principle of equality, then shown how it can be realized in small group interactions, Cohen goes on to claim that this demonstrates the desirability of a socialist organization of the economy.[4] The only question that remains is one of feasibility: how do we "scale up" the system from a small group to a complex modern economy? Intuitively, we can all understand the idea. And yet the question of why certain sorts of cooperative arrangements are more or less difficult to scale up (i.e., to expand the number of cooperating participants) is seldom posed directly, much less answered. Thus my central objective in the paper is to present an analysis and general way of thinking about institutional scale. A consequence of this analysis, however, is that one cannot posit normative ideals that are independent of the particular scale at which they are to be realized.

The second chapter, "Why Profit Is Not the Problem," is similarly concerned with debates over the feasibility of socialism. A certain fraction of the outrage over the injustices of capitalism stems from a failure to appreciate how difficult the task is that it accomplishes (which is to institutionalize a very, very large-scale division of labour). Another large fraction is due to a lack of understanding of the particular way that markets achieve cooperative outcomes, which is not directly, by requiring individuals to act cooperatively, but rather indirectly, by placing them in a staged competition with one another. As a result, socialists have a tendency to propose alternatives to capitalism, or else improvements, that could never be institutionalized. This shows up repeatedly among those for whom the moral case against capitalism involves denouncing the evils of profit. I try to show why profit cannot be the problem, because any feasible socialist reorganization of the economy would also have to rely on profit as an organizational objective.

I switch gears somewhat in chapter 3, "Egalitarianism and Status Hierarchy," in order to consider an issue that has not been given sufficient attention by egalitarians, particularly those who are concerned about distributive justice. There is widespread recognition that the attempt to realize equality occurs against significant background inequality. Much of it is socially produced, but some of it is "natural," in the sense that it involves different capacities and propensities that individuals are born with. Thus egalitarians have worried a great deal about what to do with individuals with limited "talent." What I focus on here, by contrast, is the socially produced form of inequality conventionally referred to as status inequality. Egalitarians over the years have engaged in much wishful thinking about the possibility of abolishing this form of inequality. I begin therefore by reviewing some of the reasons for thinking that it will never be eliminated. This then raises a number of questions for egalitarians: first about how to situate the phenomenon of status inequality with respect to an egalitarian theory of justice, and then what to do about it, under the assumption that it cannot simply be abolished. These are both very basic questions, neither of which has been dealt with adequately in the philosophical literature. The second question is also very difficult to answer. Thus the central ambition of the chapter, apart from broaching the issue and offering some preliminary clarifications, is to suggest that egalitarians should be a great deal more troubled by the persistence of status inequality than they are.

Closely related to the phenomenon of status is that of stigmatization. This term is often used by academics in a way that conveys their own disapproval, as though it were always wrong to stigmatize others. The reality is a bit more complicated, in that condemnation is usually reserved for cases in which the stigma is associated with unchosen traits. With chosen traits, by contrast, there is less hesitation in applying stigma, especially if the behaviour is injurious to others. What I am interested in, in chapter 4, "A Defence of Stigmatization," is a class of cases in which the stigmatization of behaviour is controversial, despite the fact that the behaviour is clearly chosen, or subject to voluntary control. The most interesting cases involve acts that are self-destructive or self-undermining, where the perpetration involves some kind of self-control failure. One of the claims I have made, over the years, is that self-control should be seen not as a purely private matter, but as an achievement that often involves the cooperation of others. One way that people help one another is by helping each other to avoid self-control failures. Stigmatization can be an important element of this system. Thus I offer a qualified defence of stigmatization, on the grounds that de-stigmatization can exacerbate self-control failure and therefore undermine an important system of cooperation.

In chapter 5, "A Unified Theory of Border Control and Reasonable Accommodation," I turn to two questions that have been the subject of extensive debate in recent political philosophy: migration and multiculturalism. The first involves the question of what right states have to exclude prospective immigrants, while the second asks what accommodations must be made for those who are admitted. These two issues are usually dealt with separately in the philosophical literature, and so the most obvious contribution of this paper is that I deal with them jointly, using a shared normative framework. That framework is based on a single idea, which is that the economy must be understood as a system of cooperation. What migrants are asking for is not a change of scenery, but rather for admission to a successful cooperative scheme. The question of accommodation concerns how that system must be changed, or not changed, in order to incorporate these new members. Thus the idea of social cooperation provides basic orientation for thinking about both questions.

In the final chapter, "Two Dilemmas for US Race Relations," I discuss race relations in the United States. The baseline perspective I adopt, which informs the entire discussion, is that social integration in complex societies does not arise spontaneously. It is difficult to achieve. The presence of highly salient group differences within the society makes it even more challenging. As a result, there are few successful models of pluralistic integration. What one sees, looking around the world, are a large number of minor variations on the two or three basic strategies that work. The reason that the problem of black-white race relations in the United States never goes away is that Americans have been attempting to achieve a model of integration that does not fit into any of the standard templates. Thus my first objective is to encourage Americans to look at this problem from a more comparative perspective, in order to see why their approach to the problem has had so little success. My second objective is to articulate a set of dilemmas that prevent Americans from adopting one of the standard models. This is not offered in the expectation that it will make much difference to the situation in the United States. It is provided primarily as a cautionary lesson for non-Americans, especially Canadians, who have been tempted to reformulate many of the issues that have traditionally been dealt with under the rubric of multiculturalism into the American language of race (through the racialization of ethnic differences). This is puzzling on multiple levels, the most obvious being that it takes the conceptual framework associated with a policy that has a proven track record of failure and substitutes it for one that has a reasonable record of success.

NOTES

1 Thomas Schelling, *Micromotives and Macrobehavior* (New York: W.W. Norton, 1978), 32.

2 Russell Hardin, *Collective Action* (Baltimore, MD: Johns Hopkins University Press, 1982).
3 John Rawls, *A Theory of Justice*, rev. ed. (Cambridge, MA: Harvard University Press, 1999), 4; Rawls, *Justice as Fairness* (Cambridge, MA: Harvard University Press, 2001), 54.
4 G.A. Cohen, *Why Not Socialism?* (Princeton, NJ: Princeton University Press, 2009).

Chapter One

On the Scalability of Cooperative Structures

One of the oldest debates in social and political philosophy involves the question of whether humans are naturally suited for social life, or whether our individualistic tendencies are such that social order is a precarious and unstable achievement. Put in the crudest terms, are we more like bees (as Plato claimed), eager to sacrifice ourselves for the hive, or like wolves (as Thomas Hobbes imagined), fundamentally aggressive and at best loyal to the pack? The answer has proven elusive, partly because, when examined biologically, we seem to have more in common with wolves, and yet, when examined sociologically, it is obvious that we engage in a variety of interaction patterns that are seldom observed outside the order of the social insects. For example, the fact that we allow genetically unrelated individuals to care for our children, even briefly, is a pattern of behaviour that is practically unknown in the animal kingdom. That we do so routinely is a phenomenon that cries out for explanation, and yet such an explanation has proven elusive. This is, in part, because with other eusocial species, there is a relatively clear biological explanation for the behaviour. Humans, by contrast, have a reproductive biology that does not distinguish us in any significant way from other primates. And yet our closest primate relatives are notoriously unable to sustain anything resembling complex systems of cooperation.[1]

When it comes to our basic social psychology, Immanuel Kant summed up the essential ambivalence of human nature quite well with his claim that we exhibit an "unsocial sociability." We have, on the one hand, a set of instincts that are clearly "pro-social" in their orientation, which is to say, that favour the development of systems of cooperation. Our psychological openness to others, including our ability to feel sympathy, our capacity for joint attention, the innate "theory of mind" that we deploy in social interaction, as well as our facility at building social relations based on reciprocal altruism, all tend to promote cooperation.

We are, for example, by nature much more cooperative than chimpanzees (as empirical studies have demonstrated, such as the greater propensity to engage in spontaneous "helping behaviour" among human infants).[2] At the same time, we have a strong and persistent tendency to behave in ways that undermine cooperation, not just through individualistic forms of defection, but also through moralized patterns of behaviour, such as tit-for-tat retaliation, that can lock people into cycles of increasingly destructive interpersonal aggression. And while the old saying that humans are the only species that kill one another for pleasure is not true, there remains the fact that warfare has been a major curse afflicting human societies throughout our history, and as far as anyone can tell, our prehistory.[3] Thus it is clearly not correct to claim, as some have done, that we are "good natured."[4] And yet, given our nature, we have managed to get along surprisingly well, particularly in the past few centuries, in which we have constructed some far-ranging and robust systems of cooperation.

This puzzle is, of course, one of the most difficult in the human sciences, and certainly not one that will be resolved here. What I would like to do, instead, is introduce a concept to the discussion that I believe has the potential to elucidate several aspects in an extremely helpful way. The concept is that of "scalability." It is drawn from the computer science literature, where it refers rather generally to the capacity of a system to take on increased workload by integrating additional resources (i.e., to "scale up") without suffering degradation of performance. For example, the basic architecture of a computer includes an addressing system (using numbers to name each location in memory) that has an upper limit. On occasion the demands put on the system will bump up against this limit – a phenomenon that some users experienced with the architecture of thirty-two-bit computer systems, where the number of memory addresses was limited to 2^{32}. This meant that one could increase the power of the system in a fairly linear fashion by adding more physical memory, but only up to four gigabytes, at which point the system would have to use swaps to access the higher memory, resulting in a degradation of the rate of increased performance. Thus the system lacked scalability, eventually generating the need to scrap the thirty-two-bit architecture entirely and replace it with sixty-four-bit systems. The latter have 2^{64} addresses, which is so far beyond the needs of any current applications that, for now, such systems exhibit perfect scalability – any additional demand for memory can be satisfied simply by plugging in more chips.

The same concept can be applied in the domain of social interaction to systems of cooperation. Every system of cooperation is sustained by a particular institutional structure, which promotes cooperative behaviour and discourages defection. A particular structure is *scalable* to the extent that it can incorporate an increase in the number of individuals participating, while maintaining roughly constant average levels of cooperative behaviour. My central contention in this chapter will be that our evolved psychology provides us with a set of pro-social psychological dispositions that can be used rather effortlessly to establish small-scale systems of cooperation, but that the fundamental architecture of these systems lacks scalability. In other words, the systems that we are "naturally" disposed to create, or that we can manage using onboard cognitive resources, have something like an upper bound on the number of cooperators, so that as one adds new individuals to the system, its performance (which is to say, its capacity to sustain cooperative behaviour) begins to degrade.[5] This is what accounts for many of the phenomena associated with our "unsocial sociability." Various behavioural dispositions we have, which are pro-social in small groups, start to become increasingly antisocial as the size of the group increases. This puts an upper bound on the level of social complexity that can be sustained using those resources. It is only when the system is reorganized, and a new institutional structure is put in place, that cooperation can be further expanded.

The underlying idea here, it should be noted, is not new. What I am providing, rather, is a more perspicuous vocabulary for describing a phenomenon that has already been given considerable emphasis by, among others, Émile Durkheim in his analysis of mechanical solidarity, as well as Peter Richerson and Robert Boyd in their explanation of our "tribal social instincts."[6] In order to organize the discussion, I would like to focus on an issue where scalability has played a central role in political philosophy: in debates over the feasibility of socialism.[7] A central feature of the socialist project has been the desire to eliminate the competitiveness of the market economy and to replace it with a more directly cooperative economic order. This is often based on a set of moral ideas that are intuitively quite appealing in small-scale interactions. The question is whether or not institutions organized in accordance with these principles can be "scaled up" to the level of society as a whole, to govern a complex division of labour. These issues are put into rather stark relief in the work of G.A. Cohen, and so I will use it as a focal point for the discussion that follows.

1. Why Not Socialism?

G.A. Cohen's short book *Why Not Socialism?* is in many ways a curious work. Perhaps the biggest surprise is that Cohen answers his own question – indeed, the title of the book might easily have been the simple declarative: *Why Not Socialism*.[8] Cohen sets out to articulate the norms that inform the socialist project. In the service of this ambition, he asks the reader to imagine an idealized "camping trip," along with the principles that would govern relations among the individuals who participate. "People cooperate with a common concern that, so far as is possible, everybody has a roughly similar opportunity to flourish, and also to relax, on condition that she contributes, appropriately to her capacity, to the flourishing and relaxation of others."[9] He characterizes this as "the socialist way," involving a combination of "collective property and planned mutual giving."[10]

This is, of course, perfectly fine as an account of the prevailing norms on a camping trip. But to claim, as Cohen does, that it provides the moral basis for socialism as well raises the immediate question whether it is possible to take the norms of solidarity and equality that govern informal, face-to-face interactions among people who are on a first-name basis, and to project those norms onto society as a whole, to govern legally regulated, anonymous interactions among strangers – since this is what would be required in order to have a socialist society along the principles that Cohen articulates. Cohen acknowledges the difficulty this presents: "One may ... not infer, from the fact that camping trips of the sort that I have described are feasible and desirable, that society-wide socialism is equally feasible and equally desirable. There are too many major differences between the contexts for that inference to carry any conviction."[11] And yet, when it comes time to address this issue – and in particular, to explain how individual freedom or "personal choice" could be reconciled with equality in the larger society – Cohen simply punts the ball down the field. After describing a variety of market socialist schemes, which rely upon competitive exchange rather than "mutual giving," Cohen acknowledges that "the camping trip's confined temporal, spatial, and population scale mean that, within its confines, the right to personal choice can be exercised, without strain, consistently with equality and community. But while that can happen in the small, we do not know how to honor personal choice, consistently with equality and community, on a large social scale."[12] His only consolation is to point out that, even if we do not know how to reconcile this, "I do not think that we now know that we will never know how to do these things."[13] Given that the book is dedicated to the topic, this is a surprisingly tepid defence of the feasibility of socialism.

The other surprising aspect of this response is how little Cohen has to say about the more general problem. After all, it is not as though the argument is new. Concerns about the "feasibility and desirability" of extending norms that govern small-group interactions to the organization of society as a whole have been a familiar objection to socialism since at least 1879, when John Stuart Mill's "Chapters on Socialism" were published.[14] Similarly, Friedrich Hayek's well-known critique of socialism rested centrally upon the claim that the transition from a small-scale society, in which "small groups of people served known fellows for common purposes," to a complex economy with a "worldwide division of labor," would be impossible without a "change in morals."[15] It is strange that Cohen would accept, in almost the exact terms, Hayek's characterization of the natural locus of socialist moral intuitions, without considering the way that Hayek went on to use this as an argument *against* socialism.

It would also be surprising, to say the least, if our ability to respond to the "feasibility and desirability" question had not improved at all over the course of the past century and a half. In particular, it is hard to believe that the history of "actually existing socialism" could have taught us nothing in this regard, especially given the level of intellectual energy expended by several generations of Eastern Europeans grappling with these issues. Indeed, it is precisely because of this history that many of Cohen's critics, such as Richard Arneson, take it as practically self-evident that the norms of the camping trip are inappropriate to a larger society. As Arneson remarks, "It would be unwise to organize the economy as one big pot from which people may take what they think they need and to which they may contribute what they think they ought to contribute according to their own lights, freely and spontaneously. This vision of voluntary frictionless social cooperation would, with people as they are, swiftly turn into a nightmare."[16]

The term "nightmare" is appropriate, given the millions of people who died during the twentieth century in the various attempts to reorganize societies along socialist principles. But in order to avoid rehashing old debates, it is perhaps helpful to focus on a smaller, less controversial example of the sort of concern that animates Arneson's criticism. Between 1929 and 1933, it is estimated that over half of the livestock in the Soviet Union was killed, mostly as a consequence of passive resistance by peasants to the collectivization of agriculture. This included 15.3 million horses, 24.7 million cattle, 69.8 million sheep and goats, and 9.5 million pigs.[17] Soviet planners made a terrible mistake in believing that they could just amalgamate the basic units of agricultural production and expect the new farms to sustain the same level of output in the aggregate (much less realize economies of scale). Many farmers, it turned out, would rather kill their cow and eat the meat than share the milk with their neighbours. The lesson learned – at enormous cost – is that one cannot just take the motives that sustain the family farm and transfer them over to a village farm. In the terms being used here, the form of solidarity that sustained small-scale agricultural production within these communities turned out not to be *scalable*.

One need not insist that we will *never* know "how to do these things," in order to agree that several major, concerted attempts to do them failed, and that this should increase our prior probability estimate that they are not doable. One might also think that we owe it to the millions of human beings who lost their lives, as a consequence of these failures, to try to learn something from their fate. Cohen's refusal to take these issues seriously, it should be noted, was not just a matter of his personal politics. It was also encouraged by his philosophical method, which involved isolating and articulating principles of justice in a context completely divorced from all empirical facts about people or the world. He emphatically rejects Rousseau's dictum that we must take people as they are and laws as they might be (or Rawls's suggestion, that we must make certain "concessions to human nature" in formulating principles of justice[18]). Cohen instead sets out to define what we might describe as rules for the kingdom of normativland – a hypothetical state in which everyone behaves exactly as required, and where mere facts, including facts of human psychology, exercise no constraint on the formulation of normative principles. This is utopia in the literal sense – a place that does not exist. It is a methodologically necessary postulate, in Cohen's view, because we must imagine such a scenario in order to prevent our normative principles from becoming contaminated by merely empirical considerations. (Most importantly, if we allow any of the traditional concerns over "limited altruism" to intrude, then this may give some people licence to "blackmail" others, by refusing to act cooperatively unless they get a greater share.)[19]

Cohen is, of course, perfectly aware that after moral principles have been chosen they must subsequently be institutionalized. For example, one rule that is generally thought to prevail in normativland is that people should always act cooperatively and never free ride. They should be willing to work hard for the public weal, regardless of whether they derive any personal benefit from their labour ("from each according to his ability"). Yet in the world that we live in, incentives are generally required to motivate people to work, especially when the benefits accrue to others. We typically express this by saying that these moral principles of contribution must be *institutionalized*. Cohen says very little about what would be required in order to effectively institutionalize his principles. He is not alone in this regard. There is relatively little discussion of this issue in the philosophical literature.[20] It may be helpful therefore to canvass some of the functions that institutions perform. What follows is a non-exhaustive list:

1. *Motivation.* The most commonly cited feature of institutions is that they supply individuals with the motivation to act morally where it is lacking. Because morality often conflicts with self-interest, and not everyone always assigns priority to the former, individuals must often be given some extrinsic incentive to act morally. This can take the form of either a reward for acting correctly, or a punishment for acting incorrectly (the two are generally referred to, somewhat confusingly, as "sanctions" by sociologists).[21] It is also worth noting that many individuals start out lacking an intrinsic motive to act morally, and so social institutions must inculcate appropriate attitudes – a task that is generally referred to as *socialization*. One might be inclined to describe this as a separate function of institutions, except that the application of sanctions, under the correct circumstances, is widely thought to have a socializing influence, particularly upon the young. Thus the creation of complementary intrinsic and extrinsic motives for conformity to norms is often regarded as a single, complex function of social institutions. Typically, the ambition is to accomplish as much as possible through socialization, and then make up for whatever deficiencies of intrinsic motivation may remain through the application of extrinsic sanctions.
2. *Information.* The implementation of norms necessarily requires information, primarily so that individuals can determine whether the norms have been satisfied (necessary both for actors, to ascertain their obligations, and observers, to regulate the application of sanctions). Many normative principles are informationally quite demanding. The utilitarian calculus, for instance, famously requires not just a measure of individual happiness, but a way of making meaningful interpersonal comparisons of happiness levels. Egalitarian theories, as well, require some basis for comparison across individuals, because in order to determine whether people are equal, with respect to some *equalisandum*, one must be able to say how much of it they have. Cohen's demand that individuals have "equal access to advantage," for instance, requires some method of measuring how much advantage each person receives, in several different dimensions, then some way of aggregating across these dimensions.[22] One key step required to implement this would therefore involve specifying which dimensions one is actually in

a position to measure (e.g., income, leisure), and which ones are, for practical purposes, unmeasurable (e.g., social status, romantic satisfaction). One might also choose measurable *proxies* for dimensions that are unmeasurable. In the end, the type of equality that one wound up promoting institutionally would likely be only a very coarse approximation of the type of equality that one regarded as morally important, because there would not be enough information available to achieve a closer approximation.

3. *Specification.* Moral values or principles are often articulated at a very high level of abstraction, such that they cannot serve as guides to action without some further specification. In order to act upon a motive of "benevolence," for instance, one must determine what is to *count* as benevolence. In order to promote "equality," one must answer all sorts of questions about what we should be seeking to equalize, and in which domains. One important function of our institutions is to provide such specifications. For example, in his camping trip scenario, Cohen gives a variety of examples of actions individuals might perform that count as "contributing" to the group effort.[23] In so doing, he is relying upon a tacit set of institutional specifications, which stipulate that "fishing" counts as a contribution (assuming that it produces food for the group), while "whittling a stick" probably does not, and "singing" may or may not, depending upon whether it is done for the enjoyment of others, or whether it has that effect. Part of the reason that institutions must provide these specifications, and not just individual actors, is that disagreements may arise that require definitive resolution – for instance, those who owe a duty of benevolence to others may claim that a particular action satisfies that obligation, while the supposed beneficiaries of the action may deny that it does (consider, for instance, the practice of praying for the sick).

4. *Coordination.* Even after abstract duties have been fully specified, there may still be the need for coordination among individuals. Most obviously, imperfect duties may need to be translated into perfect duties. "Give money to the homeless" does not say which specific homeless person one should give money to. And naturally, there is reason to want to avoid something like the "Baby Jessica" outcome, where thousands of people donate money to the child who happens to fall down a well, resulting in a lavish trust fund for that one child, while the greater needs of many others go unmet. There is a lot to be said for having a system of rules that specifies in greater detail exactly who owes what to whom. Or in the case of

Cohen's camping trip, after the abstract concept of "contribution" gets specified as "fishing," "chopping wood," "cooking dinner," "cleaning up," and so forth, there is a need to assign one person to each of these tasks (or, more generally, a mechanism for deciding who will perform which task). Thus institutions discharge the important function of dividing up among individuals the tasks that are required to satisfy the abstract norms.

5. *Role differentiation*. Individuals who comply with institutional expectations, as specified in the previous four ways, can be confident that the way they are acting constitutes "the right thing to do," even absent that institutional specification. However, some institutions impose a "division of moral labour" in the strong sense of the term, which goes beyond the mere coordination of effort and involves setting up a complex dynamic whereby the morally desirable outcome emerges only out of the interaction of several individuals, none of whom necessarily intends that outcome. Institutions may impose what are often referred to as *role obligations*. An individual who conforms to such an obligation may wind up acting in a way that would not be "the right thing to do," absent that institutional context. This is common in cases where tasks are delegated (e.g., to soldiers or police officers), but is especially apparent in institutions that have an adversarial structure. A typical trial procedure provides an excellent example, where even though the overall objective is to secure an outcome that is just from an impartial point of view, attorneys for both the prosecution and the defence are expected to be highly partial to only one side and to make that case as vigorously as possible. This may commit individuals to acting in ways that seem wrong prima facie (e.g., striving to secure the acquittal of someone who one believes to be guilty of murder), but are right when performed in the appropriate institutional context.

There are several things worth noting about this list. The first is that all of these different aspects of implementation are interconnected, and so the way that an institution solves a challenge in one dimension will often have implications for all the others (just as changes in one dimension may impose adjustments in others). For example, a lot of the information that may be required to satisfy a particular principle will be private, known only to individuals (such as anything having to do with preferences or welfare). Much of the implementation challenge will involve getting this private information and somehow making it publicly available. Typically, the only way to do this will be to give individuals some incentive to reveal it. When it comes to doing so, however, intrinsic incentives may prove much more successful than extrinsic ones. In other words, if one can motivate people to be honest in their reports, one is likely to be more successful at getting accurate information than if one can only threaten to punish misrepresentation. Designing external incentive schemes to reward truthful disclosure (so-called revelation mechanisms) is not impossible, but is often quite difficult. But as a result, if there is a shift within an institution away from intrinsic toward extrinsic motivation, this may affect the quality of the information that is available to participants and may in turn affect the ability of the institution to effectively coordinate tasks among individuals. One could easily develop more examples in this vein, showing how changes in any one dimension could have knock-on effects that would promote changes in any other dimension. Thus any stable institution should be regarded as being in a complex equilibrium among these different requirements.

The second thing worth noting is that any one of these aspects of implementation could be sensitive to *scale* (i.e., when the institution is called upon to integrate the actions of more people). A system that works well to coordinate the actions of 10 people might not work as well to coordinate the actions of 100. Information that is easy to obtain in small groups, among people who know one another well, may be more difficult to obtain in a larger group, among individuals who do not directly or repeatedly interact with one another. Socialization processes that work in intimate settings may become ineffective in large groups. Again, the examples could easily be multiplied. Furthermore, because all of these different dimensions are interconnected, even one that happens not to be directly sensitive to scale could easily be indirectly affected by another that is, and so changes in the scale of an institution could affect its performance in every dimension.

One of the most commonly noted changes that does occur in institutions as their scale increases is a general shift away from intrinsic towards extrinsic motivation. For now we can leave this as a folk-sociological generalization, although I will have more to say later about reasons for thinking it true. It should be noted that Cohen is presupposing this, tacitly, when he asks whether it would be "feasible and desirable" to move from the camping trip to "society-wide socialism." If one understands "feasible" to mean simply "not impossible," then there are not many things that are completely infeasible – although it is worth noting that intrinsic and extrinsic sanctions are not perfect substitutes for one another, and there are limits to how much cooperative behaviour one can elicit from people by threatening them. Nevertheless, one can certainly *imagine* organizing all of society like a giant camping trip. The real question is whether that would be desirable. And, of course, the reason that Cohen – and many other people – think it might not be is that, since moral suasion is most effective in small groups, as one increases the scale of the endeavour one must rely more heavily on extrinsic incentives. This is a somewhat euphemistic way of saying that society-wide socialism would have to make rather extensive use of coercion, in order to maintain reasonable levels of compliance, and indeed, so much coercion that it might in fact vitiate the entire project – or turn it into, as Arneson suggests, "a nightmare."

Thus the concept of "feasibility" does not contribute much to the discussion, while the concept of "desirability" is one that Cohen leaves underspecified. The notion of "scalability" can be introduced as a way of articulating more precisely the idea that there are both costs and benefits involved in expanding an institution, and thus, as a way of making the "desirability" question more tractable. If we focus on institutions that promote some scheme of cooperation, then we can represent the scalability of a particular institutional structure as determined by the marginal costs and benefits of integrating a new individual into the system. Naturally, a key determinant of those costs and benefits will be whether the system is actually capable of eliciting cooperative behaviour from that person, or whether the new entrant comes and free-rides on the efforts of the others. Important sources of benefit, from a new entrant, will be not just the additional effort that a person is able to bring to various tasks, but also whatever amplification of effort is made possible if there are, for instance, economies of scale in the cooperative project. The important sources of cost will be, first, whatever additional resources must be invested in trying to secure cooperation (e.g., time and energy spent socializing new entrants, resources dedicated to imposing extrinsic sanctions, etc.), and second, the costs caused by any *failure* to integrate new entrants (e.g., losses due to shirking, dishonesty, crime, etc.). The latter includes not just the direct costs of free-riding, but also whatever losses are caused by the disruptive effects that such deviance can have (e.g., some of those who had previously been cooperating may switch to defection, upon observing others doing so).

Figure 1.1 shows the general trajectory that many institutions will have (where the y axis represents the net benefit/cost that an additional individual brings to the cooperative scheme, as a function of the number of individuals, n, currently in the scheme). The cooperative scheme depicted is one that is not worth doing until some threshold number of participants is achieved. Once that point is reached, the benefits to increased scale are strongly positive and the costs relatively low, so

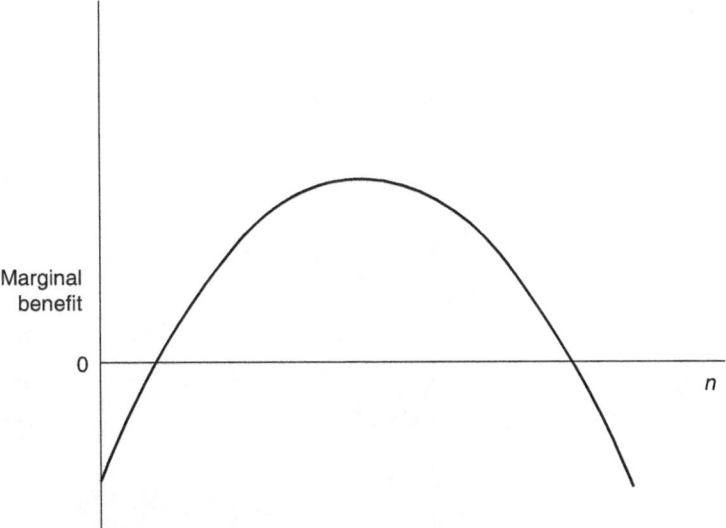

Figure 1.1. Scalability profile of an institution

there is a lot to be said for bringing new people in. As the number of individuals increases, however, the benefits decline, and/or the cost of securing compliance increases, so that the curve begins to bend downward. Eventually it will pass the zero line again, at which point bringing in new people actually reduces the benefits of the cooperative scheme.

What does an institution look like on the downward side of the curve? Typically it will be characterized by an increase in antisocial behaviour, as individuals become less willing to act cooperatively. The specific manifestations will be various, depending upon the nature of the institution: more violence, theft, lying, shirking, disrespect, and unconcern for others, less mutual assistance, trust, succour, and good-faith effort. This is often described, in general terms, as a decline in "solidarity" or "social capital." Such a rise in antisocial behaviour will typically be met with sanctions, and so participants in the scheme will make up for deficiencies of socialization by becoming increasingly punitive, again increasing the costs associated with that particular mode of social integration.

One can think of this marginal (net) benefit curve as the scalability profile of the institution. It provides, among other things, a highly abstract way of comparing different institutional forms. Figure 1.2, for instance, presents a comparison between one institution (A) that is

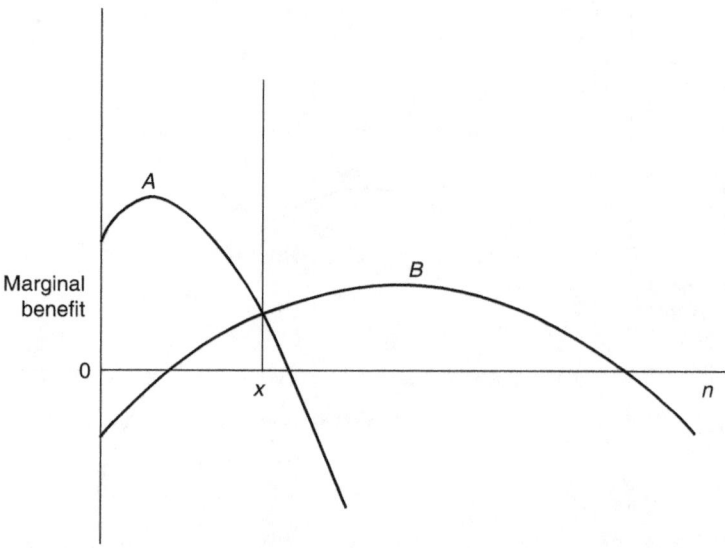

Figure 1.2. More vs. less scalable institution

highly beneficial to participants, but lacks scalability, while the second (B) is not as immediately beneficial, but is more scalable. Because of its greater scalability, the latter will in fact be in a position to deliver a greater cooperative benefit, because even though each additional person brings only a small benefit, one can continue to add more people, and so eventually the average benefit to participants will be greater than that of the smaller, less scalable scheme.

Note that the net marginal benefit of institution B in figure 1.2 starts out in negative territory, unlike A, which offers an immediate benefit to the very first individuals to initiate cooperation. Thus what one is likely to see, sociologically, is *progress* from one institution to another. A couple of individuals will start out using institution A to organize their affairs (e.g., they might form a partnership). Seeing the benefits that are being produced, others will seek to join. As the institution expands, however, the incremental benefits of cooperation will begin to decline (e.g., enmity and strife may begin to develop). Meanwhile, however, the benefits of the institutional alternative, B, are now positive, and so it will be advantageous for the group to switch from institutional arrangement A to B once the number of individuals involved is x (e.g., they may form a club with explicit rules). (In reality, this may not be so simple, as the switch may involve significant transition costs, or may have distributive effects that lead some people to oppose it.)

Now of course it is always possible to create institution *B* with a "big bang," getting *x* people together to start things up. It is just that, as a sociological generalization, this is not how things tend to occur. (Francis Fukuyama's discussion of business corporations – showing how they typically start out as family firms, before making the transition to professional management – provides a wealth of examples of this trajectory.[24]) This conception of institutional progress will become important in the discussion that follows.

2. Solidary Groups

It is somewhat unclear whether Cohen chose the example of a camping trip because he considered it normativland, or rather just a social context that closely resembles normativland. It is fairly clear that he was envisioning a system of "voluntary frictionless social cooperation" (as Arneson described it), where people do what they are supposed to do merely because they are supposed to do it, and not because they fear extrinsic sanctions. And yet it is not clear how voluntary or how frictionless such an endeavour ever really is. As anyone who has ever been on a camping trip can attest – and Cohen made it clear that he had not been on many – there are always some people who are lazier than others, who sit around instead of collecting wood, are slow to break camp in the morning, eat more than their share, fall asleep on fire watch, and so on. In order to keep things happy and harmonious, some institutional structure is required to maintain a fair distribution of the burdens and benefits of the cooperative scheme. The central feature of the camping trip is not that it features an absence of social control, but that it relies upon *informal* mechanisms of negotiation, reciprocity, and sanction to maintain order.

Indeed, one of the great achievements of mid-twentieth-century microsociology was to have demonstrated just how much work goes into the management of small-group interactions, and in particular, how much social control is still being exercised, even with action that is experienced introspectively as "voluntary" by participants. These discoveries were facilitated by the development of audio and subsequently video recording, which allowed observers to catch many of the small details of interaction that had previously eluded even participants – such as how long a person pauses before responding to a question (e.g., much longer when saying no than when saying yes to a request), or how extremely rapid changes in facial expression can be used to communicate approval or disapproval, beneath the threshold of conscious awareness.[25] One crucial technique used to reveal the underlying structure – employed to great effect in experiments conducted by Stanley Milgram and Harold Garfinkel – was to selectively violate behavioural expectations, in seemingly small and insignificant ways.[26] The fact that this often evoked a punitive response – a sometimes rather disproportionate one, given the nature of the infraction – showed that many forms of behaviour that are experienced as spontaneous and voluntarily chosen are in fact mandatory and enforced. It is just that people are so well socialized into the prevailing set of norms that they never even contemplate breaking the rules, and so never notice that there are penalties for doing so.

Certainly the norms governing camping trips are enforced. The participants employ a toolkit of organizational strategies that we might refer to as the "solidary group" structure. It is of course very familiar to anthropologists, because it is the toolkit that is used in most small-scale hunter-gatherer societies (and is, for that reason, widely thought to reflect a set of evolved psychological dispositions). Indeed, the one respect in which Cohen's example of a camping trip is well chosen is that, unlike in many other cooperative enterprises, participants in a (wilderness) camping trip are obliged to reproduce all of the basic features of a small-scale economy: they must organize the provision, preparation, and possibly production of food, as well as purification or transportation of water; they must create a shelter, protect themselves from the elements, build and maintain a fire, deal with night-time and the challenges posed by darkness, take precautions against predators, manage personal hygiene – all of this with a set of tools that must be transportable from location to location. The fact that camping trips impose this obligation to reproduce the material conditions of human existence in a relatively autarkic fashion is precisely what gives them their pedagogical value, especially for children, who often come to realize for the first time while camping just how much *work* is involved in staying warm, dry, safe, and fed. Thus the camping trip does provide a useful point of departure for thinking about economic questions, precisely because it contains most of the elements of a primitive economy. The fact that the organizational challenges confronted by participants on a camping trip parallel those confronted by hunter-gatherers goes some way toward explaining why we are able to employ roughly the same toolkit of institutional strategies to meet those challenges.

The central features of this solidary group structure are as follows:

1. *Sanctions are informal.* It is a general feature of social norms that they are sanctioned regularities of conduct, which is to say that individuals are punished for deviance and/or rewarded for

conformity. A central characteristic of the solidary group structure is that these sanctions are applied in a completely decentralized way. A person who violates a norm – e.g., who continues to relax by the fire while everyone else gets up and starts to break camp – opens herself up to sanction by *any* member of the group. Furthermore, there is no particular member of the group who is responsible for applying the sanction. When someone does take the initiative, the entire group often participates as well, by conspicuously "doing nothing," or failing to "stand up" for the person, even though the deviant is being treated in a way that would *otherwise* be prohibited.

2. *Withdrawal of cooperation is favoured over costly punishment.* When participants in a cooperative project are confronted by individual defection, there are two general ways that they can respond. The first is simply by withdrawing their own cooperation, or to the extent possible refusing to cooperate with the offender. (Game theorists refer to this as a "weak reciprocity" mechanism, because it does not require non-utility maximizing behaviour.)[27] It is often only if this fails, or is for pragmatic purposes not an option, that people will ramp up their opposition and inflict a mutually costly punishment on that person. (This is a "strong reciprocity" mechanism, because it involves non-utility maximizing action.) The second characteristic of the solidary group structure is that it tends to favour withdrawal of cooperation over costly punishment (which is to say, it uses weak reciprocity mechanisms rather than strong ones to sustain cooperation).[28] This can range from mild shunning to total ostracism and can include as well conspicuous failures to offer aid, in cases where it would normally be forthcoming.

3. *Sanctions are largely symbolic rather than intrinsic.* As Talcott Parsons observed, much of what we experience as punishments and rewards are actually actions that have no *intrinsic* significance one way or the other, but merely signal a shift in attitude.[29] Norm-violations, for instance, are almost always met with angry stares, followed often by verbal criticism or abuse. In many solidary groups, for instance, mockery, name-calling, and public shaming are used to great effect. Most people, however, are so attuned to the attitudes of others that they easily forget that being called "lazy" in front of others, or being laughed at, is not intrinsically harmful. Having someone make a rude gesture at you may feel like being slapped in the face, and yet it differs in that the action lacks intrinsic significance – and thus, it constitutes a sanction only

among those who have already internalized a set of norms and are therefore sensitive to symbolic affronts.

These three features of the solidary group conspire to make the institutional structure extremely inconspicuous, not just to observers, but even to participants, who may experience only a very diffuse sense of group pressure to conform to the prevailing norms. Sanctioning often takes the form of shifts in the attitude of others, signalled in very subtle ways. This is particularly true in contexts where individual survival depends heavily upon collective effort, and thus in maintaining "good standing" with the group – because it results in individuals developing very high sensitivity to the attitudes of others. So even when punishment does occur, it may not be easy to notice (indeed, the person being punished may have only a vague sense that "something is up").[30] As a result, it is easy for outside observers to imagine that all the behaviour is purely spontaneous and voluntary.

There are many interesting examples in the ethnographic literature of how these systems of social control operate in small-scale societies. Colin Turnbull, for instance, describes an episode among the Mbuti band, in the Congolese rain forest, in which the community responds to the violation of the norms governing cooperative hunting by one of its members. The deviant individual, Cephu, had placed his net in front of the nets of the others (instead of beside them), in order to ensure that he would catch more game. One of the other hunters spotted this and informed the group what Cephu had done. When Cephu returned to camp, he received a frosty reception: "Cephu walked into the group, and still nobody spoke. He went up to where a youth was sitting in a chair. Usually he would have been offered the seat without his having to ask, and now he did not dare ask, and the youth continued to sit there in as nonchalant a manner as he could muster. Cephu went to another chair where Amabosu was sitting. He shook it violently when Amabosu ignored him, at which he was told, 'Animals lie on the ground.'"[31]

One can see here the three key features of the solidary group structure. First, the task of punishing the offender is not delegated to any specific individual. Those who are sitting in the chairs wind up doing it, but that is only because Cephu approaches them; had he done something other, then someone else might have wound up confronting him. Second, the punishment consists largely in the withdrawal of cooperation. The first youth, in particular, does not go out of his way to harm Cephu, he simply fails to show him a courtesy that, under ordinary circumstances, a young man would show to his elder. And finally, even the more dramatic confrontation, in which Cephu is told to lie on the ground like an animal, is no more than a symbolic affront. Apart from the fact that it is verbal, there is also the fact that there is nothing inherently wrong with sitting on the ground, it is merely that, in this cultural context, doing so would have been beneath his dignity.

In this case, the punishment system worked quite effectively, and the issue was resolved when Cephu agreed to turn over the entirety of his catch to the group. There are other cases, however, in which the more informal system of social control favoured by solidary groups is insufficient, and so it is necessary to "ramp up" the punishment. For example, when merely symbolic punishments prove ineffective, or when dealing with more serious offences, it may be necessary to employ physical force. There is, for instance, the well-known account of a !Kung band imposing a targeted, intrinsic punishment, but inflicting it still in an informal fashion: "In the most dramatic case on record, a man named /Twi had killed three other people, when the community, in a rare move of unanimity, ambushed and fatally wounded him in full daylight. As he lay dying, all the men fired at him with poisoned arrows until, in the words of one informant, 'he looked like a porcupine.' Then, after he was dead, all the women as well as the men approached his body and stabbed him with spears, symbolically sharing the responsibility for his death."[32]

This is actually an unusual arrangement when it comes to capital punishment. A single murder is usually treated as something of a private matter, with the assumption that the victim's kin will exact revenge upon the perpetrator or his family. It is only with serial murderers that the community at large seems to feel threatened and therefore becomes galvanized to action.[33] Even then, the more common pattern observed among hunter-gatherers, who have decided that one of their members must be killed, is to delegate the task to a close relative of the offender. This serves the dual purpose of ensuring that there is a strong group preference for the verdict (even the offender's relatives agree), and of preventing the action from developing into a blood feud (by having the offender's own kin commit the killing). Thus solidary groups may avail themselves of more organized and coercive forms of social control. What makes this particular form of social organization distinctive is that, having done so, they revert to the more informal system. In particular, whatever specialization of role was adopted in order to handle the particular situation will be abandoned, and the group will go back to a decentralized system of informal sanctioning.

There is good reason to think of the solidary group as the "natural" (in the non-evaluative sense of the term) mode of human sociality. For instance, part of the reason that so little is made explicit in these interactions is that many aspects of our adapted psychology appear to be geared toward managing social interactions in this way and thus take place below the threshold of conscious awareness.[34] This speculation is based upon the observation that the solidary group, exemplified by the egalitarian hunter-gatherer band, constitutes the environment of evolutionary adaptation (EEA) for human beings. In the same way that we have many psychological adaptations that are clearly directed to managing aspects of the ancestral physical environment (calculating ballistic trajectories, detecting autonomous movement, maintaining colour constancy in perception, etc.[35]), it would be extremely surprising if there were not also adaptations aimed at managing aspects of the ancestral social environment (recognizing faces, detecting anger, selecting suitable mates, etc.). Consider, for instance, the way that the perception of standard infantile facial characteristics immediately evokes a "caring" response. There are important similarities between this and the way that the punitive response is evoked, in response to an observed norm-violation – again, the processing is largely unconscious, and the outcome is involuntary (although it can, of course, be overridden).

It is because of these aspects of our adapted psychology that the solidary group structure is, in many ways, the "baseline" form of social organization.[36] Most notably, it is the social structure that can be organized and maintained using purely onboard cognitive resources – for example, it does not require that anything be written down or kept track of. Perhaps for this reason, it is the pattern of social organization that people revert to when some calamity destroys more complex social structures or forms of cultural knowledge. It is also the standard form of social organization of deviant cultural groups, such as criminal gangs, who are denied access to many of the formal organizational resources of mainstream social institutions. In this respect, Hobbes's characterization of life in the state of nature as "solitary, poor, nasty, brutish and short" was mistaken only in the first term. People are not solitary, but rather "groupish" in their basic social dispositions. The solidary group is the most intuitive form of social organization, in the sense that it is the one in which actions that are socially expected and approved are the ones that directly correspond to our most unvarnished intuitions. This is just a reflection of the fact that it is the social structure that constituted the EEA, and thus best matches our adapted psychology, and hence our intuitive response to various social situations. It also goes some way toward explaining why, if one uses a philosophical method such as Cohen's, seeking to articulate moral intuitions in a completely decontextualized way, one winds up with a set of moral principles that can most easily be institutionalized in a solidary group.

The major problem with the solidary group structure is that it creates an institution that has very limited scalability. Indeed, it is a commonplace observation that egalitarian hunter-gatherer groups seem to have an upper bound of about 100 members. When they grow beyond that number they start to become dysfunctional and so either split up, forming two or more groups that preserve the solidary group structure, or else adopt some other, more formal institutional arrangement. There are no known instances of the basic solidary group structure being used to integrate a society with even as many as 200, much less 1000 individuals – neither is there any evidence of it in the archaeological record. The institutional structures that replace the solidary group are various, but one feature they all have in common is that they are more formally organized, and more coercive (which is to say, they rely less on symbolic and more on intrinsically significant punishments).

Numerous aspects of the solidary group structure limit its scalability, but four in particular are worth mentioning. The first is that many of the behavioural responses that are central to the system of social control in small groups are cued by visual information, particularly observation of the facial expression and bodily demeanour of others. This is particularly true of the means used to communicate displeasure, or a shift in attitude. As a result, these control mechanisms are most effective at regulating face-to-face interactions, amongst people who know each other reasonably well. A central feature of the solidary group structure is also that it is small enough that it contains no "strangers." As Robin Dunbar has observed, standard human cognitive competencies are such that, for up to about 150 individuals, it is possible for everyone to keep track, roughly, of who everyone else is, and what relation they stand in to each other.[37] Once that number is exceeded, however, inevitably some people in the group simply do not know who some of the other people are. Thus some interactions become *anonymous*, rendering certain systems of social control less effective. For example, it reduces the level of sympathy, generating a type of moral disinhibition. It also leads individuals to have much less concern for the attitudes that others have towards them. Both tendencies conspire to make symbolic punishments such as disapproval much less effective.

The second major feature of increased scale is that it undermines the stability of reciprocity-based cooperation, by making it more difficult to keep track of who has done what, and by making withdrawal of cooperation less effective as a punishment strategy (because it is easier for those who are being punished to find a new interaction partner). Also, by making gossip less effective, it makes it more difficult to sustain systems of indirect reciprocity based on reputation or "good standing" in the community. This pushes toward strong reciprocity. However, with the shift toward more costly punishment systems, a free-rider problem may arise. Because the punitive action is now costly to the person carrying it out, no one wants to be the one doing the punishing.

Third, there is the fact that our punitive dispositions seem to be triggered by the observation of any defection, no matter how extensive the system of cooperation. To the extent that this leads to a retaliatory withdrawal of cooperation, it can make cooperation much more difficult as group size expands, simply because the probability that someone will defect, for some reason – perhaps even by accident – increases along with the number of individuals involved.[38] If our impulse to punish were triggered by the observation of, say, more than 10 per cent of other participants defecting, then scalability might not be such a problem. But if the observation of a single person defecting gives everyone else the impulse to defect, then cooperation will become steadily more precarious, as the number of individuals involved increases.

Finally there is the phenomenon of "motivational crowding-out," which can make it impossible merely to supplement intrinsic incentives with extrinsic incentives, as the latter weaken the former. Indeed, it is a significant fallacy to think that as long as both intrinsic and extrinsic incentives are aligned, such that they promote the same forms of behaviour, their effects will be cumulative. In fact, extrinsic incentives can crowd out intrinsic ones, by encouraging individuals to think of the interaction in more instrumental or strategic terms. This means that as intrinsic motives for cooperation begin to weaken, adding in some additional material incentives, aimed at enhancing cooperation, may have the perverse effect of reducing it, because the extrinsic incentives undermine whatever residual moral incentives were in place. This is a major force limiting the scalability of institutional forms, one that explains why one cannot just add on external incentives to small-scale cooperative structures and expect the system to continue to expand in a linear fashion. Instead, the shift toward heavier reliance upon extrinsic sanctions often requires dramatic institutional reorganization.

I take these observations to be largely uncontroversial, and the examples could be multiplied – of how the techniques used to achieve social order in solidary groups become less effective as group size increases. Thus one of the more universal features of the human experience is that, as the number of individuals increases, not only does the toolkit of institutional strategies need to be expanded, with new mechanisms of social control being introduced, but many of the elements of the solidary group structure also need to be replaced. This often requires participants to override their basic intuitive or dispositional responses to social situations. Understanding this tension is the key to seeing how some of our behavioural dispositions that are pro-social in certain contexts might become counterproductive, and thus antisocial, in others.[39] This is, in turn, what generates the seemingly paradoxical characterization of our species as exhibiting an "unsocial sociability."

3. Formal Institutions

One key feature of the solidary group structure is the extent to which it relies upon implicit knowledge and understanding. Most importantly, in order for things to work well, everyone has to know what the norms are, and all have to do their part in maintaining enforcement. When these conditions are met, very little needs to be *said*, in order to impose sanctions upon a deviant. Everyone can see when a rule has been broken, and anyone can act to punish the offender, without the need for much coordination. As a result, these communities are typically rather weak at dealing with serious conflict, precisely because they have few resources for resolving disagreement when these shared understandings fail. (Even the existence of the linguistic resources needed to articulate norms, in order to make them the objects of possible contestation, cannot be taken for granted. It is, for instance, common to find communal singing or dancing, or ritualized combat, as preferred modes of dispute-resolution, rather than discussion or argumentation.) This may help to explain a feature often noted by ethnographers, which is that small-scale societies typically exhibit very low tolerance for aggression, disruptive behaviour, or even strong displays of emotion.[40] The focus is on preventing conflict from erupting at all, rather than mediating it when it does. Durkheim observed, long ago, the seemingly paradoxical fact that the societies that exhibit the strongest bonds of solidarity are also those most likely to split up or fissure. Precisely because the only way that they can stay together is by maintaining a deep normative consensus, disagreement often leaves them no choice but to break up, to form new groups, with each one then able to maintain its own internal consensus.

One can easily see how this reliance upon the implicit, the taken-for-granted, the unsaid, and the informal all limit the scale of societies integrated through a solidary group structure. One can see also why the institutional remedies that are adopted in response to these limitations all move in the direction of making things explicit, adopting formal procedures, and ultimately, creating differentiated roles. For example, any system of rules will inevitably generate conflict. Rules are not self-applying, and people are likely to interpret them in self-serving ways, producing situations in which there is disagreement over whether an offence has been committed. Similarly, there will always be excusing conditions, which are taken to exempt a rule-violator from punishment. And yet again, parties may disagree over whether those conditions are met. The classic origins of a blood feud arise when one individual drunkenly insults, assaults, or kills a member of another family. The victim's kin demand restitution or retribution, which the perpetrator rejects, on the grounds that the drunkenness constitutes an excusing condition. The victim's family rejects this excuse and imposes what it takes to be justifiable punishment on the perpetrator. This is, however, interpreted as an act of aggression by the perpetrator's kin, who then act to impose punishment upon the victim's kin, and the cycle continues. The important point is that each side interprets its own actions as punitive and the other's as aggressive, and because no injustice should go unpunished, the two families become locked into a never-ending cycle of retributive violence. What is missing is a third party able to provide a definitive *interpretation* of the events, that will establish how the (shared) norms apply.

Now there are, of course, many ways this can be accomplished, but the most common recourse is simply for the community to look to one person – ideally, one whose judgment is respected by all – to provide this interpretation. This can be thought of as the introduction of *authority*. What is important about authority, and what distinguishes it from the merely coordinating role that a leader might provide, is that the decisions of the person in authority are taken to be normatively *binding*, because they are construed, first and foremost, as interpretations of the normative order. This has a variety of consequences, the most important being that obedience to authority becomes obligatory, because that person's pronouncements acquire a force that was previously held only by social norms. Thus any who fail to obey open themselves up to sanctions from the rest of the community. (Anthropologists often advert to this in drawing the distinction between a "big-man" and a "chief": the former is an individual who is merely dominant, but whose commands enjoy no special status, while the latter is taken to have genuine authority, in the sense that his commands are normatively binding for members of the community.[41])

In the same way that there are advantages to introducing specialization to the task of interpreting the normative order, there are also advantages to having the enforcement of that order become specialized. So instead of relying upon the spontaneous reaction of group members to sanction social deviants, the task may be delegated to particular individuals, not just episodically, but permanently. There is, of course, a natural complementarity between the development of these two forms of specialization. Thus we might think of genuine *political authority* as developing when an individual or group is recognized as being entitled to make normatively binding decisions for the community and to have those decisions imposed, by force if necessary, by agents specialized in that task.

When the agents who do the enforcement are selected on the grounds of strong personal loyalty to the chief, an institutional structure may be produced that is extremely stable – indeed, the problem of succession becomes its only significant vulnerability. This may explain why there are no extant examples of sedentary societies that retain a solidary group structure. Since the latter rely so heavily on splitting up in response to internal conflict, the organizational form is better suited to a nomadic lifestyle. Once groups becomes sedentary, the development of more sophisticated conflict-resolution procedures becomes practically inevitable, which tends then to push in the direction of the emergence of political authority.[42] Thus the *tribal chieftainship* becomes almost the default mode of social organization in early agricultural societies (and even sedentary foraging societies, such as were found on the West Coast of Canada before European colonization).

Yet increased stability is not the only advantage that this sort of chieftainship enjoys over the solidary group. Once genuine political authority is constituted, it can be used not just to provide binding interpretation and enforcement of the pre-existing normative order, it can also be used to undertake new initiatives, and ultimately, to modify the normative order. This *leadership* function of political authority gives the society the capacity to expand the scope of cooperation and to achieve new forms of collective action. Historically, one can see this primarily with the emergence of organized warfare. With solidary groups it is very difficult to draw any sharp distinction between murder and war, mainly because all violence takes place in a very disorganized and episodic way.[43] With chieftainships, on the other hand, one begins to see more concerted efforts by communities to commit acts of aggression or predation against their neighbours. This is one reason that hunter-gatherer societies that retain a solidary group structure all live in very marginal environments – they have almost all been forcibly displaced by more highly organized tribal societies.

A second major advantage enjoyed by chieftainships over solidary groups is that, with the latter, each individual member of the community must have internalized the prevailing norms to a very high degree, sufficient to motivate a great deal of unforced compliance. With the introduction of specialized enforcement, by contrast, the punishment mechanism becomes so much more effective that the level of internalization required, and hence the burden of socialization, is reduced. Those who are imposing the punishments still need to be highly motivated, but once their compliance is assured, the rest of the population can be motivated, to a much greater degree, by the threat of punishment. This makes coercion a much more prominent feature of the social order, but it also allows the society as a whole to make more economical use of its socializing energies. The result is a social structure that exhibits much greater scalability (e.g., by making it easier to integrate new members).

At the same time, tribal chieftainships are subject to well-known factors that limit their scale. The major problem is that they have only a single locus of decision-making and implementation, and so easily become bottlenecked. The most obvious way to overcome this is through recursive application of the authority relation, to create an organizational *hierarchy*. Instead of both deciding and implementing, the chief may designate to a subordinate a particular task or area of jurisdiction. This subordinate may do the same again. This creates a "chain of command," where orders may be given centrally but then implemented in a more decentralized fashion. It also creates the possibility of a division of labour when it comes to formulating and implementing plans for collective action.

The effectiveness of hierarchies is further enhanced once it becomes possible to produce a written record of the commands being issued, a development that leads to the emergence of law. These are the institutional developments that we associated with the rise of *the state*, which provides an institutional toolkit that, historically, allowed for the integration of even more large-scale societies and systems of cooperation. Despite the obvious advantages of this form of organization, the task of constructing a state has historically been experienced as extremely difficult.[44] This is partly because of the need to break with the system of personalistic loyalty that supports the enforcement system in a chieftainship and shift it over to the more impersonal institution (since it is in the nature of a hierarchy that the individuals occupying the positions of authority can be replaced piecemeal, while the institution as a whole persists). More importantly, however, there is the fact that the state – at least in its early stages – seems to have offered very little improvement in the quality of life of the average subject. As Michael Mann has argued, given the obvious disadvantages of living in a coercive authority structure, early states emerged in areas like the Nile delta, where for geographic reasons newly settled agriculturalists became "trapped," because surrounding territory could not support anything like the population densities that developed. As a result, unlike hunter-gatherers or pastoralists, farmers were not able to escape the emergent power structure through migration.[45]

Once formed, these states quickly acquired far greater organizational capacity than their neighbours. This is why, again, one of the most important forces driving secondary state-formation was military conflict. The society that does manage to form an integrated hierarchical authority structure comes to possess superior ability to project military force, making it a threat to its neighbours, who in turn come under pressure to set aside their own differences and accept a unified system of authority. Thus the conditions required for "pristine" state-formation are generally thought to be quite different from those that produce secondary state-formation.

Figure 1.3 provides a sketch of what the marginal benefits of these different institutional forms might look like at different scales. If they have the general form that I have suggested here, it would explain why social scientists have often posited a developmental sequence or hierarchy in social formations. What is crucial is that, when the number of individuals involved is small, the benefits of organizing a chieftainship, much less a state, are actually negative. Thus initially people will naturally gravitate toward the solidary group structure, because it offers the greatest net benefits. And yet as the solidary group becomes larger, and the returns to scale begin to decline, the benefits of a chieftainship become positive. If it is not possible to split up and form new solidary groups, then eventually a point will be reached at which the group is better off switching over to the new institutional form. The same occurs later on, as the scale of the chieftainship increases – the benefits of that form begin to decline, while those of the state become positive. It is noteworthy, however, that at the time it becomes worthwhile switching over to a chieftainship, the benefits of a state are still negative. Thus the society will follow a path that moves it through a set of institutional forms in sequence.[46] This is why we do not observe, in the historical or archaeological record, any instances of societies moving directly from solidary groups to states, but instead they always pass through the tribal form before arriving there. This gives the impression of it being a "development," when in fact it can be understood as merely a consequence of the scalability profiles of the relevant institutional forms.

It should be noted that the labels identify only the "top-level" organizational structure of the society. Smaller-scale social formations will often continue to thrive, interstitially, within the larger-scale social

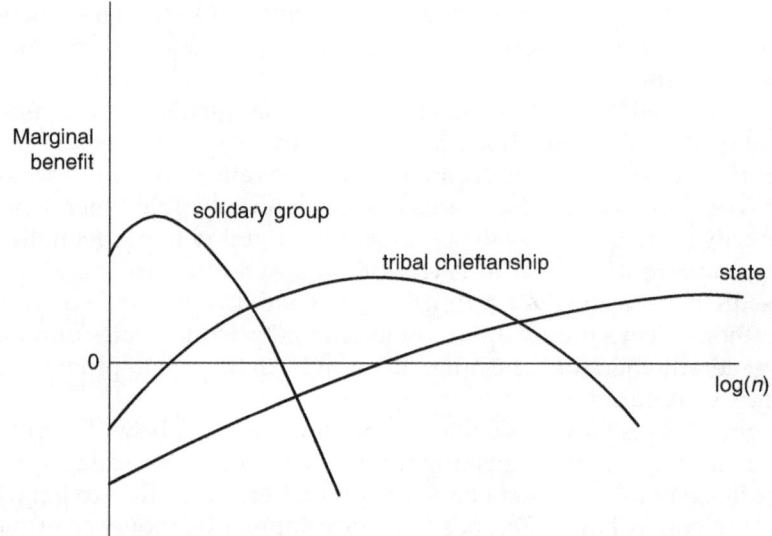

Figure 1.3. Three institutional forms

structure that is enabled by the top-level formation.[47] In the same way that a military organization will preserve the solidary group structure at the level of the "platoon," or a large corporation in the form of a "work group," more complex societies will continue to preserve within themselves, and in many cases encourage the formation of, smaller-scale social structures (typically on the grounds that they are more intensely solidaristic and are thus able to cultivate and make greater use of intrinsic motivation). This is, however, a complicated issue, because at the same time that there is reason to preserve these smaller-scale social formations, they must also remain subordinated to the top-level structure. In many circumstances, however, the more intense loyalties generated at the lower levels can pose a threat to social integration at the higher one, producing fragmentation and conflict. This may be why states that are stable in the long term are traditionally supported by a universalistic ideology that justifies the subordination of more particularistic loyalties (Confucianism, Christianity, Islam, etc.).[48]

Because the smaller-scale formations generate more intense solidarity, they are often able to challenge and subvert the more diffuse forms of solidarity generated by formal, large-scale institutions. And yet while they can undermine large-scale institutions, they tend to fragment them as well, since they are unable to reproduce solidarity and cooperation on the same scale. This is what explains the phenomenon of social collapse. Indeed, the analysis presented here fits with and supports the well-known thesis, advanced by Joseph Tainter, that the phenomenon of declining marginal returns to modes of social organization explains the collapse of complex societies. In his view, vulnerability to collapse occurs when "demographic and/or socio-political factors limit the option of dispersal for a large segment of a population," and yet new institutional forms are not available. As a result, the society becomes "locked in" to a particular mode of organization, even as marginal benefits decline and, eventually, become negative.[49] At some point, replacement of the large-scale social structure with multiple instances of the "previous" small-scale structure becomes more advantageous or stable, and so the former collapses. Regression of an integrated hierarchical state into a set of fragmented tribal chieftainships is the most common instance.

4. Further Observations

The transition between forms of social organization is not nearly as simple or painless as one might like. In particular, the movement from a tribal structure to the state can be extremely difficult and has been the subject of extensive analysis and speculation.[50] In order for the very abstract schema presented in the previous section to elucidate the progress of real institutions, something must be said about these difficulties and their underlying source.

If human psychology conformed to the metaphor of a blank slate, one might expect the transition from one form of social organization to another to follow something close to the optimizing path. The major reason it does not is that we have a number of psychological adaptations that are specifically geared toward maintaining solidary groups. This is why we are able to organize them so effortlessly on a small scale. But as the scale increases, these aspects of our innate psychology become increasingly dysfunctional. One can think of this as a variant of Peter Richerson and Robert Boyd's dictum that culture was "built for speed, not comfort."[51] Evolution has equipped us with a set of dispositions that allow for very rapid and effortless formation of cooperative structures, but at the expense of limiting the scale of these institutions. This kind of "design trade-off" is extremely common in adapted systems and lies at the heart of our unsocial sociability. The problem is that, being implemented at the level of automatic, intuitive processes, these elementary pro-social dispositions cannot simply be unlearned and replaced. In order to render a new institutional form stable, these intuitive responses must be in some way suppressed, overridden, or circumvented. But they never go away and thus remain a potentially disruptive force in every large-scale society. As Azar Gat puts it, the persistence of "evolution-shaped behaviours in radically altered cultural settings is at the core of human historical development. Consciousness of the fact that the original conditions no longer apply often has little effect on patterns of behaviour determined by deeply engrained, evolution-shaped, proximate stimuli."[52] The formal structures that we put in place in order to extend human sociality consist largely in kluges or work-arounds to the limitations of our adapted psychology.

From this perspective, we can identify several different behavioural tendencies that are highly pro-social in small-group settings, but that become increasingly antisocial as group size increases:

1. *Familism*. So far I have said little about one of the strongest and most reliable sources of social solidarity, which is the family. I have ignored it in favour of the solidary group as the smallest type of social structure, simply because one almost never encounters families as autarkic social units. This is probably just for pragmatic reasons, in that families are generally too small to be able to reliably fill all positions required for an effective division of labour, even in a foraging economy. Furthermore, non-incestuous marriage quickly results in families forming ties to other kin groups. Thus even among the Inuit of northern Canada, where there were very low population densities and considerable social isolation, the smallest functional group tended to consist of five or six families, cross-bound by marriage relations. The family, however, does provide a set of extremely robust resources for forming small groups, and – via these marriage relations – a relatively powerful resource for knitting them together into a larger network. At the same time, the structures created in this way have limited scalability, most obviously in the case of the strong ties shared by family members. Furthermore, because it serves as such a powerful source of solidarity, the family can sharply limit the development of larger-scale institutions. Indeed, as Fukuyama has emphasized, the family serves as the major obstacle to state-formation, because it generates intense particularistic loyalties.[53] He provides a number of examples of how early states, or hierarchical institutions, achieved loyalty and stability only by suppressing family formation – creating, in effect, "sterile castes," such as eunuchs in imperial China, the mamelukes in medieval Egypt, or the celibate clergy in Western Christendom. There also appears to be a functional

relationship between the rise of the state and the development of universalistic ideologies (typically religious) that serve as a basis for suppression of familistic loyalties.

2. *In-group bias.* Closely related to familism, but distinct, is a certain disposition toward coalition-formation, which results in heightened solidarity among in-group members, combined with reduced cooperativeness toward out-group members. This disposition is easy to replicate experimentally in public goods games. Merely by dividing players up into two groups and providing some basis for identification of in-group and out-group members, one can observe a higher-than-baseline level of cooperation within the group combined with a higher-than-baseline level of defection directed toward non-members.[54] In a small-scale society this can be a useful disposition, as there will typically be neighbours down the road who can serve as an object of antagonism, but where interactions with this group are sufficiently uncommon that it will not be overly disruptive in day-to-day life. One can find a reflection of this in the moral codes of small-scale societies, which in all known cases exhibit an in-group bias. This shows up in various ways. For instance, a survey of normative attitudes towards violence in ninety small-scale societies revealed significant differences in attitude, depending upon the in-group/out-group status of the victim – with a full 60 per cent of societies approving of violence directed toward members of other ethnolinguistic groups.[55] Again, one can see how this disposition can be highly functional in a small group. Finding a common enemy is a fast and easy way of generating increased solidarity, and thus, eliciting more cooperative behaviour (up to and including self-sacrifice for the group). And yet it creates an institutional structure that becomes increasingly dysfunctional, when the attempt is made to bring disparate groups together under a single authority structure. Not only do the antagonisms serve as a source of direct disruption, but to the extent that they are successfully dissolved, it may lead to a decrease in solidarity within the groups that had traditionally been held together by the antagonism toward outsiders.

3. *Zero-tolerance punishment.* There is good reason to think that the desire to punish that we experience when we witness a violation of the normative order is psychologically deep-seated, rather than being socially learned. As a result, even when the enforcement of norms has become specialized – so that it becomes the responsibility of only a subset of the members of the community – the punitive response continues to be triggered among all members

of the population who witness a norm violation. This is why people continue to take a keen interest in matters of criminal justice and derive enormous vicarious satisfaction from the punishment of offenders, even though in a complex society the task has been delegated to others. (Compare that to say, street cleaning, where once the task has been delegated most people lose interest in it.) And yet because the punitive response has such a low threshold of activation, larger-scale institutions must often leave unpunished forms of behaviour that individuals still feel an impulse to punish. Thus there is often a tension between the institutional demands that are imposed and the more basic social intuitions that individuals bring to bear upon interactions.

4. *Dependence on visual system.* As a result of our adaptations for face-to-face interactions with identifiable individuals, people have a tendency to discount harms caused to strangers or unknown individuals. This appears to be a major factor, for instance, in the formation of permissive attitudes towards certain crimes among juvenile delinquents. According to one study, "There seems to be a core rule that physical injury to a familiar person is unacceptable; but whereas delinquent reasoning stops here, non-delinquents generalize the rule to unfamiliar persons, institutions, and organizations, and find material damage as unacceptable as personal injury."[56] In other words, our *tendency* is to classify as "ignorable" harms that are diffused over a large number of people, or that fall upon unknown or unfamiliar individuals. There is also the well-known (and well-replicated) "watching eyes" effect, where individuals are more likely to act in a cooperative or pro-social fashion when they are being observed. There appears to be a measure of involuntary neural activation involved in this, since the effect can be reproduced even in cases in which the eyes in question are known to be artificial.[57] Again, this is a clear-cut example of an adaptation geared toward the EEA, where the persons with whom one is expected to act cooperatively would almost always have been physically present, and thus identifiable, when the action is performed.

From the standpoint of modern social engineering, these dispositions are rather similar to the "bugs" in our other heuristic problem-solving systems. Consider an analogy to the way that we anticipate movement. Everyone has a system of "innate physics," which allows us, inter alia, to anticipate ballistic trajectories.[58] It contains, however, several well-known bugs, such as the expectation that dropped objects will descend straight down, regardless of forward momentum at the time of release. As a result, our intuitions about physical motion are consistently wrong in this situation, and so we must exercise a conscious override whenever dealing with dropped objects. Similarly, the "accessibility heuristic" that we use to estimate frequencies has known flaws, such as the one caused by our tendency to log repeat viewings of an image as new instances of the event portrayed, which leads us to drastically overestimate the frequency (and hence probability) of events that receive significant media coverage. Despite these flaws, one can understand how these heuristics might have evolved, since they are extremely fast, demand little effort or attention, while nevertheless providing solutions that were "good enough for practical purposes in the EEA." In other words, the circumstances under which they produce the wrong answer would have been sufficiently uncommon, in the EEA, that it would not have made any adaptive sense to slow down the whole process in order to perform the additional calculations needed to avoid those errors.

Much the same can be said for our cooperative dispositions. In an environment in which one is almost never called upon to cooperate with physically distant individuals, there is very little cost to a disposition that uses visual processing of facial cues to prompt pro-social behaviour. Again, it provides a fast, low-effort solution that is "good enough for practical purposes in the EEA." Unfortunately, our social environment has undergone drastic changes – far more than the physical environment. For instance, many of us live in urban contexts in which the majority of social interactions that we have are with strangers.[59] In order to maintain even baseline cooperation in such contexts, formal institutions must be created that in some way correct the tendencies enumerated above. We cannot merely eliminate these dispositions (any more than we can rid ourselves of the erroneous intuitions generated by our onboard physics simulator). At most we can override them, or work around them, so that the outcome produced is closer to what would be achieved if we lacked these tendencies. Often this is done by creating an explicit, coercive institutional structure that forces individuals to behave in large-scale societies in ways that they would naturally be inclined to behave in smaller-scale contexts.

In other cases, it is possible to extend systems of cooperation, not by overriding our innate dispositions directly, but rather by "spoofing" them, or tricking them into producing desired output in circumstances that would not normally elicit it. For example, one technique used by tribes or clans to create allegiance among their members is to focus on a distant ancestor – or sometimes even invent a mythic one – in order to persuade a larger number of individuals to treat one another as family.⁶⁰ Symbolic marking is also used – universally – as a way of differentiating in-group from out-group members. One can think of this as a way of tricking our kin-recognition mechanism, which focuses on resemblance, into responding positively to an individual who is in fact non-kin, as a way of generating increased cooperativeness.⁶¹ So, for example, whereas without the tribal marking, the most salient cue for assessing resemblance might be some bodily trait, the introduction of facial tattooing, or a particular hair style, or clothing of a particular colour, can be used to shift the salient cue toward something that can be reproduced artificially among non-kin. Similar methods are used by gangs or subcultural groups within mass societies. States also accomplish a comparable trick, creating "imagined communities" among their citizens in ways that enhance social solidarity. Thus the institutional toolkit used to create more extensive systems of cooperation can be thought of, without too much distortion, as a bag of tricks, designed either to fool or to override our more primitive social instincts, in order to induce cooperative behaviour in circumstances in which individuals would otherwise tend to act in an antisocial fashion.

Thus the institutions that permit more extensive sociality function as workarounds to the bugs in our more basic psychological dispositions. This is an extremely powerful idea that has been developed by Richerson and Boyd:

> If we are correct, the institutions that foster hierarchy, strong leadership, inegalitarian social relations, and an extensive division of labor in modern societies are built on top of a social "grammar" originally adapted to life in tribal societies. To function, humans construct a social world that resembles the one in which our social instincts evolved. At the same time, a large-scale society cannot function unless people are able to behave in ways that are quite different from what they would be in small-scale tribal societies. Labor must be finely divided. Discipline is important, and leaders must have formal power to command obedience. Large societies require routine, peaceful interactions between unrelated strangers. These requirements necessarily conflict with ancient and tribal social instincts, and thus generate emotional conflict, social disruption, and inefficiency. Consequently, social innovations that make larger-scale society possible, but at the same time effectively simulate life in a tribal-scale society, will tend to spread.⁶²

The extent to which our innate dispositions complicate the task may be reflected in the fact that only a relatively small number of tricks work very well. While there is enormous variation in human *culture*, the degree of variation in social structure is much less extensive. This can be seen in the fact that there are so few genuinely different trajectories of development in human civilizations. For example, the development of Mesoamerican civilization prior to European contact exhibits remarkable similarities to the development of Chinese – and subsequently European – civilization, even though it developed completely independently (and so defies "diffusionist" explanation). For example, no human society has ever developed a state without a functionally differentiated class of priests. It is not difficult to imagine why states might require a specialized military class. But why priests? And yet clearly they arise endogenously, since one can see priests taking on a very similar role in Aztec or Mayan civilization as in Sumerian or Egyptian. This suggests that the number of different ways of organizing human societies is surprisingly narrow – because the number of tricks that actually work is not large.

Indeed, one of the most striking features of utopian schemes, or even "experiments in living," is that they almost all fail. Even though many of them may seem very attractive on paper, they can be extremely difficult to institutionalize. (For example, of the thousands of communes that were created in the United States during the 1960s, very few survived more than a decade.[63] Among those that did, most either had a strong religious character or else reproduced significant institutional features of the dominant society, such as formal laws and bureaucratized decision procedures.) This explains why, again, social formations admit of evolutionary explanation. Because almost everything fails, it is practically impossible to say in advance what will work. And so people try thousands of different arrangements, with the one or two innovations that are successful then being retained and copied by others, with greater or lesser degrees of success.

Again, it is important to recognize that the copying and diffusion of social formations can be either voluntary or involuntary. Historically, to the extent that new institutional arrangements permit the development of more extensive systems of cooperation, it will tend to increase military strength, and so neighbouring societies will fall under pressure to either copy the innovation or have it imposed upon them – either way, they wind up adopting it. This is true of both the basic tribal pattern and of the modern hierarchical state. (Thus the fact that state-formation is largely driven by warfare is perfectly consistent with the view that states enhance the capacity for cooperation. Wars in the modern era have usually been won by societies with greater organizational capacity – such as the ability to conscript and pay soldiers, to move supplies, to manufacture weapons, and even to borrow money.)

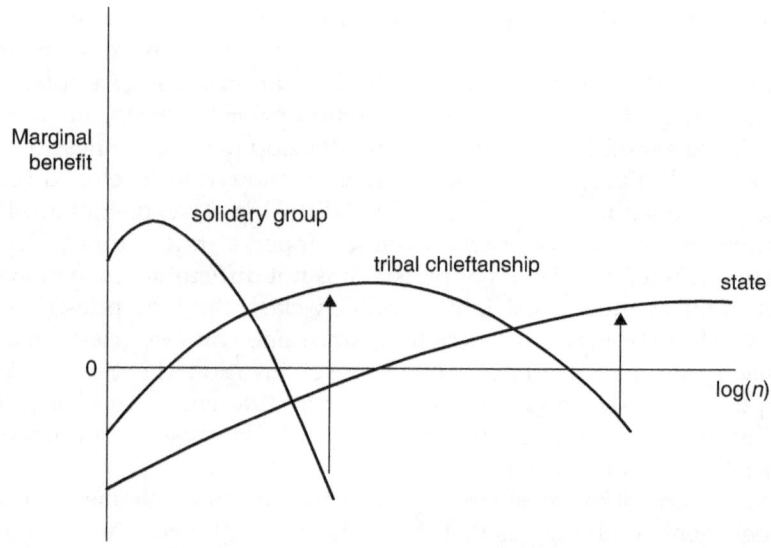

Figure 1.4. Transition points between institutional forms

Thus societies often cling to an organizational form long after the net benefit of increased scale is negative and sometimes make the transition to a more scalable form only when forced to do so. Figure 1.4 shows a typical trajectory of institutional development.

There is, it should be noted, no inevitability about the direction of change in human societies. Talk of development has a tendency to turn into a debate over progress, and whether there is a teleological aspect to the emergence of large-scale systems of cooperation. I have no strong views on this question. Perhaps the wisest words on the subject have been written by Mann, who observed that "there has been unsteady growth of human collective powers through history, not yet reversed, although different parts of the world have provided the leading edge of development at different times. This is because, once invented and adopted, innovations that extend human collective powers ... almost never disappear."[64] So while institutional decay and collapse is always a possibility, reconstruction is easier than the initial construction, because the items in the institutional toolkit used to extend cooperation need not be reinvented. This, combined with the benefits that individuals derive from extending the system of cooperation, means that the succession of forms of organization in human history will not resemble a random walk, but rather a directional process.

5. Socialism Again

This analysis goes some way toward explaining why, when one asks individuals living under any particular social structure what their intuition tells them about some simple interaction, the response will correspond rather closely to the norms that structure the solidary group. Thus the philosophical method of eliciting moral intuitions in decontextualized or highly stylized hypothetical scenarios encourages atavism in the most literal sense of the term. It is in large part because of our evolved psychology that, despite growing up and living in more complex societies, which make very different demands of us, we nevertheless continue to feel the pull of the norms that structure Cohen's camping trip. This is also why highly moralized critiques of institutional arrangements are so easy to come up with, and thus why "utopian socialism" is such a persistent tendency (as each generation rediscovers anew).

If instead of just polling our intuitions, we try to think through systematically what some abstract moral norm might require of us in different institutional contexts, our answers are likely to deviate quite significantly from those that structure Cohen's camping trip. For instance, if one takes what he refers to as the commitment to the principle of "community," then the way that it will be expressed in different institutional contexts is likely to be very different. In a solidary group it may take the form of "mutual giving," as he suggests. But in a chieftainship it may take the form of loyalty and unconditional obedience to authority. The difference is that the solidary group institutes reciprocity in a decentralized fashion – and thus each person is responsible for the needs of everyone else – while in a chieftainship there is a division of moral labour, such that the system of reciprocity is mediated through the central authority. Instead of individuals giving to each other, everyone makes payments to the central authority, who then redistributes in accordance with the prevailing conception of entitlement. Thus "mutual giving" may turn into "obedience to authority" as one scales up the social formation from a solidary group to a tribal chieftainship. Despite the superficial difference between the two norms, they may turn out to be just different instantiations of our commitment to the principle of community.

Of course one might reasonably doubt that there are any values or principles at the level of abstraction at which Cohen posits them. They do so little work, relative to the institutions that supposedly implement them, that one might wonder whether they do any work at all. But even setting this potential objection aside, it seems to me clear that it is question-begging to think that, if we were to scale up our institutions from those of the camping trip to those of a modern industrial economy, the norms we would wind up implementing in the latter case would bear much resemblance to those that elicit our approval in the former. The fact that we do not organize our economy through "mutual giving" in modern mass societies may not reflect a lack of commitment to community. Rather, it may just be that the commitment appears in a different way, pragmatically adjusted to meet the motivational, informational, and logistical demands of a complex economy.

This is, in fact, precisely what I would like to suggest. In what is obviously an unfriendly amendment to Cohen's view, I would argue that "mutual giving" actually turns into "buying and selling" when one moves to a large-scale economy, in which reciprocity occurs between anonymous individuals far removed from one another in space and time. In the discussion above, I rather conspicuously omitted any discussion of the most recent innovation for the extension of cooperative relations: the market. The introduction of "buying and selling," however, raises the question of the moral status of the market. (I say "the market," for the moment, and not "capitalism," because as Cohen himself makes clear, one could also use the market to coordinate economic activity in a society in which the ownership structure of firms was collective. Cohen's vision of socialism, however, excludes not just capitalist ownership structures, but also use of the market as a coordination mechanism – he rejects "market socialism.")[65] Indeed, it is the market that has made possible the creation of the global system of cooperation that has recently allowed humanity to surpass ants as the most "ultrasocial" species on the planet.[66] (There are, of course, state-based systems of global cooperation as well, but they tend to be more limited in scope and more difficult to organize.)

The advantages of the market, as an institutional mechanism for organizing economic cooperation, are often described in terms of its ability to reduce the motivational burden that is placed upon individuals. (This point is often made with reference to Adam Smith's observation that, once a system of exchange is institutionalized, "it is not from the benevolence of the butcher, the brewer, or the baker, that we expect our dinner, but from their regard to their own interest."[67]) Again, this is a perfect example of a kluge or workaround to the problem of limited cooperativeness. The invisible hand of the market essentially tricks individuals into acting in a pro-social way, despite its being no part of their intention. Communist revolutionaries in the twentieth century were clear on this point as well, understanding that, in order to abolish the market, they would need to find some way of eliciting a higher level of directly cooperative behaviour from workers. Thus they put considerable faith in the potential for improvements on the motivational front achievable through socialization and education (e.g., the vision of "new socialist man," or *"conciencia"* in Cuba), and how much international solidarity they would be able to produce (e.g., through the Communist International, or the various international brotherhoods). In retrospect, much of this was overly optimistic.

Cohen makes the rather standard observation that in emergencies, people are capable of exhibiting a high level of social solidarity, even with strangers, and so we know that it is possible.[68] This is, however, something of a culpably naive remark. The problem with the "emergency response" is that it fades rather quickly, after which all of the usual enmities re-emerge. Relying on this response as a structural feature of the social system can therefore generate perverse incentives. This could be seen rather clearly in the Communist states of the twentieth century. As their ongoing failure to elicit sufficient levels of social solidarity became evident, there was a temptation to want to *provoke* emergencies, or in some cases, to create a state of permanent emergency, for precisely this reason – as a trick aimed at eliciting higher levels of social solidarity. Yet unlike other strategies in the bag of tricks that we use to promote more extensive cooperation, this one proved to be highly destabilizing, and in some cases enormously destructive. The Cultural Revolution in China, for instance, apart from resulting directly in the death of at least a million people, also led to the collapse of the university system, the closure of schools across the country for several years, a sharp decline in industrial production, as well as widespread destruction of Chinese cultural heritage. Given this legacy, responsible socialists should not be appealing to people's response to emergencies as a model of how to produce heightened social solidarity, or as grounds for optimism about the possibility of more voluntarist modes of industrial organization.

There is, of course, a well-known line of apologetics, which explains events like the Cultural Revolution as a consequence of personal characteristics of the leader. There seems to me a powerful element of wishful thinking in this, simply because many of these individuals – Stalin and Mao in particular – were responding to an obvious structural problem in communist societies. They had called for reforms that required a very high level of cooperativeness (collectivization of agriculture, a "great leap forward," etc.). When the necessary level of cooperativeness proved to be unforthcoming, they responded by increasing the amount of coercion directed against "reactionary elements," who refused to play along. When this coercion failed, they chose to escalate. This also failed, and in some cases proved counterproductive, leading to the emergence of more "reactionary elements." And yet instead of backing off, they ramped it up some more. Now of course it was also a feature of the totalitarian political systems in which they operated that there were no veto points at which these orders could be countermanded. But that is not what gave rise to the problem. The core problem arose from an attempt to pursue a set of moral ideals that demanded a higher level of cooperativeness than the available institutions (much less underlying human behavioural dispositions) were able to deliver.

This is, I grant, a controversial claim, and not one that I need insist on here. In order to discuss Cohen's specific proposals, one can just as well set aside the issue of motivation and focus on a more often neglected aspect of the way that institutions implement norms. This is the second major function of institutions, outlined above, which is the provision of *information*. When Cohen describes an ideal socialist economy as involving a system of "planned mutual giving," he makes it clear that he is not envisaging a return to a system of autarkic production. A socialist economy, in his view, would feature a division of labour and thus would have some system of reciprocity, so that individuals could specialize in the production of one good, to meet the needs of others, with the confidence that others would, in return, provide for their own needs. One feature of systems of reciprocity, however, is that they require information in order to keep track of how much people have contributed, and how much they are owed.[69] This is relatively easy to do in small groups but can become much more complicated as group size increases. For example, some friends may have a tradition of taking turns buying rounds of drinks whenever they are together in a bar. Most people are able to keep track of the level of reciprocation passively, using innate competences. (That they are, at some level, keeping track is revealed by the fact that if one person defects too often – e.g., conveniently absenting himself when it comes time to pay – others will eventually notice.) However, once group size expands, it becomes impossible to ensure that the system of reciprocity is being respected using only onboard resources. At this point, the standard expedient is to introduce some sort of formal information system, such as a ledger to record how much each person has spent, in order to ensure that the benefits and burdens of the cooperative system are being distributed fairly.

When Cohen describes the principle of community as requiring a system of "planned mutual giving," the term "planned" represents a concession in the direction of realism. Rather than having a system of spontaneous giving, Cohen presumably wants the giving to be planned in order to ensure that what people give bears some relationship to what other people want. This expectation is sensible. He therefore describes the contrast between capitalism and socialism in the following way: "The relationship between us under communal reciprocity is not the market-instrumental one in which I give because I get, but the non-instrumental one in which I give because you need, or want, and in which I expect a comparable generosity from you."[70] Note that the word "expect" in the final clause must be interpreted in the rather emphatic, normative sense. As Cohen writes, "I serve you in the expectation that (if you are able to) you will also serve me. My commitment to socialist community does not require me to be a sucker who serves you regardless of whether (if you are able to do so) you are going to serve me."[71] Thus the system of mutual giving he imagines is one in which, unless certain excusing conditions are met, exchanges will satisfy a fairly strict reciprocity condition. People "get" only if they also "give." It is important to recognize, however, that in order for this reciprocity condition to be satisfied, each individual's giving must be guided by the needs and wants of others. They cannot just give whatever they feel like giving. But how is everyone to know what everyone else needs? On a camping trip this is relatively easy – people can just talk to one another, in order to communicate their needs – but as the size of the group increases, the challenge involved in knowing what others need increases.

In a complex economy, whenever anyone does some work, this can be thought of as contributing to an enormous pool of goods (and services, but to simplify I will say just goods), which constitutes the set of cooperatively produced goods that are available for consumption by others. This will include everything from food, clothing, and shelter to philosophy lectures, smartphones, massage therapy, livestock, and children's toys. Setting aside for the moment how one is supposed to know exactly what others need when there is such an enormous pool of cooperatively produced goods, it is instructive to consider the sorts of moral principles that individuals must respect, in order to sustain the division of labour that makes it possible to organize such a pool.

The first and most obvious rule is simply the reciprocity constraint, that one should take out no more than one puts in. This could take the form of a strict reciprocity condition:

1. One should be willing to draw from the stock of goods, to meet one's own consumption needs, an amount no greater than the value *to others* of what one has produced.

It is actually unclear whether Cohen favours a strict principle, such as this one, which requires that what each person takes out be exactly equivalent to what she puts in (according to some yet-to-be-specified metric). Certainly every one of these principles must be taken to apply only *ceteris paribus*, in order to ease the requirement of reciprocity in cases where individuals are, for reasons beyond their control, unable to contribute. Cohen may also have favoured only a weaker reciprocity principle, under which what one takes out need only be approximately equivalent to what one puts in. To go any weaker than that, however (such as requiring only that individuals contribute *something*), amounts to dissolving the reciprocity constraint, which he clearly does not want to do.

Regardless of whether one adopts a strict reciprocity or a weak reciprocity constraint, the following principles must also be respected, in order to sustain a complex division of labour of the sort that one finds in an industrial or post-industrial economy:

2. One must be guided in one's productive decisions by what other people want, and not just by what one enjoys doing. And if what others want changes, one should be willing to change as well to meet their new needs.
3. One should recognize when the needs of others for some good are greater than one's own, and let them have it instead of consuming it oneself.
4. If some accident of fate should result in a reduction in the ability of society to produce some good, or an increase in the amount of effort that it takes for others to produce it, one should be willing to reduce one's own consumption of that good.

Beyond this, it is also important to recognize that the pool of goods contains not just articles of consumption, but also capital goods (e.g., tools), and resources, which are used to produce final consumption goods. This stock must not be wasted – most obviously, the capital goods ought not be consumed (e.g., the seed corn should not be eaten), but also it should be used by the person who is able to use it most effectively (e.g., if there is only one fishing rod, it should be used by the person who is reasonably competent at catching fish). This generates some additional principles:

5. Production requires resources, which will have to be provided by others. One should be as economical as possible in drawing from this stock – taking no more than the absolute minimum required to produce one's goods, even if this sometimes means that one will have to work harder.

6. One should recognize when others are able to make better use of some resource than one is able, and allow them to have it.

These are obviously fairly significant moral demands. For example, the temptation to use productive resources inefficiently, when doing so allows one to exert less effort, can be very difficult to overcome. The important point, for our purposes, is that even in a society of saints, each of whom was fully motivated to comply with these principles out of pure cooperative zeal, an enormous amount of information would be required in order to know what one was required to do, and what constituted compliance. How is one to know if a lump of clay could be put to better use by oneself or someone else? How is one to know if the Central American coffee blight is sufficiently severe that one should consider switching to tea? How is one to know if the need for philosophy is great enough that one can justifiably commit oneself to producing it? And suppose one were to be challenged by others: "Why do you get to use that lump of clay?" or "Should you really be drinking coffee at a time like this?" or "Why do you get to sit around all day doing philosophy, while others are labouring in the fields?" How is one to respond? Because one's consumption necessarily imposes costs upon others, how does one begin to make the case that it is, all things considered, reasonable, given one's own contributions and needs, compared to the contributions and needs of others?

The answer to these questions is familiar. Some sort of quantitative measure is required that will indicate the total social cost of producing each good, which can then be compared to some aggregate measure of the capacity of that good to satisfy human wants. In other words, what is required is a system of *scarcity prices*, which can be used as a guide by individuals, so that they know the exact value to others of what they are contributing to the pool, and what they are taking out.[72] Otherwise it is impossible to say whether a reciprocity condition is being even approximately satisfied. The idea is rather simple: if you decide to grow carrots, rather than potatoes, at a time when people want carrots more than potatoes, then you should get more credit for doing so, because you have done more to help others. This in turn entitles you to take out more from the common pool, when it comes to satisfying your own wants. The task of tracking this sort of credit is basically what the *price system* does. In a face-to-face interaction, it is easy to find out what other people want. In an anonymous interaction, where even very small transactions can involve cooperation among thousands of people, the only way to find out what others want is to look at prices.

One can go through all six of the principles enumerated above and show in each case how, without prices, it is impossible to know whether one has satisfied them (or whether they even apply in one's situation). Thus the only interesting institutional question is how we get those prices. There are three known ways of doing so. Markets achieve it through decentralized competition amongst producers and consumers. In principle, a Walrasian auction can accomplish the same, centralizing the price-setting mechanism, yet maintaining decentralization in economic production. And finally, one can eliminate decentralization entirely and institute a system of central planning. The last option proved highly ineffective, the second is sufficiently difficult to institutionalize that it remains hypothetical, and so most countries in the world have settled on some variant of the first, where attempts are made to promote competitive markets, with the state then making adjustments to prices as required through subsidies, taxes, regulations, or in some cases outright ownership of firms. The competitive market arrangement is, of course, morally counter-intuitive, because it achieves the cooperative outcome only indirectly, as a by-product of a system of adversarial relations.[73]

What is important to recognize, for the sake of the argument at hand, is that under any of these three arrangements, Cohen's requirement that individuals must maintain a "non-instrumental" attitude toward exchange is impossible to satisfy. Smith's invisible hand permits mutual disinterest in transactions ("I give because I get"), whereas for Cohen, exchange should be based on a system of mutual giving ("I give because you need, or want"). But either way, individuals will wake up every morning facing a set of prices. These prices specify how much each individual must be paid, when she "gives" something to someone else, in order to ensure that the requirements of reciprocity are satisfied when it comes time to "get" something from someone else. Whether she is giving it to that person *in order* to get paid, or whether the payment is interpreted as a gift that expresses the appreciation of the nameless beneficiaries, is a distinction without a difference. Apart from being unknowable and unenforceable, it simply does not make any difference to how the relevant economic institutions are organized. In other words, it is perfectly open to people living in a capitalist society to think of the market as a system of "planned mutual giving," since it would not cause them to behave any differently.

Finally, it is worth noting that unlike a camping trip, in which all participants always act as both consumers and producers in roughly equal proportion, a complex economy is one in which individuals may over-contribute to the pool as they like, on the understanding that this will allow them to under-contribute at some later time (and vice versa). In other words, individuals have a balance, which represents their net contribution, which they are allowed to run up or down as they see fit. The most obvious manifestation of this is retirement savings, where individuals over-contribute throughout their working lives, in order to live as pure consumers during old age. One might think of this system as governed by two further moral principles:

7. If, in the past, one has contributed more to the pool than one has taken out, one is entitled, in the future, to draw out an amount equivalent to one's over-contribution.
8. One is allowed to draw more from the pool than one contributes, so long as one is prepared to make it up later by contributing more than one withdraws.

It is worth noting that these two principles are just extensions of the fundamental reciprocity principle. Together they are what underlie the institutions of "savings" and "debt" in our society. There is much to be said for having a flexible system that both permits individual over- and under-contribution, but that keeps track, in order to ensure that individuals do not exceed their balances. (Principle 8, which allows individuals to live at the expense of others, based on a promise to make up for it later, is particularly vulnerable to abuse once one begins to contemplate the possibility of individuals acting on self-interested motives.) The fact is that, at various periods in their lives, individuals may have needs that greatly exceed their capacity to make productive contribution (i.e., during childhood, when raising small children, and in old age). Thus a system that permits them to incur debt, or draw down savings, has obvious advantages. Somewhat less obvious is the fact that individuals are often in a position, at certain periods of their lives, to produce much more than they need to consume. This creates an opportunity to direct their efforts, not just to the production of consumption goods for others, but to the creation of capital goods, which will make it easier to produce consumption goods in the future.

I am dwelling upon this point because, while contemplation of the practical implications of principles 1–6 leads to the conclusion that one must have some kind of a market economy, principles 7–8 tend to push in the direction, not just of a market, but a specifically *capitalist* mode of economic organization. Once it is recognized that over-contribution is what permits reproduction of the capital stock, it is not so far to the conclusion that when these individuals subsequently withdraw their contribution, they should be able to take, not just the amount put in, but rather the economic value of the *investment* that their over-contribution permitted. At this point, one has basically accepted the idea that holders of capital (i.e., savers) are entitled to the return of their investment (i.e., to "profit" in the Marxian sense of the term). This is the feature of capitalism that, historically at least, socialists have found most difficult to accept.

What this analysis shows is that if one begins with the moral principles elicited by Cohen's camping trip thought-experiment, but then takes seriously the scaling-up problem, focusing on institutional arrangements that have an actual track record of success at promoting large-scale cooperation, and in particular, at instituting a complex division of labour, it is not difficult to make the case that a market economy constitutes a realization of those principles. It is not a direct realization – and therefore will be experienced by participants as morally counter-intuitive – only because of the kluge-like way in which these institutions bring about the desired cooperative outcome.

6. Conclusion

With this discussion of the market in place, the full picture that I have been trying to sketch out of the scalability of cooperative structures can now be presented (figure 1.5), although the limitations of the graphical mode of representation that I have been using also become clear. One of the most perplexing aspects of the market is the way that it forms a system of cooperation that is in certain respects separated from, "decoupled," or "disembedded" from the other major systems of cooperation in society.[74] One way of characterizing this development, suggested by Jürgen Habermas, among others, is to see it as a *functional differentiation* among systems of social cooperation.[75] Rather than there being a single, overarching structure of authority, that coordinates and integrates all other systems of cooperation, the society becomes decentred, with different functionally specialized subsystems organized around different modalities of cooperative benefit. Of course, it is important not to produce an overly static or simplistic framework for this analysis. For instance, while "the market" becomes increasingly differentiated from the state, the market still contains within it an enormous number of corporations, which achieve cooperative benefits through an administrative hierarchy that very much resembles that employed by the state. Thus it is important that the institutional differentiation not be regarded as overly neat.

If the focus is on the scalability of cooperative structures, perhaps the most useful way of characterizing these developments is in terms

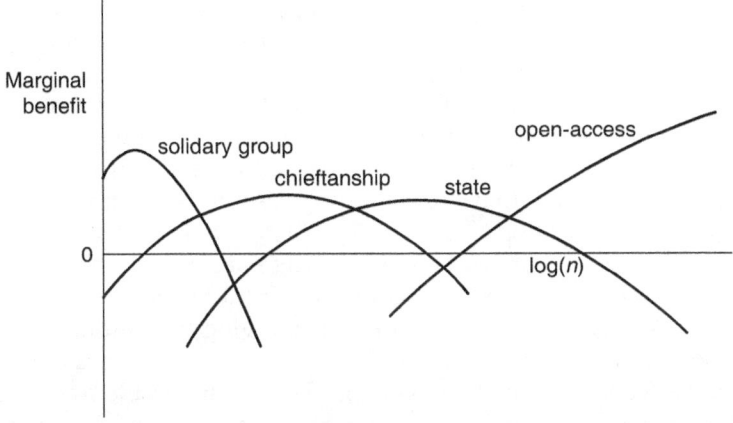

Figure 1.5. Developmental trajectory

of the concept, articulated by Douglass North, John Wallis, and Barry Weingast, of an "open access order."[76] In their view, the primary feature of early social orders is that the "natural state" is directly involved in the integration of every primary system of cooperation (e.g., providing specification and interpretation of the rules, enforcing compliance, etc.). In an open access order, by contrast, the state shifts away from this direct role, toward a system in which it merely provides individuals with a set of resources for creating their own organizations (e.g., legal templates, enforcement of contracts, etc.). When combined with the imposition of a set of ground rules that limit the chances of these organizations falling into collective action problems, the result can be another dramatic expansion in the scalability of the overall system of cooperation.

What has emerged under conditions of open access are numerous variations on the arrangement in which private ownership and decentralized economic decision-making is favoured whenever the conditions of a competitive market can be approximately satisfied, but where the state and third-sector groups play a significant complementary role. This is the familiar constellation of "welfare state plus market economy" that has proven to be such a successful model over the past several decades.[77] It may have been premature to declare, as Fukuyama did, that this particular institutional configuration represents "the end of history." In a similar way, it would be premature for a computer scientist to announce that sixty-four-bit systems represent the ultimate or final architecture. The point, however, is rather similar, which is that the scalability of these open access systems so vastly exceeds that of any near rivals, and we are so far from hitting their theoretical limits, that they are, for all practical purposes, here to stay.

This much is rather straightforward. With regard to Cohen's work, my argument has been somewhat less direct. There are many defences of the market economy that have a structure that mirrors Cohen's defence of socialism – they simply point to some small-scale aspect of the institution that people like and say, "Isn't capitalism wonderful?" Deirdre McCloskey, for instance, in order to accentuate the virtues of economic exchange, paints a picture of a local farmer's market on a sunny weekend, with happy farmers exchanging wholesome produce with the locals.[78] John Tomasi and Jason Brennan point to the morally uplifting effects of small business ownership.[79] The problem with these arguments is that they fail to accommodate or even explain the *persistence* of the moral intuitions that underlie Cohen's camping trip and that motivate anti-capitalism. If one could settle the debate over the moral status of capitalism just by pointing to happy people exchanging goods – or, more abstractly, to the fact that economic exchange is Pareto-improving – then the debate would have been over a very long time ago. There is, I suppose, a temptation to want to defeat anti-capitalist moral intuitions just by lining up other, pro-capitalist intuitions, and hoping that the latter are stronger. This argumentation strategy, however, fails to address the deeper question, which is why certain anti-capitalist intuitions prove so recalcitrant in the face of these arguments, or why each new generation – despite growing up in a thoroughly capitalist society, to which there are no plausible or coherent alternatives – manages to reinvent utopian socialism for itself.

The analysis that I have presented here attempts to answer this question. My goal was to explain why, despite living under a particular institutional arrangement, one that most reflective people regard as all-things-considered justified, so many people still have moral intuitions that are in tension with it.[80] My answer has been that many of these intuitions represent evolved dispositions that were adaptive in the EEA, in which humans lived in solidary groups. The present institutional environment, by contrast, is profoundly unnatural. It is, as Keith Stanovich describes it, like a sodium vapour lamp, a highly unnatural form of light that causes our innate colour-correction algorithms to malfunction.[81] In the case of socialism, it is mass society that functions like a sodium vapour lamp. Our "onboard" resources are not geared toward handling large-scale cooperation with strangers. The level of cooperation we have achieved is the result of thousands of years of (cultural) evolution of institutional structures, which function as kluges, allowing us to work around the limitations of these innate dispositions. Thus support for it rests upon a rational insight into the compromises that are required, in order to implement a scheme of cooperation on such a large scale.

From this perspective, Cohen's half-hearted plea for socialism bears a certain similarity to that of the weary soldier, surveying the battlefield, who asks, "Why can't we all just get along?" This is a perfectly reasonable question, but it does not provide any traction on real-world problems. And while a perfectly coherent form of pacifism can be founded upon this perspective, it does not really constitute a profound critique of the human condition. The first step to wisdom involves acceptance of the fact that people cannot "just get along," and so we need to figure out some way to manage conflict. The socialist, in Cohen's version, is someone who looks at the economy and says, "Why can't we all just cooperate?" Again, this is a perfectly reasonable question, but also one that has a relatively straightforward answer. The first step to wisdom involves the recognition that we cannot all "just cooperate," any more than we can all "just get along." As the scale of our institutions increases, certain perversities of human nature become more manifest, and these need to be managed. As a result, capitalism is not a moral ideal. Voluntary, direct cooperation, without competition, remains the ideal. Unfortunately, we simply lack the onboard resources to achieve that ideal at scale – this is the unsocial sociability of human nature. And yet even if it is not ideal, markets remain the most powerful workaround yet discovered to this unfortunate aspect of our nature.

NOTES

1 Robert Boyd and Peter J. Richerson, "Solving the Puzzle of Human Cooperation," in *Evolution and Culture*, ed. S. Levinson (Cambridge, MA: MIT Press, 2005), 105–32.
2 Michael Tomasello, *A Natural History of Human Morality* (Cambridge, MA: Harvard University Press, 2016).
3 Azar Gat, *War in Human Civilization* (Oxford: Oxford University Press, 2006). On intraspecific violence among non-human animals, see 7–10.
4 Franz de Waal, *Good Natured: The Origins of Right and Wrong in Humans and Other Animals* (Cambridge, MA: Harvard University Press, 1997).
5 The concept of "onboard" resources is from Andy Clark, *Being There* (Cambridge, MA: MIT Press, 1997), 207.
6 Émile Durkheim, *The Division of Labor in Society*, trans. W.D. Halls (New York: Free Press, 1997); Peter J. Richerson and Robert Boyd, *Not by Genes Alone* (Chicago: University of Chicago Press, 2005).

7 See, e.g., Alec Nove, *The Economics of a Feasible Socialism Revisited* (New York: Taylor & Francis, 1991); Joseph Stiglitz, *Whither Socialism?* (Cambridge, MA: MIT Press, 1994).
8 Thus I have always been mystified by the weirdly defensive reaction to Cohen's work found in Jason Brennan, *Why Not Capitalism?* (New York: Routledge, 2014).
9 G.A. Cohen, *Why Not Socialism?* (Princeton, NJ: Princeton University Press, 2009), 4–5.
10 Cohen, *Why Not Socialism?*, 10.
11 Cohen, 10–11.
12 Cohen, 76.
13 Cohen, 76. Note that this could be said of many things, such as faster-than-light travel. Even though we do not now know that we will never know how to do it, we certainly have grounds for suspicion that it is not doable.
14 John Stuart Mill, *Socialism* (Chicago: Belfords, Clarke, 1879).
15 Friedrich A. Hayek, "The Moral Imperative of the Market," in *The Unfinished Agenda: Essays on the Political Economy of Government Policy in Honour of Arthus Seldon*, ed. Martin J. Anderson (London: Institute of Economic Affairs, 1986), 56–89.
16 Richard J. Arneson, "'Equality of What?' Revisited" (5 August 2010), 4, SSRN, https://ssrn.com/abstract=1653981. Miriam Ronzoni expresses a similar view: "I cannot really believe that human beings, given what they are like, could freely and voluntarily sustain a social scheme of this kind, and I therefore suspect that horrible things would have to be done to them in order to achieve this goal" "Life Is Not a Camping Trip: On the Desirability of Cohenite Socialism," *Politics, Philosophy and Economics* 11, no. 2 (2011): 183.
17 Robert William Davies, Mark Harrison, and S.G. Wheatcroft, *The Economic Transformation of the Soviet Union, 1913–1945* (Cambridge: Cambridge University Press, 1994), 289, cited in Robert Allen, *Farm to Factory* (Princeton, NJ: Princeton University Press, 2003), 99.
18 John Rawls, "Justice as Fairness," in *Collected Papers*, ed. Samuel Freeman (Cambridge, MA: Harvard University Press, 1999), 55.
19 This is the major takeaway of Cohen's "kidnapper's argument." G.A. Cohen, *Rescuing Justice and Equality* (Cambridge, MA: Harvard University Press, 2008), 39–41.
20 Allen Buchanan, "Perfecting Imperfect Duties: Collective Action to Create Moral Obligations," *Business Ethics Quarterly* 6, no. 1 (1996): 27–42.
21 Talcott Parsons, *The Social System* (New York: Free Press, 1951), 38–40.
22 G.A. Cohen, "On the Currency of Egalitarian Justice," *Ethics* 99, no. 4 (1989): 906–944.

23 Cohen, *Why Not Socialism?*, 7–9.
24 Francis Fukuyama, *Trust* (London: Penguin, 1996).
25 See David Silverman, *Harvey Sacks: Social Science and Conversation Analysis* (Oxford: Oxford University Press, 1998).
26 See Harold Garfinkel, "Studies of the Routine Grounds of Everyday Activities," in his *Studies in Ethnomethodology* (Cambridge: Policy, 1984), 35–75. See also Stanley Milgram, *The Individual in a Social World* (New York: McGraw Hill, 1992).
27 Samuel Bowles and Herbert Gintis, *A Cooperative Species* (Princeton, NJ: Princeton University Press, 2011).
28 Just to be clear on the distinction, if someone were to ask you, "Can you please pass me that stick beside you?" and you were to say, "No," that would be a weak reciprocity mechanism, since you don't really have any independent reason to pass him the stick. On the other hand, if you were to pick up the stick and throw it at him, that would be a strong reciprocity mechanism, since you don't really have any reason to throw it at him either, other than as punishment for some transgression. Bracketing the question of what this person has done to deserve sanction, in the former case you are acting in accordance with your preferences (and thus, as you otherwise would be acting), in the latter you are acting contrary to them.
29 Parsons, *Social System*, 272–3.
30 See, e.g., Jean Briggs, *Never in Anger* (Cambridge, MA: Harvard University Press, 1971), 218–26.
31 Colin M. Turnbull, *The Forest People* (New York: Simon and Schuster, 1963), 105, cited in Christopher Boehm, *Moral Origins* (New York: Basic Books, 2012), 39.
32 Richard B. Lee, *The !Kung San: Men, Women, and Work in a Foraging Society* (Cambridge: Cambridge University Press, 1979), 130. Cited in Boehm, *Moral Origins*, 180.
33 Boehm, *Moral Origins*, 259. See also Jared Diamond, *The World until Yesterday* (New York: Viking, 2012).
34 The relationship between "adapted" and "unconscious" that I am relying on here is based on the work of Timothy Wilson, *Strangers to Ourselves* (Cambridge, MA: Harvard University Press, 2004).
35 See Jerome H. Barkow, Leda Cosmides, and John Tooby, eds., *The Adapted Mind* (Oxford: Oxford University Press, 2003).
36 There are two smaller patterns of association: the family and friendship. These fall below the threshold of modes of "social organization" because they do not generally incorporate enough members to discharge all of the functions associated with reproduction of human life. Thus the smallest nomadic societies on record consist of a small group of allied families.

Similarly, although "friendship" is an institution that permits the rapid formation of cooperative relations, it is rather strikingly non-scalable, being usually confined to dyadic relations, or very small networks of dyadically linked individuals. The goal of creating a "society of friends" (as the Quakers put it) has been a persistent ambition throughout human history, but has never been achieved.

37 Robin Dunbar, "Neocortex Size as a Constraint on Group Size in Primates," *Journal of Human Evolution* 22, no. 6 (1992): 469–93.
38 Robert Boyd and Peter Richerson, "The Evolution of Reciprocity in Sizable Groups," *Journal of Theoretical Biology* 132, no. 3 (1988): 337–56.
39 In my view, this explains the phenomenon observed by Jonathan Haidt, that people living in modern liberal societies draw upon a narrower range of resources in making moral judgments than people living in traditional ones (or yearning for a return to traditional ones). See Jonathan Haidt and Jesse Graham, "When Morality Opposes Justice: Conservatives Have Moral Intuitions That Liberals May Not Recognize," *Social Justice Research* 20, no. 1 (2007): 98–116. Haidt does not consider the possibility that there may be functional dependencies between the types of moral judgment and elements of social structure, such that large-scale cooperative arrangements can be institutionalized only by *suppressing* certain moralizing impulses that people have.
40 Christopher Boehm, *Hierarchy in the Forest* (Cambridge, MA: Harvard University Press, 1999), 43–7; Richard Wrangham, *The Goodness Paradox* (New York: Pantheon, 2019).
41 Kent Flannery and Joyce Marcus, *The Creation of Inequality* (Cambridge, MA: Harvard University Press, 2014); Morton H. Fried, *The Evolution of Political Society* (New York: Random House, 1967).
42 Boehm, *Moral Origins*, 255.
43 Gat, *War in Human Civilization*, 133–46.
44 See Francis Fukuyama, *Origins of Political Order* (New York: Farrar, Straus and Giroux, 2011), 92–4; James C. Scott, *Against the Grain* (New Haven, CT: Yale University Press, 2017).
45 Michael Mann, *The Sources of Social Power*, vol. 1, 2nd ed. (Cambridge: Cambridge University Press, 2012).
46 This is why, as Steven Pinker observes, Peter Singer's attempt to compare the "expanding circle" of human sociality to an escalator is a poorly chosen metaphor. "The only problem with Singer's metaphor is that the history ... looks less like an escalator than an elevator that gets stuck on a floor for a seeming eternity, then lurches up to the next floor, gets stuck there for a while, and so on" (*The Better Angels of Our Nature* [New York: Penguin, 2011], 649).
47 See Emile Durkheim, *Professional Ethics and Civic Morals*, trans. Cornelia Brookfield (London: Routledge, 2003).

48 This is a strong theme in Fukuyama's work, both *Trust* and *Origins of Political Order*.
49 Joseph A. Tainter, *The Collapse of Complex Societies* (Cambridge: Cambridge University Press, 1988), 123.
50 Boehm, *Hierarchy in the Forest*, 106–12; Fukuyama, *Origins of Political Order*, 90–4; Daron Acemoglu and James Robinson, *Why Nations Fail* (New York: Random House, 2012).
51 Richerson and Boyd, *Not by Genes Alone*, 188.
52 Gat, *War in Human Civilization*, 130. He goes on to give the example of our taste for sweet foods.
53 Fukuyama, *Origins of Political Order*, 229–39.
54 Roderick M. Kramer and Marilynn B. Brewer, "Effects of Group Identity on Resource Use in a Simulated Commons Dilemma," *Journal of Personality and Social Psychology* 46, no. 5 (1984): 1044–57. For classic study, see Henri Tajfel, M. Billig, R.P. Bundy, and Claude Flament, "Social Categorization and Intergroup Behavior," *European Journal of Social Psychology* 1, no. 2 (1971): 149–77. For discussion, see Jack Deavid Eller, *Cruel Creeds, Virtuous Violence* (Amherst, NY: Prometheus, 2010), 37.
55 Marc Howard Ross, *The Culture of Conflict* (New Haven, CT: Yale University Press, 1993), 79–80.
56 Johannes A. Landsheer, Harm 't Hart, and Willem Kox, "Delinquent Values and Victim Damage," *British Journal of Criminology* 34, no. 1 (1994): 53.
57 Terence C. Burnham and Brian Hare, "Engineering Human Cooperation," *Human Nature* 18, no. 2 (2007): 88–108.
58 Michael McCloskey, "Intuitive Physics," *Scientific American* 248, no. 4 (1983): 122–30.
59 See Paul Seabright, *The Company of Strangers* (Princeton, NY: Princeton University Press, 2004).
60 For discussion, see Fukuyama, *Origins of Political Order*, 57–9; Gat, *War in Human Civilization*, 180.
61 Leda Cosmides, John Tooby, and Robert Kurzban, "Perceptions of Race," *Trends in Cognitive Science* 7, no. 4 (2003): 173–9. As Gat observes (*War in Human Civilization*, 135) military organizations are a good place to look for the exercise of these techniques, because of the high level of solidarity they must inculcate, in order to motivate soldiers to give up their lives for the group (and the relative weakness of external incentives).
62 Richerson and Boyd, *Not by Genes Alone*, 230.
63 Timothy Miller, *The 60s Communes* (Syracuse, NY: Syracuse University Press, 1999), xviii–xx.
64 Mann, *Sources of Social Power*, 1:x.
65 Cohen, *Why Not Socialism?*, 69–70. He makes this clear as well in G.A. Cohen, *If You're an Egalitarian, How Come You're So Rich?* (Cambridge, MA: Harvard University Press, 2001), 181.

64 Cooperation and Social Justice

66 Peter J. Richerson and Robert Boyd, "The Evolution of Human Ultra-Sociality," in *Indoctrinability, Ideology, and Warfare*, ed. Irenäus Eibl-Eibesfeldt and Frank Kemp Salter (New York: Berghan Books, 1998), 71–95.
67 Adam Smith, *An Inquiry into the Nature and Causes of the Wealth of Nations*, ed. R.H. Campbell and A.S. Skinner (Oxford: Oxford University Press, 1976), 26–7.
68 Cohen, *Why Not Socialism?*, 54.
69 Which Cohen acknowledges, *Why Not Socialism?*, 61.
70 Cohen, 43.
71 Cohen, 43.
72 On this, see Joseph Heath, *Filthy Lucre* (Toronto: HarperCollins, 2008), 159.
73 Joseph Heath, "An Adversarial Ethic for Business: or When Sun-Tzu Met the Stakeholder," *Journal of Business Ethics* 72, no. 4 (2007): 359–74.
74 Karl Polanyi, *The Great Transformation* (Boston: Beacon, 1957). Mark Granovetter, "Economic Action and Social Structure: The Problem of Embeddedness," *American Journal of Sociology* 91, no. 3 (1985): 481–510, shows how difficult it is to characterize the precise sense in which modern economies are disembedded from more general social structures.
75 Jürgen Habermas, *The Theory of Communicative Action*, vol. 2., trans. Thomas McCarthy (Boston: Beacon, 1987).
76 Douglass C. North, John Joseph Wallis, and Barry R. Weingast, "A Conceptual Framework for Interpreting Recorded Human History," NBER working paper 12795 (2006). See also Douglass C. North, John Joseph Wallis, and Barry R. Weingast, *Violence and Social Orders* (Cambridge: Cambridge University Press, 2009).
77 See Joseph Heath, "Three Normative Models of the Welfare State," *Public Reason* 3, no. 2 (2011): 13–44.
78 Deirdre McCloskey, *The Bourgeois Virtues* (Chicago: University of Chicago Press, 2006).
79 John Tomasi, *Free Market Fairness* (Princeton, NJ: Princeton University Press, 2012); Brennan, *Why Not Capitalism?*
80 The most striking example of this is Daniel Kahneman, Jack L. Knetsch, and Richard Thaler, "Fairness as a Constraint on Profit Seeking: Entitlements in the Market," *American Economic Review* 76, no. 4 (1986): 728–41, showing that a majority of Canadians polled considered it morally impermissible for merchants to raise prices in response to an increased need for their goods.
81 Keith Stanovich, *The Robot's Rebellion* (Chicago: University of Chicago Press, 2005), 134.

Chapter Two

Why Profit Is Not the Problem

On 20 April 2010, a sudden release of methane gas from a deep sea oil well led to a massive explosion in the Macondo oil field in the Gulf of Mexico. The blast killed eleven workers, sank the BP-owned Deepwater Horizon drilling platform, and created an uncapped oil wellhead on the sea floor, which poured crude oil into the Gulf for almost three months. When it was finally brought under control, the well had leaked 4.9 million barrels of crude oil, the largest marine oil spill in history. A US presidential commission called to investigate the disaster concluded that the accident was a consequence of decisions made by the three companies involved in contracting and operating the well, which created risks that were both "unreasonably large" and entirely "avoidable." The report outlined numerous examples of the firms having systematically "cut corners" in the construction of the well, with the goal of saving time and expense.[1] Furthermore, there appeared to have been no policies in place at BP to assess the safety consequences of these decisions. The commission noted, "Unless companies create and enforce such policies, there is simply too great a risk that financial pressures will systematically bias decisionmaking in favor of time- and cost-savings."[2] Finally, the relationship between BP and the US federal government, in particular the Minerals Management Service (MMS), which was the primary regulator, turned out to be a textbook case of "regulatory capture," and in some cases outright corruption.[3] Apart from the usual industry gifts, junkets, and free tickets to sporting events, the commission noted many conflicts of interest, such as an MMS employee who "had conducted inspections on a company's oil platforms while in the process of negotiating (and later accepting employment) with the company."[4] The result was safety oversight that was deficient, and environmental regulation that was almost entirely non-existent.[5]

The entire episode was a good example of a privately owned corporation engaging in activities contrary to the public interest. There are certain risks inherent in deep sea oil drilling, and if the public wants to consume those fossil fuels, then such risks must be accepted. However, the investigation revealed that the risks that led to the Deepwater Horizon accident were all undertaken *unnecessarily*. Furthermore, the firms involved took action aimed at undermining the government agencies responsible for protecting the public interest, aggressively lobbying against regulation, and then evading or undermining enforcement of the regulations that were enacted. This type of corporate behaviour is of the sort that leaves many people wondering why anyone would choose to act this way. And, of course, when searching for an answer to this question, it seldom escapes notice that the incentives for acting this way were all, in one way or another, pecuniary. Put in more prosaic terms, one cannot help noticing that the firms involved saved money by cutting corners, and that this enhanced their profitability. Furthermore, these firms were already quite profitable. Their reckless actions were undertaken as part of a more general objective of *maximizing* profit.

There is nothing wrong with these observations. However, many people go on to draw a further conclusion, which I do think should be contested. They suggest that, since this sort of antisocial behaviour – let us call it "corporate misconduct" – is aimed at enhancing profitability, we should eliminate the profit orientation of firms (or eliminate the institution of the profit-oriented firm entirely) and replace it with something else, in order to reduce the incidence of such behaviour. According to this view, the profit orientation of firms is essentially a standing inducement to engage in misconduct. It follows that the incidence of antisocial firm behaviour can be reduced by eliminating the profit orientation, or preventing such firms from operating in certain sectors. Indeed, the impulse to denounce the evils of "profit" sometimes shades over into a fixation. (The corporation, according to Joel Bakan, is a sociopathic "machine" that is "programmed to exploit others for profit.")[6] This generates a very common rhetorical trope, in which the profit orientation of firms, or "corporate greed," is blamed for everything from environmental damage and workplace accidents to income inequality and global poverty.[7]

In a sense, this view is an optimistic one, in that it suggests that many large-scale problems in our society admit of *structural* solutions. In other words, it amounts to the suggestion that by changing laws and making other formal modifications to the way that our institutions are organized, we can eliminate certain persistent social problems. After all, if it were the ownership structure of the corporation, along with the system of incentives that this provides to management, that was the source of corporate misconduct, then the problem could be fixed just by replacing that structure with something else. Unfortunately, this optimistic view is not well supported, either by theory or by evidence. Indeed, many people who are not particularly enthusiastic about the structure of the standard business corporation nevertheless think that there is no organizational form that is likely to do better. Many of the ownership structures proposed as an alternative – such as cooperatives, or even state ownership – exhibit essentially the same problems. Meanwhile, structures that are genuinely different – such as non-profit firms – have other problems, which are sufficiently severe that they generally outweigh the advantages of the organizational form.

Furthermore, many of the supposed benefits of eliminating the profit orientation of firms are illusory. For instance, one often hears repeated the view that shareholders are like parasites, contributing nothing to production, yet nevertheless demanding a cut.[8] It follows from this that the elimination of profit from the list of organizational objectives should represent a pure saving, so that, for instance, a firm that does not have to pay out profits should be able to pay higher wages.[9] This is unfortunately not the case. If capital is not obtained from shareholders, it must be obtained from somewhere else, and whoever else provides it – even if it is the workers themselves – will need to be paid a return on the investment. There is always a cost of capital, even if it is only an opportunity cost.

My goal in this chapter is to systematically work through the alternatives to the profit-oriented capitalist firm, showing how they have failed to provide a viable, or desirable, alternative. I begin with cooperatives, which are undoubtedly the most commonly cited alternative. They are, I will argue, not an alternative at all, since they are also profit-oriented. It is just that the profits are disbursed to a different class of owners (and are often not called "profits"). I turn then to public ownership and observe that the dominant trend in Western welfare states, since the early 1970s, has been toward "corporatization" of state-owned enterprises, which usually includes the imposition of a profit-maximization objective on managers. I will discuss some of the motives for these reforms, which were, I should note, quite independent of the wave of privatizations that occurred in subsequent decades. Finally, I will discuss the non-profit firm, which represents the only organizational form that completely breaks with the profit-maximization imperative. Although appropriate in some sectors, non-profits do not represent a general solution to the problem of corporate misconduct, not least because most individuals lack any incentive to create them.

Throughout this discussion I will be assuming the basic desirability of the price system, and thus of markets generally, as a way of mediating exchanges and allocating resources, goods, and services. This is, of course, not entirely uncontroversial, but taking into account more radical socialist projects would move the discussion too far afield.[10] What I am interested in are proposals that seek to keep the basic structure of the market in place, while eliminating the investor-owned capitalist firm. (This includes, then, most proposals classified as "market socialist.")[11] It is within this framework, I will claim, that there is no organizational form that can provide any structural solution to the problems generated by the capitalist firm. This is primarily because abolishing investor ownership does not entail eliminating profit-maximization as an *organizational objective*, and so most of the plausible alternative ownership structures proposed wind up maintaining the profit orientation. Rather than serving as a source of despair, however, I will suggest that it serves instead as an argument for better ethical governance of firms. Since there is little to be said for restructuring the firm, we should focus our energies rather on encouraging better behaviour from the firms that we have, structured as they are. Specifically, rather than trying to eliminate the profit orientation, we should instead be pressuring firms to exercise greater restraint in the profit-maximization strategies they employ. From this perspective, cases of corporate misconduct like the Deepwater Horizon disaster were caused, not by the pursuit of profit as such, but rather from the pursuit of profit in the wrong way.

1. What Is Profit?

Before getting into the details of this discussion, it is worth taking the time to develop an accurate account of what is meant by "profit," and the sense in which modern corporations are said to maximize it. My intention here is not to obfuscate the issue by bringing in unnecessary technicalities, but rather to get clear on what we are talking about, since there is a great deal of loose talk about the evils of "profit," with different implicit definitions of the term being used. Furthermore, the current trend in the business world is to regard the concept of profit as somewhat outdated and to describe business corporations as seeking rather to maximize "shareholder value." Similarly, the search for profit is often described by critics as the primary, or even sole, objective of the firm, although the reality is significantly more complicated than that.

The first and more important thing to understand about profit is that it is a residuum. It is sometimes defined as the excess of revenue over expenditure, but this can be misleading, depending upon how expenditure is understood. It is best therefore to think of profit as what is left over after all of the firm's contractual obligations have been met. This is, I should note, not the Marxist definition, since Marx used the term "profit" to describe any payment to the providers of capital (whom he assumed to be also owners of the firm). In contemporary finance, by contrast, it is standard to distinguish two forms of capital provision: equity and debt. Debt includes both loans made to the firm and bonds that it has sold. The central characteristic of debt is that its holders are paid an amount that is contractually fixed, what is commonly known as *interest*. Equity, by contrast, also involves the provision of capital to the firm, but on terms that are contractually unspecified. Instead of getting a fixed interest payment, equity investors (i.e., shareholders), get a residual claim, which is to say, an entitlement to what is left over after all others – including all bond-holders and creditors, but also workers, suppliers, etc. – have been paid. This is what we call "profit." The most obvious feature of equity, in this regard, is that it is much riskier than debt. There is a lot more upside, because in principle shareholders get everything left over, but also a lot more downside, because shareholders are the last to get paid (and in the case of bankruptcy, lose their stake entirely).

A more intuitive way of illustrating the distinction between equity and debt is to compare it to the collaboration that normally takes place in the purchase of a home. There are usually two sources of capital involved in the purchase, the first supplied by the owner, who is expected to put up a "down payment" representing some fraction of the value of the home; the second supplied by a bank, which provides the balance of capital required in the form of a mortgage loan. The owner, in this case, is essentially providing equity, while the bank is supplying debt. This is reflected in the fact that the owner gets the residual claim, which means that if the value of the house goes up, all of that increase in value accrues to the owner, and if the value of the house goes down, the owner suffers the entire loss. The bank, meanwhile, gets no greater payment than the interest rate that was contractually agreed upon. At the same time, it has the right to demand payment, so that if the homeowner fails to meet the terms of the contract, the bank can force sale of the asset in order to recover the sum that it is entitled to. Its position therefore is less risky – it has significantly less upside, but also enjoys significant protection against the downside risks. In effect, in return for getting to keep any increase in the value of the home, the owner also agrees to absorb 100 per cent of the losses that the property may suffer – the bank begins to absorb losses only after the owner's stake has been completely wiped out (i.e., the foreclosure value of the home becomes less than the outstanding mortgage).

Similarly, the key to the bargain accepted by shareholders in the firm is that they get significant upside to their investment, in return for accepting considerable downside risk. What makes the arrangement attractive for the firm is the flexibility that it gets from having a significant amount of equity capital. Firms often experience fluctuations in revenue. The problem with debt is that it is inflexible. Banks demand regular payments of interest on loans and may force the firm to liquidate assets if payment is not forthcoming. Shareholders, on the other hand, need not be paid. And so if the firm hits a rough patch, the equity serves as a "cushion," protecting it from the demands of creditors, as well as any other group with a contractual claim on the firm, such as workers. (It is for this reason that shareholders are often also described as "residual risk-bearers.") Similarly, the firm may, at its discretion, decide to retain profits in order to finance new investment, knowing that shareholders need not be paid right away, or on a regular basis. The firm may be punished for such a decision by a lower stock price, if investors decide that on balance they are not getting a sufficient return, but none of this represents an existential threat to the firm – unlike with creditors, who can force the firm into bankruptcy if they are not being paid.

One can see then why it is inaccurate, or at least very misleading, to describe the earning of profit as the sole objective of the firm (or to claim that corporations "only care about profit"). In fact, corporations normally assign greater priority to their contractual obligations – meeting payroll, making payments to suppliers, servicing their loans – precisely because they have no discretion in these matters, and failure to make these payments threatens their ability to remain in business. They do, of course, also try to make a profit. It is just that the only legitimate way to do so is by first meeting all of these other obligations. This is, in part, why profit is taken to be a measure of success, because it shows that the firm is managing to meet all of its diverse obligations, with room to spare, so to speak. Naturally, significant profits will increase the share price, allowing the firm to raise capital by creating and selling new shares, and thereby to expand its business. In the process, it provides a mechanism through which – from a social point of view – investment funds are channelled to those who are likely to make the best use of them.

Also, it should be noted that while profits that are not reinvested are often disbursed to shareholders in the form of dividend payments, many firms elect not to do so. Indeed, there are many firms that technically have never paid out any "profits" to shareholders at all. They may simply accumulate the funds, in order to finance acquisitions, research and development, or other growth strategies. Indeed, many investors buy stock not because they expect it to pay dividends, but because they expect the value of the stock to appreciate. (For instance, Microsoft Corporation paid out no dividends from 1986, when it first went public, until 2003. It is often a symptom of a firm becoming "mature," "blue chip," or perhaps "stagnant," that it begins to pay dividends.) It is also common, in jurisdictions where capital gains are taxed more lightly in the hands of individuals than dividends, for firms to buy back their own shares as an alternative to paying dividends. The buyback leads to appreciation in the value of all outstanding shares, allowing the remaining shareholders to take their profits in the form of capital gains (i.e., an increase in the value of the shares they own), rather than dividends. Apart from being taxed at a lower rate in many jurisdictions, this also allows the owners to choose when they want to book the profit (i.e., by deciding when to sell their shares). Because of the widespread use of such strategies, it is standard now to speak about "shareholder value" rather than "profit," in recognition of the fact that there are multiple ways in which benefits can be directed to investors.

The idea that corporations are nothing but profit-making machines is often encouraged (particularly by critics of capitalism) through reference to the 1919 Michigan Supreme Court decision, *Dodge v. Ford*, which ordered the Ford Motor Corporation to pay out dividends, asserting that "a business corporation is organized and carried on primarily for the profit of the stockholders."[12] And yet, as Lynn Stout has argued (in her aptly named paper, "Why We Should Stop Teaching *Dodge v. Ford*"),[13] this is a complete misrepresentation of the state of corporate law (in America, but also elsewhere).[14] Despite being widely taught and cited by legal theorists, *Dodge v. Ford* has almost never been cited as a legal precedent in any Delaware court decision – which is the jurisdiction in which important US corporate law cases are decided. Furthermore, whatever doctrinal value it may have had has been entirely superseded by the "business judgment rule," which US courts use to grant enormous discretion to firm executives.[15] This rule essentially instructs courts to avoid second-guessing management and board decisions (in many areas, including the payment of dividends). As Stout puts it, "Courts shield directors from liability under the business judgment rule so long as any plausible connection can be made between the directors' decision and some possible future benefit, however intangible and unlikely, to shareholders. If the directors lack the imagination to offer such a 'long-run' rationalization for their decision, courts will invent one."[16] This is the rubric, for instance, under which charitable and political donations by corporations are protected from shareholder lawsuits. Corporations may also accumulate enormous piles of cash ("retained earnings"), which can be used, inter alia, to finance mergers and acquisitions. Many of these are of extremely dubious value to shareholders, but it is difficult to imagine circumstances under which courts would intervene and force the money to be disbursed to shareholders instead.

It is also worth noting that the maximization of shareholder value, or even the intention to seek profits, is seldom mentioned explicitly in corporate charters. There is, of course, an implicit understanding that this is what the firm intends to do, but there is no explicit contractual commitment, and thus no legally enforceable obligation. There is also nothing to prevent businesses from assigning other objectives priority in their charters, and there are celebrated examples of corporations that do. (Perhaps the most high-profile is the *New York Times* Corporation, which assigns highest priority to its news-reporting functions, and secondary importance to profits.)[17] This is why certain progressive corporate law scholars have opposed the development of "benefit corporations" in the United States, which are investor-owned but have an explicit commitment to certain eleemosynary objectives, as well as to consideration of the interests of non-shareholder groups. The central argument against them is that they are redundant, since there is nothing to prevent the organization of a standard business corporation in the same way.

As Frank Easterbrook and Daniel Fischel put it, "If a corporation is started with a promise to pay half of the profits to the employees rather than the equity investors, that ... is simply a term of the contract. It will be an experiment.... Similarly if a bank is formed with a declared purpose of giving priority to loans to minority-owned businesses or third-world nations, that is a matter for the venturers to settle among themselves. So too if a corporation, on building a plant, undertakes never to leave the community."[18] This is, of course, somewhat tongue-in-cheek, since it would be rather difficult for a standard business corporation to attract investors if it were to announce straightaway that it is not going to be seeking to maximize shareholder value. The essential point, though, is an important one. The firm is established through contractual relations between the involved parties, and corporate law grants them extremely wide discretion in deciding the terms of these contracts. The image of a legal straitjacket, forcing firms to pump out profits for investors, is entirely illusory.

Finally, it may seem rather obvious, but it nevertheless bears repeating, that the slippage one often encounters, in popular rhetoric, between "profit" and "self-interest" or "greed," is extremely misleading.[19] Adam Smith may have used the two terms interchangeably, when discussing the "interest" of the butcher or the baker, but that is because he was writing at a time before the emergence of the modern business corporation. With the development of professional management, the people who are making the profits and those who are receiving them are usually two different groups. Indeed, many firms go to great trouble in attempting to align the incentives of the two, by giving managers an equity stake in the firm, or stock options in lieu of salary. Nevertheless, a major structural feature of the modern business corporation is that senior executives have discovered various ways of enriching themselves at the expense of shareholders.[20] (The cost of stock options, for instance, is born almost entirely by shareholders, in the form of share dilution.) Thus all the loose talk about corporate "rapaciousness" or "greed" is in many ways quite unhelpful, because it obscures the complex mixture of incentives that structures the actions of the various parties involved in the firm, and in particular, it fails to take seriously the fact that managers often do not stand to gain personally from the various forms of corporate misconduct that they suborn. Even talk of the "profit motive" is potentially confusing, since it blurs the distinction between profit as an *organizational objective* and the specific incentives that individuals within the firm are given (e.g., salary, bonuses, equity-based compensation, etc.) This becomes extremely important when it comes to thinking about alternatives to the profit-maximizing firm, because even where it is possible to eliminate profit as an organizational objective, this does not automatically eliminate the incentives that may have been pushing managers to engage in malfeasance.

To illustrate the point with a specific example, BP (formerly British Petroleum) actually has a very long history of acting in antisocial and counterproductive ways, dating back to the period in which it was under the majority ownership of the British state.[21] It is not as though the firm or its managers suddenly became "greedy" when the firm was privatized. Thus in order to understand the behaviour of the firm, it is not obvious that looking at its ownership structure, or at the top-level managerial objective, is going to be all that illuminating. The best place to start would be to look more carefully at the corporate culture, and at the incentives faced by managers – which arguably have not changed all that much, with the various shifts in ownership structure. Terms like "corporate greed," however, blur all of the important distinctions, and perhaps more importantly, shift attention away from the incentives that managers face on an individual level.

2. Cooperatives and Profit

With these preliminaries out of the way, we can turn to the central question, which is whether we can find a *structural* solution to the problem of corporate malfeasance by eliminating the profit objective (understood as shareholder value maximization). There are three basic ways that this can be done: through state ownership, by requiring firms to be incorporated as non-profits, or by promoting cooperatives. The last is by far the most popular suggestion, largely because it leaves the market mechanism untouched and is therefore thought to generate only minimal interference with the price system. Thanks to a general awareness of the pitfalls of central planning, many critics of capitalism are actually not keen to abolish the main feature of capitalism, which is the use of a decentralized, competitive exchange system to make the primary allocative and productive decisions in the economy. Their goal is just to reform ownership structures, so that market actors will behave less antisocially (and ideally, income will be distributed less unequally).

It is worth noting that this idea – market socialism based on worker cooperatives – has been in circulation for over 150 years and has been the subject of both extensive experimentation and critique. Among those who worry about practicality, or who would like to avoid a sudden collapse in living standards, it is generally thought to be subject to rather significant difficulties. For present purposes, however, the crucial point to observe is that an economy dominated by cooperatives is not sufficiently different from the existing system to be able to claim, with any plausibility, to represent a solution to the specific problem of corporate malfeasance. Most importantly, it does not abolish the profit orientation of the firm, it merely conceals it to varying degrees.[22] It follows that, if profit truly is the problem, then such a reform would merely replace corporate misconduct with cooperative misconduct.

To see why this is so, it is important to understand the legal structure of cooperatives.[23] Most jurisdictions have statutes that permit individuals to incorporate as a cooperative, and indeed, most capitalist economies have cooperatives in various sectors, competing on all fours with standard business corporations. It is common, in contemporary discussions, to characterize the firm as a "nexus of contracts" between individuals, who can be grouped together, for convenience, into four primary "patron groups": workers who provide labour, investors who provide capital, suppliers who sell inputs to the firm, and customers who purchase the firm's outputs. A standard business corporation has an ownership relation with its investors. All other inputs, including some portion of the firm's capital, are obtained through contractual relations. There is, however, no requirement that the owners of the firm be the investors. In fact, many firms start out as partnerships, or as small "closed held" corporations, which are often quite ambiguous in structure, involving individuals from different patron groups in the ownership class. For instance, it is very common for partnerships to form among workers (restaurant workers, software programmers, etc.), or else for them to create a corporation in which all the founders are assigned shares, but then to bring an "angel investor" into the firm at some later point. As a result, more than one class of patron winds up having representation within the ownership group. It is often only when the firm "goes public" – offering shares to the general public in return for an investment – that it assumes the unambiguous structure of an investor-owned capitalist firm.

A cooperative is similar to a public corporation in that it has an unambiguous ownership structure. The chief difference is that one of the patron groups other than the investors assumes ownership of the firm.[24] As a result, most cooperatives come in one of three different "flavours," depending upon which patron group exercises ownership. In some cases it will be the suppliers – as in a dairy cooperative, where the farmers who supply milk will own the firm that processes it into cheese, butter, or yogurt. A "credit union" (or "building society" in the United Kingdom) is also, somewhat counterintuitively, a supply cooperative, in that it is owned by depositors, who are not actually customers, but rather suppliers, since they supply the credit to the firm's real customers, who are the borrowers. A more common arrangement is for customers to own the firm – this is the structure of a standard "farm supply" cooperative, as well as a "mutual" insurance society. And finally, there are worker cooperatives, an arrangement that is not all that common, but can be found in the taxi industry and in travel agencies. What makes a particular patron group the "owners" of the firm is that they exercise control over the board of directors and have a residual claim on the firm's earnings.[25]

In certain cases, the similarity between a cooperative and an investor-owned firm is obvious, because the cooperative will literally pay out "profits" to its owners. In a dairy cooperative, for instance, farmers will typically supply milk to the firm at a below-market rate (in the same way that shareholders provide capital to the firm on generous terms). They will, in turn, receive a profit-share at the end of the year, based on the amount of milk that they have provided. Thus the firm gets the advantage of being able to secure its primary input on flexible terms, in a way that essentially guarantees its solvency in the face of market fluctuations. In effect, the ability to buy its primary input at below-market rates functions as a cushion, in the same way that equity capital does in an investor-owned firm. The farmers accept some downside risk – if the cooperative does not make a profit, then they will have lost money by failing to sell their milk on the open market – but in return they get the upside benefit of the profit share.

One can see the same structure in an insurance cooperative, although here the residual claim is not labelled as "profit." A mutual insurance scheme is a customer cooperative – it is owned by the policyholders. Again, the owners will contract with the firm on generous terms. In the case of insurance, this means that they will typically *overpay* for their policies, making premium payments often twice as high as the market rate for comparable insurance (which, again, provides the equivalent of an equity cushion). In return, however, they each receive a "rebate" at the end of the year, based on how much money the firm has left over after paying all claims. The upside is that, in a typical year, the premium *minus the rebate* will be less than the price of a comparable policy from an investor-owned insurance company. The downside is that, in a bad year, the policyholders receive no rebate and thus shoulder the entire cost of the excess claims.

This rebate paid by a cooperative insurance scheme is, rather obviously, a profit-share in everything but name, since the firm is disbursing its residual earnings to members of the ownership group. Similarly, when workers in a worker cooperative receive a year-end "bonus," this is also a profit-share. Cooperative members may also appropriate the residuum in more subtle ways, such as in-kind payments. Workers, for instance, may benefit from a superior-but-costly-to-provide work environment. More commonly, members of a customer co-op receive a nominal profit-share, whereas the true benefit of the co-op lies in being able to purchase superior-quality or price-discounted goods. (This is the business model of outdoor leisure retailers such as REI in the United States, which sells what is, for the price, technically superior gear.) There are certain limits to this strategy, however, in that for a worker cooperative simply to pay higher wages, or a customer cooperative to have lower prices, risks undermining the primary advantage of having an ownership group with only a residual claim. The key feature of a bonus payment to workers is that the firm is not under any contractual obligation to pay it, and so the firm is able to respond more flexibly to changing market conditions. If workers are simply paid higher wages, then the cooperative winds up having all the same disadvantages of a capitalist firm (i.e., a fixed wage bill) and none of the advantages (i.e., the equity cushion).

The central attraction of a cooperative, it should be noted, does not always rest with the financial benefits that it provides to its members, but rather the opportunity it creates to develop a different sort of relationship between members and the firm. The conventions of ownership include the understanding that the management of the firm "works for" its owners and so is under a duty to assign priority to their interests – in the same way that shareholder-owned firms are governed by a norm of shareholder primacy, worker cooperatives are governed by a norm of worker primacy, and customer cooperatives are governed by a norm of customer primacy, etc. This allows members of the ownership group to develop much stronger trust relations with the firm – an opportunity that is particularly valuable when the firm exercises market power over (and is thus in a position to act opportunistically toward) them. This is a key motive in cooperative formation in certain sectors, such as farm supply cooperatives in the early twentieth century. A contemporary example would be cooperative day-care centres. For-profit (i.e., investor-owned) day-cares have not been particularly successful, largely because parents do not trust such firms to care for their children properly (and to refrain from cutting corners). Cooperative day-care centres (i.e., customer cooperatives) remain extremely popular, despite chronic management difficulties caused by the fact that few of their owners expect to have ongoing relations with the firm. The difference is that parents are more comfortable leaving their children in the care of a firm whose management works for *them*, rather than some anonymous group of investors, because it reduces the chances that they will be the targets of opportunistic firm behaviour.

It is this altered structure of managerial loyalty that is responsible, I suspect, for the perception that cooperatives are more virtuous than standard business corporations. It is, however, to some degree an illusion.[26] While the cooperative has an ownership relation, and thus exhibits loyalty toward, a different patron group, it retains contractual relations with all of the others. A worker cooperative will typically treat its workers better, and a customer co-op will treat its customers better, but there is no reason to expect that a worker cooperative will treat its customers better, or a customer cooperative will treat its workers better. For the customer, the difference between taking a "co-op" taxi and an ordinary capitalist taxi is entirely imperceptible. Indeed, part of the reason that most people underestimate the number of cooperatives already operating in market economies is that, unless they are dealing with a consumer cooperative, they simply do not notice any difference in the way they are treated when transacting with a cooperative rather than a standard business corporation.

Furthermore, the cooperative retains three of the essential qualities of the capitalist firm. First, it is profit oriented and so has the same incentive to act in a "rapacious" or "exploitative" fashion. It is, of course, not going to be acting rapaciously toward its owners, but that doesn't mean that it is not going to act opportunistically when dealing with other patron groups. The taxi industry, for instance, has been extremely aggressive in securing and defending the economic rents it receives from municipal licensing arrangements. Dairy supply cooperatives in Canada have led the fight to defend "supply management," a cartel arrangement that is highly inimical to the interests of consumers. More generally, the history of labour unions provides no reason to think that workers are any less self-interested, or less bloody-minded in the pursuit of their interests than investors.

Second, cooperatives have essentially the same incentives as capitalist firms to externalize costs. As Joseph Stiglitz has observed, negative externalities (such as pollution) are a consequence of the decentralization of decision-making, rather than the specific ownership structure of capitalist firms.[27] (For example, departments within a university are constantly making decisions that have a negative impact on other departments, simply because nothing forces them to take an all-things-considered perspective on whether their budgets, or their faculty complement, or their program requirements are justified.) Because decision-making in the market is decentralized, cooperatives will still have powerful incentives to lay off workers during economic downturns, to raise prices when it is profitable to do so, to pollute, or otherwise offload costs onto others when they think they can get away with it, to deter competition, and to cut corners and engage in sharp practices when it benefits their owners to do so. They are, in other words, not committed to the general interest, but are just as committed to advancing a particular set of interests as the capitalist firm is. The only difference is that they are committing to advancing a different set of particular interests. The group whose interests they are committed to advancing may be a more sympathetic one, from the standpoint of many observers, but this should not be permitted to obscure the fact that cooperatives and capitalist firms exhibit the same partiality toward the interests of their owners.

Third, as cooperatives become larger and more successful, they come under increased pressure to make the transition to professional management. These managers are typically salaried employees, even in worker cooperatives. (Worker cooperatives often opt to hire managers on contractual terms, in order to avoid some of the tensions and conflicts that would result from authority relations being established among members of the ownership group.) As a result, many of the same problems of incentive alignment that arise within capitalist firms can occur within cooperatives. Under the current state of affairs, in which cooperatives represent a relatively small segment of the economy, cooperative managers tend to be a self-selecting group. Because they are paid less, relative to private-sector managers, cooperatives tend to attract individuals who have an ideological commitment to cooperative principles, and that approach reduces internal agency problems. If cooperatives became more widespread, however, one would expect that managers would come to represent the broader spectrum of human motivations, and so there is no particular reason to think that cooperatives would not begin to experience many of the problems that have afflicted investor-owned firms.

Finally, it should be noted that the superior virtue of cooperatives is often said to flow from the fact that they are "more democratic" than capitalist firms. Stated baldly, this is simply not true. Formal control of the firm is always exercised democratically *by the ownership group*. Thus a shareholder-owned firm is controlled democratically by the shareholders, just as a customer-owned cooperative is controlled democratically by the customers, and a worker-owned cooperative is controlled democratically by the workers. Under no circumstances do individuals outside the ownership group get to vote. Thus it is simply confused to claim that a standard business corporation is "undemocratic" because workers do not get to decide democratically how the firm is to be managed.[28] It would make as much sense to complain that worker cooperatives are "undemocratic" because investors do not get to decide democratically how their money is to be spent. Democratic control is part of a bundle of rights associated with ownership: the residual claim, formal control over management (typically mediated by a board of directors), fiduciary duties of management, and voting rights in selecting board members and dealing with major questions confronting the firm.

A slightly more subtle version of the criticism points to the fact that many cooperatives allocate voting rights to individuals, rather than basing them on the number of "shares" that an individual possesses. There is actually much confusion on this point, so it is worth dwelling upon for a moment. The basic claim, as a factual matter, is again not true. The original Rochdale principles of cooperative management required "one member one vote," but the International Cooperative Alliance, which functions as the current custodian of these principles, has modified the "democratic member control" principle to permit other arrangements.[29] For example, certain dairy cooperatives allocate shares to farmers based on how much milk they supply to the cooperative, and then use a one-share-one-vote rule.[30] The reasons are not difficult to discern, since there may be vast differences among farmers in how much of a stake they have in the success of the firm. In other cases, with cooperatives in which the members have roughly the same stake, the one-person-one-vote rule is uncontroversial. In a standard worker cooperative, such as a taxi company, all of the drivers are similarly situated vis-a-vis the firm, and so it makes sense that they would be given equal say. But if some were full-time, while others were part-time or casual members, an arrangement under which everyone had equal say might become the source of considerable tension.

From this perspective, it is easy to see why a standard investor-owned firm uses a one-share-one-vote principle – it is because different investors can have vastly different amounts at stake in the firm. It would be absurd to give a small punter who purchases a single bank share the same say in the direction of the firm's management as a large pension fund, which is investing the life savings of thousands. So while the one-person-one-vote rule may seem more democratic, because it bears greater resemblance to the way that the political system is organized, it is difficult to see why it should apply to the firm, and indeed, in many cases it would seem to violate basic principles of fairness to give equal say to all members of the ownership group when they are differently situated. (That having been said, it would be easy for a capitalist firm to reproduce this feature of cooperatives, simply by issuing a very restricted number of shares, with the specification that no individual can own more than one share. At the same time, it is also easy to come up with objections, both practical and moral, to such an arrangement.)

It is worth emphasizing that none of this is intended as a criticism of the cooperative form, or of the cooperative movement more generally. My objective is simply to show that there is no basis for thinking that cooperatives are any less likely to produce the same sort of social problems as the investor-owned business corporation. The main reason is simply that they are not sufficiently *different* from business corporations. The most important similarity is, of course, the fact that cooperatives, just like business corporations, are organized around the pursuit of profit and therefore do not represent an alternative to the profit-maximizing firm.

3. Cooperatives and Capital

There is another point about cooperatives that should be made, which is sufficiently complex in the details that it merits its own discussion. Cooperatives still have need of capital. The general principle governing the firm is that inputs can be obtained either from the ownership group or through market contracting. If workers, customers, or suppliers form the ownership group, then the availability of capital from the ownership group is going to be quite limited. As a result, the primary recourse of the firm will be to obtain its capital through market contracting, which is to say, in the form of bank loans or through the sale of investment bonds. Unfortunately, many cooperatives have difficulty raising capital in this way, a situation that produces what some call "the capital conundrum."[31]

As an aside, it should be noted that cutting out the shareholder does not mean eliminating the capitalist, in at least one sense of the term. The firm still has investors, and these investors are still earning a return (or a "profit," in the Marxian sense of the term).[32] The only difference is the *terms* on which capital is being obtained. Instead of being secured on flexible terms, in return for the residual claim, the residuum is being appropriated by some other patron group, and so capital must be secured on fixed and inflexible terms, in return for an interest payment. As a result, the firm does not save any money with the elimination of shareholders. It may be relieved of the duty to pay out profits to investors, but it substitutes for this the duty to pay interest to creditors. One might note that the rate of interest is typically lower than the long-run rate of return on equities, and so there is still some savings there. These savings are, however, illusory, because along with the elimination of shareholders comes the elimination of their role as residual risk-bearers. Once capital is being obtained on inflexible terms, then the risks associated with market fluctuations and general uncertainty must be borne by the new ownership group. They will either have to shoulder this risk or purchase insurance against it – either way, the cost to them will tend to be the same as the "spread" between the interest rate and the return on equities (which is why that spread is often referred to as the "risk premium" on equity investments). One can see this very clearly in the insurance industry, where mutuals have to purchase "reinsurance," to protect themselves from the risk of a spike in claims that outstrip their ability to pay, even with the high initial premiums paid by members. Through demutualization (i.e., transformation into a standard business corporation), some of this tail risk is transferred to investors, which in turn reduces the amount that the firm must spend on reinsurance. The important point is that there is no free lunch in all of this.

Cooperatives face challenges in securing bank loans because they have difficulty finding collateral. In a standard business corporation, the firm's equity serves as collateral (which is why lenders often look to the debt/equity ratio of the firm to determine its creditworthiness). The problem of finding collateral is most acute in the case of a worker cooperative, where the prohibition on indentured servitude means that workers cannot pledge their own input to the firm (i.e., their labour) as collateral.[33] Supply and consumer cooperatives have the same problem, although often in a less acute form if they are able to somehow pledge their input to the firm as collateral. For instance, a wind power cooperative may raise capital to purchase turbines by having its owners (electricity consumers) sign long-term purchase contracts, which can either be pledged as collateral or, in some cases, directly resold on secondary markets. But when arrangements like this are not possible, cooperatives have to pay a higher interest rate on loans, based on the perception (and in many cases the reality) that it is riskier to lend to them. This explains why cooperatives, especially worker cooperatives, tend to flourish in less capital-intensive sectors of the economy. It is difficult to imagine an arrangement under which firms in highly capital-intensive sectors, such as telecommunications, shipping and railroads, automobile manufacturing, or petroleum extraction and refinement, could be organized as worker cooperatives, simply because workers have so little at stake in the firm compared to investors.

An alternative to bank finance is for cooperatives to raise capital from their members, even though the latter are not primarily investors. In principle, cooperatives could require members to pay a large membership fee (and thus, in effect, make a capital investment in the firm) in order to join.[34] (There are also, of course, pseudo-cooperatives, such as standard business corporations that are owned by their employees through an Employee Stock Ownership Plan [ESOP]. These differ from worker cooperatives in that employees enjoy ownership rights only in their capacity as investors, and not in their capacity as workers.) This is often regarded as undesirable, however, from a socialist perspective because it limits membership to the relatively affluent (trying to get a loan to pay the membership fee has the same collateral problem), and from a prudential perspective because it heightens the members' exposure to risk, so that now they face a potential loss of capital in addition to fluctuation in the value of their residual claim. Another option is to have cooperatives paired with a credit union (in the same way that Japanese *zaibatsu* or *keiretsu* would have a slaved bank within the industrial conglomerate). This is how the Mondragon cooperative network in the Basque region of Spain operates. All it means, however, is that the credit union, to the extent that it makes loans to the cooperatives on better terms than those offered by commercial banks, is tacitly accepting either more risk or a lower return for its depositors.

Thus what many proponents of cooperatives seem to have in mind, when thinking about access to capital, is that cooperatives will be largely self-financing. In other words, rather than disbursing residual earnings (i.e., profits), to their members, the firm will retain them and use these funds to make capital investments. This is essentially identical to the process through which a standard business corporation reinvests profits, although in the case of cooperatives it generates a number of complexities. The important thing to note is that the firm is still paying for its use of this capital, although less conspicuously so. After all, the firm could take its retained earnings and invest them elsewhere, such as the stock market. Thus when it chooses to finance its own capital investment, it is foregoing the stock market rate of return (which constitutes, therefore, the opportunity cost of this use of capital). It could also put the money into the pension fund of its members, where it could earn the same rate of return. Or it could disburse the profits to its members, who could invest it privately. Either way, there is obviously no free lunch to be had – the firm's own earnings are not a zero-cost source of capital. All it means is that the investment is funded, ultimately, by the members of the cooperative (i.e., those with the residual claim on those earnings).

However, a complication arises when cooperatives engage in self-financing. It stems from the fact that there is no secondary market for ownership of cooperative shares, the way that there is with standard business corporations. To see the problems this can create, consider a worker cooperative with 1,000 members, which decides to invest $10 million in new plant equipment, financed through retained earnings. This means that each worker will receive $10,000 less in wages (i.e., profit-share, bonus, etc.), in order to finance this investment. The situation is essentially the same as one in which the workers are paid the money but then forced to reinvest it in the firm. The difference is that, with the latter arrangement, the workers would presumably have some title, certificate, or document, giving them a claim on a fraction of the firm's capital. With self-financing, on the other hand, workers are tacitly investing in the firm, and yet they get no claim on the firm's capital, only the claim on the revenue stream that they enjoy in their capacity as workers. As a result, if they quit their jobs (or worse, are laid off), they wind up with nothing.

At best, this can create unwanted labour-market rigidity, as workers become locked into employment at firms in which their investments are held (because the only way they can earn the profits from those investments is to remain members in the cooperative). At worst, it can create grievous conflict within the cooperative. For instance, it is a recipe for intergenerational conflict, as older workers will not be interested in forgoing wages in order to finance long-term investment, while younger workers will tend to support it. Members of the cooperative will also be unwilling to bring in new members, for the obvious reason that doing so dilutes their ownership share and thus tacitly gives away some fraction of their invested capital. The only real way to manage this is to have some arrangement in which workers are "bought out" when they quit or retire (i.e., are given a payment equal to their invested capital), and in which workers must buy their way in with an equivalent sum of capital. This is, of course, how a standard business corporation operates – with owners being able to buy and sell their shares – but it is often felt to be in tension with the ideals of a worker cooperative.

Finally, it is worth mentioning that any type of financing arrangement that relies upon members, in one way or another, for access to either collateral or capital tends to diminish the attractions of the cooperative form (or as Henry Hansmann says, it increases the "costs of ownership").[35] Investment is extremely risky, particularly with modern bankruptcy law, which offers debtors significant protection against creditors. Equity investors protect themselves against this risk primarily by holding a diversified portfolio, as well as by availing themselves of natural hedging strategies that present themselves. Of course, other patron groups are exposed to risk as well. Workers face labour market risk, most obviously, a decline in demand for their services (and thus, the prospect of being laid off). As Margaret Blair has observed, workers also make a variety of "asset-specific investments" in the firm that employs them, such as learning to master complex systems (e.g., inventory, file storage, bookkeeping, etc.) that are unique to the firm, and thus of no value elsewhere.[36] Ideally, workers should be able to protect themselves from the risk exposure generated by dealing with only one firm. It is, however, difficult to do so in the case of their labour investments. At very least then, they should hold their *capital* investments elsewhere. (For instance, they could avail themselves of the natural hedging strategy of investing their savings in their employer's most prominent competitor.) The last thing they should be doing is doubling down, by investing their savings with their own employer. This is the fatal flaw in ESOPs – they make it so that when the firm goes bankrupt, employees lose *both* their jobs and their retirement savings.

Member-financed cooperatives have the exact same flaw, which may be one of the reasons that workers in particular have not proven overly enthusiastic about them. Because of the typical structure of household finance, with fixed mortgage and car payments eating up a very large fraction of monthly income, workers tend to be extremely risk-averse when it comes to the possibility of a wage reduction. A standard business corporation offers them hostile management and "exploitation" at the hands of capitalists, in return for a guaranteed wage (that is given higher priority, in the firm's schedule of payments, than the profits going to shareholders). Cooperatives, by contrast, substitute friendly management and a profit share, but increase the worker's risk exposure (or "precarity") by taking some fraction of the wage and turning it into a residual claim, which may or may not be paid, according to market conditions. Self-financing ratchets up the risk some more, by tying up the worker's capital (in practice, retirement savings) with the firm, and in some cases making it impossible to withdraw. All of this risk is, of course, invisible, and so it is possible to pretend that it is not there – even though workers are aware of it, although more so in the former case than the latter. None of this is to say that there should not be worker cooperatives. It is merely to observe that they have rather significant drawbacks and that these are, in many cases, structural features of the cooperative form.

4. State Ownership

There is another recourse for critics of the profit orientation of firms, which is to push for greater state ownership. Indeed, many people would like to preserve the essential structure of a market economy, as far as the price system is concerned, and yet see much greater state involvement in the ownership of firms, particularly in sensitive sectors such as banking, energy, and transportation. Indeed, one can imagine an arrangement under which capital-intensive sectors of the economy were under state ownership, with privately owned firms, such as cooperatives and perhaps a smattering of capitalist firms, occupying the retail and service sectors. For many this seems like a "best of both worlds" arrangement.

There are, of course, well-known objections to such proposals. Proponents of state ownership also sometimes claim that there is a free lunch to be had, in that the state can access capital at lower cost by cutting out profits to investors. But this is again an illusion, as the state that supplies the capital also winds up bearing all the risk (which either takes the form of an implicit cost, or becomes an explicit one, when it purchases insurance in order to offload it). There are also some well-known challenges involved in public management, due to the fact that the state cannot go bankrupt. This generates, inter alia, a "soft budget constraint" that can result in severe agency problems, making it difficult to control managers.[37] Finally, even if it were possible to leave the basic structure of a competitive market in place, the state often has difficulty responding appropriately to price signals, because interest groups may use the political process to engage in rent seeking. As a result, even when the state is as good as the market at rewarding success, it is invariably worse at punishing failure.

These issues are all well known, and rather than rehearsing the details here, I would instead like to make a less obvious point, which is that state ownership often does not involve as much of a break with the profit orientation of firms as many people have imagined. There is a popular perception, according to which privately owned firms are selfish, and so maximize profits, while publicly owned firms are altruistic, and so promote the common good. Because of this perception, many people are surprised to learn that the current best practice recommendation in public management involves insulating state-owned enterprises (SOEs) from political control as much as possible, then giving managers the injunction to maximize profits (and judging their performance by their success in this regard). In other words, profit-maximization is often retained as an *organizational objective* in the state sector, and so the mere fact of public ownership often does not translate into any difference in management objective or incentives. It is also one of the reasons that SOEs almost always need to be regulated externally through law, in exactly the same way that capitalist firms are, rather than being controlled internally through the political process.[38]

One might wonder why this is so. Given that there are no investors demanding returns, why should publicly owned firms care about profits? The answer has to do with a somewhat subtle, and thus underappreciated virtue of the profit orientation in privately owned firms, which is that it gives owners an important tool for evaluating managerial performance, and thus for reducing agency costs. In order to understand the significance of this, it is important to recognize how serious the problem of managerial incompetence or malfeasance can be in large organizations. Consider, for example, the 2001 accounting scandal involving the Enron corporation. This is often presented as a case study of corporate greed run amok. And yet the problems at Enron had very little to do with the search for profit or "corporate greed." The problem was actually one of individual greed. Rather than making profits for investors, senior managers at the firm were in fact enriching themselves, while running up enormous corporate debt that they concealed from investors. At the time of bankruptcy, Enron was carrying about $10 billion in hidden debt. And while the firm may have participated in a range of unethical practices (such as the gaming of the California electricity market), this was often not done with the goal of increasing *firm* profits, but rather to maximize bonus payments to individual employees – indeed, the major problem with the firm was that it had no profits, because it had made a series of money-losing investments (such as the Dabhol power plant in India).[39]

Thus the structural problem with Enron was actually that it suffered from severe internal agency problems. Because of an ill-considered bonus system, which rewarded individuals upfront for the anticipated value over many years of contracts signed, with no mechanism to claw back payments in cases where the anticipated gains did not materialize, employees simply failed to exhibit any concern for the long-run performance of the firm's investments. Part of the function of the profit orientation, at the level of the firm, is to control these agency problems by providing a single metric that can be used to measure managerial performance, in order to ensure that organizational objectives are given precedence over individual self-interest. As Michael Jensen has argued, "Every organization has to ask and answer the question: What are we trying to accomplish? Or, to put the same question in more concrete terms: How do we keep score? When all is said and done, how do we measure better versus worse?"[40] If we take the *creation of economic value* to be the primary purpose of the firm – whether it be a business corporation or a cooperative – then the obvious way of measuring success is to look at the balance of expenditure and revenue, which is conveniently summarized in the profit and loss statement. This is, of course, a rough and ready measure, and it is not difficult to think of ways in which it fails to represent the primary goal. Nevertheless, it has one advantage over a very large number of other measures, which is that it generates a single "bottom line," which can be used to assess and compare performance across the organization.[41] It therefore serves as what Jensen describes as an "objective function" for measuring firm performance.

It is not difficult to think of more nuanced measures of firm performance that are multidimensional, prescribing a list of different objectives (such as one finds in "balanced scorecard" or "triple bottom line" accounting). The problem with these systems is that they generate "multitask" agency problems, which in turn make it difficult to assess managerial performance. When managers are given two objectives that are not strictly complementary (such as making a profit *and* promoting domestic employment), they are essentially being freed from the obligation to do their best with respect to either. When asked to explain their failure to achieve one objective, they can point to the constraints imposed by the other, and it is essentially impossible for an observer to determine whether the manager has in fact made the best effort, or chosen the best policies. Furthermore, it becomes impossible to compare the performance of managers at different firms, because each will be balancing the objectives in a different way. As a result, competition becomes useless as a revelation mechanism for assessing managerial performance.

The "multiple objectives" issue is widely understood to be a problem in the private sector, which is one of the reasons for insistence upon a single firm objective. In the public sector, however, it is an even more serious problem. Indeed, in the first half of the twentieth century, many industries were nationalized, or developed in the public sector, precisely so that they could serve multiple objectives – not just generating revenue for the public purse, but also pursuing regional development strategies, enhancing national security, fighting unemployment, providing macroeconomic stability, and favouring domestic industry, to name a few. But as a result, many nations found themselves struggling to control these firms, and in particular, to impose discipline upon managers. For example, not having to worry about the cost of capital, many of these firms became overcapitalized, as managers undertook massive investments, knowing that the state would pick up the tab. More commonly, with SOEs being structurally incapable of bankruptcy, they simply failed to cover their own operating costs, creating losses that the state (and thus taxpayers) wound up having no choice but to cover.

The primary response, beginning in the 1960s, was a series of reforms of the SOE sector, where instead of being treated as just another branch of government operations, SOEs were transformed into stand-alone corporations, which were then set in an arm's-length relationship to elected politicians. In the earlier model, the activities of the SOE had been integrated into one or more government departments, elected officials were actively involved in operational decision-making, and there was no separation between the budget of the "firm" and the department (ministry, etc.) in which it was embedded. "Capital investment by state enterprises was, alongside road building, current expenditure on police and so on, part of public expenditure programmes, whilst their operating surpluses were, along with taxes, social security payments and so on, part of government income."[42] Beginning in the late 1960s, however, a large-scale shift began, with countries moving away from this model toward an arrangement that involved: (1) greater managerial autonomy, (2) creation of a board of directors to mediate relations between elected officials and managers, (3) partitioning of assets and liabilities between the SOE and line departments, (4) the demand for self-financing of capital investment by the SOE, (5) increased focus on economic efficiency (i.e., break-even, or profitability) as a managerial objective, and finally, (6) the use of contracting to implement the "social responsibility" mandate of the firm. Many of these reforms were pioneered in France, following the release of the Nora report in 1967, and were imitated by other countries, such as Canada, during the 1970s. This overall period is often described as the "corporatization" phase of SOEs.

The reason that these reforms were undertaken had to do with agency problems that arose with public sector managers. The most conspicuous symptom of these agency problems was that SOEs lost a great deal of money.[43] The Nora report, for instance, was commissioned after the annual operating losses being absorbed by the French state from its SOEs more than doubled over a period of only four years, from 2.3 billion francs in 1961 to 5.2 billion in 1965.[44] The 1967 U.K. white paper *Nationalised Industries: A Review of Financial and Economic Objectives* was motivated by similar concerns and arrived at nearly identical conclusions.[45] The underlying problem was a breakdown of managerial discipline, resulting from the combination of multitask and multi-principal agency problems – managers were being given too many different objectives and were held accountable to too many different actors.[46]

To provide a concrete example that illustrates the general problem, consider Canada's national airline (Trans-Canada Airlines, subsequently renamed Air Canada). It was initially established with a clear public-interest mandate. (As C.D. Howe, the minister responsible, described it in 1937, "The company will be protected against loss, but its profits will be very strictly limited. In other words, it is organized to perform a certain national service, and it is expected that the service will be performed at or near cost.")[47] It was created with a board of directors, but one that exercised very little authority. Key management decisions were made by the Department of Transportation, the Department of Finance, the Treasury Board Secretariat, and in some cases Cabinet as a whole. Most dramatically, the purchase of new aircraft was, over the years, almost always a political decision, made by the minister, or Cabinet, sometimes over the opposition of airline management.[48] Key route decisions, both international and domestic, were also made by Cabinet, with a number of "social routes" to remote regions – routes that were too uneconomical to be serviced by a private carrier – imposed on "national interest" grounds. (These were not always imposed. The airline sometimes took the initiative and created "social routes" on its own, introducing direct flights to the ridings of powerful Cabinet ministers from remote regions.)[49] And finally, the location of the airline's major maintenance operations was decided politically, as part of a regional development strategy (most controversially, to maintain employment in Winnipeg, instead of consolidating operations in Montreal, as the airline's management had proposed).[50]

I think it is fairly easy to see the problems that this organizational structure can create. How can anyone tell whether the airline is being well managed or not? Naturally, Air Canada lost a great deal of money, and passengers were constantly complaining about the quality of service. But was this justifiable or not? If the government is forcing an airline to fly money-losing "social routes," or to maintain uneconomical maintenance facilities, *and* it wants fares to be kept low, then it cannot really complain when the airline loses money. The question of whether the loss is larger than it necessarily had to be becomes effectively unanswerable. This is the conclusion that was also arrived at in the Nora report, on similar grounds, particularly in its discussion of SNCF (the French national railway operator). On the one hand, SNCF managers were supposed to run their operations efficiently, but on the other hand, they were expected to keep fares low, to maintain service to low-population areas, and to create employment in depressed regions. This made it impossible to determine whether the organization was being effective in its pursuit of *any* of these ends.

Nora's enormously influential recommendation was that the objectives imposed upon the firm be disaggregated and separately costed. The firm should adopt a standard business model – choosing routes, for instance, where passenger revenue is sufficient to cover expenses, including capital outlays – as its baseline strategy. It should then take any deviations from the strategy – running "social routes," for instance, to underserviced regions – and determine how much it costs to achieve those particular objectives. The state should, in turn, determine how much it is willing to pay to achieve the public interest objectives it would like to see the SOE pursue. The two parties should then negotiate, and work out an explicit contract, with the state essentially paying the SOE an agreed amount for each public interest objective it imposes.[51] In return, it can demand that the firm show an overall operating surplus, and that it maintain its own balance sheet, carrying its own losses. This arrangement makes it possible to impose a standard auditing regime upon SOEs, and to hold managers accountable to a single objective.[52]

In 1978, the Air Canada Act instructed the airline to run its operation with "due regard to sound business principles and, in particular, the contemplation of profit."[53] Similar decisions were made in every other Western nation, by both left-wing and right-wing governments. Thus the introduction of the profit objective to SOEs arose endogenously out of the practice of public management. It was not imposed from without, nor was it part of any broader "neoliberal" agenda. In Canada, for instance, the decision to restructure Air Canada was made by the left-of-centre Liberal government of Pierre Trudeau, long before there was any discussion of privatization.[54] Of course, once these firms had been insulated from political control through the creation of an independent board of directors, and their managers were given the instruction to pursue profits, it became difficult to say why they should remain under exclusive public ownership. Thus the corporatization of SOEs that took place in the 1970s wound up laying the groundwork for many of the privatizations that occurred beginning in the 1980s, but it is anachronistic to imagine that the latter supplied the motive for the former. It is also important to note that the change in ownership associated with privatization did not result in a sudden introduction of the profit objective to these organizations.

It remains the case that vast segments of the public sector are not currently organized around the pursuit of profit, and not all SOEs have been fully corporatized. This is in part a selection effect, because many sectors that could be corporatized were subsequently privatized, and so most of the operations that have remained in the public sector are ones that necessarily have a multitask or multi-principal structure. (An example often given is the passport office, which has a dual mandate: there is the customer service objective of providing fast and reliable service in issuing passports, but also the security objective, of ensuring that passports do not wind up in the hands of those who are not entitled to them.) This tends to generate the illusion that the public sector is run on principles vastly different from those that govern the private sector. If one looks, however, at areas in which the state is engaged in activities broadly similar to those undertaken by private firms – such as state-owned oil companies, or electricity generation facilities – one can see that there is now very little difference in the way that public and private organizations are managed.

This is important, for our purposes, because if one wants to push for state ownership of sectors of the economy as an alternative to management by private, profit-oriented firms, then the experience of the twentieth century suggests that the most effective management model for these SOEs will involve the imposition of a profit orientation on those firms as an organizational objective. To the extent that they pursue social objectives, this will typically be done through explicit contracting, with the state essentially paying the SOE to pursue these goals. Thus the difference in the behaviour of SOEs and standard business corporations will wind up being rather slight. In effect, once the management structure has been standardized, then the difference between being owned by the state and being owned by a collection of large pension and mutual funds (which is typically what private ownership amounts to for major firms) turns out to be not that great.[55]

5. Non-profits

There is a final option that must be discussed, more for completeness than anything, which is the non-profit firm. I am not aware of anyone having suggested that non-profits could be a systemic alternative to profit-oriented firms. There has, however, been much enthusiasm for the "third sector" in recent years, a term that is used to refer to voluntary and community organizations, non-governmental organizations (NGOs), as well as non-profits. Non-profits are best known as the preferred organizational form for charities, advocacy groups, and professional or trade organizations. There are also some sectors of the economy in which non-profit corporations are a common organizational form, with the two leading examples being hospitals and daycare centres, as well as universities in certain jurisdictions. A survey of developed countries in 2000 found that, on average, the non-profit and voluntary sector employed 7.6 per cent of the active workforce in these countries.[56] Thus it is worth making a few observations about this organizational form, largely as a way of explaining why, despite playing an important role in the economy, it remains largely confined to these niche sectors.

The central feature of a non-profit organization (whether it be a corporation, a trust, or a foundation) is that it is legally prohibited from disbursing residual sums to any of its patron groups.[57] This does not mean that it cannot pursue profits, or that it is penalized for making them. It simply means that it is forced to retain them. As a result, there is a sense in which such a firm has no owners, because there is no residual claimant. As far as governance is concerned, it is typically run by a self-perpetuating board of directors (i.e., where new directors are chosen by old ones).

This management structure works quite well with organizations that have a strong mission or eleemosynary purpose, sufficient to constrain the behaviour of insiders. The weaknesses become apparent, however, with non-profit organizations that are involved in more ordinary economic activities, or that lack a tightly focused mission. There are three basic problems. First, the fact that the organization cannot disburse profits *as such* does not stop it from doing so in more indirect ways. The most common end-run around the constraint is simply to pay exorbitant salaries to insiders – including bonuses (although these are normally subject to some constraint). This has become a serious problem with non-profit hospitals in the United States, which often fundraise as though they were charities, then use the money to pay multi-million-dollar salaries to top managers. Similarly, it has been argued that many universities, despite being officially incorporated as non-profits, in fact function as worker cooperatives run by faculty. Not only do faculty exercise control by reserving access to top managerial positions for members, they have a de facto residual claim on firm earnings, simply because any excess revenue is absorbed, by hook or by crook, by increased faculty salaries.

Second, because non-profit organizations have no investors, they are not under any pressure to justify the cost of capital of what they possess. As a result, they also have a tendency to become overcapitalized, e.g., by earning a great deal of money, then using it to construct more and more lavish headquarters or facilities. Any visitor to an exclusive American university, such as Princeton, Duke, or Stanford, can see this pathology on display, as the physical infrastructure on these campuses is often one that could handle a student population an order of magnitude larger. The arrangement persists only because there is no one worrying about the ROI ("return on investment") of the infrastructure. Finally, there is the possibility of the organization becoming captured by an interest group that is able to gain control of the board of directors. Because the organization is unaccountable to any broader constituency, there is often nothing that can be done in these circumstances.

For all three of these reasons, non-profit firms often suffer from poor management. Indeed, the fact that executive positions at non-profit organizations often serve as sinecures for retired politicians, civic leaders, and other worthies, is a symptom of this problem. The important point is that there are very few structural constraints on the abuse of this organizational form. To the extent that non-profits are effective, it is typically because the members are guided by a set of moral constraints arising from the organizational mission. If one were to extend the non-profit form into other domains of the economy, where there is no comparable moral purpose, one can only imagine that abuse of the organizational form would become more prevalent. The case of hospitals in the United States provides an instructive example in this regard. (As with any organizational form, it is a helpful exercise to imagine what uses it could be put to once Wall Street bankers and lawyers got their hands on it.)[58]

Finally, it is worth noting one other problem with non-profit firms, which is that, absent some humanitarian mission, individuals often lack the incentive to create them. When demand for a particular good increases, in a standard competitive market with standard business corporations, this creates higher-than-average rates of return for the firms in that sector. This in turn motivates new firms to enter these markets, thereby increasing supply. It is the pursuit of windfall profits that serves as the inducement for firms to enter underserviced sectors. With non-profit firms, by contrast, the mere fact that a particular good is in short supply provides no particular incentive to expand production of it. One can see this clearly in the case of non-profit day-care centres, which are often very well run but typically in short supply, with those that are created often a side operation of an enterprise with an established constituency, such as a church or university. One very seldom sees the creation of a self-standing non-profit day-care centre, even in areas of chronic shortage where this would constitute an important public service.

Thus it is important to recognize that non-profits are not quite as compatible with the price mechanism as cooperatives are, precisely because they lack the organizational commitment to maximizing profits. This difference is unimportant in an economy dominated by profit-oriented firms, with non-profits operating largely in marginal and uneconomic sectors. Any proposal to expand non-profits into core sectors of the economy, however, would have to deal with the problem of maintaining the price system, with firms that lack the crucial incentive to engage in price competition with one another, or even to expand supply in response to increased demand. This is another way of making a more basic point, which is that the desire to keep the price system while eliminating the profit orientation of firms is problematic, because it is the profit orientation of market actors that pushes prices toward market-clearing levels. Unless one is willing to introduce some sort of socialist planning system, such as a central agency that instructs firm managers to engage in marginal cost pricing, then the attempt to restructure firms in a way that genuinely abolishes the profit orientation winds up, *eo ipso*, undermining the price system.

6. Conclusion

One of the more under-appreciated features of capitalism has been the extraordinary creativity it has exhibited, in generating new forms of private property, as well as new forms of association involved in owning property.[59] Not only has it produced an enormous range of generic corporate forms, such as sole proprietorships, partnerships, limited liability partnerships, private corporations, public corporations, as well as a number of different forms of cooperative, it has also given rise to an array of special-purpose forms, such as condominiums, mutual funds, and real estate investment trusts. So while it is sometimes tempting to think of the "capitalist firm" as a hegemonic type, what modern market societies actually provide is set of enabling statutes, which allow individuals to choose the organizational form that seems most appropriate to the economic activity that they intend to undertake, as well as to restructure the firm as it develops, or as conditions change.

Despite the existence of a large menu of choices, the standard investor-owned firm remains by far the most popular organizational form – whether it be a publicly traded business corporation, or increasingly, a closed-held firm owned by private equity.[60] Although the hegemony of investor ownership is sometimes portrayed as a consequence of some nefarious plot on the part of capital, the considerations surveyed here suggest that it has more to do with the intrinsic advantages of the organizational form. This judgment must be modulated by the recognition that there remain, in many jurisdictions, legal constraints on cooperatives that might be thought to bias decision-making in the direction of investor ownership. The cooperative movement has been fighting for the elimination of such barriers (including, for instance, promoting legislation to enable the formation of multi-stakeholder cooperatives). Such efforts should be applauded, on the grounds that the ideal arrangement is one in which corporate law (understood broadly) remains essentially neutral between different organizational forms, focusing rather on enabling the parties themselves to structure their economic relations in a way that maximizes the benefits of the administrative arrangements they seek to establish. There are grounds for scepticism that such neutrality would in fact result in the formation of many more cooperatives, but that is not a question to be settled at the level of normative theory. Rather, it is an issue to be decided piecemeal by those who are actually involved in the enterprises. The commitment to legal neutrality is, of course, based on the claim defended here, that no single organizational form is likely to result in increased production of social benefits, or an overall reduction in the incidence of misconduct. In other words, "society" has nothing at stake in the question, whether there are more cooperatives or more business corporations in the economy, since only the parties involved stand to benefit or lose. This is what licenses the general presumption in favour of whatever arrangements arise out of free contracting among individuals.

It should be noted as well that most advanced welfare states go to great lengths to discourage corporate misconduct, and yet the primary mechanism through which they seek to achieve this is the external regulation of firms, not internal governance reform or changes in ownership structure. If a non-capitalist organizational form offered significant advantages, from a social point of view, it would be reasonable to expect that governments would have done more to encourage individuals to organize themselves in this way. Cooperative and non-profit formation has been encouraged in particular sectors, such as renewable energy, where governments have promoted consumer cooperatives as a way to secure greater community acceptance (or "social licence") for such projects. But there has been little general effort to promote cooperatives as an alternative economic model. Certain policies do favour non-capitalist organizational structures, of which the tax deduction offered to those who donate to non-profits is perhaps the most well-known.[61] There is also the less-often-noted fact that cooperatives are largely exempt from corporate taxation, because the rebates or bonuses disbursed to members can be counted as a tax-deductible expense, unlike the profits paid to shareholders in a business firm. The fact that cooperatives remain relatively rare in core sectors of the economy, despite these inducements, suggests that they have significant countervailing deficiencies.

When assessing the normative significance of these facts, it is important not to lose sight of the basic role that the firm plays in a market economy. Firms exist, fundamentally, in order to enable forms of team production that cannot be achieved, or cannot be achieved as efficiently, through market contracting.[62] As private organizations, they cannot compel participation, and so the only way that they attract transaction partners from any of their patron groups is by offering up some share of the benefits of the cooperative system that they institutionalize, a share that is better than that offered elsewhere. It is in this sense that a firm serves as something like a "public good" for its patron groups, regardless of what sort of legal form the relationship between those individuals and the firm takes. A successful firm provides valuable products to its customers, stable and remunerative employment to its workers, as well as reliable returns to its providers of capital. But more importantly, a successful firm allows all who are involved to focus their energies and resources on *the production of economic value*, rather than on distributive conflict, office politics, competitive shirking, bureaucratic obstruction, managerial nest-feathering, and the myriad other pathologies that can afflict large organizations. Firms organized around the maximization of shareholder value have proven highly effective – which is to say, more effective than their rival organizational forms – at discharging this basic task in a wide range of different contexts. They provide relatively clear lines of authority, a transparent metric for assessing performance, a unified ownership group, and an active "market for control" that provides an extra layer of discipline on management.[63]

Of course, these advantages of the corporate organizational form come with offsetting disadvantages, one of which is the tendency to be overly partial to the interests of its ownership group, or to insiders, and thus to pursue profits in ways that do not actually rest upon the production of economic value, but involve merely transferring costs to other patron groups, or else to uninvolved third parties in the form of externalities. While it is perhaps an exaggeration to describe the modern business corporation as an "externality machine," as Kent Greenfield does, a very large number of firms have invested exceptional amounts of time and energy in developing business strategies that can best be described as conspiracies against the public.[64] It is also worth observing, however, that such corporate misconduct is not an intrinsic feature of the market system, in the way that, for example, price competition is. Indeed, governments work very hard to eliminate these undesirable profit-seeking strategies through regulation, and there is no contradiction in imagining an ideal market in which the *only* way to pursue profit would be through the production of economic value.[65]

Once it is recognized that no other organizational form is likely, on balance, to do a better job of coordinating the production of value, then what the critique of corporate malfeasance amounts to is a plea for *business ethics*. There is nothing wrong with encouraging other ownership forms, such as cooperatives and non-profits, and the question of whether a particular economic activity belongs in the private or public sector must continually be posed, as productive technology and organizational costs change. At the same time, we must recognize that, for the foreseeable future, the core of the economy will be organized and operated by profit-oriented investor-owned firms. The lack of any structural alternative to this arrangement, rather than serving as a source of despondency, should instead be seen as highlighting the critical importance of business ethics in a market economy. Because the law is a blunt instrument, it is impossible for the state to provide extrinsic incentives sufficient to deter all corporate misconduct – indeed, even securing compliance with existing laws is an enormous and ongoing challenge.[66] Thus every market society relies, to varying degrees, upon the willingness of business enterprises to exercise self-restraint in taking advantage of opportunities for misconduct. The central task of applied business ethics is to specify the occasions on which such self-restraint should be exercised, and of theoretical business ethics, to provide an intellectual framework within which such self-restraint can be justified.

There is much to be gained from this turn away from a "political economy" toward an "ethical" framing of the problem of corporate misconduct.[67] Most of the time, what critics of the profit orientation of firms actually want is for individual economic actors to behave more ethically. Their mistake lies in thinking that this can be achieved by eliminating profit as an organizational objective. Their reasoning usually begins with the conflation of profit and self-interest. They assume that if firms are seeking profits, then individuals within those firms must be acting in a self-interested manner. But since acting ethically often requires setting aside one's self-interest, the pressure to maximize profits amounts to a pressure to act unethically. So the best way to get people to act more ethically is to abolish the profit motive. Furthermore, trying to put pressure on these people to act more ethically without structural reform aimed at relieving the pressure imposed on them by the profit motive is likely to be ineffective.

This reasoning is fallacious, as we have seen, because of the way that it confuses profit as an organizational objective with self-interest as an individual motive. Unfortunately, business ethicists have not always been as clear as they ought to be in insisting on the distinction. For example, in their recent book, *The Ethics of Business*, Al Gini and Alexei Marcoux start out by conflating the two, describing the gain in utility that individuals achieve through economic exchange as a type of "profit," and then treating the profit earned by firms as merely an extension or aggregate of these individual gains.[68] Although they intend this as a way of legitimizing the profit orientation of firms, the argument tends rather to have the reverse consequence, of delegitimizing profit, by suggesting that it represents nothing more than individual selfishness writ large. The correct approach is to insist on a strict distinction between individual utility-maximization and the maximization of profit as an organizational objective, in order to show that moral imperatives, understood as impartial constraints on individual utility-maximization, may be perfectly compatible with the organizational imperative of profit-seeking business corporations.

In the same way that profit is not identical to self-interest, we have seen as well that the profit orientation of firms does not force managers to act without regard for moral principles. Competition certainly imposes constraints upon managers, but economic models that use the ideal of perfect competition as a benchmark for thinking about markets tend to give a very distorted picture of how much discretion corporate managers actually enjoy. Gary Becker, it may be recalled, deduced from first principles of microeconomics that any firm that engaged in racial or gender discrimination would be forced out of business by the competitive pressures of the marketplace.[69] And yet we know that firms are perfectly capable of engaging in discrimination without going bankrupt. Firms are also capable of acting morally – in particular, refraining from engaging in misconduct – and remaining in business, for precisely the same reason, that markets are simply not as competitive in real life as they are in economic models. Furthermore, as we have seen, the "business judgment rule" offers blanket protection for managers from any legal consequences of such decisions, should aggrieved shareholders try to press the issue.

Indeed, to the extent that cooperatives have a track record of behaving more "virtuously" than capitalist firms, this shows that a formal commitment to profit-maximization at the organizational level – a feature that cooperatives share with standard business corporations – is perfectly compatible with maintaining high standards of morality. Thus the only significant tension between business ethics and the profit-maximization imperative rests on the concern that the focus on investor returns, and on the competitive virtues that a market economy promotes, will create an ethos or culture that will tend to crowd out moral incentives.[70] This is the old complaint that capitalism, while not actually requiring selfish behaviour, nevertheless does a great deal to encourage it. There is much to be said for this concern. At the same time, it is important to remember that most individuals in a capitalist economy do not actually work at the "coal face," where market exchange occurs and adversarial norms prevail. Most work as employees deep in the interior of large bureaucratic organizations, where all of the transactions they engage in are administered. These large organizations are capable of cultivating their own corporate culture, and ones that do typically promote traditional cooperative norms (e.g., agreeableness, industriousness, professionalism, honesty, tolerance, etc.). This helps to explain why corporate malfeasance is not evenly diffused across the economy, but tends rather to cluster in very specific sectors and firms. For example, back in 1980, Marshall Clinard and Peter Yeager had identified three key industrial sectors that appeared to be particularly prone to white collar crime: pharmaceuticals, automotive, and petrochemical.[71] This list has remained surprisingly stable over the past few decades (although one might want to amend the list now to include finance and banking). Knowing that certain industries are ethically challenged reduces the surprise value of corporate scandals like the Deepwater Horizon disaster, or the emissions fraud that was disclosed at Volkswagen. At the same time, it shows that much can be achieved by working internally at these firms, striving to reform the corporate culture in order to improve ethical standards, or at least bring it into conformity with the standards that prevail elsewhere in the economy.

There are, of course, limits to what can be achieved through moral suasion. Precisely because it relies upon voluntary self-restraint, business ethics offers no guarantee against corporate misconduct. When low-cost legal or regulatory solutions are available, they should be preferred. At the same time, we should resist the temptation to look for a deeper structural solution, or some sort of "big bang" that would eliminate the problem of corporate malfeasance at its source. This is what drives much of the opposition to the profit-oriented capitalist firm. The considerations advanced here are intended to show that this opposition is largely a waste of time, simply because there are no viable or attractive institutional alternatives. Rather than responding to specific instances of corporate misconduct with abstract complaints about profit and greed, it would be better to respond by complaining about the specific forms of corporate misconduct involved, showing how they fail to live up to the standards that are already implicit in the operations of the market economy. This will often be useless as well, because of the weak motivational force of moral suasion, but unlike the complaints about profit, it at least has the *potential* to be useful.

NOTES

1 National Commission on the BP Deepwater Horizon Spill, *Deep Water: The Gulf Oil Disaster and the Future of Offshore Drilling* (Washington, DC: US Government Printing Office, 2011), 125.
2 National Commission, *Deep Water*, 126.
3 National Commission, 77–8.
4 National Commission, 78.
5 National Commission, 84.
6 Joel Bakan, *The Corporation: The Pathological Pursuit of Profit and Power* (Toronto: Penguin, 2004), 69.
7 An example, chosen almost at random: "Privatization means that a public service is taken over by a for-profit business, whose highest goal is profit. Investors expect a profit when a business moves into a new venture. The new corporation operating the hospital or the prison or the fire department cuts costs by every means to increase profits.... The consequences can be dangerous to ordinary citizens. Doctors in privatized hospitals may perform unnecessary surgeries to increase revenues or avoid treating patients whose care may be too expensive." Diane Ravitch, "When Public Goes Private, as Trump Wants: What Happens?," *New York Review of Books*, 8 December 2016, 58. The key assumption is that doctors in public or non-profit hospitals do not perform unnecessary surgeries to increase revenue.
8 David Schweickart, *Capitalism or Worker Control?* (New York: Praeger Publishing, 1980), 11.
9 David Schweickart, *After Capitalism* (Oxford: Rowman and Littlefield, 2002), 30. Richard Wilkinson and Kate Pickett, for instance, suggest that a shift from capitalist firms to worker cooperatives would generate "a substantial redistribution of wealth from external shareholders to

employees and a simultaneous redistribution of income from that wealth," in *The Spirit Level* (London: Penguin, 2010), 260. To see the problem with this claim, one need only consider two simple questions: Without shareholders, where does the firm get its capital? And who bears the risk of losses?

10 This constraint not only limits the discussion to a manageable set of institutional proposals, it also limits the range of *normative* considerations that must be considered germane. The price system is best thought of as a special-purpose institutional mechanism aimed at promoting Pareto efficiency, by maximizing the number of Pareto-improving exchanges that occur. See Joseph Heath, *Morality, Competition and the Firm* (New York: Oxford University Press, 2014), 187–9. Corporate malfeasance, in the sense in which I am using the term, represents a type of market failure, which is to say, a failure of the market to promote Pareto-improving forms of behaviour. As a result, all of the proposals canvassed below, to the extent that they are aimed at eliminating corporate malfeasance, are tacitly governed by, and are being assessed in terms of, the norm of Pareto efficiency. Thus I will not be concerned about whether, for instance, other firm structures might be better at promoting distributive justice.

11 E.g., see Schweikert, *After Capitalism*.

12 E.g., Bakan, *Corporation*, 35–7.

13 Lynn A. Stout, "Why We Should Stop Teaching *Dodge v. Ford*," *Virginia Law and Business Review* 3, no. 1 (2008): 165.

14 For a comparative perspective, see Reiner Kraakman, John Armour, Paul Davies, Luca Enriques, Henry Hansmann, Gerard Hertig, Klaus Hopt, Hideki Kanda, Mariana Pargendler, Wolf-Georg Ringe, and Edward Rock, *The Anatomy of Corporate Law*, 2nd ed. (Oxford: Oxford University Press, 2009).

15 Frank H. Easterbrook and Daniel R. Fischel, *The Economic Structure of Corporate Law* (Cambridge, MA: Harvard University Press, 1991), 90–108.

16 Stout, "Why We Should Stop Teaching *Dodge v. Ford*," 170–1.

17 Easterbrook and Fischel, *Economic Structure of Corporate Law*, 13.

18 Easterbrook and Fischel, 36.

19 E.g., "The corporation's legally defined mandate is to pursue, relentlessly and without exceptions, its own self-interest, regardless of the often harmful consequences it might cause to others" (Bakan, *Corporation*, 1–2). More generally, see Anthony Flew, "The Profit Motive," *Ethics* 86, no. 4 (1976): 312–22.

20 Lucian Bebchuk and Jesse Fried, *Pay without Performance* (Cambridge, MA: Harvard University Press, 2009). Note that the point of stock options was to give managers a form of compensation that would provide an incentive to increase the share price, but that stopped short of giving them

actual shares. In other words, it was to align their interests with those of the owners without actually making them owners. The alignment is imperfect, however, in part because those who hold options can benefit from volatility in a way that owners do not.

21 Harvey B. Feigenbaum, "Public Enterprise in Comparative Perspective," *Comparative Politics* 15, no. 1 (1982): 111.
22 E.g., see Schweickart, *Capitalism or Worker Control?*, 51.
23 Henry Hansmann, *The Ownership of Enterprise* (Cambridge, MA: Harvard University Press, 2000).
24 The truth of this generalization has been somewhat eroded, of late, by the introduction in some jurisdictions of multi-stakeholder cooperatives. See Catherine Leviten-Reid and Brett Fairbairn, "Multi-Stakeholder Governance in Cooperative Organizations: Toward a New Framework for Research?," *Canadian Journal of Nonprofit and Social Economy Research* 2, no. 2 (2011): 25–6.
25 This is the definition provided by Hansmann (*Ownership of Enterprise*, 11–12). It is worth noting that many of the rights traditionally associated with property ownership are absent in the case of firm ownership, and so there has been considerable debate over whether shareholders can be said to "own" the firm in a meaningful sense.
26 There may also be a selection effect, where those who are drawn toward the cooperative form, in the current economy, tend to be more idealistic or public spirited. In this case, cooperatives may actually act more ethically. The question, however, is what would happen if the cooperative form was extended to the entire economy. This would presumably bring in many people who have no ideological commitment to the cooperative form, and so are merely looking to exploit whatever angles they can find. In this case, there is no *structural* reason to think that cooperatives will be less prone to misconduct than capitalist firms.
27 Joseph Stiglitz, *Whither Socialism?* (Cambridge, MA: MIT Press, 1994), 163.
28 For a classic instance of this confusion, see Robert A. Dahl, *A Preface to Economic Democracy* (Berkeley: University of California Press, 1985). See also Schweikert, *After Capitalism*, 48.
29 As the ICA explains it, "In 1995 when the Principles were last reformulated, most primary co-operatives had a single homogeneous group of members. In these co-operatives the rule for equal voting rights, one member, one vote, is self-evident. In multi-stakeholder or hybrid primary co-operatives different voting systems may, for good reason, need to apply," *Guidance Notes to the Cooperative Principles*, 16, https://www.ica.coop/sites/default/files/2021-11/ICA%20Guidance%20Notes%20EN.pdf.
30 Hansmann, *Ownership of Enterprise*, 15.

31 International Cooperative Alliance, "The Capital Conundrum for Co-operatives," 25 February 2016, https://ica.coop/en/media/news/new-report-capital-conundrum-co-operatives.
32 Note that, using a Marxist definition of "profit," cooperatives that succeed in raising capital from external sources are, to that extent, still profit-oriented firms that "exploit" workers – because they make payments to the providers of capital. This provides a good illustration of why the Marxist terminology is no longer widely used – it makes it very difficult to articulate many of the important distinctions that structure contemporary debates over firm structure, such as the distinction between equity and debt, control of the residuum, the legal ownership of the firm, etc.
33 Gregory Dow, *Governing the Firm: Workers' Control in Theory and Practice* (New York: Cambridge University Press, 2003).
34 Benjamin Ward, "The Firm in Illyria: Market Syndicalism," *American Economic Review* 48, no. 4 (1958): 566–89.
35 Hansmann, *Ownership of Enterprise*, 35.
36 Margaret M. Blair, "Firm-Specific Human Capital and the Theories of the Firm," in *Employees and Corporate Governance*, ed. Margaret M. Blair and Mark J. Roe (Washington, DC: Brookings, 2000), 58–90.
37 Joseph Heath and Wayne Norman, "Stakeholder Theory, Corporate Governance and Public Management: What Can the History of State-Run Enterprises Teach Us in the Post-Enron Era?," *Journal of Business Ethics* 53, no. 3 (2004): 247–65.
38 Christopher Hood, Oliver James, George Jones, Colin Scott, and Tony Tavers, eds., *Regulation inside Government: Waste-Watchers, Quality Police, and Sleazebusters* (Oxford: Oxford University Press, 1999).
39 Bethany McLean and Peter Elkind, *The Smartest Guys in the Room* (New York: Penguin, 2003), 79–83.
40 Michael Jensen, "Value Maximization, Stakeholder Theory, and the Corporate Objective Function," *Journal of Applied Corporate Finance* 14, no. 3 (2001): 8.
41 Wayne Norman and Chris Macdonald, "Getting to the Bottom of the 'Triple Bottom Line,'" *Business Ethics Quarterly* 14, no. 2 (2004): 243–62.
42 Robert Milward, *Private and Public Enterprise in Europe* (Cambridge: Cambridge University Press, 2005), 261.
43 Or to put it in more precise language, "The inability of state enterprises to reconcile the break-even target with the non-commercial obligations of state enterprises manifested itself in a consistently large shortfall of earnings below operating costs and capital charges" (Milward, *Private and Public Enterprise in Europe*, 296).

44 Groupe de travail du comité interministériel des entreprises publiques *Rapport sur les entreprises publiques* (Nora Report), (Paris: La Documentation française, Éditions de Secrétariat Général du Gouvernement, 1967), 45.
45 H.M. Treasury, *Nationalised Industries: A Review of Financial and Economic Objectives*, cmd. 3437 (London: HMSO, 1967).
46 For discussion, see Heath and Norman, "Stakeholder Theory, Corporate Governance, and Public Management."
47 John Langford and Ken Huffman, "Air Canada," in *Privatization, Public Policy and Public Corporations in Canada*, ed. Allan Tupper and G. Bruce Doern (Montreal: Institute for Research on Public Policy, 1988), 99.
48 Langford and Huffman, "Air Canada," 116.
49 John Langford, "Air Canada," in Tupper and Doern, *Public Corporations and Public Policy*, 267.
50 Langford and Huffman, "Air Canada," 116.
51 Nora Report, 37–9.
52 On the importance of a single objective, see Jensen, "Value Maximization."
53 Langford and Huffman, "Air Canada," 99.
54 Tupper and Doern, *Privatization, Public Policy and Public Corporations.*
55 Saul Estrin and Virginie Pérotin, "Does Ownership Always Matter?," *International Journal of Industrial Organization* 9, no. 1 (1991): 55–72.
56 Michael H. Hall, Cathy W. Barr, M. Easwaramoorthy, S. Wojciech Sokolowski, and Lester M. Salamon, *The Canadian Nonprofit and Voluntary Sector in Comparative Perspective* (Toronto: Imagine Canada, 2005), 10.
57 Henry Hansmann, "The Role of Nonprofit Enterprise," *Yale Law Journal* 89, no. 5 (1980): 835–901.
58 In this context, the problem of "pseudo" or "fraudulent" cooperatives in countries such as Brazil should serve as an important cautionary example. In order to do an end-run around labour law, many firms began to organize their employees into a formally autonomous "worker cooperative," then outsource employment to the cooperative. See Roberto R.C. Pires, "Beyond the Fear of Discretion: Flexibility, Performance, and Accountability in the Management of Regulatory Bureaucracies," *Regulation and Governance* 5, no. 1 (2011): 53–6.
59 Hernando de Soto, *The Mystery of Capital* (New York: Basic Books, 2000).
60 This observation is due to Hansmann, *Ownership of Enterprise*, 287–97.
61 See Ryan Pevnick, "Democratizing the Nonprofit Sector," *Journal of Political Philosophy* 21, no. 3 (2013): 260–82.
62 This is another way of saying that they are "transaction cost minimizing" devices. See Alan Shipman, *The Market Revolution and Its Limits* (London: Routledge, 1999).
63 Abraham Singer, *The Form of the Firm* (New York: Oxford University Press, 2019), 210–12.

64 Kent Greenfield, "The Puzzle of Short-Termism," *Wake Forest Law Review* 46, no. 3 (2011): 627–40. On conspiracies against the public, see James Surowiecki, ed., *Best Business Crime Writing of the Year* (New York: Random House, 2002).
65 See Joseph Heath, "Three Normative Models of the Welfare State," *Public Reason* 3, no. 2 (2011): 13–43.
66 Sally Simpson, *Corporate Crime, Law and Social Control* (Cambridge: Cambridge University Press, 2002); Ian Ayres and John Braithwaite, *Responsive Regulation* (New York: Oxford University Press, 1992).
67 Wayne Norman, "Business Ethics as Self-Regulation: Why Principles That Ground Regulations Should Be Used to Ground Beyond-Compliance Norms as Well," *Journal of Business Ethics* 102, no. 1 (2011): 43–57.
68 Al Gini and Alexei Marcous, *The Ethics of Business* (Lanham, MD: Rowman & Littlefield, 2012).
69 Gary Becker, *The Economics of Discrimination* (Chicago: University of Chicago Press, 1957).
70 See Waheed Hussain, "Why Should We Care about Competition?," *Critical Review of International Social and Political Philosophy* 21, no. 5 (2018): 570–85.
71 Marshall B. Clinard and Peter C. Yeager, *Corporate Crime* (New York: Free Press, 1980), 340–1.

Chapter Three

Egalitarianism and Status Hierarchy

It is standard practice in sociological research on class and inequality to refer to members of what are conventionally known as the "lower classes" using the slightly euphemistic term "low-SES individuals." SES is an acronym that stands for "socioeconomic status," and it is used in recognition of the fact that social stratification is based upon much more than just economic standing (i.e., income or wealth). The "socio-" prefix is a catchall, which is usually operationalized by specifying education level and occupational status. These are meant to approximate something more ephemeral, or at least difficult to measure, which is the amount of "social status" that an individual possesses.[1] We all understand this notion of status implicitly, on the basis of our own lives and social relationships, but it is very difficult to articulate explicitly. Status is, in our society, an informally maintained system of ranking, or of dominance, based on an invidious comparison between individuals. There is no single basis for this ordering, although there are strong correlations between individual positions in the rankings, because high standing in one dimension can often be parlayed into improvements in some other.[2] (To take just one example, physical attractiveness is an important source of status, both directly, through the psychological effects it has on others, but also indirectly, because it can be used to obtain greater wealth, influence, and opportunity.[3] And so if one compares the difference in average level of physical attractiveness between, say, the members of an expensive tennis club and the customers at a Walmart store, the contrast is dramatic.[4]) Social status is also closely tied to self-esteem, because the categories under which individuals evaluate their own qualities are typically contrastive, such that thinking one is "good" in some way usually amounts to thinking that one is "better than" certain other people.[5]

In the period before the egalitarian political revolutions of the modern age and their ensuing social consequences, the status hierarchy in Western societies was both explicit and publicly recognized. It was universally understood and acknowledged that some people were better than others, not just in specific ways, but in general. It was common for individuals to appeal unselfconsciously to their own "rank" and to demand that others give way or defer to their "betters." Political and economic institutions reflected and reinforced this status hierarchy. Certain economic advantages, such as land ownership, and political positions, such as military leadership, were reserved for those who belonged to the higher orders of society. Thus both informal and formal institutions worked together in a mutually reinforcing way to sustain the status hierarchy. Because of this entwinement, it was not absurd for early social and political reformers to think that the abolition of status inequality in the formal institutions of society would lead to the collapse of the informal status order as well. And yet the latter has proven surprisingly resilient. Despite decades of social and political reform, most people in our society remain acutely aware that they occupy a certain position in the social hierarchy, even though these positions are seldom explicitly acknowledged or recognized and obviously have no legal standing. Furthermore, it is not difficult to discern the consequences of this informal hierarchy, in terms of access to other advantages, ranging from marriage partners to life expectancy. If anything, the major consequence of our commitment to equality has been to turn us all into hypocrites about status, where none of us officially endorses the hierarchy, and yet all continue to participate in the practices that sustain it.

The persistence of status hierarchy in the informal social sphere poses a serious challenge to any egalitarian project that hopes to establish more than just formal political equality among citizens. There is every reason to think that occupying a low-status position will remain a major source of unhappiness and resentment for many people, in part because of the connection to self-esteem, but also because status markers mediate many aspects of interpersonal relations. High-status individuals simply get treated better by others, and in turn demand better treatment, which makes every aspect of their lives go better.[6] Status inequality skews the distribution of benefits in every other domain of social interaction, ranging from workplace promotion to the opportunity for a fair trial. As a result, inequality of status constitutes a serious obstacle to the creation of more comprehensive social equality. This is why, I believe, egalitarian political movements have maintained a certain optimism about the possibility that status hierarchy can be abolished. Although the frustrations experienced by many egalitarian political experiments of the twentieth century – ranging from worker cooperatives to labour kibbutzim – have done much to diminish this optimism, it does retain some currency. Thus I will begin my discussion by explaining why I think the impulse to order social relations through status hierarchy is a feature of human nature that, for all practical purposes, cannot be eliminated. It is, of course, impossible to prove this definitively. What I would like to do instead is provide grounds for thinking it reasonable to assume that status inequality will persist in the informal social sphere. The interesting question then becomes how egalitarians should respond.

Five major strategies for dealing with status inequality have been put forward, or are implicit in the literature. I refer to these as elimination, recognition, compensation, neutralization, and insulation. The first is the view that underlying status there is something fungible, such as the "social bases of self-respect," and so inequality can be abolished through redistribution. The second view is also eliminativist but relies on some variant of the Hegelian "mutual recognition" formula as a way to resolve the problem of status inequality. The third, compensation, is implicit in the view that goods are to be distributed in a way that promotes equality of welfare. It follows that individuals who derive less satisfaction from their status position will have to be given a larger allocation of other goods in order to bring their welfare up to the target level. The fourth view, neutralization, suggests that the proliferation of status hierarchies in the modern world can be used to bring about something like "undominated diversity" in this domain, where each individual is able to win at least one status competition, and thus something like an egalitarian outcome is achievable. The fifth and final view, insulation, is in a sense the most pessimistic, in that it is based on the assumption that most people are destined to remain dissatisfied with their status position. The objective then is to limit the collateral damage this causes to the broader egalitarian project, by attempting to insulate the formal institutions of the basic structure from the patterning effects of status hierarchy. This last view, I will argue, is the best that we can hope to achieve, and even then it faces formidable obstacles.

1. What Is Status?

One puzzle in contemporary anthropology is why, despite the fact that our nearest primate relatives live in societies ordered by a dominance hierarchy, small-scale human societies are almost invariably "egalitarian" in their social relations.[7] Given that the last shared ancestor between humans and chimpanzees lived only five million years ago, it seems implausible that the repertoire of behavioural dispositions associated with maintenance of dominance relations has disappeared from our evolved psychology. Thus theoretical speculation has tended to focus on "overrides," or emergent features of human social interaction that would leave the basic set of psychological dominance instincts in place, and yet prevent them from finding social expression, or of generating a full-blown dominance hierarchy. Perhaps the most well-known hypothesis in this vein is Christopher Boehm's conception of a "reverse dominance hierarchy," which suggests that an aversion to being bullied results in informal coalitions being formed to oppose overly aggressive or dominant individuals.[8] Individuals in this view still seek to establish dominance, it is just that they are blocked from achieving it in any but ephemeral forms. This theory explains how a social structure could emerge among humans that no longer mirrors the underlying set of behavioural dispositions.

One very plausible way of understanding human status relations would be to regard them as a vestigial consequence of these archaic dominance instincts, which persist in the informal social sphere even when they are being overridden by institutional mechanisms.[9] There is, after all, good reason to think that dominance behaviour is psychologically deep-seated. The formation of a dominance hierarchy is the default mode of social organization throughout much of the animal kingdom, and certainly in our own lineage. The literature on this is vast, but particular attention has been focused on the role that dominance hierarchy plays in the social relations of various fish, birds, bovines, dogs, horses, frogs, wasps, ants, and primates.[10] Farmers are familiar with the very strict, linear dominance hierarchy among domestic fowl (the aptly named "pecking order"). More familiar perhaps, to anyone who has owned a dog, will be the greeting ritual that dogs enact when they first meet, which is used to establish a dominance relation. Failure to establish dominance through symbolic confrontation will often lead to fighting, which ends when one dog adopts a fully submissive posture. Either way, the dogs will not return to "normal" activities until a dominance relation has been established. Once this is done, that relation structures all subsequent interactions.

Warder Clyde Allee, in his classic study "Dominance and Hierarchy in Societies of Vertebrates," defined a dominance hierarchy as "any social rank order established through direct combat, threat, passive submission, or some combination of these behavior patterns."[11] Although it originates in dyadic relations between individuals, the agonistic interaction establishes a pattern of deference, which then governs future interactions. To the extent that transitivity of relations is respected, this generates a relatively stable social structure that assigns each individual a rank.[12] Once established, this structure mediates access to most other resources, in particular, food and reproductive opportunities. When food becomes available, for instance, the submissive individual will defer to the dominant one, allowing him or her to eat first. Both do better under this arrangement than in an unstructured relation, in which they risk open conflict that is likely to result in injury. The weaker individual, for instance, is going to wind up with the leftovers whether he chooses to contest or not. The question is only whether he wants to run the risk of sustaining injury as well.

At its core, what distinguishes dominance from simple aggression is that, with dominance, both individuals try to anticipate who would win a fight, on the basis of either observation of traits or recollection of past interactions. They then move directly to what they are able to establish as the *expected* outcome of a fight, skipping the actual fight. Given the advantages associated with being in a dominant social position, one can see how this leads to the development of characteristic forms of dominance displays or behaviour, designed to *signal* to the other individual that "if you fight me, I will win." For example, physical size is one of the most basic predictors of success in conflict. This generates the practically ubiquitous behaviour of animals getting "puffed up" at the outset of a confrontation (such as dogs raising their hackles) in order to increase their perceived size. (Humans, despite being largely hairless, retain the same neurophysiological response, which is why one can feel the hair stand up on the back of one's neck when experiencing threat or fear. Bipedalism has, of course, rendered this particular display completely pointless, and so it is a good example of behaviour grounded in vestigial dominance instincts.) The fact that one can find the same type of behavioural display in reptiles, avians, and mammals is rather astonishing, given the evolutionary distance that separates us all from our last common ancestor.

One other noteworthy feature of dominance behaviour is that, in many species, it is deployed in circumstances in which there is no immediate basis for conflict, but where the behaviour is aimed merely at "reinforcing" the hierarchy.[13] Thus one finds ritual displays of intimidation and submission becoming a part of everyday social interaction, even when there is nothing objective at stake. This is what contributes to the sense that there is an independent ordering of individuals, or a social *structure* in place, and not just a series of agonistic dyadic interactions generating winners and losers.

The primary reason for thinking that the psychological underpinnings of status hierarchy among humans lie in these archaic dominance instincts, apart from structural homologies between the two systems, is that human status competition employs many of the same signals that establish dominance relations in the animal kingdom. In particular, human status signalling relies upon morphological features, bodily posture, threat displays, and behaviour sequences that can easily be observed in other primates. An example is the "sneering" facial display – often associated with downward status judgments in humans – which in other primates results in the baring of canine teeth, but in humans is obviously a vestigial reflex. A more colourful example involves the way that U.K. politician Nigel Farage described Donald Trump's body language in his second debate with Hillary Clinton in 2016 (the format was a peculiar one, which allowed the candidates to move freely about the stage): "I thought he was like a big silverback gorilla prowling the stage.... He took control. He dominated Hillary Clinton."[14] While not everyone shared Farage's enthusiasm for Trump's performance, no one could fail to recognize the behaviour that he was describing, or the aptness of the comparison. Indeed, part of the reason that primates are so fascinating to observe is that we find much of their body language and facial expressions easily interpretable, on the basis of our own social relations and intuitions.

More fundamentally, humans share with other animals much of the physiological system associated with dominance behaviour, in particular, the hormonal regulatory system. For instance, although there is a great deal that we do not know about the neuroendocrine system and its behavioural effects, serotonin is clearly involved in dominance behaviour across the animal kingdom.[15] Not only are serotonin levels affected by dominance rank, but manipulation of serotonin levels has been shown to affect dominance behaviour and relations in multiple species. More importantly, it appears to regulate status rank and behaviour among humans in much the same way that it regulates dominance in other species. And, of course, many humans manipulate their own serotonin levels pharmacologically, particularly through the use of selective serotonin reuptake inhibitors (SSRIs), in order to moderate depression, anxiety, and social phobias. (This is another reminder of the humbling fact that much of the basic "hardware" of the human brain is shared with other animals. Functionally and physiologically, our brain is not some precious evolutionary anomaly. It is, as Frans de Waal observed, "essentially a linearly scaled-up monkey brain."[16]) Many of the negative health effects associated with low social status among humans, such as high blood pressure, have also been shown to be experienced by primates with low dominance rank.

Thus there is good reason to think that dominance is a biologically deep-seated feature of human psychology. It is not merely a part of an ideological superstructure, or a peculiar feature of certain cultures.[17] Our desire for status is more like sexual appetite, which, despite taking very different forms and expressions in different cultural contexts, is nevertheless a profound and fundamental feature of the human motivational system. The fact that human social relations are not always governed by a rigid dominance hierarchy, as they are among other primates, is due to the fact that these instincts can be overridden by other institutional arrangements (as Boehm and others have suggested).[18] But they have not gone away. They have merely been repressed or sublimated. This explains why status hierarchy persists in the informal sphere, despite formally egalitarian social relations.[19]

By conceptualizing status in this way, I am adopting a somewhat narrower focus than one sometimes encounters in the philosophical literature. For example, Geoffrey Brennan and Philip Pettit have written extensively on the subject of "the economy of esteem."[20] Their concept of "esteem," however, is much broader than the notion of "status" that I am using, as it includes forms of social approbation that extend beyond the dominance ranking and the deference it induces, which I take to be the central feature of the status hierarchy. In particular, they consider both moral behaviour and norm-conformity to be sources of esteem and therefore fail to distinguish between behaviour aimed at producing an invidious comparison, or based on an emulative motive, from behaviour that is pro-social in orientation (e.g., cooperative or altruistic).[21] Indeed, one problem with traditional virtue theory is that Aristotle's concept of "excellence" fails to distinguish traits of character that are a source of social status (e.g., having a deep voice, sponsoring feasts), from traits that are primarily of benefit to others. In this respect, it is like the traditional concept of "honour," which also blends moral ideas with notions of social standing in ways that are very difficult to disaggregate. Brennan and Pettit, far from seeing this as a problem, essentially reproduce the ambiguity in their notion of esteem. Thus they risk losing track of the most troublesome feature of social status, which is that its invidious character makes it intrinsically zero-sum and competitive, in a way that morally based forms of esteem are not.

Over the course of the twentieth century, the idea of social rank also became somewhat muddied by egalitarian social movements that sought its abolition. The nineteenth-century style of talking, in which people spoke openly of having a "position" in society, and routinely chastised others for acting in ways incompatible with their rank, became socially unacceptable. But even though most overt forms of status hierarchy were officially suppressed, status inequality tended to re-emerge in more subterranean ways. For example, classification according to level of "cool" became the central status hierarchy among young people, and eventually urban society in general. Many find this confusing, because despite being a very strict and competitive hierarchy, based entirely on invidious comparison with the "square" (later "uncool," later "normie"), "cool" was officially anti-establishment, and so many people failed to recognize it as a dominance hierarchy.[22] In more recent years, the emergence and growing popularity of the terms "winner" and "loser," as a way of describing people and positioning them in the social structure, has worked to re-establish something closer to the nineteenth-century level of clarity about status relations. The advantage of this vocabulary is that it is binary, focuses on conflict, and serves no expressive purpose other than to denigrate or elevate individuals. In this respect, it sums up the essence of status.

Finally, although it was Max Weber who first drew attention to the importance of status in generating social inequality or "stratification," my definition of status is somewhat narrower than Weber's notion of *Stand* (and *Stände*), which is often translated as "prestige" or "status group."[23] I take there to be two quite distinct aspects of our evolved psychology involved in status *groupings*. First, there is the concern over rank, which is a legacy of our archaic dominance instincts. Second, there is what is sometimes described as "groupishness," which involves our tendency to divide the social world into "in-group" and "out-group" members, adopting an antagonistic orientation toward the latter.[24] These two tendencies have different psychological underpinnings, and although they sometimes work in concert, they are also often at cross-purposes.[25] In particular, formation of a strong in-group identity can have a levelling effect, by making status differences less salient (as can sometimes be observed in sports teams or military units). This may be why modern egalitarian societies are often highly nationalistic.[26] On the other hand, individuals who occupy roughly equivalent status positions may use this as a basis for in-group differentiation, thereby forming what is conventionally known as a "status group" (or a "clique"). When this occurs, the status hierarchy is best envisioned, not as a ranking, but as a set of concentric circles.

The distinction between status and groupishness is important to understanding a social phenomenon such as racism, which is often articulated in ways that evoke group identity, but more often involves a status contest. For example, racism among American whites, far from serving as a source of in-group solidarity, is strongly stigmatized, in part because it is seen as low-status behaviour. This is based on the recognition that the most prominent motivation for overt racism is the desire of low-SES whites (i.e., people who are often openly referred to as "white trash") to maintain the position of someone else below them in the status hierarchy. This is generally a sign of desperation, since the expression of overt racism constitutes a self-inflicted status injury within the group of whites and so is typically made only by those who are downwardly mobile and seeking to establish a "floor" that limits how much farther they can sink. Similarly, a certain amount of racial discrimination is actually evoked by status cues, and not racial identity per se, but because race serves as a negative status marker, the status discrimination is disproportionately directed toward racial minorities, making it easy to confound the two. In both cases, misrepresentation of the status conflict as being concerned with group identity leads to a fundamental misunderstanding of the phenomenon.

2. Why Status Matters

Philosophers have been inclined to underestimate the difficulties that the persistence of status hierarchy creates for egalitarian political projects. There are several reasons for this, but one that should be noted, if only in passing, is that most philosophers are university professors, and university professors are not generally blessed with the greatest level of insight into status, because they have so much of it. After all, if wealthy donors are willing to spend millions of dollars to endow university research chairs, effectively converting some fraction of their fortune from money to status, it seems reasonable to suppose that the individuals who are eligible to occupy these chairs have much *more* status to begin with. And like most other good things, status is subject to diminishing marginal returns, as a result of which people who are at a very high level tend not care much about small changes either up or down. This is often experienced introspectively as a type of high-mindedness, or as a lack of concern over status, when it is actually just a consequence of being in a dominant position.

The only way to appreciate the importance of status to most people is to consider what it is like to be at a low level. In this respect, status is also like wealth. The only way to fully understand the importance of money is to spend at least some time living in poverty. Only then can one experience what it is like to be denied access to most things in society – to know that one does not have the option of living in most apartments, because they are too expensive, that one cannot shop in most stores, because they are too expensive, that one cannot eat in most restaurants, because they are too expensive, and so on. The wealthy often underestimate the importance of money, because they have never had, or have forgotten, the experience of living without it. This is also often experienced as a kind of high-mindedness (e.g., only the very wealthy are impressed by pseudo-profundities like "Money is not important, it's what you *do* with your money that matters"). The same is true of status. To have low social status is to live in a society in which most neighbourhoods, buildings, stores, restaurants, etc., are inaccessible, on the grounds that they are too "fancy" or "posh." Even though the barriers are not rigid, as they are with money, psychologically they are just as important. Low-status individuals may not be denied entry to high-status establishments, but they are generally made to feel so foolish or uncomfortable that they eagerly avoid them. For a university professor, by contrast, the thought that anyone might experience intense status anxiety visiting an art gallery, or even just walking around a university campus, is so entirely foreign that most are blissfully unaware that anyone feels this way, or give wide berth to these places in order to avoid that feeling.

This point about the diminishing marginal utility of status is enormously important and is one of the reasons that Thorstein Veblen's classic work, *The Theory of the Leisure Class*, cannot easily be assigned a political valence. We tend to associate status displays with the upper classes, and indeed, much of Veblen's book is a send-up of upper-class status signalling (e.g., he describes hobbies such as "cards, yachting, golf" as designed to avoid any display of "indecorous usefulness";[27] he suggests that learning "certain of the dead languages of southern Europe" serves primarily "as evidence of wasted time and effort, and hence of the pecuniary strength necessary in order to afford this waste";[28] etc.). His major focus was on the shift underway, in the late nineteenth century, from the conspicuous *leisure* of the sedentary aristocracy to the conspicuous *consumption* of the more mobile, and thus anonymous, urban bourgeoisie. Like Weber, Veblen was making an anti-Marxian point, by showing how these changes in consumption patterns had nothing to do with "material" conditions, but were driven by status preoccupations. In a similar vein, he argued that the living standard of the poor was not determined by the material conditions of reproduction of their labour, but rather by what he referred to as the "pecuniary standard of decency," which was the level of expenditure required in order to appear in public without shame. He observed that members of the lower classes were often willing to make major compromises in their material standard of living in order to avoid falling below the standard of decency.[29] (In this he is echoing a point made famously by Adam Smith, regarding the willingness of some workers to go hungry, in order to avoid having to appear in public without a linen shirt or leather shoes.[30]) This is because the poor care more about status than the rich – in the sense that they are willing to make greater sacrifices in order to obtain an increment of it – precisely because they have so little to begin with. This results in status having greater *marginal* utility. It follows that, even if conspicuous consumption is less flamboyant among the lower classes, the competition is likely to be more intensely felt. As a result, Veblen observes, the poor are partially complicit in their own deprivation, because they care more about status than they do about certain aspects of their material well-being.

This analysis suggests that status differentials will be an extremely important dimension of social inequality. This is a very serious problem for proponents of "social equality," as well as certain forms of "relational equality," who insist that individuals must interact with one another as equals.[31] Indeed, Carina Fourie describes "an opposition to ranking people according to hierarchies of social status" as "*the* central tenet of social equality."[32] Similarly, David Miller describes the ideal as that of achieving "*equality of status*."[33] If status is as persistent and deep-seated as I have claimed, then this egalitarian ambition is hopeless. For the most part, relational egalitarians have avoided confronting this difficulty using two strategies.[34] The first involves formulating the egalitarian ideal in such an abstract way (e.g., as the requirement that citizens be able to "look one another in the eye," or that they treat each other as having equal "moral standing") that it is compatible with all but the most extreme forms of status hierarchy.[35] The second involves focusing only on the most formal or rigid types of status inequality, while ignoring the informal order entirely. Thus T.M. Scanlon dedicates an entire chapter of his book *Why Does Inequality Matter?* to the topic of status inequality, but the only forms of self-standing status inequality that he considers are those based on overt discrimination (e.g., racism and sexism).[36] The type of status that he enjoys as a Harvard professor is not problematized.

If the analysis presented here is correct, this relational egalitarian ideal is hopeless, because status comparisons are psychologically ineradicable, intrinsically invidious, and inseparable from other supposedly meritorious hierarchies. My objective, however, is not to criticize relational egalitarianism. Although proponents of this view have spoken a great deal about the importance of equalizing status, they have not advanced any original proposals for doing so. They appear to subscribe to the same batch of remedies that have been advanced over the years by proponents of the more traditional "distributive justice" conception of equality. Thus I will focus my remarks on distributive egalitarianism (i.e., the view that "there is something that justice requires people to have equal amounts of"[37]). Status poses a problem for this view because, unlike inequalities of income and wealth, three features make it particularly intractable: it cannot be redistributed, the supply cannot be expanded, and the process of economic growth increases its relative importance. This creates a further problem, because as status competition becomes more intense, it increasingly contaminates other domains of interaction, transforming them into zero- or negative-sum interactions.

2.1. Status Is Non-Fungible

Status is notoriously resistant to explicit social interference. A teacher can order other children to play with an unpopular child, but it is impossible to *make* the child popular in this way. On the contrary, ordering others to play with the child is likely to be itself stigmatizing, or to generate a backlash, leading to even more profound social ostracism, further reducing the child's popularity. Similarly, the state cannot just take away status from some people and give it to others, the way that it can effect transfers of wealth. Even private individuals are unable to transfer any fraction of their own status to others.[38] Particularly high-status individuals can attempt to raise the status of others by associating with them, but they cannot alienate or "gift" some fraction of their own status. For the same reason, the willingness of others to offer consideration in return for someone else's status is irrelevant, since the status cannot be transferred, and the willingness to pay for status, like the willingness to pay for sex, is socially stigmatized (as a sign of desperation of those unable to obtain it on their own merits). The closest one can come to purchasing status is to pay a high-status individual to associate with one, in the hope that others will mistake the relationship for one based on free association, rather than on economic exchange.

Closely related to non-fungibility is the fact that status seems to be subject to the "teleological paradox," which arises when adopting a particular outcome as one's explicit aim is incompatible with obtaining that outcome (and is thus self-defeating).[39] Being seen as status-seeking, or as being excessively concerned with status, has the effect of lowering one's status. Being unconcerned about status, and yet obtaining it nevertheless, is a source of increased status. Herein lies the difference between "vulgarity" and "sophistication." (One can see this in the strong taboo in academic circles against being explicitly concerned with status. Only the naive mistake this for genuine disregard. Pretending that status does not influence one's choices is itself a form of status display, a way of establishing one's superiority over others.) This may explain why deals of the sort "I will do this for you, and in return, you accord me higher status" do not work when made explicit, even though many arrangements have this implicit structure (such as the relationship between wealthy donors and universities, or "big fish in small pond" work relations).[40]

This non-fungibility is presumably why John Rawls chose to include "the social bases of self-respect" in his list of social primary goods, and not "self-respect" itself.[41] It is easy to see why his distributive justice framework is not well equipped to handle status. Unlike the dominance hierarchies among other animals, the status hierarchy among humans serves no functional purpose, because it has been largely supplanted by other institutional arrangements as a way of mediating access to resources and resolving disputes. Given the option, it seems obvious that individuals choosing social arrangements in the original position would choose not to have a status hierarchy at all.[42] On the other hand, if there is going to be a status hierarchy, then it is not clear how the sort of maximin reasoning that generates the difference principle can be applied. If status generates an ordinal ranking, then there is no way to improve the situation of the worst-off individual, other than by making someone else the worst-off individual. This is presumably what motivates Rawls to shift attention away from status itself, to focus on the type of resources that people use to obtain status (or its correlate, "self-respect") and to suggest that they be distributed in accordance with the same principles that govern wealth and income.

Unfortunately, the issue is somewhat more difficult than Rawls makes it seem. Even redistributing the "social bases of self-respect" can be difficult, because they have been known to shift, and if redistribution itself changes them, they may turn out to be just as non-fungible as "self-respect" itself. One of the greatest challenges of welfare policy arises from the fact that being in receipt of a redistributive transfer tends to undermine recipients' self-respect. This is closely related to the fact that social assistance generates a status injury – being "on the dole" or "getting pogey" is stigmatized. This is why many welfare state programs take great care to describe transfers as earned entitlements. Opinions may vary about how important it is that income be earned, but most people are quite insistent that status, or self-respect, must be earned.[43] It is therefore unclear how anyone's self-respect could be increased through redistribution, since anything transferred is likely to be considered unearned. For instance, having one's own living space is an essential component of self-respect, but social housing tends to attract stigma, and so living in "projects" or "council flats" becomes associated with the same opprobrium that might once have come from sleeping in a "flophouse" or being homeless.

To put the problem in somewhat more precise terms, consider some object x, which is owned or consumed by individuals with high social status, and some individual y, who has low social status. It is tempting to think that one can improve the status of y by taking some of object x and giving it to this person. The idea, of course, is that y, being now in possession of x, will benefit from the status associations of x, in a way that will raises y's social status. It is important to realize, however, that the opposite may occur. Instead of y's status being raised though the status associations of x, the transfer may instead contaminate x, eroding its status associations. In other words, instead of x raising up y, y may lower x. This effect may be exacerbated by high-status individuals divesting themselves of x as soon as it becomes the object of transfer. (This dynamic is familiar to any luxury brand manager, who has to worry about goods being appropriated by "chavs" or their equivalent. Indeed, the "chav" phenomenon reveals precisely the problem, since the term is used specifically to express derision toward low-class individuals who engage in a conspicuous display of high-class consumer goods.)

So not only is it impossible to redistribute status, but the requirement that status transactions not be made explicit makes them peculiarly resistant to social intervention. As a result, it is difficult to see how a society committed to equality could adopt any *policy* that would deal with status inequality effectively.[44]

2.2. Status Is Zero-Sum

Unlike status, redistribution of wealth is possible, at least in principle. In practice, however, it can be quite difficult, because of the resistance put up by those who stand to lose from the redistribution. To the extent that they have more resources than those who stand to gain from the redistribution, and are willing to "burn" those resources rather than see them given to others, they will be able to make redistribution costly, and in some cases infeasible.[45] And yet even if our capacity for material redistribution is limited in this way, we are still able to pacify conflict over material goods by producing *more* of them. Most people, it turns out, are happy to see their own consumption grow. The fact that someone else's consumption may be growing by more is seldom enough, as such, to negate these gains. As a result, economic growth has a number of salutary effects, not the least of which is that it diminishes distributive conflict.[46] The supply of status, on the other hand, cannot easily be expanded. Because it is a ranking system, the only way for one person to move up is to bump at least one other person down. This means that the status of one person can be increased only by reducing the status of others, resulting in net gain of zero. As a result, the competition for status is, at best, fixed-sum.

Competitions in which the outcome is fixed-sum are generally seen as undesirable, because they quickly become negative sum from the standpoint of social welfare. If it is possible to obtain advantages over others through the expenditure of resources (including time, energy, and attention), then a race to the bottom can easily develop, in which more and more resources are expended, even though the sum of benefits awarded through the competition remains the same. This expenditure is wasteful, as Veblen observed.[47] One argument for limiting expenditures during political campaigns, for instance, is that most of the spending is wasteful from a societal point of view. The total amount of campaign spending in US congressional races, for instance, has increased from $1.6 billion in the year 2000 to over $4 billion at the time of writing, but when all of the ballots are counted, the same number of congressional representatives are elected. So the extra $2.6 billion spent does not accomplish anything, it is merely the product of a collective action problem among the parties.

In general, societies do better by avoiding competitions with fixed or zero-sum rewards. For instance, one of the most powerful arguments against the practice of polygyny is that the supply of women is basically fixed. Polygyny makes access to wives more competitive, with a number of pernicious consequences. Patriarchy is often described, misleadingly, as a system of male domination. In practice, it is usually a system of dominance by *older* men over women and younger men. As a result, polygyny creates a large pool of unmarried young men in a society, which is, in general, a recipe for instability and violence. It is certainly not an accident that the top twenty countries on the "fragile states" index are all ones in which polygyny is practised. "If a rich man has a Lamborghini, that does not mean that a poor man has to walk, for the supply of cars is not fixed. By contrast, every time a rich man takes an extra wife, another poor man must remain single. If the richest and most powerful 10% of men have, say, four wives each, the bottom 30% of men cannot marry. Young men will take desperate measures to avoid this state."[48] This generates constant pressure to bring younger girls onto the marriage market, or to dispose of the young men (through warfare or other means).

Thus the standard objection to status competition is that, like other fixed-sum competitions, it is wasteful and potentially destabilizing. Because the total quantity of status cannot be increased, any resources expended in the pursuit of status gains will fail to increase the sum of well-being. The social pathology of *consumerism* – where the level of material consumption in society increases, without perceptible gains in average satisfaction level – is often attributed to the effects of competitive consumption in pursuit of status gains.[49] There are other pernicious effects as well. For instance, by far the most serious impairment in quality of life in lower-class African-American communities in the United States is the constant threat of interpersonal violence.[50] A surprisingly large fraction of this arises out of conflict over social status, most notably "dissing," or failing to show proper respect to someone. Lethal violence is often precipitated by slights that "seem petty to middle-class people (maintaining eye contact for too long, for example)."[51] Again the observation that status is subject to diminishing marginal returns offers a parsimonious explanation of the phenomenon – those with low social status are far more concerned to avoid further losses, often to the point of violence when challenged. It reaffirms Veblen's depressing conclusion that the lower a person stands in the status hierarchy of a society, the more likely that person is to become embroiled in wasteful and destructive conflicts over status. The problems that stem from this are extremely resistant to policy intervention, because while it is possible to raise the material standard of living of these communities, it is not possible to expand the amount of social status within them.

2.3. Things Are Getting Worse

One foundational work on the economics of status is Fred Hirsch's *The Social Limits to Growth*. Hirsch's best-known contribution is the distinction he introduced between material and "positional" goods. The former are defined simply as goods whose output can be increased, or more narrowly, as "output amenable to continued increase in productivity per unit of labor input."[52] Goods that lack this characteristic are referred to as "positional" because, being in fixed supply, the only way of gaining access to them is to be willing to pay more than others are. For example, the 2005 Chateau Pavie is considered a particularly fine vintage of Bordeaux wine, but only 7,000 cases of it were made, and it is impossible to produce any more. As a result, the only way to obtain some is to offer more than others are willing to pay. Thus it is one's *position* in the ranking of wealth, and not one's absolute wealth per se, that determines access to it. As a result, economic growth, which increases only the supply of material goods, has the effect of raising the prices of positional goods, sometimes dramatically (a fact that has been lamented by oenophiles, who complain that they must now pay three or four times more than they used to, a decade or two ago, in order to purchase the higher quality vintages). Of course, wine is a somewhat peculiar example, because past vintages are strictly limited in supply. In practice, the distinction between positional and material goods is not hard-and-fast, and goods may be valued for different qualities, some of which are positional, some of which are material. Thus it is more helpful to think of positional goods as being, not strictly limited, but rather extremely inelastic in supply.

Hirsch's most important observation is that many of the qualities that make certain goods positional are not natural features of the object, but rather are social in origin. For example, he observes that real estate values are determined, not so much by intrinsic features of a building, or the land it is on, but rather its relationship to surrounding land uses (hence the real estate agent's slogan for determining value, "Location, location, location"). Urban real estate is, in this sense, intrinsically scarce, because cities are simply the location where most people want to live. If everyone wants to live at the place where everyone else wants to live, not all can satisfy their preferences simultaneously. As a result, economic growth will drive up the price of urban real estate far more than it does land in surrounding areas.[53] Of course, it is not *impossible* to create more urban real estate – one can always increase density. What Hirsch's analysis captures is the sense in which urban property will always be expensive, with price increases often disproportionate to average income gains, because the inelasticity of supply means that access to it will be determined largely by one's ability to outbid others for it.

The most common source of social scarcity is status. Because status is zero-sum, any good consumed as a way of achieving status thereby becomes positional, and access to it will be determined by one's ranking in the order of "pecuniary strength." Membership in an exclusive club, a table at the hottest new restaurant, ownership of a luxury car, tasteful redecoration of one's home, an elite education, are all essentially positional goods, because a large fraction of the value of these goods comes from the social status that individuals derive from their consumption. Expanding the material supply of these goods is self-defeating, because it only produces dilution of the status they confer (or as Hirsch says, it produces "quality erosion"). If the exclusive club starts selling more memberships, it becomes less exclusive, forcing existing patrons to decamp to a new, more exclusive club, in order to preserve their status. Objects that are a sign of good taste become bad taste as they are acquired by more people. Many of the cycles of obsolescence that we associate with consumerism are produced through this social dynamic, whereby expansion of the supply of a good produces a decline in the status that it confers, leading high-status consumers to abandon that good in favour of some other, more supply-restricted alternative.[54]

The positional economy is a source of enormous frustration for many people, because the history of economic growth has produced the expectation that, over time, we will have greater access to the goods enjoyed by those in the classes above us. This was the dynamic at the time when the primary difference between classes rested in their level of material consumption. At the end of the nineteenth century, for instance, it was common for members of the working classes to have only one set of clothes, and certainly only one pair of shoes, while those who were wealthier had many. Economic growth lifted this constraint, so that the poor became able to enjoy many of the luxuries previously affordable only to the rich. And yet this increased accessibility does not occur in the positional economy. As people become wealthier, they find that positional goods continue to recede over the horizon, because the price goes up at a rate that either matches or exceeds their income gains. Or they find that, by the time they can afford them, most of these goods have lost their cachet, as the elite have moved on. (For instance, brightly coloured cloth was at one time very expensive, and so coloured clothing was not only unaffordable to most people, but reserved for the elite through sumptuary laws. By the time it became affordable to all, through a combination of technological change and economic growth, the cultural valuation was reversed, making brightly coloured clothing "tacky.") This is, as Hirsch observes, a structural feature of these goods. The only way to gain access to them is by improving one's position *relative to others*. Broad-based economic growth, enjoyed by all, leaves superior positional goods as inaccessible as ever.

Hirsch also noted a harmful dynamic, whereby economic development tends to increase, over time, the importance of the positional economy. Not only does the supply of material goods expand, but being subject to diminishing marginal returns, the value of an additional increment of material goods declines relative to positional goods. In part this just serves as a source of frustration, as positional goods become more expensive, and economic growth fails to deliver the benefits that people have come to expect from it. As Hirsch puts it, "What the wealthy have today can no longer be delivered to the rest of us tomorrow; yet as we individually grow richer, that is what we expect."[55] What is more troublesome are the resources that are wasted, as individuals compete for positional advantage. Economic growth will tend to result in increased spending on intermediate goods, which do not directly produce welfare, but are merely instrumental to the attainment of other goods. Intermediate spending on access to positional goods by different consumers unfortunately cancels out, resulting in a waste of resources and no net gain in welfare.

2.4. The Problem for Egalitarianism

One major problem caused by status hierarchy, which is assumed in the work of both Veblen and Hirsch but not stated explicitly, is that our quest for status does not remain confined to the realm of personal behaviour, but tends to bleed over into other areas of social life, so that other goods become recruited to serve in the battle for increased status. One consequence of human cultural plasticity is that almost anything, it would appear, can be transformed into a status signal.[56] Most obviously, the quest for status colonizes the sphere of material consumption, so that people begin to care for goods more for the status they confer than for their material properties. As a result, over time the economy *becomes* more positional, and so economic growth becomes less effective at increasing social welfare.

It is a commonplace among anthropologists that societies tend to have both a "material" and a "prestige" economy, with often quite different rules governing the exchange or distribution of goods in the two sectors.[57] In many traditional or small-scale societies there is a strict partition between the two. Among the Ponapaens of Micronesia, for example, ordinary yams are a staple foodstuff, but giant yams are grown strictly for the sake of prestige (there is a competition to see who can grow the largest yam).[58] As prestige goods, yams are eaten at feasts and cannot be exchanged for everyday comestibles (or not without terrible loss of honour). Families have been known to go hungry, despite having a surfeit of oversized yams, for the familiar reason that they rank status more highly than their "lowly" bodily needs.[59] There is no tendency to confuse the two spheres:

> Each head of a farmstead contributes a yam, in addition to other food, when a Section feast is given. Everyone present examines and compares the yams as they are brought into the feast house, and praises the largest yam for its size and quality. They go up to the man who, in their opinion, brought the best yam to tell him that he is "Number One." The commoners praise him for his skill and ability as a farmer; the chief praises him for his generosity. As far as any standards of generosity are concerned, the

rules of competition are artificial and arbitrary. Contributions of fresh breadfruit, fish and other seafood, coconuts, taro, bananas, and other foods do not count. It is the size of the individual yam, and not the quantity of yams that is important.[60]

What has happened in our society – and in many other complex economies – is that the partition between these two economic spheres has broken down, so that every type of good has become a potential object of prestige. The existence of a cash economy is important in this development, because it offers a common metric in which traits like "generosity" can be assessed. Of course, some goods are more *obviously* status-oriented than others. And yet even the most utilitarian of devices, such as a corkscrew or a T-shirt, now comes with a story to edify the consumer and, not incidentally, to advertise that same consumer's higher aesthetic or moral sensibility. (As David Brooks observes, "Nobody wants to talk about a diamond necklace over dinner, but it's charming to start a conversation about the host's African-inspired salad serving forks. The smaller an item is, the more praiseworthy it is to have thought deeply about its purchase."[61]) Furthermore, the explosion of productivity in the material sector, not to mention the globalization of trade, has meant that the basic requirements of life can be met at a trifling cost. As a result, in wealthy countries the positional or prestige economy has practically occluded the material.

This has a number of important consequences, perhaps the most obvious being that it tends to neutralize the effectiveness of economic growth as a way of pacifying distributive conflict. As far as more utopian egalitarian schemes are concerned, it implies that "post-scarcity" conditions, such as Marx was counting on to bring about a classless society, will never be achieved. This is something that Veblen foresaw long ago:

> In the nature of the case, the desire for wealth can scarcely be satisfied in any individual instance, and evidently a satiation of the average or general desire for wealth is out of the question. However widely, or equally, or "fairly" it may be distributed, no general increase of the community's wealth can make any approach to satiating this need, the ground of which is the desire of every one to excel every one else in the accumulation of goods. If, as is sometimes assumed, the incentive to accumulation were the want of subsistence or of physical comfort, then the aggregate economic wants of a community might conceivably be satisfied at some point in the advance of industrial efficiency; but since the struggle is substantially a race for reputability on the basis of an invidious comparison, no approach to a definitive attainment is possible.[62]

Veblen went on to declare, prophetically, that "the need for conspicuous waste stands ready to absorb any increase in the community's industrial efficiency or output of goods, after the most elementary physical wants have been provided for."[63] This is, when one thinks about it, a stunning claim, one that most economists found completely unbelievable at the time. Surely, it seemed, a tenfold increase in per capita wealth would eliminate scarcity and render distributive conflict otiose. And even if it falls somewhat short of eliminating all conflict, it should at least make people less possessive and thus take some of the anger out of distributive conflict. And yet Veblen's prediction has been fully borne out over time. Surprising as it may seem, it is possible to increase the average level of wealth tenfold, without gaining even a tiny reduction in the average level of possessiveness or hostility to redistribution.

The centrality of status considerations in consumption also creates a serious problem for sufficientarianism (i.e., the view that the demand for equality can be satisfied by ensuring that everyone is above a certain threshold level of consumption or welfare), which is often based on a distinction drawn between the "basic needs" of the person, which establishes the threshold of sufficiency, and the more optional set of "wants" that extend beyond. The problem is that in developed countries, even among those who are very poor, the majority are well above what can be considered a plausible standard of sufficiency. Among US households below the poverty line, 95 per cent have electricity, indoor plumbing, a refrigerator, stove, and colour television. More than 80 per cent have an air conditioner, video recorder, and a cell phone, while two-thirds have their own a washing machine and dryer.[64] This is not "poverty" as understood historically. And yet one would not want to say that, because so many Americans are above a plausible sufficiency threshold, that the distribution of wealth in America raises no issues of justice. The very idea of sufficiency seems to imply that there is a point of satiation, at which one can unproblematically say that people have "enough," and so further inequalities do not matter. The implicit framework is one in which consumption is aimed at satisfying material needs, which admit of satiation. With positional goods and status, on the other hand, there is no point of satiation, and that is why people never seem to regard themselves as having "enough" material possessions, no matter how much they have.

These reflections suggest that, from a strictly pragmatic perspective, equality will not become any easier to achieve over time, because people's possessiveness, and their resistance to redistribution, will not decline with any increase in wealth. But beyond this, the analysis also casts doubt upon the usefulness of the principle of equality proper.

That is because the standard sort of redistributions undertaken in the name of equality, such as transfer programs funded by progressive income taxation, do not actually change the ranking of individuals. All they do is compress the income gap between them. So while they promote greater equality of income, they do nothing to promote greater equality of status. To the extent that goods are valued for the status they confer, this means that the redistribution will not improve anyone's satisfaction with the distribution of goods either.

Hirsch observes that, throughout the history of capitalism, growth has largely served as a substitute for redistribution. By making the economic pie larger, it was possible to offer everyone a larger slice, sufficient to forestall the question of how the pie was being divided up.[65] This is the insight underlying Robert Lucas's famous remark, that "of the vast increase in the well-being of hundreds of millions of people that has occurred in the 200-year course of the industrial revolution to date, virtually none of it can be attributed to the direct redistribution of resources from rich to poor. The potential for improving the lives of poor people by finding different ways of distributing current production is nothing compared to the apparently limitless potential of increasing production."[66] And yet the transition from a material to a positional economy risks undermining the effectiveness of this growth strategy. As Hirsch puts it, "Just as there was a tendency in times of material poverty to exaggerate what redistribution of income could do to diffuse what was then the most sought-after prerogative of the contemporary rich, their material comfort, so there is a tendency in times of material affluence to exaggerate what growth can do for diffusion of the new distinctive preserve of the rich, their positional prerogatives."[67]

If Hirsch is right, then one might conclude that the emphasis should shift over time, in the conception of economic justice, away from efficiency toward equality. Lucas may have been right about poor countries, that they should focus on creating more wealth, rather than redistributing it. But in rich countries the opposite situation prevails, so they should focus less on creating wealth, and more on redistributing it. This is a tempting conclusion. And yet unfortunately, it is not obvious that redistribution will accomplish much in a positional economy. As long as it stops short of creating perfect equality, redistribution serves only to change the *slope* of the social gradient (as Hirsch acknowledges). While it may compress the income distribution, so that the "distance" between individuals is not as great, it does nothing to change anyone's *rank*, and as a result, does not improve anyone's access to positional goods, nor does it create greater equality of status. The problem would appear to be the existence of the gradient, not the slope of the gradient. So not only does redistribution of goods fail to create greater equality of status, it may not even improve anyone's satisfaction with the distribution of goods. Thus the idea that redistribution "reduces inequality" turns out to harbour an important ambiguity. Redistribution can compress inequality, but if inequality is understood in terms of ranking, then there is a sense in which it will not reduce the amount of inequality.

There is, unfortunately, reason to be concerned that people care more about rank than about absolute income level. There are, for instance, many well-known instances of people demanding to be paid a purely nominal sum more than their nearest rivals (such as Maria Callas's requirement that, wherever she sang, she be paid at least one dollar more than the next-highest-paid singer[68]). This suggests that it is the mere existence of a gap between individuals, and not the size of the gap, that serves as the basis for status differences.[69] If the issue is rank, the only way to reduce inequality is to abolish it entirely – anything short of that will have little or no effect. Thus the increased positionality of the economy not only neutralizes the effectiveness of economic growth as a way of pacifying social conflict, *it also neutralizes the effectiveness of redistribution*. This is something that should be of considerable concern to egalitarians.

We are often reminded that the average compensation of chief executive officers (CEOs) in Fortune 500 US business corporations increased dramatically during the late twentieth century, from 30 times the wage of an average production worker in 1970 to more than 300 times the average wage at the end of the century.[70] Some have recommended a surtax on the income of very high earners, such as the top 1 percent, as a way of reducing the inequality caused by runaway compensation. And yet even if an implausibly large tax were implemented, which resulted in CEOs losing 50 per cent of their pay package, they would still be making 150 times more than the average worker. The wage structure would be compressed, but wage differentials would not be eliminated. (Indeed, an income tax system with increasing *marginal* rates is structurally incapable of doing anything other than compressing the income distribution.) While this may improve the government's revenue position, it is not clear that it reduces economic inequality in a way that matters to anyone in society, if what people care about is primarily status.

The problem that this creates for egalitarians has often been overlooked. In one of the few philosophical discussions of the topic, Harry Brighouse and Adam Swift argue that recognition of the positionality of many goods may resolve a traditional conundrum for egalitarians, which is to explain why anyone might prefer an equal distribution of some good to an unequal one in which the worst-off receive a share that is larger in absolute terms.[71] This is easy to explain, they claim, if the value of the good is a function of one's position or rank in the distribution.[72] What they fail to consider, however, is that even if this argument works as a reason for preferring a distribution that is exactly equal, it does not generate any reason for preferring a more-equal to a less-equal distribution. For instance, equality so construed offers no support for the Pigou-Dalton transfer principle.[73] Thus their defence of equality fails to satisfy an important desideratum for any theory of justice, which is that it should provide not just a specification of the ideal, but also a way of ranking second-best states.

One can find similar oversights in more empirically oriented literature. Consider, for instance, Michael Marmot's celebrated Whitehall study, which examined the effect of status differentials on the long-term health and longevity of British civil servants. It established the existence of a clear "health gradient," based on employment grade (and thus, position in the organizational hierarchy), even when controlling for all other obvious factors – including the fact that all of them had equal access to the same health care through the British National Health Service. On the basis of this observation, Gopal Sreenivasan has suggested that, if the goal is to promote greater equality in health outcomes, the best strategy may not be to introduce a national health insurance scheme, but rather to focus on "equalizing the distribution of social status – on equalizing the distribution of income, say, or of education."[74] Sreenivasan assumes that, because income is a "component" of status, improving the distribution of income will improve the distribution of status, or somehow diminish status inequality.[75] And yet short of perfect equality, it is not clear that income compression will have any such effect. One reason that Marmot chose the British civil service for study is that its members are alike in so many regards. In particular, salary differences between grades of British civil servants are minimal and are quite compressed compared to the private sector. (There are, as Marmot observes, "no private jets, and no unemployed or unemployable" in the civil service.)[76] And yet "the social gradient in health in Whitehall is steeper than in the country as a whole."[77] The unwelcome implication, which Marmot fails to note, is that it is possible to reduce economic inequality without actually making the health gradient less steep. Observers are sometimes misled by studies showing different countries with more income inequality (e.g., higher GINI coefficients) having a steeper health gradient. But this does not show that reducing the gradient in income will lower the gradient in health. Even if income is correlated with health outcomes, if the relationship is mediated by status rank, then compressing the distribution of income may not reduce the disparity in health outcomes.

I am not suggesting that these observations represent a decisive defeat for egalitarianism. My goal is only to show that egalitarians should be much more *worried* about status inequality than they appear to be. If one considers the intensity and detail of the famed "equality of what?" debate, it is striking how little energy and attention was directed toward the problem of status inequality. For instance, instead of the platitudinous claim that "gradients are bad," what needs to be shown is that "steeper gradients are worse than shallow ones." Some portions of Richard Wilkinson and Kate Pickett's *The Spirit Level* can be read as supporting this claim, although there are difficulties with the analysis that would need to be worked out, and considerable additional research would be required to establish the claim definitively.[78] Similarly, there are interesting empirical questions about how individuals assess their own status positions. Do they compare themselves to people in adjacent positions, or do they think about "distance from the top" or "distance from the bottom"? Do they care more about one or the other, or is there some point in the rank at which the concern switches? What is the effect of population viscosity (e.g., residential and occupational segregation), or media exposure to other lifestyles?[79] What sort of variation is there among individuals? These are all questions that require answers, before one can begin to think normatively about what it would mean to reduce status inequality, or the harms that it causes.[80]

3. Egalitarian Strategies

I have been speaking throughout of status inequality as a problem for egalitarians. This of course rests on an important presupposition, which is that egalitarians are not satisfied just to engage in abstract normative denunciations of inequality, but are hoping rather to do something about it. This ambition is front and centre in Rawls's work, when he describes justice as the "first virtue of social institutions," or discusses the basic structure as the "subject" of justice. It is clear that his goal is to develop a conception of justice that is capable of being *institutionalized*. Thus his normative principles must be capable of being rendered motivationally effective (hence his concerns over the "strains of commitment.") The basic structure of society institutionalizes a system of cooperation, which in turn has distributional consequences. The thought is that, if there is something wrong with the resulting outcome – for instance, if it violates equality – then the institutions should be changed, so that the outcome comes closer to satisfying the egalitarian constraint. If status hierarchy turns out to be a major impediment to the achievement of this outcome, then that constitutes a problem for egalitarianism in this sense.

There is, however, another strand of thinking in the egalitarian literature, which is content to dwell upon equality as an abstract moral ideal, without any particular concern for its institutional realization. G.A. Cohen gave considerable encouragement to this tendency, with his insistence that normative ideals must be specified without any admixture of concern over "facts," and in particular, without regard for the motivational limits of human psychology.[81] From this perspective, status inequality does not really pose a problem, it is simply a bad thing, one that we would all be better off without. One can find this thought in the writings of relational and social egalitarians as well, who for the most part have remained content simply to condemn status inequality, or to catalogue its legitimate and illegitimate forms.[82] Some may believe that moral condemnation alone will be sufficient to eliminate it. Some may not care and consider themselves to be engaged in merely a philosophical exercise of clarifying the relevant concepts or moral intuitions. My comments are obviously not addressed toward those who hold such views; I am focusing my remarks on those who are thinking about inequality in more institutional terms, with an interest in taking practical steps toward reducing it.

With some egalitarians, it is difficult to know what they think about status, because they write about inequality as though status inequality did not exist. Typical of this sort of work would be Anthony Atkinson's *Inequality: What Can Be Done?*, which, despite being admirable in many respects, is preoccupied exclusively with economic inequality and says nothing at all about status. In other cases, status inequality is mentioned, but without much detail, and often with vague suggestions as to how it might be dealt with.[83] These generally fall some distance short of being programs or strategies for dealing with the problem and might best be described as "grounds for hope" that it *can* be dealt with. There are, as far as I have been able to discern, at least five (non-exclusive) suggestions in this vein that enjoy some currency:

3.1. Elimination

In his short book, *Why Not Socialism?* Cohen develops an extended reflection upon the principles that a group of friends use to organize their daily activities on a camping trip. Labour is undertaken through an equal division of tasks, and distribution is achieved through "mutual giving." These seem like natural principles for the organization of a camping trip, and so, Cohen asks, why would we not want to extend them to society at large? And yet, early on in the exposition, Cohen strikes a discordant note by mentioning that despite his use of this example, he personally does not enjoy camping very much, and that he "would rather have my socialism in the warmth of All Souls College."[84] Anyone attuned to the intricacies of academic status will find this statement rather off-putting. Cohen could have chosen to say that he prefers the warmth of his own living room, and yet instead, he decided to highlight his appointment at All Souls College (he does not deign to mention the university, because as *everyone* knows, All Souls College is a part of Oxford University). Consider, by contrast, how peculiar the remark would sound if Cohen had been a professor at even a slightly less prestigious institution: e.g., "I would rather have my socialism in the warmth of the faculty club at the University of Wisconsin-Madison." But of course, no one would ever say such a thing, because Cohen's remark makes sense only in the context of the not-so-subtle status signalling that he was engaged in. He was reminding the reader, in case anyone had forgotten, that he was not just a political philosopher, but rather one of the most important political philosophers in the world. What is striking is not that he was preening in this way – academics do it all the time – but that he was doing so in the opening pages of a book whose official purpose was to make the case for "socialist equality."[85]

Episodes such as this, in my view, provide grounds for pessimism about the possibility of extirpating status hierarchy from human affairs. The more optimistic view holds that status differences are merely a by-product of *other* sets of inequalities, in a realm that does admit of redistribution, and so can be eliminated indirectly. For instance, while Marx did not articulate this view explicitly – "status" was not one of his concerns – he did believe that most trappings of class identity, along with nationalism, marriage, and religion, were part of the "superstructure," since they existed only in the realm of consciousness. The implication is that once class relations are abolished, through a change in the mode of production, status hierarchy will disappear as well. Although seldom expressed in these terms any longer, economic determinism of this sort remains extremely common in egalitarian writings on status. The hope is that if low-SES groups are given sufficient "economic opportunity," or perhaps just material resources, the status injuries that they suffer will fade away.

A slightly less optimistic view would recognize that status is not likely to disappear, but that it might nevertheless be overcome through some kind of targeted, effortful intervention. For instance, one might recognize that status inequality is not merely a by-product of unequal material relations, that it is anchored in deep-seated features of our evolved psychology, and yet think that through intensive socialization practices individuals might be trained to repress it. To put it in Freudian terms, dominance impulses might be treated as just one of the many instincts that are in tension with the demands of civilization and that therefore must be overcome, even on pain of some increase in psychological repression.[86]

Although possible in principle, socialization projects of this sort have frequently been a recipe for disappointment. In the same way that, with respect to nationalism, the working class has proven peculiarly resistant to the ideals of the *Internationale*, status has always found a way of reasserting itself, so that attempts to eliminate it acquire something of a "Whac-A-Mole" quality. The basic eliminativist claim is, of course, not straightforwardly falsifiable. Since we have never created anything resembling a classless society, there is no way to prove that these purportedly superstructural elements will not someday disappear, and it is always possible to explain away their persistence as a consequence of conditions being less than ideal. Similarly, no system of education or socialization is ever complete, so it is always possible that a bit more effort is all that is required to banish status hierarchy to the dark ages.

At the same time, there have been a very large number of utopian experiments undertaken, particularly during the twentieth century, none of which provide any grounds for optimism about the possibility of eliminating status hierarchy.[87] As Robert Nozick argued (and many others have observed), when the distribution of some desirable good (or quality, etc.) serves as the basis of an invidious comparison, it is tempting to think that the status difference can be eliminated by equalizing distribution of that good. However, when the equalization is performed, the basis of comparison often simply shifts to some other good, and the same basic hierarchy is preserved.[88] For instance, one motivation for favouring school uniforms is to dampen competitive consumption over clothing among schoolchildren. And yet this is generally acknowledged to have little effect on the status hierarchy, as competitive consumption simply shifts to other items not covered by the uniform policy, such as backpacks.[89] Or the result may simply be that everyone puts greater emphasis on non-consumption goods, such as physical attractiveness or athletic ability.

Perhaps the most perverse form of status displacement that occurs, within communes or other egalitarian communities, is that the basis of invidious comparison may be shifted to rigorous adherence to the moral ideals of the community itself. Most incredibly, as anyone who has participated in a commune or cooperative can attest, people in egalitarian communities often use *the intensity of their commitment to equality* as grounds for invidious comparison, and hence as a basis for status inequality. Thus it is common to encounter various forms of ostentatious "I care more about equality than you do" behaviour, which function as a status display. The fact that the moral commitment to equality can itself serve as a basis for status inequality should, I think, encourage a certain pessimism about the human capacity to overcome these impulses.

The term "political correctness," it may be recalled, was coined *on the left*, in order to criticize those who used the strictness of their conformity to left-wing political ideals to engage in "one-upmanship" over others, and thus to engage in a type of status competition. (This represents an instance of the form of social deviance that Talcott Parsons referred to as "hyperconformism.")[90] The development of complex, ever-changing speech codes, for instance, arises out of this competition for positional advantage, driven by the "calling out" of those who are unable to reproduce the performance. Elaborate codes of etiquette have served the same status function in many different societies. They not only mark status distinctions (e.g., between "woke" and "basic"), but also serve as a powerful device for excluding others from high-status positions, because the code is effectively unlearnable by those who are not already members of the superior class.[91] The code is also typically moralized, so that insiders are persuaded that the status distinctions they are drawing coincide with real differences in merit. One can see this clearly with contemporary woke culture, where those who have mastered the relevant speech codes find the hostility they experience from others uninterpretable as anything other than the expression of racism, sexism, homophobia, transphobia, etc. The possibility that others might be responding to a status injury – that by using these complex, unfamiliar locutions, those on the inside are performing the rituals of an exclusionary status system – is an entirely foreign thought.[92]

These forms of status competition among egalitarians have been familiar to insiders for a long time, but the development of social media has both intensified them and made the essential dynamic observable to the broader public. The ability to "like" and "retweet" messages on social media platforms has led to the development of virtue signalling, as well as an extremely competitive call-out culture, in which individuals scrutinize the communications of others, looking for opportunities to criticize them for moral violations and thereby to establish their own superiority.[93] Mark Fisher described the basic dynamic as "driven by a priest's desire to excommunicate and condemn, an academic-pedant's desire to be the first to spot a mistake, and a hipster's desire to be one of the in-crowd."[94] For instance, many people would be surprised to discover that it is a moral transgression to use the term "Hispanic" rather than "Latinx," or to mention that Caitlyn Jenner once went by the name Bruce. And yet these are faux pas for which one can (at the time of writing) be furiously called out on social media, and even in some corners of the academy.[95] What many neutral observers are struck by is the intensity of the language and sentiment expressed (adjectives commonly used to describe it include "furious," "vindictive," "savage," "vicious"). This is largely because the interaction is a status competition, and status is zero-sum. Angela Nagle describes the basic dynamic as follows:

> At first, self-righteously or snarkily denouncing others for racism, sexism or homophobia was the most instantaneous and certain way to achieve social media fame. Something about public social media platforms, it turned out, was conducive to the vanity of morally righteous politics and the irresistible draw of the culture wars. But soon the secret was out and everyone was doing it. The value of the currency of virtue that those who had made their social media cultural capital on was in danger of being suddenly devalued. Thus, the attacks increasingly focused on other liberals and leftists often with seemingly pristine progressive credentials, instead of those who engaged in any actual racism, sexism or homophobia.[96]

Again, the fact that this sort of status competition can take place among individuals who take themselves to be engaged in a struggle for social justice should be enough to give pause to anyone who envisions a future in which human beings have transcended their archaic concern for social dominance.[97]

3.2. Mutual Recognition

A large number of political theorists have sought to move away from the distributive paradigm of social justice associated with Marxism, on the grounds that it fails to offer a plausible reconstruction of the claims made by many of the new social movements of the twentieth century, such as feminism and the civil rights movement.[98] Many of these movements were not centrally concerned with economic issues, but focused rather on the way that members of various groups (women, visible minorities, homosexuals, etc.) were *treated* by others, both institutionally and in everyday social interaction. The central objection was to the way that they were *discriminated against*. There is obviously an egalitarian concern here, since discrimination seems to involve a type of unequal treatment, and yet it is not easily characterized as distributive inequality. Furthermore, the assurance from Marxists and others that these harms could be expected to disappear, once the "underlying" economic issues were addressed, struck many as wishful thinking.

Among social scientists, one influential current of thought chose to characterize these issues as involving a conflict over status. Erving Goffman, for instance, analysed forms of discrimination in terms of social stigma, which he interpreted as essentially a negative status marker.[99] Among political philosophers, however, there was some resistance to the analysis of these conflicts in terms of status. The more popular way of thematizing the issues was to move back from Marx to the early Hegel and to understand the basic dynamic as involving a *struggle for recognition*.[100] Normatively, this might have seemed to be a more attractive framework, because one can find in Hegel the suggestion that inequality and domination are only a stage of the development of this struggle, one that is ultimately unstable, and will be surpassed by a final resolution involving mutual recognition. This lends support to the essentially optimistic view that an equality of relations can be achieved that will allow society to transcend status hierarchy. The result is, in a sense, another type of eliminativism, but not one that relies upon an indirect mechanism of redistribution to correct inequality.

Hegel's analysis of recognition suggests that the type of asymmetric relations established through domination are unsatisfying to the parties and hence unstable. In his parable of the "master and slave," when two individuals meet, they set out to dominate one another, producing a conflict that results either in the death of both or the successful enslavement of one to the other.[101] The recognition that the master achieves from the slave is crucial, Hegel believed, to the development of the former's self-consciousness. Implicit in this is the idea – which many have felt to be correct – that our personal identity, or self-esteem, is constituted by coming to see ourselves in the way that others see us. And yet the recognition offered by the slave is ultimately inadequate, because it is not given freely. A natural conclusion to draw, on this basis, would be that the relationship of domination between master and slave must be replaced with some framework that permits symmetric or mutual recognition. Many have followed Alexandre Kojève in thinking that the status of undifferentiated citizenship established in modern democratic states achieves this objective.[102]

Optimistically, then, one might argue that the type of domination associated with primitive status competition is ultimately self-defeating, since it embodies an internal contradiction. It involves the craving for a certain recognition, but by establishing dominance over the one who is supposed to provide it, the dominant party ultimately deprives the gesture of its significance. This insight creates the possibility of moving to a higher stage or level, in which the quest for domination is set aside and individuals enter into relations of mutual recognition as equals. Dialogue or discourse is often recommended as a way of achieving this goal.[103]

There is, it should be noted, something to the basic point about the tension between the desire to dominate others and the fact that domination devalues the recognition one receives. Even in animal dominance hierarchies, what an individual gains from winning a confrontation is a function of the dominance rank of the loser. This is why, for most individuals, there is little to be gained from picking on those who are at the bottom of the dominance hierarchy. Primatologists have found that an Elo rating system does a good job of predicting the dynamics of dominance ranking in a number of species, including macaques.[104] (The Elo rating is best known as the rank system used in chess, where the number of points that one gains from a victory is a function of the number of points possessed by the person defeated. Thus one gains more points by beating someone who has, in turn, beaten more people.) The amount of status one gains from dominating others is a function of the amount of status possessed by those whom one dominates. But one cannot conclude from this that, because domination reduces the status of those being dominated, hierarchy is internally contradictory, and reciprocal recognition is the only equilibrium arrangement. Hegel's parable makes it seem this way because the scenario he considers involves only two people. In a larger society, those who are dominated will, in turn, dominate others, and so their recognition will always have value. Furthermore, if the basis of status is multidimensional, there may be no one who is entirely devoid of status. Thus the claim that there is a natural or internal tendency to progress toward mutual recognition is essentially unmotivated.

Others have criticized the mutual recognition model on the grounds that it winds up misconstruing the nature of the demands made by historically marginalized or oppressed groups. Nancy Fraser, in particular, has argued that the "recognition model" espoused by Axel Honneth and Charles Taylor, among others, should be rejected in favour of a Weberian "status model."[105] She faults the recognition model for encouraging a form of identity politics that seeks positive, mutual affirmation of all "group specificities."[106] This has the effect of increasing the salience of differentiating characteristics such as race in everyday interaction, which may have perverse consequences. In many cases, Fraser maintains, eliminating specific status inequalities may require a "universalist" or "deconstructive" strategy, which involves dissolving or making less salient individual differences, so that they can no longer serve to demarcate status groups.[107] With respect to race, for instance, the insistence on mutual recognition may foster an unrealistic optimism about the possibility of achieving equality. If the issue is one of status, a "deconstructive" strategy, which seeks to problematize or obscure the relevant racial markers, may be more effective at eliminating inequality.

While Fraser is persuasive in her critique of the "recognition model," she says surprisingly little about the tension between the Weberian status model that she recommends and her commitment to equality. As Christopher Zurn has observed, in his comments on Fraser, "For Weber, status is essentially a matter of honor, and honor is essentially a matter of differential judgments of worth. To put it another way, there can be no status apart from judgments that those who have honor are worth more than others; there is no possibility of egalitarian status relations."[108] If Fraser is correct, that modern identity politics is essentially a conflict over group status, then the only egalitarian solution should be for these groups to be "put out of business" as distinct groups.[109]

Fraser avoids this politically explosive consequence of her view only by watering down her conception of equality to make it compatible with significant status inequality. She endorses what she refers to as the "parity of participation" norm, according to which all individuals must be able to "participate as peers in social life."[110] On the distributive justice side, the principle is sufficientarian – it requires that everyone have enough "to ensure participants' independence and voice."[111] On the status side, it requires only that "institutionalized patterns of cultural value [must] express equal respect for all participants and ensure equal opportunity for achieving social esteem."[112] Significantly, equality of respect is mandated directly – this is the sort of formal equality that can be achieved through equal legal standing – while the principle requires only equal "opportunity" to achieve esteem, which is the more variable form of status that is maintained informally. Needless to say, providing people an equal opportunity to achieve social status is compatible with the persistence of an entirely hierarchical status ordering. Thus there is an element in Fraser's critique of the "mutual recognition" paradigm that is actually just scepticism about the possibility of resolving the problem of status inequality, coupled with a retreat from the normative commitment to doing so.

3.3. Compensation

Suppose one were to accept that status inequality cannot be eliminated in the informal social sphere. This in itself is not fatal to the egalitarian project. One obvious way of responding would be to compensate individuals for having low status by giving them more of some other good, so that their total allocation wound up being equal to that of others (according to whatever metric of interpersonal comparison is chosen). This is a well-known strategy for handling other non-fungible goods, such as natural talents and handicaps. Ronald Dworkin, for instance, includes in his egalitarian scheme a hypothetical insurance market that would offer individuals indemnity against various handicaps.[113] This could be extended to include coverage against having low status. A similar transfer would be mandated by any form of egalitarianism that seeks to achieve equality of welfare, opportunities for welfare, total capabilities, etc. To the extent that having low status impairs a person's attainment of the *equalisandum*, and yet status is non-fungible, a larger quantity of other, fungible goods would have to be allocated to that person in order to raise him or her to the target level.

Consider, for example, the way that the envy-freeness standard works as a conception of equality. This represents an attractive way of specifying what counts as an equal allocation when confronted with a heterogeneous collection of goods, along with individuals having differing preferences. Suppose that the goods can be grouped into two broad classes: x and y (e.g., income and leisure). Unless everyone is given an identical bundle, it is difficult to say what an equal allocation amounts to. If some people are receiving more x and less y, while others are receiving more y and less x, it will be necessary to specify the value of x relative to y, in order to determine whether the allocation respects or violates equality. Envy-freeness uses a purely subjective standard, specifying that if the allocation of bundles to individuals is such that no one wants to switch bundles with anyone else, then that allocation is equal. If someone does want to switch places, then the "egalitarian planner" must adjust the assignment of goods to bundles, in order to make the envied bundle less attractive, the assigned bundle more attractive, or both, until neither the discontented individual nor anyone else wants to switch places. Suppose, however, that one person has a special talent that allows her to make use of x in a way that the other person cannot. We might then feel that the allocation in which she receives the preponderance of x is intuitively unfair, because the other person would be envious of all that x, save for the fact that he is unable to make use of it. One solution is to introduce the talent to make use of x as a third category of good, z, and then specify that allocations of all three goods must be envy-free, but that individuals can only be assigned a bundle that contains the measure of talent that they, in fact, possess.[114] This resolves the intuitive unfairness in the example under consideration – the second person would have to be given a great deal more y, in order to prevent her from envying the generous allocation of x and z being assigned to the first. There is no guarantee that there will be a solution – there may not be enough fungible goods to fully compensate an individual for his deficit in non-fungible ones – but if there is a solution, it will be equal. So even though the talent cannot be redistributed, it can be treated as part of the agent's allocation when determining whether the distribution satisfies the principle of equality.

If we suppose that status hierarchy is maintained in the informal social sphere and so cannot be modified or redistributed, then it should still be possible to maintain overall equality by treating the individual's status position like a talent or handicap, which can be added to the overall bundle of goods that constitutes that person's endowment. Something like this is implicit in any form of welfare egalitarianism that seeks to make everyone equally happy. To the extent that low status is a source of unhappiness, individuals who are assigned to those positions will have to be given more of something else in order to increase their happiness to the target level. The crudest but most direct proposal would simply be to give them cash as compensation for occupying a low-status position.

There are, it should be noted, some private social and economic arrangements that appear to have this structure. Robert Frank, for instance, has observed that the best employees in an organization often forego the opportunity to earn a great deal more money working at a better firm.[115] He suggests that there is a tacit bargain: the "big fish" gains the status of being the best employee, while the others benefit by appropriating some fraction of the economic rent that would otherwise have gone to that individual. Thus the big fish is tacitly paying the small fish, in return for the latter being willing to accept a subordinate status. This transaction, however, is implicit – most people in the subordinate position would find the offer too humiliating to accept if made explicit. In this respect, it resembles the "trophy wife" arrangement, which normally must be couched in a great deal of self-deception on both sides in order to be successful.

There is, however, good reason to think that this model cannot be generalized to redistributive programs administered by the state. Obviously, there is no way of administering such a compensation system without making the structure of the transaction explicit. This means that the program would have very complicated dynamics, since the offer of compensation would itself be denigrating. The bigger problem, however, is the tendency, already noted, for status to bleed over into other domains of social life, and to change the value of other goods. Suppose that our three goods, x, y and z, stand for income, leisure, and status.

In order to compensate an individual for having very little z, it will be necessary to give her more of x and y. Unfortunately, being of low status may *change the value* of x or y in such a way as to make this compensation impossible. For instance, both upper and lower classes possess leisure in abundance. As Veblen observed, what people in higher social classes value about leisure is not the absence of work – on the contrary, they often invent for themselves highly labour-intensive hobbies, such as sailing or horseback riding, in order to stave off boredom. Leisure is valued as a signal, indicating "conspicuous exemption from productive labor."[116] Thus it may be impossible to compensate low-status individuals by giving them more leisure, because leisure is not always valued intrinsically, and the very act of offering it as compensation transforms it into a signal of low status. The transfer therefore winds up only adding insult to injury.

Similar problems may afflict the transfer of ordinary goods, particularly if they are identifiable as part of a transfer scheme. This is, as we have seen, one traditional problem with social housing, as well as programs like "food stamps" (now the Supplemental Nutrition Assistance Program, or SNAP) in the United States, which used to humiliate its recipients by requiring the use of special coupons at the point of purchase. Low-status individuals can have their welfare improved by ensuring that their material living requirements are satisfied. Beyond this, however, it is difficult to compensate them for having low status, because a major function of consumption goods is status signalling, and so unless it is possible to change the actual status position of these individuals, any goods transferred to them will simply be recoded to reflect the lower status of their new owners.

These reflections are not meant to show that it is impossible for an individual to be fully compensated for having low status, but merely that it may be very difficult and perhaps infeasible to do so, particularly for the state. The problem stems from the peculiar way that status interacts with goods in other categories, turning them into markers that reinforce status inequality. Whether this can be worked out or not will depend upon the specific conception of equality under consideration, as well as the specific institutional strategies being contemplated for achieving its realization.

3.4. Neutralization

Earlier in the discussion I skated over a rather complex issue, when I mentioned that the basis of status ordering is "multidimensional." There are a variety of personal traits that are associated with higher status: physical prowess, strength, and agility; sexual attractiveness; intelligence and verbal acuity. There are also social and institutional positions, particularly power, wealth, and fame. The way that these qualities and positions are evaluated differs at different periods of life, and are also, to some degree, evaluated differently according to gender. This is true of other animals as well, but the number of different dimensions is far more pronounced among humans. One might think that the overall ranking represents nothing but an aggregate or average of an individual's ranking in each of these single dimensions. However, several factors complicate the rankings. First there are the effects of what can be referred to as population viscosity. This reflects the fact that not everyone interacts with everyone else. Since status is maintained in the informal sphere, the most powerful determinants of status occur in face-to-face interaction. So while there is a society-wide status ordering, which slots individuals into broad classes and furnishes the basic set of status stereotypes, there is also a more fine-grained local status hierarchy maintained in every school, workplace, club, or neighbourhood.[117] Individuals who are "losers" in the larger scheme of things may still be "winners" within a local one, and vice versa. The "big fish in small pond" phenomenon plays upon this, as individuals choose a less competitive reference group, so that their relative status will be higher. The arrangement may be attractive, to the extent that the global status position is basically an abstraction, which, unless one dwells upon it, has little effect on day-to-day life, while local status provides gratification and advantages in everyday interaction.[118] The same phenomenon occurs in even more localized interactions, such as social clubs, sports teams, offices, and so on.

Complicating things further is the fact that individuals are subject to various forms of optimism bias, which leads them to overestimate their position in the status hierarchy. To some degree this is just false belief, based on distorted perception of how others perceive them. But some of it exploits the fact that status is multidimensional, and there is no consensus method for reconciling the various orderings. As a result, individuals often engage in ego-protection by assigning greater weight to the dimension in which they happen to do well, while downgrading or denigrating the dimension in which they do poorly.[119] For instance, a fairly reliable source of amusement in the literature on optimism bias is a study of university professors, which showed that 94 per cent rated themselves as above-average teachers, while 68 per cent considered themselves to be in the top 25 per cent.[120] One suspects, however, that this is not entirely delusional. Teaching is a complex activity, which relies upon a mix of skills and produces a range of desired outcomes.

Some professors may be quite interesting speakers and so enjoy greater success at keeping the attention of students. Others may be very well-organized and so may present more coherent lectures. Others may be better at promoting student understanding, while others may achieve better knowledge-retention. It is possible (although not entirely likely) that 94 per cent are above average in *some* dimension. And so if each individual ranks that dimension as the most important, then each can say, with some degree of plausibility, that he or she is an above-average teacher.[121]

The question is whether this infirmity of human nature could become a remedy to itself, by providing a solution to the age-old problem of status inequality. If people are more concerned with their local status than their position in the global status ordering, then achieving pre-eminence in a particular task, activity, or community may be sufficient to support a robust self-esteem.[122] By assigning greater importance to the status competitions in which they excel, and ignoring or discounting those in which they do poorly, everyone is able to conceive of himself or herself as a "winner." And so, even if there is still a status hierarchy, it might be possible to achieve the outcome that Rawls recommended, when he specified that "there should be for each person at least one community of shared interests to which he belongs and where he finds his endeavors confirmed by his associates."[123]

More technically, it is possible that the effects of status hierarchy can be neutralized through the attainment of something like the condition that Philippe Van Parijs refers to as "undominated diversity."[124] Under this arrangement, individuals will be status-ranked along multiple dimensions, at multiple localities, which we may think of as status micro-orderings. One person will be *dominated* by another if the second person enjoys a higher rank than the first in every single micro-ordering in which the first is ranked. In this case, the position of the second person will be unanimously preferred to that of the first. If, however, for any two people, there is at least one micro-ordering in which the first ranks higher than the second, and one micro-ordering in which the second ranks higher than the first, then with sufficient pluralism neither person's position will be unanimously preferred, in the broader society, to that of the other. Thus the two individuals are *undominated* in status ranking with respect to one another. This might then plausibly be thought to neutralize the pernicious effects of these hierarchies. Society still ranks people, classifying them as winners and losers, but it provides everyone with the opportunity to be a winner in at least one contest. And if individuals are disposed to think that the contests in which they are winners are more important than those in which they are losers, then everyone will be happy.¹²⁵ Alternately, one might think of undominated diversity as a conception of equality that is compatible with ongoing status hierarchy.

It seems fairly clear that traditional social structures, in which people live in small communities and interact very seldom with strangers, fail to provide a sufficient number of status competitions for the condition of undominated diversity to obtain. One of the things that people find oppressive about rural communities and small towns is that there is something close to a consensus status ordering. Greater population density, pluralism, and anonymity fragment this status ordering. Within ethnic groups, and with the formation of subcultures, status hierarchies develop that are completely independent of those maintained by "mainstream" society and institutions and are often non-comparable to one another. Thus it is not difficult to think that there has been significant movement in the direction that would be required, in order to achieve undominated diversity in status. Nevertheless, there are a lot of people in the world, and it is difficult to imagine circumstances in which literally each one could score a "win." At very least, a society committed to achieving this ideal would want to encourage greater fragmentation and pluralism, in order to generate a proliferation of status micro-orderings. The thought would be that, by creating more ponds, we make it possible for each person to be a big fish in at least one.¹²⁶

Some have argued that the rise of online communities has made it possible, for the first time, for these conditions to be satisfied. Status-seeking drives a great deal of online behaviour. Consider, for instance, a site like Reddit, which allows individuals to create online communities of interest (or "subreddits"). Commentators and "redditors" provide content, which fellow users can either upvote or downvote, causing it to be displayed more or less prominently. Each upvote gives the user a karma point, which has purely notional value, but functions for many people as a powerful signal of social approval. Over the twelve-year period from 2008 to 2020, the number of subreddits increased from around 10,000 to over 2.2 million. Each functions very much like a community, with dedicated moderators and commentators seeking to acquire reputation and earn karma. While the global status competition takes place on the "front page" of Reddit, most people are content to toil away in the obscurity of various subreddits, seeking the approval of that small set of users. The elimination of geographic boundaries makes it possible for the small handful of people who share some obscure interest or skill to find one another, and to form an audience that appreciates what would otherwise be an individual peculiarity.

These are important developments, but their normative significance is difficult to assess. On the one hand, the internet has given rise to a self-conscious "beta" culture, of individuals who accept that they are losers in the real-life (RL) game of status competition and so turn to online communities for validation instead. Given the enormous weight that physical attractiveness carries in determining RL-status, it is unsurprising that online interactions wind up generating very different rankings. At the same time, the difference between the two has the capacity to generate for some people profound alienation from all aspects of RL interaction. Perhaps more importantly, while certain aspects of online interaction have the effect of fragmenting social hierarchies, others have the exact opposite effect. It has long been observed that the growth of transportation, communication, and mechanical reproduction have led to the emergence and consolidation of "winner-take-all" markets.[127] For instance, at the beginning of the twentieth century most professional sports leagues earned their revenue from ticket sales, and as a result, were able to provide a modest living to a fairly large number of athletes. The development of radio, and to a larger extent television, consolidated audiences, focusing them on the top-tier league, along with a very small number of star players. Similar dynamics occurred in music, theatre (acting), and other sectors of the entertainment industry. As a result, hundreds of local status hierarchies were consolidated into a single, vastly more competitive status hierarchy, which provides a very generous living to a small number of "superstars" and nothing for anyone else.[128]

The development of social media has intensified this dynamic, with platforms like Instagram, TikTok, and YouTube basically just reinforcing existing RL status hierarchies, while at the same time vastly expanding the scope of the competition. (There is a reason that TikTok is the favourite app of the traditional popular teenagers – it allows them to draw upon traditional RL status assets, such as physical attractiveness, then vastly amplifies *and quantifies* their resulting status attainment.) In the same way that consumerism turns everyday objects into status symbols, social media posting extends this phenomenon, so that everyday experiences and services become the focus of intense lifestyle competition. Furthermore, the ability of viewers to directly signal their approval (by "liking," "following," or the equivalent), and to provide feedback to the originator, makes these interactions the perfect vehicle for global status competition. Quantification also constrains self-deception, making it much more difficult to overestimate one's status attainment. As a result, many users find their online experiences depressing (and yet addictive, which is why they persist in seeking them out).[129]

Contrary to the optimism bias that people have about certain social traits, there is evidence to suggest that a majority tends to think that others have better and more active social lives – a perception that is obviously exacerbated by social media in which individuals present "curated" selections of their lived experiences.[130]

As a result of these developments, it is not obvious that the neutralization strategy, of promoting undominated diversity in the field of status, is being facilitated, rather than impaired, by the fact that a significant fraction of human interactions are being shifted into virtual environments. While it is able to produce fragmentation, it also consolidates audiences on a vast scale – two dynamics that push in exactly opposite directions, as far as the individual experience of status competition is concerned. The likely effects are unclear. One might be inclined to call for more research, but even this seems pointless at the moment. The development of technology, along with human use of that technology, is too fast-moving to be worth researching any particular modality in detail. For the most part we have no choice but to see how it unfolds.

3.5. Insulation

Anyone who is troubled by status hierarchy cannot help but be struck by the perverse ingenuity human beings exhibit when inventing and sustaining ways of drawing invidious comparisons with one another. As a result, the formula that Rawls adopts – which rests on a combination of legal equality and the neutralization strategy – seems overly optimistic ("In a well-ordered society the need for status is met by the public recognition of just institutions, together with the full and diverse internal life of the many free communities of interests that the equal liberties allows").[131] There is, however, another template for managing inequality that can be found in Rawls's work, which he adopts for dealing with problems arising from inequality of talents. This involves accepting the inevitability of the inequality and resisting the impulse to offer redress, but instead focusing on preventing that inequality from ramifying throughout the basic structure.[132] Using this model, the goal would be to contain status inequality within the informal sphere, preventing it from generating inequality in other domains – and thus to *insulate* the basic structure from the effects of status inequality.

Rawls, it may be recalled, insisted that the "distribution of natural talents" was "neither just nor unjust," so there was no obligation to compensate those who received an inferior natural endowment.[133] Furthermore, he claimed that "the more advantaged have a right to their natural assets, as does everyone else."[134] What he objected to in the system of "natural liberty" is that it gives individuals with superior natural endowments access to a cooperative scheme "that enables them to obtain even further benefits in ways that do not contribute to the advantages of others."[135] In other words, he objected to any arrangement that allows individuals to leverage these natural advantages, in order to obtain greater advantages in the distribution of socially produced goods. Such an arrangement favours "the more fortunate twice over" – they get the superior natural endowment, and then they are able to use it to get a disproportionate share of the cooperative surplus.[136] Thus the normative ideal seeks to insulate the social sphere (or the domains of interaction governed by the basic structure, and hence regulated by principles of justice) from the effects of natural inequality.

This model, I would like to suggest, can also be used as a way of thinking about status inequality. Rather than optimistically trying to abolish the inequality, or to provide individuals with compensation for its effects, the goal would be to arrest the aforementioned tendency for status to bleed over into other spheres of social life, and thus to influence the distribution of the benefits of the cooperative schemes that we are involved in. This is, of course, a more limited objective than any of the ones considered in the previous sections, which might seem odd, given that status inequality is not beyond human control in the way that the distribution of natural talents is. Of course, both status and natural talents share the common feature of being outside the basic structure, which means that the inequality can be treated as exogenous from the standpoint of justice. There is, however, a mistaken tendency to think that if something is social, then it can be changed at will, and so accepting the inevitability of status inequality would be an unacceptable capitulation. This is, however, precisely the position that I am recommending, based on the observation that many social phenomena are just as resistant to social planning as natural ones. (Those who are less pessimistic might instead favour insulation as an interim strategy, to be adopted until we discover how to abolish status hierarchy once and for all.)

This insulation strategy, it should be noted, rules out more comprehensive forms of egalitarianism that seek to promote overall equality of condition. In order for insulation to make sense, it would have to be possible to say that a particular sort of cooperative benefit, such as wealth, education, or access to certain advantages, was distributed equally, even though some other benefits were distributed unequally. Forms of welfarism or luck egalitarianism that look only at overall equality of condition are unable to break things down in this way, and so recognition of the inevitability of status hierarchy leaves only the compensation strategy available to them.[137] Forms of egalitarianism that focus on equalizing the distribution of particular resources, or of the benefits of cooperation, by contrast, are able to distinguish different cooperative schemes from one another and to recommend that the terms of cooperation of as many as possible be as equal as possible. Thus the strategy of insulating one domain of interaction from the others makes sense (such that, even if *life* is unfair, access to education, health care, or employment opportunities can still be fair).

This sort of insulation might seem too modest an ambition, until one stops to consider what would be involved in its attainment. In the previous section, I focused on the way that status concerns bleed into the domain of consumption and economic well-being, but this is only a small part of the picture. It is actually extraordinarily difficult to prevent status from intruding into every domain of social interaction. In part this is the result of "status generalization," whereby high-status individuals are assumed to have superior qualities in other domains. Within groups this affects "such behaviors as deference, choices for group leader, estimation of individuals' contributions to group problem solution, being given and accepting chances to participate in discussions, exerting influence over others, being granted respect or esteem, and *proacting* in task oriented categories of interaction rather than *reacting* in social-emotional categories."[138] As a result, high status outside a group is converted into high status within the group, even when there is no rational basis for this importation.[139] This makes it very difficult to contain status inequality within a particular sphere.

For instance, a central feature of the major systems of cooperation in society is that they are regulated by law. And yet if one looks at the enforcement of the law, starting with the police and moving all the way up through the courts, one can see the effects of status inequality at every level. To take just one example, status differences are often easily detected through variations in the way that people speak. This is true not just in the United Kingdom (where the entire nation seems to have a finely honed ability to identify an individual's precise class background on the basis of spoken accent), but in every society, where certain differences of idiom, vocabulary, and speaking style are strongly correlated with status. This has predictable effects on access to various advantages, particularly those allocated through face-to-face exchanges. An influential study conducted by William O'Barr looked at courtroom testimony, categorizing it according to different speech styles. O'Barr identified a distinctive form of hedging that he described as the "powerless" style, employed primarily by housewives and men in low-status jobs or unemployed.[140] He found that this speech style was systematically disadvantaging to the speaker. "Whether the witness was male or female, he or she was thought to be less convincing, less believable, less competent, less intelligent, and less trustworthy when the powerless style was used."[141] He found also that the effects on jury members were quite persistent and were not influenced by any instruction from the judge to ignore aspects of verbal presentation.[142]

Similarly, in analysing police discretion, Mary Pat Baumgartner has argued that this discretion is exercised in a way that systematically reinforces background social hierarchies.[143] While citizens may enjoy formal equality before the law, offences perpetrated against high-status individuals are taken far more seriously, testimony offered by high-status individuals is found to be more believable, and transgressions perpetrated by them are far more likely to be excused. This confirms a point often made in the sociology of policing, which is that the police normally interpret their function not only as enforcement of the law, but also the maintenance of a particular conception of respectability and order.[144] Police use their statutory discretion as a source of power, which can be applied to enforcement of the informal social order. This may have its benefits, but it also has the effect of taking status inequalities that are maintained in the informal sphere and importing them into the more formal institutions of the basic structure. The result is a dilemma for egalitarians. It is impossible to avoid a great deal of discretion, in both the interpretation and enforcement of the law. Yet as Baumgartner puts it, "If discretion can never be totally abolished from law, then, and if social discrimination inevitably arises from discretion, it follows that law will always be discriminatory to some extent.... An end to social inequities in the handling of legal cases may well require nothing less than an end to law itself."[145] Since there is no reason to think that any alternative to a legal ordering will be less discriminatory, the overall effect of her reflections is merely to cast doubt upon our ability to make much progress in the direction of equality.

There are, of course, some things that can be done. As Cecilia Ridgeway has observed, particular emphasis should be put on eliminating the influence of status on "gateway" processes, such as educational admissions, that determine access to major social and economic institutions.[146] Here there is much to be learned from initiatives to reduce racial or gender discrimination, since, as I have argued, a portion of what people are responding to in racial differences, and to a lesser extent gender differences, are actually status signals. Abolishing the practice among job applications of including a photograph with a curriculum vitae is an obvious move. Similarly, the abolition of face-to-face interviews for many positions (such as medical school admissions) is motivated in part by the desire to eliminate the biasing effects of these interactions. Indeed, personal interviews seem to have very little predictive value for many outcomes, and yet they serve as a rich source of potentially misleading information, and an obvious vehicle for status generalization.[147] The fact that online interactions screen out many status signals creates new possibilities as well. Thus there is no reason to think that the situation is entirely hopeless, or sufficiently so that it undermines the normative ideal of insulation.

Finally, it should be noted that because status concerns are relatively myopic, it is sometimes possible to redirect the relevant competitive energies so that instead of producing socially undesirable effects, they actually generate pro-social behaviour. "Efficient status competitions" occur when actions that have positive social value serve also as status signals.[148] A good example of such an institutional arrangement is the charity auction, which encourages wealthy individuals to engage in a competitive display of "pecuniary strength," but where the proceeds all go toward some worthwhile cause. Certain aspects of traditional etiquette, which served as markers of status, but also encouraged more genteel modes of social interaction, had a similar structure. Thus it is not always necessary to quarantine status competition to prevent it from infecting other spheres of interaction. In some cases it is possible to redirect it – by encouraging cultural value systems that confer status for altruistic or cooperative behaviour – so that its influence becomes positive rather than negative.

4. Conclusion

My central contention in this chapter has been that egalitarians should be more worried about status inequality than they traditionally have been. While Marx is not entirely to blame for the prevailing insouciance, he did contribute to an intellectual environment that has been governed by wishful thinking – the belief that status inequality will simply go away once a more egalitarian distribution of wealth is achieved. More generally, there is a widespread tendency to believe that economic inequality is the primary form of inequality in our society, and that status inequality is somehow secondary, or less important. Certainly economic inequality is easier to *measure* than status inequality, but that does not make it more important. Given that people often make enormous material sacrifices in order to avoid loss of status, it is not clear that income and wealth should be accorded such priority. Furthermore, there is every reason to think that the importance of status inequality is growing. If one looks at the consumption habits of the poor in developed countries, what stands out is not the material deprivation, but rather the status injury. The rich do not always have that much more stuff than the poor, but it is much nicer stuff. In the face of these inequalities, it is not obvious that the traditional politics of distributive justice actually address the issues that people care about most.

I have laid out and provided some analysis of five different ways that egalitarians have responded to this state of affairs. Much of this response, however, has been implicit, and even when explicit, underdeveloped. This is why most of my discussion has been focused on what egalitarians *could* say. There is simply not enough serious literature on the question to be able to engage effectively with what they *do* say. Of course, different forms of egalitarianism have different resources for responding to the difficulty. My discussion here has been constrained in part by my desire to address the issue at a high level of generality, in terms of the problem that status poses for distributive egalitarianism in general, rather than focusing on the problems that status inequality creates for any particular conception of equality. Similarly, the analysis raises important questions about the extent to which these strategies are incompatible with one another. Obviously some are and some are not, but it is difficult to be more precise without specifying the particular conception of equality that one is committed to.

I am inclined to think that status inequality, especially if it is persistent, creates more serious difficulties for some egalitarian views than others. Indeed, one argument that lends support to my favoured conception of egalitarian justice, which focuses on the benefits of cooperation as the appropriate *equalisandum*, is that it handles the problem of status inequality better than other views, because it works well with the insulation strategy. These more fine-grained debates must at some point be entered into, before progress can be made on the basic problem of status. But before that happens, the broader issue must be taken more seriously by egalitarians of all persuasions. My ambition in this discussion has been merely to make the case for such an investment of attention and energy.

NOTES

1 August de Belmont Hollingshead, *Two Factor Index of Social Position* (New Haven, CT: Hollingshead, 1957).
2 Cecilia L. Ridgeway, "Why Status Matters for Inequality," *American Sociological Review* 79, no. 1 (2014): 1–16.

3 Patricia Roszell, David Kennedy, and Edward Grabb, "Physical Attractiveness and Income Attainment among Canadians," *Journal of Psychology* 123, no. 6 (1989): 547–59. For a more inside discussion, see Ashley Mears, *Very Important People* (Princeton, NJ: Princeton University Press, 2020).
4 There is an entire subgenre of misanthropic humour focused on sharing photographs of lower-class customers at US Walmart stores: Reddit, "People of Walmart," https://www.reddit.com/r/peopleofwalmart/. Another useful resource for observing status judgments is Reddit, "All Things Trashy!," https://www.reddit.com/r/trashy/.
5 Leon Festinger, "A Theory of Social Comparison Processes," *Human Relations* 7, no. 2 (1954): 117–40; Susan T. Fiske, *Envy Up, Scorn Down* (New York: Russell Sage, 2011). It is becoming increasingly standard in the philosophical literature to distinguish self-respect from self-esteem by treating the former as tied to human capacities that are universally shared, and thus as subject to equal distribution, the latter as variable, determined by achievement and other relative measures. See David Sachs, "How to Distinguish Self-Respect from Self-Esteem," *Philosophy and Public Affairs* 10, no. 4 (1981): 346–60.
6 E.g., "The most general conclusion from research is that the world must be a more pleasant and satisfying place for attractive people because they possess almost all types of social advantage that can be measured." See Murray Webster Jr. and James E. Driskell Jr., "Beauty as Status," *American Journal of Sociology* 89, no. 1 (1983): 141.
7 I put the term "egalitarian" in quotation marks because social relations in these societies are not egalitarian in the sense that modern, normative egalitarians use the term. Most obviously, almost all these societies have a gendered division of labour and exhibit various features of male dominance over females. They are "egalitarian" in the sense that they do not have an explicit or formal hierarchy or leadership. Thus the contrast in non-state social formations is normally drawn between egalitarian societies, those with a "big-man" structure (explicit, informal dominance), and "chieftainship" (explicit, institutionalized dominance). For classic discussion, see Morton H. Fried, *The Evolution of Political Society* (New York: Random House, 1967).
8 Christopher Boehm, *Hierarchy in the Forest* (Cambridge, MA: Harvard University Press, 2001).
9 Laura Van Berkel, Chris Crandall, Scott Eidelman, and John C. Blanchar, "Hierarchy, Dominance, and Deliberation: Egalitarian Values Require Mental Effort," *Personality & Social Psychology Bulletin* 41, no. 9 (2015): 1207–22.

10 Eric Bonabeau, Guy Theraulaz, and Jean-Louis Deneubourg, "Mathematical Model of Self-Organizing Hierarchies in Animal Societies," *Bulletin of Mathematical Biology* 58, no. 4 (1996): 662.
11 W.C. Allee, "Dominance and Hierarchy in Societies of Vertebrates," in *Structure et physiologie des sociétées animales : colloques internationaux*, 34, ed. P.P. Grasse (Paris: CNRS, 1952), 157–81.
12 Irwin S. Bernstein, "Dominance: The Baby and the Bathwater," *Behavioral and Brain Sciences* 4, no. 3 (1981): 421.
13 Bernstein, "Dominance," 422.
14 Nick Allen, "Nigel Farage Says Donald Trump Was 'Like a Silverback Gorilla' in US Presidential Debate," *Telegraph*, 10 October 2016, https://www.telegraph.co.uk/news/2016/10/10/nigel-farage-says-donald-trump-was-like-a-silverback-gorilla-in/.
15 Dominik Kiser, Ben Steemers, Igor Branchi, and Judith R. Homberg, "The Reciprocal Interaction between Serotonin and Social Behavior," *Neuroscience and Biobehavioral Reviews* 36, no. 2 (2011): 786–98; Donald H. Edwards and Edward A. Kravitz, "Serotonin, Social Status and Aggression," *Current Opinion in Neurobiology* 7, no. 6 (1997): 812–19; Joan Y. Chiao, "Neural Basis of Social Status Hierarchy across Species," *Current Opinion in Neurobiology* 20, no. 6 (2010): 803–9.
16 Frans B.W. de Waal, "Natural Normativity: The 'Is' and 'Ought' of Animal Behavior," in *Evolved Morality*, ed. Frans B.W. de Waal, Patricia Smith Churchland, Telmo Pievani, and Stefano Parmigiani (Leiden: Brill, 2014), 54.
17 Thus I disagree with Ridgeway's description of status inequality as grounded in "cultural beliefs." See "Why Status Matters for Inequality," 3. This implies that it is propagated through social learning, which I find unduly optimistic.
18 Boehm, *Hierarchy in the Forest*; Robert Boyd and Peter Richerson, *Not by Genes Alone* (Chicago: University of Chicago Press, 2005).
19 For instance, North American university professors have three official status ranks. But *within* any given rank, there is still a status ordering. It is common knowledge within a given department, or at any academic conference, who the high-status professors and who the low-status professors are, even though the ranking is maintained informally and seldom explicitly articulated.
20 Geoffrey Brennan and Philip Pettit, *The Economy of Esteem* (Oxford: Oxford University Press, 2006).
21 Note that I am using the word "emulation" in its older sense (such as it is used by Thorstein Veblen), according to which emulation involves reproducing a certain behaviour while at the same time demonstrating one's superiority (the sort of display often prefaced by the phrase "let

me show you how it's done.") The meaning of the word has changed, under the influence of twentieth-century computer science. Setting up one computer system to run software designed to work with another was described as "emulation," under the assumption that the motive for doing so would be to do a better job at running it. Over time, however, the notion of doing it better was lost, and so emulation came to mean roughly the same thing as "copying."

22 Joseph Heath and Andrew Potter, *The Rebel Sell* (Toronto: HarperCollins, 2004), 200–5.
23 Max Weber, *Economy and Society*, ed. Claus Wittich and Guenther Ross (Berkeley: University of California Press, 1978), 305–6.
24 Henri Tajfel, "Social Psychology of Intergroup Relations," *Annual Review of Psychology* 33 (1982): 1–39.
25 Gwyneth H. McClendon, *Envy in Politics* (Princeton, NJ: Princeton University Press, 2018), 139.
26 Yael Tamir, *Liberal Nationalism* (Princeton, NJ: Princeton University Press, 1993).
27 Thorstein Veblen, *The Theory of the Leisure Class* (Oxford: Oxford University Press, 2007), 65.
28 Veblen, *Theory of the Leisure Class*, 257.
29 Veblen, 70.
30 Adam Smith, *An Inquiry into the Nature and Causes of the Wealth of Nations* (Oxford: Oxford University Press, 1976), 870.
31 Carina Fourie, Fabian Schuppert, and Ivo Wallimann-Helmer, eds., *Social Equality* (Oxford: Oxford University Press, 2015); W.G. Runciman, "'Social' Equality," *Philosophical Quarterly* 17, no. 68 (1967): 221–30; Elizabeth Anderson, "What Is the Point of Equality?," *Ethics* 109, no. 2 (1990): 287–337.
32 Carina Fourie, "What Is Social Equality? An Analysis of Status Equality as a Strongly Egalitarian Ideal," *Res Publica* 18, no. 2 (2012): 111.
33 David Miller, "Equality and Justice," *Ratio* 10, no. 3 (1997): 224.
34 For more complete discussion, see Kasper Lippert-Rasmussen, *Relational Egalitarianism* (Cambridge: Cambridge University Press, 2018). Lippert-Rasmusen also observes that, having formulated their doctrine primarily as a critique of luck egalitarianism, relational egalitarians have tended to neglect the task of offering an affirmative statement of their own view.
35 Lippert-Rasmussen, *Relational Egalitarianism*, 63–70.
36 T.M. Scanlon, *Why Does Inequality Matter?* (Oxford: Oxford University Press, 2018), 26. All other forms of status inequality that he considers are downstream effects of economic inequality. One can see in this selective emphasis another important aspect of relational egalitarianism, which is that it represents an attempt by egalitarian liberals to annex some

portion of the moral high ground currently occupied by identity politics in American left-wing thought.
37 G.A. Cohen, "On the Currency of Egalitarian Justice," *Ethics* 99, no. 4 (1989): 906.
38 As Brennan and Pettit observe (with respect to esteem instead of status), "The very idea of supplying esteem on an intentional basis, whether as a gift or trade, or by way of transmitting the esteem of a third party, is incoherent" (*Economy of Esteem*, 55).
39 Brennan and Pettit, *Economy of Esteem*, 35–7.
40 Robert Frank, *Choosing the Right Pond* (Oxford: Oxford University Press, 1999).
41 John Rawls, *A Theory of Justice*, 2nd ed. (Cambridge, MA: Harvard University Press, 1999), 54. He describes "self-respect" as a primary good (e.g., 386). For clarification, see Rawls, *Justice as Fairness: A Restatement*, ed. Erin Kelly (Cambridge, MA: Harvard University Press, 2001), 58–9.
42 Rawls, *Theory of Justice*, 128–9.
43 I am using the term "self-respect" here because that is what Rawls uses, even though the better term would be "self-esteem." See W.G. Runciman, "'Social' Equality," *Philosophical Quarterly* 17, no. 68 (1967): 221–30; Stephen L. Darwall, "Two Kinds of Respect," *Ethics* 88, no. 1 (1977): 36–49.
44 A critical theorist with the capacity for self-criticism might suspect that the enthusiasm for egalitarianism one finds among academics is due, at least in part, to the fact that the thing academics care most about – status – cannot be redistributed, and so they need not contemplate losing the hard-earned fruits of their own labour. The way that cognitive skills are rewarded in a modern economy, most academics are individuals who have, through their training or career path, foregone extremely lucrative opportunities outside of the university. It is therefore no surprise that they are willing to contemplate confiscatory taxation of income with equanimity – they are a self-selecting group of people who care less about money than most others do. Impugn their status, on the other hand, and they react like any other powerful interest group.
45 This is what generates "Okun's leaky bucket." See Arthur Okun, *Equality and Efficiency: The Big Trade-off* (Washington, DC: Brookings, 1975).
46 Benjamin Friedman, *The Moral Consequences of Economic Growth* (New York: Penguin, 2006).
47 Veblen, *Theory of the Leisure Class*, 67. Also Joseph Heath, "Thorstein Veblen and American Social Criticism," in *Oxford Handbook of American Philosophy*, ed. Cheryl Misak (Oxford: Oxford University Press, 2008), 235–53.
48 *Economist*, "The Link between Polygamy and War," 19 December 2017.
49 Robert Frank, *Luxury Fever* (Princeton, NJ: Princeton University Press, 1999); Heath and Potter, *Rebel Sell*.

50 See Ta-Nehisi Coates, *Between the World and Me* (New York: Penguin Random House, 2015).
51 Elijah Anderson, "The Code of the Streets," *Atlantic*, 1 May 1994; also Jill Leovy, *Ghettoside* (New York: Penguin Random House, 2015).
52 Fred Hirsch, *The Social Limits to Growth* (London: Routledge and Kegan Paul, 1977), 27.
53 This is what leads to the lament, voiced by each new generation, that it has become impossible to afford a home. Typically this means that they are unable to afford a home in the specific urban area and neighbourhood that they would like to live in. This is just because older people generally have more money and so are able to outbid them. When they become older, they will outbid younger people for those same homes.
54 Heath and Potter, *Rebel Sell*.
55 Hirsch, *Social Limits to Growth*, 68.
56 For instance, if one looks at what Michael Walzer identified as the different "spheres of justice" in our society, one can see that status skews the distribution of goods in each of these different spheres away from what he regarded as the appropriate distributive principles. Michael Walzer, *Spheres of Justice* (New York: Basic Books, 1983).
57 Baron Isherwood and Mary Douglas, *The World of Goods: Towards an Anthropology of Consumption* (London: Routledge, 1979).
58 William R. Bascom, "Ponapean Prestige Economy," *Southwestern Journal of Anthropology* 4, no. 2 (1948): 211–21.
59 Bascom, "Ponapean Prestige Economy," 212.
60 Bascom, 215.
61 David Brooks, *Bobos in Paradise* (New York: Simon and Schuster, 2000), 91–2.
62 Veblen, *Theory of the Leisure Class*, 26.
63 Veblen, 75.
64 Steven Pinker, *Enlightenment Now* (New York: Penguin Random House, 2018), 117.
65 Hirsch, *Social Limits to Growth*, 177.
66 Robert Lucas, "The Industrial Revolution: Past and Future," *2003 Annual Report Essay* (Minneapolis: Federal Reserve Bank of Minneapolis, 2004), https://www.minneapolisfed.org/article/2004/the-industrial-revolution-past-and-future.
67 Hirsch, *Social Limits to Growth*, 68.
68 Christopher Freiman, "Priority and Position," *Philosophical Studies* 167, no. 2 (2014): 341.
69 Christopher J. Boyce, Gordon D.A. Brown, and Simon C. Moore, "Money and Happiness: Rank of Income, Not Income, Affects Life Satisfaction," *Psychological Science* 21, no. 4 (2010): 471–5.

70 Brian J. Hall and Kevin J. Murphy, "The Trouble with Stock Options," *Journal of Economic Perspectives* 17, no. 3 (2003): 63.
71 Harry Brighouse and Adam Swift, "Equality, Priority, and Positional Goods," *Ethics* 116, no. 3 (2006): 472.
72 This claim is actually more confusing than it might first appear, because Brighouse and Swift use the term "positional good" in a different sense than Hirsch does. They define it as a good for which the absolute value is determined at least in part by one's rank in the distribution *of that good*. In this view, education is a positional good, because one benefits from having more of it than others, but things like diamonds, fine wine, and memberships in expensive golf clubs are not positional, because their value is not determined by having more of those goods than others. People do not get extra status from having many golf club memberships, and so equalizing the distribution of golf club memberships does not help anyone. It is one's position in the distribution of *other goods* (i.e., income) that allows one access to membership in an exclusive golf club. As a result (and *pace* Brighouse and Swift), there is nothing to be gained from equalizing the distribution of any particular positional good (in Hirsch's sense); one must equalize the distribution of *all* goods. Failure to recognize the difference between the Brighouse-Swift definition of a positional good and the Hirsch definition has increasingly become a source of mischief in the literature.
73 Matthew D. Adler, "The Pigou-Dalton Principle and the Structure of Distributive Justice," SSRN working paper (2013), https://ssrn.com/abstract=2263536.
74 Gopal Sreenivasan, "Health Care and Equality of Opportunity," *Hastings Center Report* 37, no. 2 (2007): 25.
75 Sreenivasan, "Health Care and Equality of Opportunity," 29.
76 Michael Marmot, *The Status Syndrome* (New York: Henry Holt, 2004), 40.
77 Marmot, *The Status Syndrome*, 40.
78 Richard Wilkinson and Kate Pickett, *The Spirit Level* (London: Penguin, 2009). For discussion, see Marmot, *Status Syndrome*, 79.
79 Cameron Anderson, Michael W. Kraus, Adam D. Galinsky, and Dacher Keltner, "The Local-Ladder Effect: Social Status and Subjective Well-Being," *Psychological Science* 23, no. 7 (2012): 764–71.
80 Marmot, *Status Syndrome*, 97.
81 G.A. Cohen, *Rescuing Justice and Equality* (Cambridge, MA: Harvard University Press, 2008).
82 Carina Fourie, "To Praise and to Scorn," in Fourie, Schuppert, and Wallimann-Helmer, *Social Equality*, 88–106.
83 See the chapter entitled "Status Inequality" in Scanlon, *Why Does Inequality Matter?*

84 Cohen, *Why Not Socialism?*, 10.
85 Along similar lines, consider Amartya Sen, *The Idea of Justice* (Cambridge, MA: Harvard University Press, 2009). Before discussing John Rawls's *A Theory of Justice*, Sen takes time to explain how intimately acquainted he was with the author, and thus how much it pains him to have to advance any criticism of the work. "Rawls, Kenneth Arrow and I had in fact used an earlier draft of the book in a joint class that we taught on political philosophy while I was visiting Harvard for the academic year 1968–69 (from my then home base at Delhi University)," 52–3. If one were to ignore the status signalling and focus strictly on the informational content of this sentence, it would be very difficult to understand why Sen thought that it was something that the reader needed to know.
86 Sigmund Freud, *Civilization and Its Discontents*, trans. James Strachey (New York: W.W. Norton, 2010).
87 For the classic discussion of informal hierarchy within these groups, see Jo Freeman, "The Tyranny of Structurelessness," *Berkeley Journal of Sociology* 17 (1972–3): 151–64.
88 Nozick, *Anarchy, State and Utopia*, 243. See also Freiman, "Priority and Position," 350.
89 For instance, Louis Vuitton does a brisk business in school backpacks, with prices starting at US$1,800 and ranging as high as – in all seriousness – $79,000. See https://us.louisvuitton.com/eng-us/men/bags/backpacks/ (page discontinued).
90 Talcott Parsons, *The Social System* (New York: Free Press, 1951). It is helpful in this context to recall the nineteenth-century origins of the phrase "holier than thou," which was used among puritans to describe essentially the same phenomenon, this time with respect to asceticism within religious communities.
91 There is an astute bit of dialogue in season 2 of the *Downton Abbey* television series, in which the wealthy Sir Richard Carlisle presses the impecunious aristocrat Mary Crawley to marry him, after she points out a minor sartorial error in his outfit when he joins her family on a hunting expedition. Despite his great wealth, he observes, it is impossible for him to fully master the code of etiquette that governs the British upper classes. With her superior "breeding," she would be bringing something to the union as valuable as he would with his vast fortune, making them equal partners.
92 Angela Nagle, "A Tragedy of Manners," *Baffler* 36 (5 September 2017). See also Yascha Mounk, "Americans Strongly Dislike PC Culture," *Atlantic*, 10 October 2018.
93 Conor Friedersdorf, "The Destructiveness of Call-Out Culture on Campus," *Atlantic*, 8 May 2017; Mark Fisher, "Exiting the Vampire Castle," *OpenDemocracy*, 24 November 2013.

94 Fisher, "Exiting the Vampire Castle."
95 On "Latinx" and Twitter, see Angela Nagle, *Kill All Normies* (Winchester, UK: Zero Books, 2017), 77. The latter issue (i.e., "deadnaming" a trans person) figured prominently in the "Tuvel affair," involving a group of academics trying to cancel an article in a philosophy journal. See Jesse Singal, "This Is What a Modern-Day Witch Hunt Looks Like," *New York Magazine*, 2 May 2017; José Luis Bermúdez, "Defining 'Harm' in the Tuvel Affair," *Inside Higher Ed*, 5 May 2017.
96 Nagle, *Kill All Normies*, 77.
97 See also McClendon, *Envy in Politics*, 117.
98 The most influential work here was Iris Marion Young, *Justice and the Politics of Difference* (Princeton, NJ: Princeton University Press, 1990).
99 Erving Goffman, *Stigma* (New York: Simon and Schuster, 1963).
100 Axel Honneth, *The Struggle for Recognition*, trans. Joel Anderson (Cambridge, MA: MIT Press, 1992).
101 G.W.F. Hegel, *The Phenomenology of Spirit*, trans. A.V. Miller (Oxford: Oxford University Press, 1977).
102 Alexandre Kojève, *Introduction to the Reading of Hegel: Lectures on the Phenomenology of Spirit* (Ithaca, NY: Cornell University Press, 1980); Francis Fukuyama, *The End of History and the Last Man* (New York: Free Press, 1992). Fukuyama describes the agonistic social relations associated with status competition as the problem of "thumos" and suggests that mutual recognition solves this by creating something of a post-thumotic condition.
103 Charles Taylor, "The Politics of Recognition," in *Multiculturalism: Examining the Politics of Recognition*, ed. Amy Gutmann (Princeton, NJ: Princeton University Press, 1992), 25–73.
104 Christof Neumann, Julie Buboscq, Constance Dubuc, Andri Ginting, Ade Maulana Irwan, Muhammad Agil, Anja Widdig, and Antje Engelhardt, "Assessing Dominance Hierarchies: Validation and Advantages of Progressive Evaluation with Elo-Rating," *Animal Behavior* 82, no. 4 (2011): 911–21; Noah Snyder-Mackler, Jordan N. Kohn, Luis B. Barreiro, Zachary P. Johnson, Mark E. Wilson, and Jenny Tung, "Social Status Drives Social Relationships in Groups of Unrelated Female Rhesus Macaques," *Animal Behavior* 111 (2016): 307–17.
105 Nancy Fraser, "Rethinking Recognition," *New Left Review* 3 (2000): 107–20; Axel Honneth and Nancy Fraser, *Redistribution or Recognition?* (London: Verso, 2003). For discussion, see Christopher Zurn, "Identity or Status? Struggles over 'Recognition' in Fraser, Honneth and Taylor," *Constellations* 10, no. 4 (2003): 519–37.
106 Fraser, "Rethinking Recognition," 115.
107 Fraser, 115.

108 Zurn, "Identity or Status?," 522.
109 Nancy Fraser, "From Redistribution to Recognition? Dilemmas of Justice in a Post-Socialist Age," *New Left Review* 212 (1995): 68–93.
110 Fraser, "Rethinking Recognition," 115.
111 Nancy Fraser, "Recognition without Ethics?," *Theory, Culture and Society* 18, no. 2–3 (2001): 29.
112 Fraser, "Recognition without Ethics?," 29.
113 Ronald Dworkin, *Sovereign Virtue* (Cambridge, MA: Harvard University Press, 2000), 92.
114 Christian Arnsperger, "Envy-Freeness and Distributive Justice," *Journal of Economic Surveys* 8, no. 2 (1994): 165.
115 Frank, *Choosing the Right Pond*, 68–70.
116 Veblen, *Theory of the Leisure Class*, chap. 3.
117 On the society-wide system, see Bill Bishop, *The Big Sort* (New York: Houghton Mifflin, 2008).
118 For evidence that individuals often care more about local status, see McClendon, *Envy in Politics*. She shows that preferences for redistributive policies are strongly affected by the impact they will have on the individual's position in a local (intra-ethnic group) ranking, leading individuals to sometimes oppose policies that will benefit their group as a whole, if it erodes their status position within the group.
119 My son has always been perfectly content with the grades that he receives in school, because while all those who do worse than him are "dumb," all those who do better are "sweats" who "have no life." I am invited to believe that only he has achieved the optimal balance of intellectual achievement and broader self-cultivation.
120 Patricia Cross, "Not Can But Will College Teaching Be Improved?," *New Directions for Higher Education* 17 (1977): 9–10; discussed in Thomas Gilovich, *How We Know What Isn't So* (New York: Free Press, 1991), chap. 4.
121 Julie J. Exline and Anne L. Zell, "Antidotes to Envy: A Conceptual Framework," in *Envy: Theory and Research*, ed. Richard H. Smith (Oxford: Oxford University Press, 2008), 315–31.
122 Canadians of a certain age refer to this as the "King of Kensington" phenomenon. See *King of Kensington*, aired 1975–80 on CBC, title sequence, 12 April 2008, YouTube video, 1:00, https://youtu.be/NrP8mjsmy8U.
123 Rawls, *Theory of Justice*, 388.
124 Philippe van Parijs, "Equal Endowments and Undominated Diversity," *Recherches économiques de Louvain* 56, nos. 3–4 (1990): 327–55.
125 Some have suggested that academic status has essentially this structure. Particular philosophical topics or arguments, for instance, are essentially

micro-status competitions. Most professors will never achieve significant status in the discipline as a whole – much less the broader society – but there is at least one argument that they can win. Naturally, they are inclined to regard this argument as more important than any other taking place. As a result, they are able to remain persuaded that they are making an important contribution to human knowledge, even in the face of substantial contrary evidence.

126 The cognitive bias that leads us to overestimate the importance of the micro-status competitions we are able to win is an important feature of this proposal. Multiplication of status competitions could actually be quite depressing, as Carina Fourie observes, if it merely gives the individual thousands of new ways of losing (see Fourie, "To Praise and to Scorn," 101). In order for the arrangement to work, individuals must care much more about a single win than many more losses.
127 Robert H. Frank and Philip J. Cook, *The Winner-Take-All Society* (New York: Penguin, 1995).
128 Sherwin Rosen, "The Economics of Superstars," *American Economic Review* 71, no. 5 (1981): 845–58.
129 For an interesting survey of user experience with various apps by the Center for Humane Technology, see "App Ratings," https://www.humanetech.com/app-ratings.
130 Sebastian Deri, Shai Davidai, and Thomas Gilovich, "Home Alone: Why People Believe Others' Social Lives Are Richer than Their Own," *Journal of Personality and Social Psychology* 113, no. 6 (2017): 858–77.
131 Rawls, *Theory of Justice*, 477.
132 Rawls, 89.
133 Rawls, 87.
134 Rawls, 89.
135 Rawls, 88.
136 Rawls, 88.
137 See Joseph Heath, "Contractualism: Micro and Macro," in *Morality, Competition and the Firm* (New York: Oxford University Press, 2014).
138 Murray Webster Jr. and James E. Driskell Jr., "Status Generalization: A Review and Some New Data," *American Sociological Review* 43, no. 2 (1978): 221.
139 Webster and Driskell, "Status Generalization," 221.
140 William M. O'Barr, *Linguistic Evidence: Language, Power and Strategy in the Courtroom* (New York: Academic Press, 1982), 69.
141 O'Barr, *Linguistic Evidence*, 96.
142 O'Barr, 96.
143 M.P. Baumgartner, "The Myth of Discretion," in *The Uses of Discretion*, ed. Keith Hawkins (Oxford: Clarendon, 1992), 129–62.

144 P.A.J. Waddington, *Policing Citizens* (London: Routledge, 1999), 43–55.
145 Baumgartner, "Myth of Discretion," 161–2.
146 Ridgeway, "Why Status Matters for Inequality," 10–11.
147 Jason Dana, Robyn Dawes, and Nathaniel Peterson, "Belief in the Unstructured Interview: The Persistence of an Illusion," *Judgment and Decision Making* 8, no. 5 (2013): 512–20.
148 Roger D. Congleton, "Efficient Status Seeking: Externalities and the Evolution of Status Games," *Journal of Economic Behavior and Organizations* 11, no. 2 (1989): 175–90.

Chapter Four

A Defence of Stigmatization

Several terms function in contemporary social science as "crypto-normative" concepts – terms that communicate the author's moral judgment, but where the normative basis of the assessment is seldom articulated.[1] One of those terms is "stigmatization," which is almost always regarded as a *bad thing*, even if no explicit justification of this normative assessment is provided. Use of this term has become widespread in sociology and social psychology, since Erving Goffman's pioneering 1963 book, *Stigma*. But while Goffman maintained a tone of moral neutrality throughout his discussion, so studied that it sometimes bordered on affectation, subsequent literature has drifted toward forthright social and political advocacy, despite maintaining many of the stylistic conventions of traditional social science. For instance, the highly influential *Annual Review of Sociology* article "Conceptualizing Stigma," by Bruce Link and Jo Phelan, starts by defining the concept and discussing the theoretical approaches to its study. It moves on to an analysis of the interrelation between stigma and power structures, and the role of stigma in discrimination. By the end of the review, the discussion becomes explicitly prescriptive, describing stigma as a "persistent predicament" and tackling the difficult question of how it can be changed or overcome.[2] No explanation is given for how the authors have moved from the "is" claim, about the nature of stigma, to the "ought" claim, that it is something that needs to be eliminated.[3]

Of course, the fact that the normative claims are left undefended does not mean that they cannot be defended – perhaps elsewhere. And yet, if one turns to the philosophical literature, where one might be more likely to find explicit moral argumentation, one finds that stigmatization is discussed much less frequently, but that when it is, one finds that the term also has a negative moral valence, the basis of which is not explained or explored.[4] The central objective of this chapter will be to rectify this omission, by developing a normative analysis of stigmatization. Although the question of how stigma should be defined is a topic of considerable debate, the simplest working definition is the one provided by Goffman when he describes it as a *negative status symbol*.[5] It is, in this sense, the opposite of a "prestige symbol," in that rather than providing the bearer with a gain in social status, it results in a loss. This can be based upon either an unchosen characteristic of the individual or an action undertaken. If the latter, then the stigmatization involves generalization from the action to some quality of the actor. An example would be when a person moves from having merely broken the law to being regarded as a "criminal," which is a conventionally stigmatized social category.

As soon as one draws this distinction, however, between unchosen and chosen characteristics, it becomes obvious that there are going to be important normative differences between different types of stigma. Having darker skin is not the same thing as committing domestic assault, and most people would consider it perfectly reasonable to stigmatize the latter, but not the former. Working through these distinctions, however, a more nuanced picture of the normative status of stigma emerges. There are many circumstances in which stigmatization is not only morally indefensible, but merits condemnation in the strongest of terms. There are other circumstances, however, in which stigmatization would appear to be quite easily justified, particularly when it relates to behaviour that is antisocial or harmful to others. Between these extremes there is a class of difficult cases, which will serve as the primary focus of my analysis. These involve forms of stigmatized behaviour that are clearly chosen but are primarily self-destructive, as opposed to actively harmful to others. In such cases, I would like to suggest, stigmatization by others may be an important instrument of individual self-control and should therefore be conceived of as a type of "social scaffolding" that may in the long run promote individual autonomy. The result is a defence of stigmatization in a set of cases that have recently attracted controversy, such as drug addiction, petty criminality, child abandonment, voluntary unemployment, and dropping out of school. The central problem with de-stigmatization, in these cases, is that it shifts a greater part of the burden of self-control onto individuals, and onto the exercise of individual willpower, to resist the temptations that give rise to these patterns of behaviour. It therefore represents an abdication of a traditional function that social institutions have discharged in the behavioural economy of individuals.

1. The Simple Extremes

The most fundamental distinction, in any discussion of stigma, is between cases in which the object of stigma, or what gives rise to the stigma, is a chosen or an unchosen characteristic of the individual. Gerhard Falk, for instance, distinguishes "existential" from "achieved" stigma, where the former is "stigma deriving from a condition which the target of the stigma either did not cause or over which he has little control," whereas "achieved" stigma is "stigma that is earned because of conduct and/or because they contributed heavily to attaining the stigma in question."[6] As we shall see, this seemingly common-sense distinction quickly gets bogged down in difficulties about freedom of the will, and what it means to "have control" over a particular characteristic. Nevertheless, everyone is familiar with the traditional objects of "existential" stigma. The history of racial discrimination provides a plethora of examples of how minor variations in inherited physical characteristics, such as darker skin pigmentation, or the presence of an epicanthic fold, become objects of opprobrium, the presence of which leads to a reduction of the social status of the individual who possesses it (and thus, an elevation in social status of those who do not).

For many people, these instances form the canonical class when characterizing the phenomenon of stigmatization. And yet there is widespread agreement in our society – and essentially complete consensus among cultural elites – that this type of stigma is not only unjustifiable, but that the propensity to stigmatize individuals for such traits is morally reprehensible.[7] That is because stigmatization is seen as an essentially punitive social response (since it involves lowering the individual's social status). Punishment, however, is seen as being merited only when the individual can reasonably be held responsible, and in the case of inherited physical traits it is obvious that the individual cannot be held responsible for them. Without responsibility, there ought not be punishment, and so "existential" stigmatization turns out to be just a form of social aggression or status seeking. Of course, there is seldom a rational connection between the trait in question and the supposed grounds for the status demotion, but this is usually beside the point. Stigmatization is ruled out *ab initio*, by the mere fact that individuals are not responsible for existential traits.

This may seem obvious, but it is worth pausing for a moment to observe what a recent achievement this insight has been. In the world that Goffman describes, half a century ago, not only is racial discrimination rampant and homosexuals a despised minority, but even the disabled are assumed to be incompetent in ways that extend far beyond their specific impairments. (It was, for instance, long assumed that the deaf or the blind must also be intellectually deficient.) Among the examples Goffman gives, of social stigma at work, is that of a restaurant denying service to a man in a wheelchair, on the grounds that the other patrons should not have to be "depressed by the sight of cripples,"[8] or an individual with cerebral palsy being summarily dismissed from a job interview by a manager who was "shocked" that such a person "had the gall to apply for a job."[9] The fact that it is no longer officially acceptable to act in this way – that such attitudes are not avowable, even if they are sometimes still implicitly acted upon – is rightly regarded by many as evidence of significant moral progress in our society.

Again, it is important to emphasize that existential stigmatization has not been eradicated, but that it is now strongly contra-normative. Homosexuality, for instance, is still widely stigmatized in Western societies, among members of various religious and ethnic minority groups, as well as in the lower and working classes. Among the "bourgeois" classes and cultural elites, by contrast, it is the opposite vice – homophobia, or the possibility that one holds less than fully tolerant attitudes toward homosexuals – that is now stigmatized. The same has occurred with racism, particularly in the United States, where being a "racist" is a now widely stigmatized social category – a sign of, at very least, poor breeding, but more likely a malevolent temperament. And indeed, since it takes only one or two off-colour remarks to earn the designation, American elites are willing to take great precautions to avoid the stigma, by refraining from saying anything that could be in any way construed as racist. This is one current that contributes to the phenomenon often described as "political correctness," which sometimes involves using elaborate circumlocution to avoid vocabulary that could be construed as stigmatizing (e.g., "differently abled" in lieu of "disabled," "autonomous" instead of "single" parenting, "sex work" instead of "prostitution," etc.)[10]

Of course, if it is illegitimate to stigmatize a person for being a member of a particular race, but perfectly legitimate to stigmatize someone else for harbouring prejudicial views towards members of that race, there is a tacit distinction being drawn between justifiable and unjustifiable forms of stigmatization. The reason that it is permissible to stigmatize racists, but not races, is that racists are thought to have control over their attitudes, or failing that, at least the expression of those attitudes. Because they have control, they can be held responsible. This is, however, a necessary but not sufficient condition for the punitive response. The second element is that the behaviour must be harmful to others, and thus racism is rightly regarded as a pernicious character flaw, one that merits social censure. Similarly, it is considered conventionally appropriate to apply such labels as "wife beater," "rapist," "child molester," "misogynist," "back-stabber," "deadbeat," "bully," "liar," or "creep," to individuals who engage in the relevant sort of activities, without anyone bemoaning the fact that these labels can have a stigmatizing effect.

One might regard this type of stigmatization as merely an extension of the negative sanctions that are associated with the violation of any social norm.[11] In any society, there are rules – social norms – that prohibit people from engaging in certain forms of behaviour, especially forms that are harmful to others. These norms are enforced by positive sanctions for compliance and/or negative sanctions for violation. The sanction, however, is punctual – it matches a particular norm-violation on the part of ego to a particular response on the part of alter. Thus it need not have consequences that extend beyond the specific interaction. A person can get caught telling a lie, for instance, and be forced to engage in some "repair work" vis-à-vis those who have been deceived, which then brings the episode to a close. Repeat or habitual violation of a norm, however, can have effects that extend beyond the particular interaction. Rather than just punishing the behaviour, observers may begin to generalize from the action and ascribe a character trait to the individual. The person who has lied repeatedly, for instance, may come to be seen as a "liar." This can in turn affect future interactions, as individuals let the trait-ascription guide their expectations of the individual's behaviour (e.g., refusing to believe what the person says). These effects are often propagated beyond the immediate circle of observers, through informal mechanisms such as gossip, or by formal mechanisms such as credit records or employee files. It is in these cases that we say that the individual's status has been lowered, and thus that the ascribed trait or label is stigmatizing. In this respect, stigmatization is a common response to *recidivism* in the violation of a social norm and may rightly be regarded as a structural feature of the basic system of social control operating in all societies.[12]

Some actions, of course, are so deeply taboo that merely performing them once is taken to be evidence of an abnormal psychology. Thus it takes only a single violation of the prevailing norms to earn the lifetime designation of "child molester" or "rapist." In other cases, it takes a very consistent pattern of contra-normative behaviour to earn a particular designation, such as "bully" or "creep." Others are in transition, as social mores change – e.g., the zero-tolerance term "adulterer" has fallen into abeyance, while it remains unclear exactly how much infidelity is required to earn the mildly stigmatizing reputation of being a "philanderer." What all of these cases have in common, however, is that the justifiability of the stigma is simply an extension of the justifiability of the negative sanction, which is in turn a function of the justifiability of the norm itself, which is grounded in the *harm that is done to others* when the norm is violated. This chain of connections – leading from an action that is harmful to others, to the prohibition of that action, to the punishment of those who violate that prohibition, to the stigmatization of those who have a standing disposition to engage in such violations – is not unassailable, and yet it is, as these things go, relatively unproblematic. The only significant normative issue that arises then involves the question of *proportionality*, viz. whether certain stigmatizing categories involve an over- or under-reaction, given the magnitude of the offence involved. For example, the "sex offender" category, as used in the United States, is widely regarded as over-stigmatizing, relative to the harm involved in a number of the offences that fall into that category. Meanwhile, it is often lamented that various forms of white collar crime, such as antitrust violations, are under-stigmatized, relative to the magnitude of the harm they cause to society.[13]

This account, however, leaves unanalysed a vast range of behaviour that is currently subject to stigmatization and that forms the controversial core of the literature. These involve cases of self-regarding action, which involve little or no harm to anyone other than the actor, or consensual action, where those who are affected have agreed to it, and so the *volenti non fit injuria* principle implies an absence of harm. Obesity is a very clear example of the former, homosexuality of the latter. John Stuart Mill argued, influentially, that such actions should be exempt from social "censure."[14] The impulse to punish, in such cases, is likely just an expression of intolerance, or the desire to impose one's own conception of the good on someone else who disagrees with it. After all, if the action is in fact harmful to the individual, then the punishment is unnecessary – ego's self-interest alone should be sufficient motive to refrain from doing it. So to the extent that ego persists in doing it, the perception of harmfulness is most likely the expression of a disagreement between alter and ego about where ego's true interests lie. There are good reasons, both epistemic and practical, to want to defer to ego's judgment in these matters.

Mill's argument has been extremely influential in guiding legal reasoning and has been the basis for the overturning or repeal of much paternalistic legislation, particularly in the domain of sexuality or private sexual behaviour. Widespread decriminalization of contraception, adultery, homosexuality, as well as a range of non-procreative sexual acts, are testament to Mill's influence in twentieth-century jurisprudence. Mill, however, presented his principle much more broadly, claiming that both legal and social censure of self-regarding behaviour were equally impermissible. If two people no longer want to be married, for instance, the state should not hesitate to offer them a divorce. But neither should they suffer any sort of social sanction, Mill argued, for precisely the same reason – it is, quite simply, no one else's business whether they choose to continue their marriage. Thus Mill was opposed to both legal and *social* paternalism.[15] It follows from this view that stigmatization, in all of these cases, would be indefensible. If the social sanction is unjustified, then the stigma, which represents a generalization of that sanction, must also be unjustified.

Mill was, of course, well aware that there are very few actions that affect no one other than the person who performs them, and depending on how broadly one interprets "harm," it is always possible to find some sort of harm to someone. Obesity, for instance, may be primarily self-regarding, but it also creates costs for the health care system. Alcoholism and drug addiction, while primarily self-destructive, can have a negative impact on loved ones or dependent children. The problem with this line of thinking, Mill argues, is that such an expansive conception of harm essentially eliminates the space for individual experimentation and freedom. It amounts to declaring "that it is the absolute social right of every individual, that every other individual shall act in every respect exactly as he ought."[16] Thus Mill recommends narrowing the category of admissible harms, to cases in which an individual violates some "distinct and assignable obligation" to another specific individual. Thus, for example, the failure to serve as a good role model, by appearing drunk and dissolute in public, does not count as a harm, in Mill's view, because one has no specific obligation to any particular person to serve as such a model.

Such reasoning has informed the more permissive social atmosphere that has prevailed, to varying degrees, in Western countries since the late 1960s. It has resulted in the elimination of many achieved stigmas from the social mainstream, such as the ones associated with having sex outside of marriage, cohabitation and common-law marriage, remaining unmarried beyond a certain age, having eccentric interests or hobbies, being an atheist, and perhaps more importantly, being divorced or homosexual (subject to the usual qualifications about persistence within certain classes and subcultural groups). There are, however, a set of actions that are primarily self-regarding, but where the stigma has been much more persistent. These involve cases in which individuals would appear to have control, in the sense that their behaviour is consciously chosen, and yet they also appear to be suffering some form of self-control failure. Not only have many stigmas persisted in these cases, but some new ones have emerged (such as the stigmatization of cigarette smoking, obesity, or having a large number of children).[17] In such cases, Mill's clear-cut distinction between what individuals conceive to be in their own interest, and what *others* perceive to be in their interest, breaks down, because individuals themselves change their minds or suffer from weakness of the will. People will undertake a commitment to extinguish a particular behaviour and yet fail to follow through, or act in a particular way and subsequently express deep regret. In such cases, alter's judgment that the behaviour is harmful seems to be more than just a disagreement; it is a judgment that, at least some of the time, is shared by ego as well – it is simply not acted upon, or not acted upon consistently.

It is noteworthy that many of the most bitterly contested social stigmas in our society involve inconstancy of this form. Consider, for instance, behaviours and characteristics such as obesity, drug addiction, teen pregnancy, family breakdown, poor educational attainment, delinquency or petty criminality, poor dental hygiene or health, explosive temper, violent or abusive interpersonal relations, and the maintenance of personal habits that, in effect, preclude active participation in the workforce. Each of these involves self-inflicted suffering. And yet they also involve failure of self-control (by and large and in general – which is to say, sufficient to form public perception). Most are contrary to intentions that individuals formed ex ante, and in many cases, they are unlikely to be defended ex post. As a result, these cases are confounding. They do not fit into any of the simple categories, which makes them difficult to assess. And despite Mill's entreaties, many people feel strongly that they should remain stigmatized, but have enormous difficulty explaining why.

2. The Standard Debate

There is a lot to be said about these cases. However, before getting on to this, it is necessary to set aside two very stylized and traditional views, which have formed the poles of an acrimonious debate between "liberals" and "conservatives," or between "left-wing" and "right-wing" positions on these questions – with the former favouring abolition and the latter favouring maintenance of the stigma surrounding various forms of self-destructive or self-undermining behaviour.

The traditional left-wing argument for de-stigmatization essentially tries to avoid the complex issues that are raised by self-defeating behaviours, by assimilating these forms of achieved stigma into the category of existential stigma. In other words, it takes outcomes that arise as a consequence of individual choices – and thus, would appear to be subject to voluntary control – and argues that they are in fact unchosen. The most common way of doing this is simply to take the achieved status (e.g., becoming pregnant while in high school) and showing that it is correlated with some existential trait or status (e.g., having been raised in a single-parent household). Since the former cannot cause the latter, the lines of causation must run (it is claimed) from the unchosen trait to the chosen one. This is, in turn, taken to suggest that the individual is not responsible for the apparently chosen trait (or perhaps has diminished responsibility, depending upon the strength of the correlation).[18] Because the conditions for attribution of responsibility are not satisfied, there are no grounds for sanctioning, and thus, no legitimate basis for the attribution of stigma.[19]

This style of argument is so pervasive that it hardly requires much further elaboration. In case anyone requires a specific example, however, one may consider the normative structure of an article by Esther Rothblum entitled "'I'll Die for the Revolution, but Don't Ask Me Not to Diet': Feminism and the Continuing Stigmatization of Obesity."[20] She begins by lamenting the difficulty experienced by a colleague in persuading young feminist students to abandon their "antifat prejudice." She then presents the case for de-stigmatization in four short paragraphs. "In Western society, it is universally believed that the 'causes' of obesity are eating too much and exercising too little." This is, she claims, not the case. In fact, "researchers have not found differences in the food intake of fat and thin people."[21] "Weight differences appear to reflect differences in physiologically determined 'set points,' which are unique for each individual. One person's set point may be 80 pounds, and that of another may be 350 pounds. Set point mechanisms counteract individual efforts to change weight through dieting; in fact, repeated dieting may result in a higher set point, as the body adjusts to this modern form of 'famine' by storing more fat."[22] She goes on, in the final paragraph, to cast doubt upon the claim that obesity causes any particular health problems and that the appearance of such problems may actually be a consequence of dieting, or the "stress" suffered by the overweight due to the "stigmatization and discrimination" that they experience.

Without belabouring the point too much, it is worth noting the extremely casual standards of argumentation and inference that are deployed in these passages. Setting aside the dubious health claims, the author's appeal to "set points" being "physiologically determined" is clearly intended to suggest that they are outside the individual's control (with the implicit contrast being, presumably, between the "psychological" and the "physiological" – although she goes on to obscure the issue somewhat by observing that the individual's dieting behaviour can change the set point). Her general view seems to be that the body has a homeostatic mechanism that counteracts the effects of dieting. She says nothing about exercise, or about the possibility that if an individual's actions could raise her set point, they might also be able to lower it. Nevertheless, she takes these "facts about weight" to be sufficient to establish the case for de-stigmatization of obesity, without further argument.

My goal in drawing attention to the weakness in this chain of reasoning is not to take issue with the specific conclusion, but rather to consider why it might be presented so casually. My suspicion is that the case advanced here is just a specific instance of an argument template that has become so common, and so widely accepted, that one need only gesture toward it, in order to persuade much of one's audience of the conclusion.[23] In other words, people have become so familiar with this strategy for denying the conditions of responsibility-attribution – or to put it less charitably, they have become so accustomed to the suggestion that nothing is ever anyone's own fault – that they accept these claims on the basis of evidence that is often weak or non-existent. It is this tendency that has been attacked so vociferously by conservative critics, and that has given rise to much of the acrimony in these debates. It is also what underlies the increasing common political attacks on "sociology," as a discipline committed to cultivating a "culture of excuses."[24] For instance, the study of the "social determinants" of crime – itself a legitimate endeavour – is often disparaged by the observation that these "root causes" inevitably lie outside the individual and thus are used to suggest that criminals are not responsible for their actions. According to this view, the left-wing de-stigmatization argument uses a scorched-earth strategy. It tries to show that people should be held blameless for a particular outcome, but rather than trying to present specific grounds for why they should not be blamed, it instead denies that they satisfy the conditions of responsible human agency, or asserts that they are unable to control aspects of their own conduct.

This conservative critique is quite forceful, although the polemical version of the argument, as it is usually presented, also has its weaknesses. The left-wing de-stigmatization argument essentially tries to show that an individual has "no control" over a particular outcome, and so what appears to be an achieved stigma is actually an existential one. The idea of having no control is, of course, intensely problematic, but one common way of interpreting it is in terms of the claim that the individual "could not have done otherwise."[25] Thus the standard response of the right-wing critic, when presented with a correlation between a particular form of behaviour and its "social determinant," is to find one example of a person who shares the unchosen trait, and yet does not go on to exhibit the stigmatized condition. This is then presented as proof that the stigmatized individual *could* have done otherwise (which implies, in turn, that the condition is not existential, and so the conditions of responsibility-attribution do obtain).

Here is a typical example of this argument, from Theodore Dalrymple, discussing Indian immigrants to the United Kingdom embracing "underclass" values and lifestyle:

> The liberal would no doubt argue that the formation of an Indian underclass is the inevitable response to poverty and prejudice and the despair they evoke. With the path to advancement blocked by a racist society, young Indians drop out of school, shave their heads, tattoo their skin, inject themselves with heroin, father children out of wedlock, and commit crimes. But if they are caught in a vicious cycle of poverty and prejudice, why do so many of their compatriots succeed, and succeed triumphantly? Why do the children of successful Indian parents also choose the underclass way of life? And why may stunning success and abject failure so often occur in the same family? The explanation must surely involve conscious human choice.[26]

Implicit in this argument is a rather black-and-white view of the will – that actions are either determined, or they are freely chosen, with nothing in between. The natural response would therefore be to argue that both control and responsibility admit of degrees, which suggests the rather simple compromise position that while racism and exclusion may not *determine* the life chances of Indian immigrants to the United Kingdom, they exercise a significant probabilistic influence, and are, to that extent, *mitigating* circumstances when it comes to attributions of responsibility or blame.

The deeper problem with the left-wing argument, therefore, is not that it can be disproven by counter-example, as Dalrymple and many conservative critics suppose. A more serious objection would involve pointing out that it relies upon a causal theory of responsibility that is not obviously compatible with a scientific or materialist world view. One central tenet of materialism is that human decision-making does not lie outside the natural order, but that psychological states have material correlates that are produced through ordinary causal processes. It follows that any choice an individual makes will be caused, at some point, by something that is itself unchosen. If, however, the existence of such a causal chain is sufficient to demonstrate that the agent had no control over the action, and thus bears no responsibility for it, it follows that no one has control over anything, and no one is ever responsible for any of their actions. In other words, underlying the left-wing de-stigmatization argument is a form of general scepticism about freedom of the will and moral responsibility.

This issue with responsibility, it should be noted, is a longstanding problem with the scientific world view and was widely recognized as a significant sceptical challenge in early modern philosophy (by Descartes, Locke, Hume, etc.). The left-wing de-stigmatization strategy takes this essentially sceptical argument about responsibility and applies it selectively, to undermine *particular* claims about individual responsibility. The victory, however, is pyrrhic. The argument shows that a particular class of sympathetic individuals are not responsible for some form of self-destructive behaviour, but only by setting up a notion of responsibility that no human action could ever satisfy. Thus the argument has no useful normative implications. To the extent that it can be used to show that some people "cannot help" but act in some self-destructive way, it can just as easily be used to show that others "cannot help" but stigmatize them for doing so.

This is why philosophers generally reject causal theories of responsibility, or views that treat responsibility as an empirical fact about the agent, that could be discovered by examining the causal aetiology of his actions. Since Peter Strawson's pioneering work in the 1960s, the dominant view among philosophers has been that responsibility is a normative status, ascribed to agents when some appropriate set of conditions is satisfied.[27] In a normative view of responsibility, under standard circumstances, barring gross ignorance or coercion, teenagers are responsible for getting pregnant, the obese are responsible for their weight, and even addicts are responsible for their substance abuse. The standard left-wing de-stigmatization strategy, in other words, is ruled out. One can, of course, imagine more subtle arguments being developed against stigmatization in certain of these cases. For instance, one could appeal to recent work in personality psychology, developed under the rubric of "situationism," to argue that observers vastly overestimate the extent to which individual behaviour is determined by character traits. One might argue, on this basis, that the generalization from the specific sanction, associated with the norm violation, to the attribution of a status-reducing personality trait to the individuals, which is the hallmark of stigmatization, rests upon a psychological illusion (and is perhaps a hold-over from the medieval view, in which sin is thought to leave a mark upon the body of the sinner).

One might also appeal directly to Mill's argument, that the punitive social response is unwarranted, simply because it is no one else's business how individuals conduct their private affairs. One might update this point by drawing on Elliot Turiel's distinction between personal rules, conventional norms, and morality, in order to argue that there is a type of category error at work in the stigmatization of self-regarding behaviour.[28] In effect, the violation of a personal rule is being treated as though it were a moral fault.

Given the range of arguments available, it is striking how heavily proponents of de-stigmatization have relied upon the global "de-responsibilization" argument, especially given that it is highly contested.[29] Whatever its basis, the availability of these alternative argumentation strategies makes one thing clear. Refutation of the global anti-stigmatization argument does not constitute positive justification for stigmatization. The mere fact that individuals are responsible for their behaviour shows that they are *eligible* for punitive social responses, such as stigmatization, but stops well short of establishing the claim that these people *deserve* to be stigmatized. Indeed, to the extent that their behaviour is self-regarding, and in certain ways self-destructive, it is not clear what purpose it serves to punish them further. Drug addicts, for instance, may be ruining their own lives, so why do they need to be stigmatized on top of that? Stigmatization would appear to merely compound their suffering.[30] This feeds the suspicion that stigmatization is driven by a sort of irrational vindictiveness, or a desire to kick people while they are down, or to blame the victim.

Against this charge, the standard conservative defence of stigmatization is not particularly compelling. The suggestion is sometimes made that, because these habits lead individuals to become a public charge, or a burden upon society, the behaviour is actually harmful to others, and this justifies the stigma. This is, however, so implausible that it seems more like a fig leaf, or a rationalization of the stigmatizing response. Smoking, for instance, is not really costly to "society." On the contrary, it is generally thought to reduce costs on the health care system (by leading to a relatively rapid death from one of two frequently untreatable conditions, lung cancer or heart attack). Or to take a particularly illustrative example, in Canada the health care system is public, while dentistry remains entirely private, and yet having "bad teeth" is just as strongly stigmatized as obesity, perhaps even more so, despite the fact that the costs of dental care are borne entirely by the individual. Thus one need not even summon Mill's point about the danger of indulging an overly broad conception of harm to see that these arguments should not be taken seriously.

Consider then Dalrymple, who has written extensively on the topic. The central theme of his work is the way that "poverty" in Britain has become characterized, not so much by material deprivation, but by a set of essentially self-destructive personal habits. Working in a public hospital in a poor neighbourhood, as well as in a prison, Dalrymple observes a consistent pattern among the "underclass": "Their personal lives are in disarray, to put it kindly.... They indulge in self-destructive, antisocial, or irrational behaviour: they drink too much, involve themselves in meaningless quarrels, quit their jobs when they can't afford to, run up debts on trifles, pursue obviously disastrous relationships, and move their home as if the problem were in the walls that surround them."[31]

Dalrymple is insistent that these people are responsible for the consequences of their choices, and thus for much of the circumstances, in which they find themselves. For instance, he is particularly critical of the pattern of family breakdown he observes, of single mothers with several children, each by a different father, none of whom have made any contribution to the support or upbringing of their offspring. The women, he claims, share much of the blame for this, because they choose, again and again, to develop relationships and have children with men who are obviously unsuited for fatherhood. They are, in this regard, the authors of their own misfortune. And yet, it is one thing to insist that these women are responsible for much of their own misery, and so should bear the costs, quite another to insist that they should be stigmatized by society for those choices. Dalrymple is quite keen to insist that the stigma should remain – indeed, through the calculated injuriousness of his prose, he is clearly striving to make his own contribution to the ongoing reproduction of the stigma.[32] And yet he says surprisingly little about why these women deserve punishment that goes *beyond* the misery that they have brought down upon themselves. When he does try to justify it, the language that he reaches for is that of good and evil:

> Moreover, [these women] are aware that I believe that it is both foolish and wicked to have children by men without having considered even for a second or a fraction of a second whether the men have any qualities that might make them good fathers. Mistakes are possible, of course: a man may turn out not to be as expected. But not even to consider the question is to act as irresponsibly as it is possible for a human being to act. It is knowingly to increase the sum of evil in the world, and sooner or later the summation of small evils leads to the triumph of evil itself. My patient did not start out with the intention of abetting, much less of committing, evil. And yet her refusal to take seriously and act upon the signs that she saw and the knowledge that she had was not the consequence of blindness and

ignorance. It was utterly willful. She knew from her own experience, and that of many people around her, that her choices, based on the pleasure or the desire of the moment, would lead to the misery and suffering not only of herself, but – especially – of her own children.[33]

What Dalrymple is obviously eliding in this passage is the distinction between harm to others and harm to self. It is somewhat dramatic, but certainly not an abuse of terms, to describe making choices that will foreseeably lead to the misery and suffering of one's own children as "evil." But what about bringing suffering upon oneself? Most of the behaviour patterns that Dalrymple is lamenting among the underclass are primarily self-destructive, not actively harmful to others ("public drunkenness, drug-taking, teenage pregnancy, venereal disease, hooliganism, criminality"[34]). They almost all involve failures of self-control. Calling these "evil" is one way of explaining why they should be punished, or stigmatized, but there is a serious question as to whether they merit that description. Why is it "evil," and not merely "tragic"?

It should, of course, be acknowledged that the failure to draw a moral distinction between harm to self and harm to others is a long-standing feature of the Christian tradition. Of the "seven deadly sins," for instance, sloth and gluttony are listed alongside wrath and greed, despite the fact that the former are self-regarding, the latter other-regarding. Much of this is due to the influence of classical Greek morality, where the ideal of "self-mastery" was considered central to the ethical life.[35] Many of the medieval catalogues of sin were just Christianized versions of Aristotle's table of virtues and vices – a table that listed rashness and intemperance as vices, alongside more evidently other-regarding traits. Furthermore, Aristotelian virtue theory is a moral framework that encourages stigmatization, precisely because of the way that it categorizes actions as right or wrong only through reference to character traits (i.e., the "virtues" or "vices") of the individual who performs them. In this view, bad actions are the sort of thing that bad people do, not the other way around. Thus the generalization from a specific sanction to the ascription of some impairment of the person, which is the hallmark of stigmatization, is actually the recommended form of moral reasoning within the Aristotelian system. Despite the Christian injunction to "hate the sin, not the sinner," much of this Greek ethos was absorbed into Christian ethics. The result is a framework that encourages significant *moral* disapproval of the character of individuals who suffer from self-control failure.

This is what I suspect is going on in Dalrymple's thinking. At certain points, he claims that the misery he sees all around him is a consequence of declining belief in an objective order of values. ("Life in the British slums demonstrates what happens when the population at large, and the authorities as well, lose all faith in a hierarchy of values.")[36] And indeed, in order to make his argument, such an objective order of values is what he requires. To make the case that the behaviour of the heroin addict is "evil," and thus deserving of punishment, he must say that drug abuse is intrinsically wrong, above and beyond whatever impact the addict's choices have upon anyone's welfare, including his own. Drug abuse is a vice, vice is evil, and evil deserves to be punished. The problem is that Dalrymple makes no attempt to articulate what sort of intrinsic wrongness these actions might possess. Instead, he merely points to the negative social consequences that follow when people lose faith in such intrinsic, welfare-transcendent values. In doing so, however, he tends to undermine his own position. In effect, he tries to establish the importance of belief in welfare-transcendent values by pointing to the negative welfare consequences of not believing in such values. Apart from doubts one might have about the validity of such an argument, the structure of it tends to reinforce the impression that what *ultimately* counts is just human welfare. And since stigmatization, at least prima facie, reduces human welfare, the problem of how it could be justified in the case of self-regarding action remains.

There is, however, a more promising line of argument to be found in Dalyrmple's work, as well as that of many other conservative writers. This involves the claim that the left-wing de-stigmatization strategy, to the extent that it is motivated by a desire to reduce suffering, winds up failing on its own terms, because its net effect is to increase the sum total of suffering. Dalrymple lays out the argument, with characteristic aplomb, in an essay entitled "How Criminologists Foster Crime."[37] The claim, roughly, is that by suggesting that individuals who exhibit various "social pathologies" are not responsible for their actions, left-wing intellectuals have provided these individuals with an excuse for their behaviour, which in turn makes them more likely to behave in an irresponsible way. It is, for instance, a fairly well-established result in addiction research that "self-efficacy" beliefs are positively associated with successful cessation and abstinence.[38] The left-wing de-stigmatization strategy, however, directly contradicts these self-efficacy beliefs, by telling addicts that their behaviour is beyond their control (that alcoholism is, for instance, the product of a "disease," or some genetic susceptibility). Thus addicts are being offered something of a poisoned chalice. Calling their addiction a "disease" may make them feel better about their circumstances, by telling them that they are not to blame for their actions, and by removing some of the social stigma, but at the same time, it leaves them more likely to remain mired in addiction, by cultivating a psychological framework that undermines their capacity for resolute action. Being held responsible, by contrast, may produce some short-term pain, but also produces the long-term gain of helping individuals to overcome their addiction.

This argument is, I believe, one that needs to be taken very seriously. The way that it is usually articulated by conservative polemicists, however, is rather short on detail, particularly when explaining the causal mechanism that runs from the de-stigmatization strategy to the posited exacerbation of the stigmatized behaviour. What is needed is a more structured understanding of self-control failure, in order to see how these components interact.

3. The Extended Will

In order to make progress on this question, it is necessary to develop a better understanding of self-control failure. To lend some structure to the discussion, I will begin by presenting four theses about weakness of will, which I will not have space to defend in detail, but are amply discussed elsewhere in the literature.

3.1. Weakness of Will Is a "Pathology of Everyday Life"

One of Sigmund Freud's most important observations is that many clinically noteworthy forms of "psychopathology" are not idiosyncratic phenomena, but represent instead just extreme or hypertrophied versions of psychological tendencies that "normal" people exhibit as well.[39] To take a modern example, individuals with obsessive-compulsive disorder (OCD) do not exhibit any form of behaviour that is unique to those with the syndrome, since everyone engages, to some degree, in repetitious actions that are experienced as mildly compulsive (e.g., double- or triple-checking certain things before leaving the house). What distinguishes those with OCD is that they do it *a lot more* than most people, to the point where it interferes with their capacity to achieve other valued objectives. (Thus the *DSM-V* definition of the disorder includes the following: "The obsessions or compulsions are time-consuming (e.g., take more than 1 hour per day) or cause clinically significant distress or impairment in social, occupational, or other important areas of functioning.")[40] Thus the person diagnosed with OCD is not experiencing anything outside the normal human psychological repertoire. The disorder represents more of a failure of inhibition. The person who suffers from it may experience unusually strong compulsions, but a significant component of the disorder is simply an inability to suppress a behavioural impulse that is actually quite common. It is, in this respect, part of a family of "perseveration" disorders that have a similar structure.

Weakness of will (or *akrasia*) is a philosophical – not psychiatric – term used to describe the phenomenon whereby an individual might decide that, all things considered, she should perform some action x, and thus form the intention to do x, but then simply fail to follow through on this intention, performing some other action instead. This has traditionally been regarded as involving some form of motivational pathology or defect, since the individual decision that she should do x typically involves the judgment that x is, from her perspective, the best thing to do, and yet in failing to do x, the individual is thereby choosing to do something that is worse for her, by her own lights. It is not difficult to conclude that something has *gone wrong* with the agent. There is a question, however, about what sort of a failure is involved. A moment's reflection is enough to show that it is more like a "pathology of everyday life" than a sui generis psychological defect. In other words, everyone experiences weakness of the will to some degree and on certain occasions. The major differences between individuals lie only in how successful they are at suppressing or controlling the problem.

The best way to see the ubiquity of weakness of will is to observe that most instances have a temporal dimension. When the actual choice is somewhat removed from the present, individuals will resolve to choose the greater over the lesser good, but then reverse themselves in the intervening period (or at the point of decision) and choose the lesser over the greater good. This can take the form of succumbing to temptation, which involves choosing the "smaller sooner" over the "larger later" good, or else the opposite phenomenon of procrastination, which involves choosing the "larger later" bad over the "smaller sooner" one. When characterized in this way, it is easy to see that everyone exhibits these tendencies in many different areas of life. A person might resolve to go to bed early, in order to be well-rested the following day and yet wind up staying up late watching television or thumbing through social media posts. A person might open up a bag of chips vowing to eat only half, but then finish them all. A person might sit down at the computer to write a research paper, but then surf the internet and check email for an hour. These instances of everyday weakness of will are ones that we all struggle to control or manage.

There are several different models of what is going on in these familiar cases. Perhaps the simplest and most expressively robust is the hyperbolic discounting model, which attributes the phenomenon of weakness of will to a *temporary preference reversal*, caused by a "warp" in the way that we assess future events.[41] According to this view, the fact that we care more about events the closer they are to the present can be represented as a *discount* imposed upon the value of future satisfaction, depending upon on how far removed it is from the present. The rate of discount, however, is not the same for all time periods. The first periods of delay that are introduced impose a very large discount, which then declines as the delay is extended out into the future. As a result, the way that options are ranked, when they are in the distant future, is very close to the way that they would be ranked if they were to be occurring immediately. When they pass into the near term, however, small differences in their scheduled occurrence can generate significant differences in how they are evaluated, leading the agent to change the ranking. This gives rise to temporary preference reversals, which lead people to choose the "smaller sooner" over the "larger later" good, even though this does not correspond to their earlier intention, and will subsequently be regretted.

3.2. Self-Control

The phenomenon of self-control is complex, and not everything referred to under that heading is relevant to weakness of will as defined above. Inhibition, for instance, is an important component of many aspects of cognitive functioning and is closely tied to the operations of executive agency.[42] When resisting temptation, on the other hand, agents face a somewhat higher-level problem. The pattern of temporary preference reversal that we experience in various domains is relatively consistent and therefore predictable. Thus we often find ourselves knowing that, in the future, we will be required to make a choice, being able to see now (from a more dispassionate perspective) which option is best, but knowing that, in the future, we will change our minds and choose the lesser option, only to regret it later. This gives us a reason to want to lock in our choice now, knowing that even if this constrains our future self, our more distant future self will subsequently ratify the choice, and we will regard ourselves as being better off as a result.

On the hyperbolic discounting view, the same pattern that one sees in addictive behaviours – the cycle of commitment to abstinence, succumbing to temptation, followed by regret – can be seen in many different areas of life. Thus this analysis supports a "psychological" rather than a "disease" model of addiction.[43] In this view, the key characteristic of addictive substances is that they generate a pattern of stimulation that is particularly effective at taking advantage of the warp in the way that we compare present and future goods. Thus the self-control challenge that they pose is just an extreme version of the self-control problem that people encounter in all walks of life. The important point is that when individuals suffer from weakness of will in this sense, they are not "losing control" or being "overwhelmed by desire," in the way that a person might suffer a loss of intentional control and lash out when struck suddenly or startled. With weakness of will, what we are seeking to guard ourselves against is a change of mind. This change may of course be in response to a "hot" psychological state (such as the cravings experienced by an addict in withdrawal). The important point is that its effects are mediated through the intentional planning system, by inducing a preference change.[44] The problem is not that we act thoughtlessly, but that we change the way we are thinking. As a result, self-control in the face of this form of weakness of will is less about inhibition, and more a matter of resolute choice, or even just planning.[45] It involves the capacity to commit to a temporally extended sequence of actions and then stick to it, regardless of what may change in the interim.

3.3. The Extended Will

Self-control in the face of "everyday weakness of will" involves a form of self-binding, to avoid succumbing to foreseeable changes of mind that will subsequently be regretted. Because self-control, in this sense, involves guarding against one's own change of mind, there are serious limitations on our ability to use onboard cognitive resources to achieve it. This is for the simple reason that, if the weakness lies in the way that one is thinking, *more thinking* is unlikely to solve the problem (as Aristotle put it, "If water chokes us, what must we drink to wash it down?"). As a result, most people make extensive use of environmental resources and affordances in order to remain resolute in their plans. The canonical example is Ulysses ordering his sailors to bind him to the mast so that he will not be lured overboard when he hears the song of the sirens. And yet one can find many more mundane instances of the same type of strategy, of individuals manipulating the external environment, in order to constrain or modify their own future choices.

As Joel Anderson and I have argued elsewhere, individuals use the environment not just to enhance their own willpower, but in many cases to *instantiate* it.[46] Individuals are not merely bolstering their resolve through these forms of environmental manipulation, in many cases they *offload* certain decisions, or functions, onto the environment. Practical rationality, in this respect, involves "extended" cognition, similar to the forms that have been discussed under the heading of "the extended mind." As Andy Clark has observed, sophisticated cognition is achieved through "stigmergic self-modulation," which he defines as

> the process through which intelligent brains *actively* structure their own external (physical and social) worlds so as to make for successful actions with less individual computation. The coherence and the problem-solving power of much human activity, it seems, may be rooted in the simple yet often-ignored fact that we are the most prodigious creators and exploiters of external scaffolding on the planet. We build "designer environments" in which human reason is able to far outstrip the computational ambit of the unaugmented biological brain. Advanced reason is thus above all the realm of the *scaffolded* brain: the brain in its bodily context, interacting with a complex world of physical and social structures.[47]

Thus willpower – or the capacity to exercise effective self-control – must be thought of not in terms of just onboard psychological resources, but in terms of the entire system that individuals develop to structure their choices. A person's home environment, for instance, will be structured in a way that makes some choices easier and others harder. Similarly, individuals will cultivate relationships and put themselves in social contexts that make some choices much easier than others. When people exhibit great self-control it is often because they are better (either consciously or unconsciously) at such environmental manipulations than others.[48]

3.4. *Neutralizations*

There are interesting similarities between self-control failure and other forms of deviance, such as antisocial behaviour. In both cases, the individual is engaged in a type of contra-normative behaviour – even though the rules are merely personal or self-regarding in the former case, other-regarding in the latter. For instance, individuals are loathe to admit that they have failed to live up to a normatively prescribed model of behaviour (even when they are, as it were, only lying to themselves). Rather than rejecting the force or validity of the norm, they will often indulge in a significant amount of biased cognition, in order to avoid admitting that they are violating it. This is, of course, a staple observation of the "recovery" movement, with its insistence that the first step to overcoming an addiction must be acknowledging that one has a problem.[49] In general, people are strongly committed to viewing themselves as autonomous and capable, so that the occurrence of self-control failure generates significant cognitive dissonance. This is seldom resolved through straightforward admission of failure ("I am weak" or "I can't help myself"), but more often through biased or implausible beliefs ("I can quit anytime, I just choose not to").[50]

There are, as I suggested, interesting parallels between this response and the way that individuals manage other forms of contra-normative behaviour. Criminologists have long observed that people who break the law are surprisingly reticent to admit that they have actually done anything wrong, even after being tried and convicted.[51] Far from having deviant values, most criminals in fact subscribe to rather conventional moral views and also have conventionally positive ego-ideals (thinking of themselves as fundamentally "good" or "decent" persons).[52] In order to preserve these commitments, in the face of evidence that contradicts it prima facie (i.e., conviction of a criminal offence), they often adopt "vocabularies of adjustment," or rationalizations, which minimize their wrongdoing. For instance, in a classic study of incarcerated white-collar criminals, Donald Cressey observed that a significant fraction of embezzlers would not admit to having stolen, describing themselves instead as having simply "borrowed" the money.[53]

One might think that these rationalizations are merely ex post, aimed at reducing cognitive dissonance after the fact. An important advance in criminological theory lay in the recognition that criminals often adopt these sorts of rationalizations *prior* to breaking the law, in order to give themselves permission, or to overcome whatever inhibitions they might have about engaging in criminal conduct. Gresham Sykes and David Matza referred to these as "neutralizations," because they have the effect of neutralizing the force of social norms, so that deviant individuals can maintain their official adherence to these standards, while at the same time arranging things so that the norms fail to constrain their own behaviour.[54] The norms are, in this respect, not cognitively rejected, but pragmatically neutralized.

Some of these neutralizations involve vocabularies of adjustment, such as describing stealing as borrowing, but the more interesting category involve deviant use of *excuses*. An excuse, by its very nature, is neutralizing. Unlike a justification, which involves challenging the norm, or its application to one's case, an excuse involves granting that one's action was contra-normative, but appealing to some additional consideration to show that one's conduct was, nevertheless, not blameworthy.[55] In some cases, this involves denying that the conditions of responsible agency were met – for instance, with the defence of duress, or necessity ("I had no choice").[56] It is important to note that in many cases these excuses are perfectly legitimate. What characterizes the criminal is the propensity to make overly generous, self-serving use of them.

Given the parallels between different forms of contra-normative behaviour, there is reason to think that a great deal of self-control failure is also not just rationalized, but facilitated by neutralization. People confronting a particular temptation may give themselves permission to abandon earlier intentions by adopting an excuse, which allows them to perform the action while denying that it involved any self-control failure. Thus the availability of neutralizing vocabulary, in social environments that are receptive to its use, may be associated with higher incidence of self-control failure.

4. Stigmatization Reconsidered

These four claims allow us to better understand the role that stigmatization might play in regulating certain forms of self-control failure. I take it as uncontroversial that most people use *other people* as an important self-control mechanism, as part of their environmental offloading of willpower. To take an obvious domestic example, many people rely upon their spouse to tell them when they have had enough to drink, whether they have put on too much weight, that they should eat healthier food, or when they should go to bed. In some cases, the spouse is merely being called upon to correct impairments in one's judgment. In other cases, however, there is genuine motivational offloading involved. In other words, the expectation is that the spouse will not only voice her opinion about one's conduct, but will actually help one to police it, by sanctioning failure or success. Behind the statement "I think you've had enough to drink for one night," or "You should come to bed now," there is an implicit threat of punishment. This threat is, however, not entirely external to the individual's own agency. People often allow such patterns to emerge in their relationships, precisely because they know that it is easier to rely upon their spouse than on their own onboard resources, and that the threat of punishment serves as a useful motive to act in ways that they themselves would judge, in a cooler hour and all things considered, to be best.

My hypothesis is that people rely upon others, not just to provide incentives that will help them to overcome self-control problems, but also to help them avoid the cognitive biases that license these failures. We rely upon other people to serve as a check on our tendency to develop overly self-serving beliefs. As a recent study of self-deception has observed, "Individuals who are objectively poor in a behavioural domain exhibit self-enhancement due to meta-cognitive failures (i.e., the inability to self-analyse), motivational forces (i.e., the need to maintain or amplify their favourable self-views), or both."[57] Self-analysis, of course, is difficult even for the average person, just as it is difficult to avoid motivated reasoning. Other people are often better judges, in part because they are able to observe our behaviour unclouded by any knowledge of our intentions. They also lack many of the motivations that pervasively bias introspective judgment. This is, of course, what underlies the well-known fact that other people can serve as a useful source of instrumental advice. Less often noted is the fact that other people may enhance our self-control, by making it more difficult for us to engage in the type of self-deception required to maintain a neutralizing excuse.

This is an issue that arises in the criminology literature, to which there are instructive comparisons to be drawn. One central desideratum of any general theory of criminality is that it must account for the social dimension of crime, including the fact that *association with other criminals* is one of the most powerful predictors of individual criminality. This observation gave rise to early theories of criminality as learned or imitative behaviour, and later, to the "subcultural" theory of crime, which posited a set of deviant values maintained within subgroups of society (such as youth gangs).[58] Careful study, however, revealed that, for the most part, criminals do not subscribe to deviant, subcultural values, but in fact tend to have rather conventional or mainstream values. What neutralization theory suggests, by contrast, is that certain social environments might prove criminogenic because of a willingness of individuals within these groups to accept excuses that would normally be rejected, or to employ, or accept the employment of, a neutralizing vocabulary. In this view, the deviance within these groups lies not in their rejection of mainstream norms or values, but rather in their willingness to accept the cognitive distortions required to indulge certain neutralizations. This can prove criminogenic because maintaining a neutralization requires a certain measure of self-deception, and this self-deception can be difficult to maintain in isolation. Being able to convince someone *else* that one was not really stealing, or that one's victim "had it coming," or that one "had no choice" but to act as one did, can greatly enhance one's own acceptance of the excuse.

There is ample evidence to suggest that a similar phenomenon prevails in the domain of self-control. Weakness of will is often subject to neutralization, through what Anderson refers to as "self-indulgent reconstruals" of the behaviour.[59] There is a strong element of self-deception involved in this, which can more easily be maintained in a supportive social environment (i.e., one in which the relevant form of cognitive deviance is tolerated). This has two immediate consequences. First, it suggests that stigmatization of self-control failure by others may be not just an external imposition, adding insult to injury, but may serve as part of the scaffolding that individuals rely upon in order to exercise willpower. Many marriages break down, for instance, because of the infidelity of one partner – infidelity that in many cases arises from self-control failure. Those who do resist these temptations often do so, not just out of intrinsic regard for the commitments undertaken in the marriage ceremony, but also from a healthy fear of the negative consequences of being found out. Knowing this, a person might choose to organize her life in such a way that it would be difficult to carry out an affair without it being discovered. In this respect, the negative consequences become something that are no longer entirely external to the individual's own will – one may be using them to overcome one's own anticipated motivational deficits. Thus they can be seen as not just punitive, but also as having important self-binding functions. In this respect, the sanctions serve to promote what Anderson refers to as "scaffolded autonomy."

From this perspective, what does the de-stigmatization of divorce achieve? For some it is obviously an unmixed blessing. But from the standpoint of self-control it is an ambivalent development. On the one hand, it makes things better, after the fact, for those who suffer the relevant self-control failure. But at the same time, it may also increase the number who suffer from it, simply by diminishing the negative consequences associated with that failure. In today's social environment, a man contemplating an extramarital affair may hesitate, out of fear that his wife would divorce him if she found out, but he need not fear being subjected to more general social ostracism. He is no longer likely to be disowned by his parents, shunned by friends and co-workers, or expelled from his country club. This clearly reduces the incentive to refrain from infidelity. Most people are keenly aware of what others think of them and are highly motivated to maintain that regard. This fear of "what others might think" can have an important self-disciplining effect. As a result, de-stigmatization has the consequence of shifting more of the motivational burden of self-control onto the individual (and to the individual's onboard volitional resources).

Furthermore, because many self-control issues arise because of the warp in the way that we evaluate future consequences (represented as a hyperbolic discount function), merely forcing the individual to bear the full consequences of her choices – as the right-wing demand for "personal responsibility" would have it – is often unlikely to have much effect. Threatening people with massive punishments in the distant future is not a very effective remedy, as it turns out, for the problem of intemperance. This is well understood by criminologists, who have observed that the social stigmatization of criminality is a much more powerful deterrent than threats of lengthy incarceration.[60] The same is true in many domains of self-control. A smoker, for instance who ignores the increased risk of dying from lung cancer is unlikely to be much influenced by the threat of being cut off from the public health service when it comes time to pay for chemotherapy. It is all simply too far away to be taken into consideration. Stigmatization of smoking, by contrast, is an *immediate* consequence of the behaviour, and so even though the cost that it imposes upon the smoker is trivial, compared to death from lung cancer, it may actually be far more effective at deterring smoking.

The second observation to be made is that de-stigmatization, to the extent that it rests upon the standard left-wing de-responsibilization strategy, can have a secondary effect that further exacerbates self-control problems. By denying individual agency or responsibility, the strategy provides a set of neutralizations, which individuals can use to excuse lapses of self-control. It may also contribute to the creation of a social environment in which these excuses are more readily accepted. This mechanism is the plausible core at the heart of Dalrymple's claim that "criminologists foster crime" (or more generally, perhaps, that social workers cause social pathology).[61] Indeed, Dalrymple notes that many of the convicts he deals with have eagerly adopted the latest therapeutic or criminological jargon when it comes to blaming "society" for their own actions, a stance that is quickly set aside, however, if they themselves are victimized (at which point "they react like everyone else").[62] One might argue, as well, that de-responsibilization of various forms of self-destructive or self-undermining behaviour represents a failure of social institutions to provide adequate "scaffolding" for the individual will. It provides an escape route that allows individuals to fail repeatedly to live up to norms of conduct that they themselves endorse, while insulating them from any negative impact on their self-image.

If this analysis is correct, what are the normative implications for current stigmatization practices that target self-control failure? For theorists of a broadly utilitarian persuasion, the issue looks primarily like a deterrence problem. Stigmatization is good, to the extent that it deters people from the relevant sorts of self-undermining behaviour. It becomes bad, however, if the deterrent effect fails, and it begins to compound misery. Normative assessment will therefore involve doing the appropriate sums, in order to determine whether the increase in happiness caused by alleviation of the stigma from those who suffer the relevant self-control failure is greater or less than the increase in misery caused by the potential expansion of their numbers. Stigmatization, in this view, will prove justified if on balance and in the aggregate it produces positive consequences.

From a liberal egalitarian perspective, one might also be concerned about the way that de-stigmatization pushes individuals back upon their onboard volitional resources, across many different domains of life planning, and the effect that this can have on social inequality. As the well-known "marshmallow test" has shown, the ability to delay gratification can have a major impact on future success in many different areas of life, including the ability to avoid addiction.[63] The test is significant in part because it focuses primarily on differences in the volitional resources of what Clark calls the "unaugmented biological brain." Although some children use environmental expedients, such as covering their eyes with their hands, or hiding in a corner from the marshmallow, the experimental setup is one in which there are limited opportunities for environmental manipulation. Most importantly, the child is left *alone* in the room with the marshmallow, and so the option of recruiting other people to assist in the exercise of willpower is removed. To an increasing degree, this is what the broader social environment is coming to resemble as well. In expanding the domain of individual choice, and insulating self-regarding choice from social censure, we put the onus on the individual to resist temptation, using non-social and onboard forms of self-control. To the extent that there is significant variance in the distribution of these capabilities in the population, we risk seeing the development of a "self-control aristocracy," in which one particular psychological style, or strategy, receives disproportionate reward, compared to a variety of others that are, from a functional perspective, equally valid.

The problem with both of these assessments is that they ignore Mill's concern about respecting the sphere of individual freedom or autonomy. Thus they make it a little bit too easy to justify ongoing stigmatization of self-control failure. I think it is an important complement to these arguments, therefore, to observe that stigmatization in these domains is not quite the same as social censure applied to instances of minority tastes, or to individual non-conformity, which were Mill's primary concern. The difference between stigmatizing obesity and stigmatizing, say, homosexuality is that, in the former case, individuals themselves often share the judgment that the outcome is undesirable, even as they continue to make the choices that produce it. Indeed, Rothblum's inability to persuade her feminist students to abandon their "antifat prejudice" presumably stems from the fact that most people have experienced self-control failure in the domain of diet and exercise and so are unlikely to be fully persuaded that obesity is either an unchosen characteristic or an alternative lifestyle choice. In cases that involve weakness of will, individuals themselves are conflicted over where their own good lies, and their preferences shift, making it difficult to say what their authentic desire is. As a result, what seems like a paternalistic intervention from one perspective – punishing someone for failing to stick to a resolution, even when the action is primarily self-regarding – might be seen as a crucial component of social scaffolding from another. It enhances the individual capacity for resolute choice. By giving people an additional incentive to adhere to their resolutions, stigmatization allows them to achieve more effective autonomy, particularly for those suffering a relative deficit of onboard motivational resources. Furthermore, in cases in which the negative consequences of the self-control failure are in the remote future, stigmatization may serve as a "nudge" in the present – which is to say, an intervention that changes very little in the objective cost-benefit structure of the choice problem, but nevertheless can have a very significant impact on behaviour.[64]

Of course, one might have reservations about this argument, seeing in it nothing more than a fancy way of justifying what remains a paternalistic intervention.[65] Yet even if one feels this way about the incentive effects of stigmatization, one might still consider the second function of stigmatization – the cognitive task, of pushing people in the direction of greater honesty in their self-assessments – to be a valuable one, and not subject to the same Millian concerns. From this perspective, stigmatization represents, first and foremost, an insistence that failure be described as failure, and not as something else. The reduction in status that one suffers (i.e., the stigma) is an immediate and natural consequence of the perception by others that one's behaviour has fallen short of the ideal.

5. Harder Cases

One way of summarizing this analysis would be to say that de-stigmatization of self-control failure generates something like a moral hazard problem. It alleviates one form of distress, but at the expense of making the behaviour that gave rise to the stigma more likely to occur. Since individuals themselves have an interest in avoiding that behaviour, stigmatization can be seen as enhancing personal autonomy. This makes it very difficult to assess the desirability of the stigma. In the same way that the twenty-four-hour liquor store is a mixed blessing for the alcoholic, so is increased social tolerance of public drunkenness.

This dilemma arises in cases where the stigmatized behaviour is purely the product of self-control failure. There is a set of more difficult cases, however, in which the stigma is associated with a condition that is clearly mixed, in the sense that it is the product of both external causation and individual choice. This is probably true of most addictions, where even though they arise through individual choice, some individuals are more susceptible than others because of the way that they respond physiologically to the substance being abused. For example, although alcohol is a central nervous system depressant, ingestion generates an initial euphoric sensation, followed later by the depressive symptoms (which are more aversive). The timing of the two effects varies considerably between individuals, making alcohol consumption much less enjoyable for those who experience shorter delay. Similarly, individuals with the ALDH2 allele that results in "alcohol flush reaction" are much less likely to become alcoholic, simply because it makes drinking less enjoyable.

Thus there is always an *aspect* of addictive behaviour that results from unchosen factors, and some individuals will therefore face greater self-control challenges than others. This is why black-and-white notions of individual responsibility are unhelpful in discussions of the appropriate social response. Even more complicated, however, are cases in which the unchosen feature predominates, but where individual choice still plays some role in its avoidance. A particularly striking example can be seen in Talcott Parsons's analysis of the "sick role."[66] Parsons observed that, even though illness is associated with an underlying physiological condition, "being sick" is essentially a social role. Our tendency is to naively equate being sick with the physiological condition, but the two are not the same. By declaring oneself sick, and having that declaration recognized by others, one acquires exemption from some standard social obligations, while at the same time acquiring a set of new ones. Thus one is relieved of certain obligations in self-presentation, temperament, and often participation in joint labour, while acquiring the obligation to accept violations of personal space and autonomy, to strive to "get better," as well as to comply with injunctions on how to do so.[67]

Parsons describes the sick role, somewhat misleadingly, as a form of deviance, comparable to criminality.[68] This position is, as even he observes, somewhat strained, since "criminal" is not a socially legitimate role, whereas "sick" is. A more accurate statement would be that, because the sick role offers so many exemptions from everyday obligations, there is a standing temptation to make deviant use of it, either by exaggerating the severity of one's condition or extending its duration. At the extreme, this can take the form of Munchausen syndrome (or "factitious disorder"), in which individuals repeatedly fake illness in order to obtain the benefits of the sick role. Again, this is an example of everyday psychopathology, where the clinically diagnosed mental disorder is merely an extreme version of a propensity that most people exhibit. As a result, Parsons claimed, "curing" someone of an illness involves not just physiological intervention, but also the exercise of social control, including the application of sanctions. Most people are adequately motivated to get better when they are sick, but in case they are not, part of the role of the physician is to sanction that failure. Thus, for example, physicians are quite alert to common forms of "malingering" behaviour among patients (such as an unwillingness to get out of bed, or a reluctance to be discharged from hospital), and are typically quite proactive in pressuring patients to follow an expected recovery schedule.

While Parsons focuses on the aspect of social control involved in curing the sick, there is an important element of self-control as well. In many cases, striving to get better, pushing oneself, is actually an important part of the physiological recovery process. While bed rest has benefits, extended bed rest can easily become unhealthy (producing muscular atrophy, skin lesions, cardiovascular complications, etc.). "Enhanced recovery after surgery" protocols recommend early mobilization of tissue, early allowance of food intake, early removal of catheters, early transition to oral pain medication, etc.[69] ("Early" in this context almost always means "before the patient feels like it.") These transitions are all challenging and in many cases uncomfortable for the patient, but have well-established long-term health benefits. Thus the pressure to follow these protocols provides a type of volitional scaffolding for the patient who is seeking to recover from an episode of illness.

Given this characterization of the sick role, it is difficult to know what to say about the stigmatization of illness. Illness is, to use Falk's terms, *primarily* an existential condition, and yet its severity and duration, not to mention the more specific ways that the person responds to it, are partly achieved. Obviously the medieval stigmatization of illness was excessive. It was due partly to an overestimation of the effects of human agency (e.g., sin) upon illness, as well as a failure to understand disease contagion (which rewarded those who shunned the sick for doing so). Modern medicine has performed a great service by showing the extent to which illnesses ranging from cholera to cancer are outside the control of the individual. And yet the total de-stigmatization of illness in all forms may well be undesirable, precisely because it removes an important incentive to recover, or to cope more effectively with the condition. The acceptance of at least mild social stigma in cases where recovery is expected may be part of the bargain that constitutes the sick role.

6. Conclusion

I began by sketching out two sets of easy cases for normative assessment of stigmatization. On the one hand, there are stigmas associated with existential traits, which are generally regarded as unjustified, and on the other, there are achieved stigmas, associated with behaviour that is actively harmful to others, which are relatively easy to justify. There are, of course, also achieved stigmas associated with behaviour that is completely harmless, which are also unjustified. This leaves the difficult set of cases of achieved stigmas associated with harmful but primarily self-regarding behaviour. Most of the stigmas that remain controversial in our society – and that stubbornly resist de-stigmatization efforts – fall into this category. The primary response by de-stigmatization advocates has been an attempt to assimilate these to the category of existential stigma, by arguing that the conditions of responsible agency are not satisfied by those who act in this way. This has given rise to a long and acrimonious debate, along with the accusation that these advocates are "making excuses" for those who perpetuate a wide range of social pathologies. At the same time, critics of de-stigmatization have done a very poor job at explaining precisely why actions that are primarily self-regarding should be subject to social censure. Thus they have had little to say in the face of the perception that they are "piling on."

My own approach begins by affirming the common-sense view that individuals can indeed be held responsible for their choices in these domains, even in cases of addiction. The claim that they cannot relies upon a causal theory of responsibility that, when generalized, turns out to be just a form of scepticism about freedom of the will. The question, therefore, is purely the normative one, of whether stigmatization is justifiable in these cases. I argue that it may be, where the harmful action involves self-control failure. In such cases, I claim, many individuals rely upon environmental affordances – including institutional and social constraints – as a way of guarding against their own anticipated preference reversals. The fact that others may stigmatize failure provides not only an incentive to maintain resolution, but also makes it more difficult to rationalize deviation from what constitutes, in an important sense, one's better judgment. Thus stigmatization can be defended as a practice that enhances, if not individual autonomy, then at least the overall quality of individual decision-making.

NOTES

1 On "cryptonormativism" see Jürgen Habermas, *The Philosophical Discourse of Modernity*, trans. Frederick Lawrence (Cambridge, MA: MIT Press, 1987), 294.
2 Bruce Link and Jo Phelan, "Conceptualizing Stigma," *Annual Review of Sociology* 27, no. 6 (2001): 379–80.
3 It should be noted that much of this literature is American, and in that cultural context the concept of stigma immediately evokes the negative attitudes and discrimination suffered by African-Americans, the wrongness of which most American intellectuals regard as, not only axiomatic, but paradigmatic. This is, one suspects, the reason for the evidently widespread sense that no explicit argument is needed to establish the wrongness of stigmatization.
4 One of the only instances of an in-depth philosophical discussion is Martha Nussbaum, "Inscribing the Face: Shame, Stigma, and Punishment," *Political Exclusionand Domination: Nomos XLVI*, ed. Stephen Macedo and Melissa Williams (New York: New York University Press, 2005), 259–302. Nussbaum asserts that "the stigmatization behavior in which all societies engage is an aggressive reaction to infantile narcissism and to shame born of our own incompleteness" (277). More common is for theorists to use the term with negative moral valence, but without any discussion, e.g., Elizabeth Anderson. "What Is the Point of Equality?," *Ethics* 109, no. 2 (1999): 287–337; Martin O'Neill, "What Should Egalitarians Believe?," *Philosophy and Public Affairs* 36, no. 2 (2008): 119–56; Nancy Fraser, *Adding Insult to Injury*, ed. Kevin Olson (London: Verso, 2008), where it is taken for granted that stigmatization is wrong. The most striking exception is Douglas Husak, "'Already Punished Enough,'" *Philosophical Topics* 18, no. 1 (1990): 79–99, who assumes that stigmatization is appropriate and justifiable in the case of criminals.
5 Goffman, *Stigma*, 43. Focusing on status, as opposed to identity, has important normative implications. In this I am following Nancy Fraser, "Recognition without Ethics?," *Theory, Culture and Society* 18, nos. 2–3 (2001): 21–42. Note that the term "stigma" (and its plural "stigmata") historically referred to a bodily mark or injury, with particular reference to the wounds of Christ. It was also used to refer to the mark left by branding on a criminal or slave. The term is now used much more metaphorically, but the association with bodily markings often lurks in the background.

6 Gerhard Falk, *Stigma* (Amherst, NY: Prometheus, 2001), 11.
7 E.g., Elizabeth Anderson, *The Imperative of Integration* (Princeton, NJ: Princeton University Press, 2010), 59.
8 Goffman, *Stigma*, 120.
9 Goffman, 34.
10 There is also the fascinating phenomenon through which the stigma "catches up" with the new vocabulary, so that the new term introduced in order to destigmatize the phenomenon becomes, over time, stigmatizing, and so must be replaced again. One can see this most clearly with the term "idiot," which was replaced in the early twentieth century by the medical term "moron," until the latter became a term of abuse and was replaced by the more neutral "mentally retarded." This of course gave rise to "retard" as a term of abuse, which prompted a shift to the now-current "intellectual disability." The net result of these efforts at de-stigmatization has been the development of a great number of synonyms for one and the same condition.
11 On sanctions, see Talcott Parsons, *The Social System* (New York: Free Press, 1951).
12 Paul H. Robinson, "Why Does the Criminal Law Care What the Layperson Thinks Is Just? Coercive versus Normative Crime Control," *Virginia Law Review* 86, no. 8 (2000): 1862.
13 Edwin H. Sutherland, "Is 'White Collar Crime' Crime?," *American Sociological Review* 10, no. 2 (1944): 132–9. See also Richard D. Schwartz and Jerome H. Skolnick, "Two Studies of Legal Stigma," *Social Problems* 10, no. 2 (1962): 133–43.
14 John Stuart Mill, *On Liberty*, ed. Elizabeth Rapaport (Indianapolis, IN: Hackett, 1978).
15 For a development of these views, see Ruwen Ogien, *L'éthique aujourd'hui* (Paris: Gallimard, 2007).
16 Mill, *On Liberty*, 87.
17 Paul Rozin, "The Process of Moralization," *Psychological Science* 10, no. 3 (1999): 218–21.
18 For an unusually clear articulation of this view, see John E. Roemer, "Equality and Responsibility," *Boston Review* 20 (1995): 15–16.
19 Kyla Ellis-Sloan, "Teenage Mothers, Stigma and Their 'Presentation of Self,'" *Sociological Research Online* 19, no. 1 (2014): 1–13. Here the decision is blamed on the social context of "neo-liberalism."
20 Esther D. Rothblum, "'I'll Die for the Revolution, but Don't Ask Me Not to Diet': Feminism and the Continuing Stigmatization of Obesity," in *Feminist Perspectives on Eating Disorders*, ed. Patricia Fallon, Melanie A. Katzman, and Susan C. Wooley (New York: Guildford, 1994).
21 Rothblum, "'I'll Die for the Revolution,'" 54–5.

22 Rothblum, "'I'll Die for the Revolution,'" 55 (inline author-date references omitted).
23 In my morning newspaper, I came across the following, by Camille Bains, "Illicit Drug Users Try to Shed Stigma of Being Called Addicts," *Toronto Star*, 28 January 2017. The article interviews one Dr. Scott MacDonald, who refers to addiction as "the A-word" and declares, "'I won't even say it." "MacDonald said people who chronically use illicit drugs are now considered to have a substance-use disorder, not an addiction, which is more stigmatizing. 'They're just people with a medical problem, a chronic disease that's manageable with treatment,' he said."
24 Consider, for instance, Canadian Prime Minister Stephen Harper's insistence that he would not "commit sociology." Similarly, after terrorist attacks in France, Prime Minister Francois Valls declared, "I have had enough of those who are always searching for excuses or cultural or sociological explanations for what has happened." Marion Rousset, "La sociologie, une profession incomprise," *Le Monde*, 6 October 2016.
25 This is what Harry Frankfurt refers to as the "principle of alternate possibilities." See Harry Frankfurt, "Alternate Possibilities and Moral Responsibility," *Journal of Philosophy* 66, no. 23 (1969): 829–39.
26 Theodore Dalrymple, *Life at the Bottom* (Chicago: Ivan R. Dee, 2001), 118.
27 Peter Strawson, "Freedom and Resentment," *Proceedings of the British Academy* 48 (1962): 1–25.
28 Elliot Turiel, *The Development of Social Knowledge* (Cambridge: Cambridge University Press, 1983).
29 One possible explanation for the over-reliance on this one argument is that conservatives find it extraordinarily antagonizing (e.g., see David Frum, *How We Got Here: The 70s* [New York: Basic Books, 2008]). The latter, I think, can be explained by the fact that they find it extremely difficult to refute. The reason for this, however, is that it is a concealed form of general scepticism about free will – a classic philosophical conundrum, which no one is likely to resolve any time soon. The correct response, therefore, is the more indirect one recommended here, or ruling it out on the grounds that it undermines *all* ascriptions of responsibility.
30 See Lawrence Hsin Yang, Arthur Kleinman, Bruce G. Link, Jo C. Phelan, Sing Lee, and Byron Good, "Culture and Stigma: Adding Moral Experience to Stigma Theory," *Social Science and Medicine* 64, no. 7 (2007): 1528.
31 Dalrymple, *Life at the Bottom*, 162.
32 Dalrymple, 46.
33 Theodore Dalrymple, *Our Culture, What's Left of It* (Chicago: Ivan R. Dee, 2005), 12.
34 Dalrymple, *Our Culture, What's Left of It*, 14.

35 Martha Nussbaum, *The Fragility of Goodness* (Cambridge: Cambridge University Press, 1986).
36 Dalrymple, *Life at the Bottom*, 166.
37 Dalrymple, 208–20.
38 Albert Bandura, "Self-Efficacy: Toward a Unifying Theory of Behavioral Change," *Psychological Review* 84, no. 2 (1977): 191–215; John M. Majer, Leonard A. Jason, and Bradley D. Olson, "Optimism, Abstinence Self-Efficacy, and Self-Mastery: A Comparative Analysis of Cognitive Resources," *Assessment* 11, no. 1 (2004): 57–63.
39 Sigmund Freud, *The Psychopathology of Everyday Life*, ed. A.A. Brill (New York: MacMillan, 1914).
40 American Psychiatric Association, *Diagnostic and Statistical Manual of Mental Disorders, 5th Edition* (Washington, DC: American Psychiatric Publishing, 2013), 237.
41 George Ainslie, *Picoeconomics* (Cambridge: Cambridge University Press, 1992).
42 E.g., see Donald A. Norman and Tim Shallice, "Attention to Action: Willed and Automatic Control of Behavior," in *Consciousness and Self-Regulation*, ed. Richard J. Davidson, Gary E. Schwartz, and David Shapiro (New York: Plenum, 1986), 4:1–18.
43 John Monterosso and George Ainslie, "The Behavioral Economics of Will in Recovery from Addiction," *Drug & Alcohol Dependence* 90, no. S1 (2007): S100–S111. More generally, see Don Ross, Harold Kincaid, David Spurrett, and Peter Collins, *What Is Addiction?* (Cambridge, MA: MIT Press, 2010).
44 Joseph Heath, *Following the Rules* (New York: Oxford University Press, 2008).
45 On resolute choice, see Edward F. McClennen, "Pragmatic Rationality and Rules," *Philosophy and Public Affairs* 26, no. 3 (1997): 210–58; on planning, Michael Bratman, "Time, Rationality, and Self-Governance," *Philosophical Issues* 22, no. 1 (2012): 73–88.
46 Joseph Heath and Joel Anderson, "Procrastination and the Extended Will," in *The Thief of Time*, ed. Chrisoula Andreou and Mark White (New York: Oxford University Press, 2010), 233–53.
47 Andy Clark, *Being There* (Cambridge, MA: MIT Press, 1998), 191. "Creatures" changed to "creators" in second sentence.
48 David Allen, *Getting Things Done* (London: Penguin, 2001), 85–6.
49 Monterosso and Ainslie, "The Behavioral Economics of Will in Recovery from Addiction."
50 Paul Slovic, "Cigarette Smokers: Rational Actors or Rational Fools?," in *Smoking: Risk, Perception and Policy*, ed. Paul Slovic (Thousand Oaks, CA: Sage, 2001), 113. See also Marianna Masiero, Claudio Lucchiari,

and Gabriella Pravettoni, "Personal Fable: Optimistic Bias in Cigarette Smokers," *International Journal of High Risk Behavior and Addiction* 4, no. 1 (2015): e20939.

51 Gresham M. Sykes and David Matza, "Techniques of Neutralization: A Theory of Delinquency," *American Sociological Review* 22, no. 6 (1957): 664–70.

52 A recent study of incarcerated criminals in the United Kingdom found that they rated themselves, compared to the average member of the community, "more moral, more kind to others, more self-controlled, more compassionate, more generous, more dependable, more trustworthy, and more honest. Remarkably, although participants did not rate themselves as significantly more law abiding than community members, they rated themselves as equally law abiding, which may be the most surprising finding of all given their incarcerated status." Constantine Sedikides, Rosie Meek, Mark D. Alicke, and Sarah Taylor, "Behind Bars but above the Bar: Prisoners Consider Themselves More Prosocial than Non-Prisoners," *British Journal of Social Psychology* 53, no. 2 (2014): 400.

53 Donald R. Cressy, *Other People's Money* (Glencoe, IL: Free Press, 1953).

54 Sykes and Matza, "Techniques of Neutralization," 666–7.

55 Marcia Baron, "Justifications and Excuses," *Ohio State Journal of Criminal Law* 2, no. 2 (2005): 387–406.

56 Claire Finkelstein, "*Duress*: A Philosophical Account of the Defense in Law," *Arizona Law Review* 37 (1995): 251–83.

57 Sedikides et al., "Behind Bars but above the Bar," 397.

58 On "differential association," see Edwin Sutherland, *Principles of Criminology*, 4th ed. (Chicago: Lippincott, 1947). On subcultural theory, Albert K. Cohen, *Delinquent Boys* (Glencoe, IL: Free Press, 1955).

59 Joel Anderson, "Structured Nonprocrastination: Scaffolding Efforts to Resist the Temptation to Reconstrue Unwarranted Delay," in *Procrastination, Health, and Well-Being*, ed. Fuschia M. Sirois and Timothy A. Pychyl (Amsterdam: Elsevier, 2016), 53.

60 John Braithwaite, *Crime, Shame and Reintegration* (Cambridge: Cambridge University Press, 1989).

61 Consider, for instance, the story of Toronto Mayor Rob Ford, who was forced to go into "rehab" when his addiction to alcohol and crack cocaine was discovered. His greatest discovery, while in treatment, was that he could not be held responsible for his past behaviour: "It's not just an addiction. Some people can drink, some people can casually use drugs. I have a disease. I have a chronic disease. I was born with blond hair and I'm going to die with blond hair. I was born with this disease. I'm going to die with this disease." As a result, he felt that he was not to be blamed for a past incident, when he had referred to a taxi driver using a

racially pejorative term: "When you have this disease, you say things, do things that aren't you. I think that goes along with having this disease." See Robert Fulford, "Calling Alcoholism a Disease Lets Rob Ford off the Hook," *National Post*, 5 July 2014.
62 Dalrymple, *Life at the Bottom*, 218.
63 Walter Mischel, Oziem Ayduk, Marc G. Berman, B.J. Casey, Ian H. Gotlib, John Jonides, Ethan Kross, Theresa Teslovich, Nicole L. Wilson, Vivian Zayas, and Yuichi Shoda, "'Willpower' over the Life Span: Decomposing Self-Regulation," *Social Cognitive and Affective Neuroscience* 6, no. 2 (2011): 252–6.
64 Richard Thaler and Cass Sunstein, *Nudge* (New Haven, CT: Yale University Press, 2008). See also Pelle Guldborg Hansen, "The Definition of Nudge and Libertarian Paternalism: Does the Hand Fit the Glove?," *European Journal of Risk Regulation* 7, no. 1 (2016): 155–74.
65 Mark White, *The Manipulation of Choice* (New York: Palgrave Macmillan, 2013).
66 Parsons, *Social System*, 475–9.
67 Arnold Arluke, Louanne Kennedy, and Ronald C. Kessler, "Reexamining the Sick-Role Concept: An Empirical Assessment," *Journal of Health and Social Behavior* 20, no. 1 (1979): 30–6.
68 Parsons, *Social System*, 312.
69 Olle Ljungqvist, Michael Scott, and Kennet C. Fearon, "Enhanced Recovery after Surgery," *JAMA Surgery* 152, no. 3 (2017): 293.

Chapter Five

A Unified Theory of Border Control and Reasonable Accommodation

Most liberal democracies consider themselves obliged to be "open to immigration." This means that they provide a legal pathway through which non-citizens can move to the country, acquire rights to participate in the economic system (e.g., to work) and the political system (e.g., to vote), and ultimately, to "naturalize," which is to say, to acquire citizenship that grants them the same status as any member of the native-born population. Being "open to immigration" immediately poses two very difficult normative questions. The first concerns the *level* of immigration, or more precisely, how many immigrants a nation must be willing to accept in order to discharge its obligations of justice. At the moment, every liberal democracy that is open to immigration accepts far fewer immigrants than there are applicants – often by an order of magnitude.[1] Thus the question comes down to one of what reasonable limits there are, if any, on the number of immigrants that a society should feel obliged to accept. The second question arises after immigrants have arrived. Since it is no longer considered permissible to favour immigrants from particular countries of origin, openness to immigration inevitably produces, or expands the scope of, *ethnic* pluralism within the society.[2] This gives rise to the question of "reasonable accommodation" – of how much the "receiving society" must adjust its practices and laws in order to meet the demands and expectations of immigrants.[3] The fact that these societies are *liberal* makes this question very difficult to answer, because liberal societies are already structured to accommodate a great deal of internal pluralism (e.g., between Christians and Jews, between rival Christian sects, between different national and subcultural groups, etc.) and thus are not in a position to refuse all accommodation to immigrants without violating entrenched principles. Furthermore, it gives rise to a puzzle concerning the status of liberal principles, and the basis for imposing them upon groups who demand exemptions from them.

It has long been recognized that, as a matter of practical politics, the answers that are given to these two questions are interconnected. Many wealthy states, for instance, would like to increase the number of immigrants that they accept for purely demographic reasons. The major constraint on their ability to raise immigration rates is the need to secure social acceptance. The latter is, in turn, very much affected by the public perception of what sort of accommodations will have to be made for immigrants. Indeed, the perception that immigrants are going to expect, demand, and perhaps be granted significant accommodations is one of the most powerful forces driving support for political parties that seek to limit the number of immigrants. In the normative literature, however, the two questions are often treated as though they were quite separate, even though it is not difficult to see how they might be connected, not just empirically, but normatively as well. For instance, if it turns out that, as a matter of justice, states are not entitled to limit immigration, it might follow that they are also not in a position to impose many conditions on immigrants, and so the set of accommodations that immigrants can reasonably demand is quite large. Or it may turn out that, because the set of accommodations that immigrants can reasonably demand is quite large, states are entitled to limit the flow of immigrants in order to lessen the burdens imposed by these accommodations. Unfortunately, the literature tends to treat these two questions separately.[4]

My central objective in this chapter is to present a normative framework that generates an answer to both questions, about immigration levels and the limits of reasonable accommodation, simultaneously. Theoretically, I should note, these are both difficult questions that raise fundamental issues about the very basis of state authority. This is one reason they have generated such an expansive literature. Indeed, given the complexity and sophistication of this literature, it is rather unlikely that there are any decisive arguments to be made in favour of one position or another. My hope is to show how it might be possible to cut the Gordian knot, by providing a conceptual framework that is quite simple but will come to be seen as more compelling through its capacity to address both problems simultaneously. As a result, I shall be running somewhat roughshod over a vast and rather difficult theoretical literature, as well as ignoring many of the objections that could be raised. In part this is because I would like to formulate my central thesis in a way that will be policy-relevant and so want to avoid getting sidetracked into the more fine-grained details of the academic debate. Primarily, however, it is because I believe that the very simplicity of the view I will be presenting is its major virtue.

My central idea, stated roughly, is that immigrants are at risk of acting in a collectively self-defeating way, by disrupting or seeking to change the very institutions that account for the desirable properties of the societies that they are seeking to join. In order to avoid this outcome, states must have an immigration policy, which must include both a system of border control and an active approach to immigrant integration. States must also be prepared to adjust their domestic practices, in cases where laws or norms constitute barriers to integration, but should reject demands for accommodation in cases where these demands impinge upon core liberal principles. Thus the very simple idea, and normatively minimal principle, that immigration ought not be allowed to undermine the very features of the society that draws immigrants to it in the first place, provides useful guidance in thinking about the issue of border control, as well as explaining why liberal societies need not accommodate illiberal practices.

1. Wealth and Poverty

Current debates over immigration are marked by a chasm between the prevailing set of normative theories and the actual practice of sovereign states. What is broadly perceived as the moral high ground is occupied by the view that there is something deeply problematic about the contemporary practice in liberal states of controlling immigration, and thus excluding foreigners from citizenship.[5] This "open borders" view is naturally subject to qualifications – it does not require tolerating what would amount to a foreign invasion, for instance[6] – but the core idea is that border control, for the purposes of limiting migration, represents an unjust (or illiberal) use of state power. Indeed, since border control is coercive, and yet those who are subject to it enjoy none of the rights that are ordinarily thought to make state coercion permissible, there are those who believe that border control is fundamentally illegitimate – having more in common with an act of war than an ordinary exercise of state sovereignty or law enforcement.[7] This view, it should be noted, is very closely allied with the "cosmopolitan luck egalitarian" position in debates over global justice, which suggests that there is no basis for privileging co-nationals when it comes to obligations of distributive justice.[8] Since the country in which one is born is a morally arbitrary feature of persons (i.e., a matter of "luck"), the rights and entitlements that individuals enjoy should be independent of nationality.[9] Institutionally, one way of pushing things in the direction of this outcome would be to permit free movement of people across borders.

For those who are opposed to this open borders position, there may be a temptation to rest the opposition on realist grounds, that the proposal is utopian in the pejorative sense of the term. This involves surrendering the moral high ground, granting that in an ideal world such unrestricted movement might be desirable, but that in the non-ideal world in which we live – which includes, for instance, credible concerns about terrorism and organized crime, not to mention domestic hostility to both immigration and multiculturalism – it is both necessary and justifiable for states to exercise border control. In this way, the discussion over border control can easily become sidetracked into a more general debate over the merits of ideal and non-ideal theory, or of realism in political theory. There are others, however, who have opposed the open borders position on normative grounds. (It is perhaps worth mentioning, in this context, that the opposite of "open" borders is not "closed" borders. Philosophical critics of open borders all believe that countries should be open to immigration. They merely think that states can legitimately exercise *control* over their borders, a power that may be used to limit migration, should the state so choose.[10]) Unsurprisingly, many defenders of national partiality in the debates over global justice have weighed in, offering defences of border control.[11] This stands to reason, simply because the only way to effectively institutionalize such partiality is for members of the group to have some control over who becomes a member. Unfortunately, the way that the defenders of border control have made their case has typically been by offering somewhat exotic, and in some cases non-liberal, theories of state power.[12]

In other cases, critics have focused their energy on attacking the two central arguments for open borders. The first is based upon the claim that individuals have a right to freedom of movement. Since liberal states recognize freedom of movement within their borders as an important individual right, proponents of open borders have argued that it "makes no sense" (as Joseph Carens put it) to treat freedom of movement across state borders as "a matter of political discretion."[13] Yet despite being a provocative observation, this is hardly a decisive argument. After all, the rights to freedom of movement that individuals enjoy domestically are not absolute and are limited routinely by, for instance, the property rights of others.[14] Thus a number of theorists have tried to articulate ways in which a right to exclusion might arise from the nature of state sovereignty, and in particular, its territorial aspect.[15] Some of these theorists, I should note, accept the somewhat misleading characterization of the issue as one of *movement*. In an early contribution, Roger Nett formulated the open borders position as involving the right of individuals "to move freely over the surface of the earth so long as they are willing to obey local laws and respect local customs."[16] This is a description that applies more readily to tourists than to immigrants. When we talk about freedom of movement, it is not really a demand for movement that we are concerned with – this could be satisfied by issuing travel visas – but rather a demand for inclusion, or the right to *become a member* of any economic and political society.[17] It is the demand for inclusion in the labour market that is particularly contentious (e.g., the issues raised by the large populations of elderly retirees from northern countries living in southern climes is seldom considered pressing). Apart from reframing the discussion, so that the right in question no longer sounds like it could be a negative liberty, this way of presenting the issue also makes it seem much easier to override.[18] There are, after all, many forms of human association in which members are not obliged to accept anyone who comes along and demands admission.[19]

Once one recognizes the complexity of the "right" being asserted, it becomes difficult to see what sort of conceptual resources might be available to adjudicate the issue, because there is no generally accepted account of the foundation of rights. This is one reason that the debate quickly becomes mired down, as theorists have found themselves having first to lay out a theory of individual (or collective) rights, in order then to specify how rights of migration and inclusion might (or might not) fit in.[20] Furthermore, since the supposed right of migration is not recognized by any existing legal regime, proponents of the open borders position are forced to posit it at a very high level of normative idealization. They have, however, failed to recognize that, at this level of idealization, world government might also be feasible and desirable, and thus the position may not justify a right of movement *across borders*, it may simply amount to the claim that, in an ideal world, there would be no nations and no walls, and so all of humanity could exercise the rights currently enjoyed by members of a liberal polity. The burden of proof, in other words, is to show that there is a level of idealization at which one could justify state sovereignty in most of the traditional domains *except* that of border control.

Much of this argument, however, strikes me as misdirected effort, since it seems unlikely that a concern over individual rights is what is really driving the argument for open borders. For instance, no one much laments the fate of the American automotive engineer, living and working in Tokyo but denied any route to citizenship, or the Finnish computer programmer, whose US work visa has been held up in perpetuity, or even the Malian agricultural worker, hoping to normalize his status in the Ivory Coast. The sort of migration that elicits attention from normative theorists is typically from poor countries to wealthy ones. Carens, for instance, implores us to consider how the system of border control looks "to Africans in small, leaky vessels seeking to avoid patrol boats while they cross the Mediterranean to southern Europe or to Mexicans risking death from heat and exposure in the Arizona desert as they try to evade border patrols and enter the United States."[21] What the examples have in common is that they feature migrants trying to escape from poverty, encountering the barriers set up by wealthy countries to discourage precisely that sort of migration.

This set of issues is at the core of the second major argument for open borders, which appeals not to rights but rather to considerations of distributive justice.[22] Underlying it is a concern raised by the extreme arbitrariness of the distribution of wealth in the world today. To pick just one example, a person born in Mexico, who grows up to become an assembly line worker at an automobile factory, can expect to earn around $5 per hour. A person born in the United States, who goes on to do the exact same job, at a factory owned by the same company, can expect to earn closer to $30 per hour. The difference in earnings is purely an effect of luck – the American worker is basically a winner in what Ayelet Shachar calls the "birthright lottery." Citizenship, along with the practices of exclusion that sustain it, has become, in her view, a system that allows members of wealthy states to create "an enclave in which to preserve their accumulated wealth and power through time."[23] One obvious way to redress this is by permitting open migration. The wage differential between US and Mexican autoworkers, for instance, would be difficult to sustain if there were an open border between the two countries.

There is much to be said for this argument. The early discussion in the global justice literature, however, was marred by the prevalence of widespread misunderstandings about the sources of the underlying economic inequality, which in turn caused confusion in the debate over migration. Perhaps the most wrongheaded suggestion was that differences in the wealth of nations were caused by inequalities in their resource endowments. Of course nations have fought wars that were motivated primarily by the desire to control natural resources, whether it be the coal mines of Alsace-Lorraine, the farmland of Manchuria, or the oilfields of Kuwait. Yet it does not follow from this that control of natural resources has actually played an important role in the economic development of many nations.[24] It is a staple observation in the economic development literature that some countries, such as the Congo, remain poor despite their enormous resource endowment, while others, such as Japan or the Netherlands, have become very wealthy despite an absolute paucity of natural resources. Thus it would be difficult to find any economist willing to endorse the theory of development underlying Charles Beitz's suggestion that "some areas are rich in resources, and societies established in such areas can be expected to exploit their natural riches and to prosper. Other societies do not fare so well, and despite the best efforts of their members, they may attain only a meagre level of well-being because of resource scarcities."[25] Resources are traded on highly competitive global markets, where they can be obtained by all. Absent state intervention, and given the low cost of international shipping, domestic prices are roughly the same as world prices, and so there is no special advantage to be had from living in a resource-rich country. Furthermore, with the exception of oil, diamonds, and a few rare minerals, there are no supranormal rents associated with resource extraction. For these and several other reasons, there is simply no advantage to be had for states with abundant natural resources within their territory.

One suspects that the central attraction of this emphasis on resources – what motivated much of the willingness to overlook its empirical implausibility – is that it dramatically simplifies the normative question. If one imagines states being formed through some kind of unprincipled land grab, the effects of which are handed down intergenerationally, so that current inequalities of wealth between nations are a direct consequence of the unjust initial appropriation, then it is not difficult to conclude that these inequalities call for redress, and that the simplest way of doing this is to permit open migration (on the principle that it is easier to move people to natural resources than natural resources to people). For instance, the United States seized a great deal of territory from Mexico during the 1846–8 war (including the current states of California, Nevada, Utah, Arizona, New Mexico, as well as parts of Wyoming, Kansas, and Colorado). If the differences in wealth between the average American and the average Mexican worker were due to differential resource endowments caused by the unjust seizure of these territories by the United States, then Mexican nationals would have a very strong claim for admission to the United States. Indeed, rejecting this claim would amount to the suggestion that present Americans should be able to continue to benefit from the theft perpetrated by their ancestors.

This is, however, simply incorrect as an account of the inequality of wealth between Mexico and the United States. The difference in wages between Mexican and American workers is a consequence of differences in average labour productivity in the two countries. At the time of writing, the average US worker produces $68.30 of output per hour, whereas the average Mexican worker produces less than $20 (at PPP value).[26] Several factors contribute to this difference in output, but the most important is the capital stock that workers have access to. American agriculture, for instance, is highly mechanized, and so only 2 per cent of the population works in that sector, as opposed to Mexico, where the number is 13 per cent.[27] The term "capital" is the economist's shorthand way of referring to the stock of artefacts that amplify human effort, including "plant and equipment," roads and infrastructure, buildings, computers, etc. Thus, for instance, the influential "Solow growth model" represents output as a function of the quantity of labour, capital, and knowledge.[28] Since knowledge diffuses relatively easily across national borders, and poor countries typically have plenty of labour, differences in output are therefore regarded as primarily due to differences in productive capital. Although the capital stock is difficult to measure and compare between nations, intuitively the difference between countries is not hard to grasp. In poor countries, roads are built with shovels and wheelbarrows, in rich countries they are built with excavators and dump trucks. Although some fraction of the increased product goes to the owners of capital, a relatively consistent fraction goes to workers, which accounts for the higher wages paid in wealthier countries.

The fact that differences in national wealth are due primarily to differences in labour productivity is somewhat obscured by the fact that in a competitive labour market, workers are not paid a wage that reflects their own personal productivity, but one that is determined by the average level of productivity in the economy. Roughly speaking, firms pay workers no more than is necessary to keep them from quitting and working elsewhere. Thus Mexican workers at an American-owned automobile factory, despite having access to roughly the same plant, equipment, and technology as American workers doing the same job, nevertheless command lower salaries, because their outside options are worse. It is productivity levels in the rest of the economy that determine the wage level, not the productivity level in the specific firm. This is why the only way to raise wages in a sustainable fashion is to increase labour productivity in the economy as a whole. (One can see the process at work in China, over the past decade, where real wages have increased by over 10 per cent per year, closely tracking the growth in both GDP and average labour productivity.)[29]

It should be noted that, from a distributive justice perspective, it makes no normative difference that the primary inequalities of wealth between countries have nothing to do with inequalities in natural resource endowment and are instead based on inequalities in the capital stock. This is because the capital stock is largely *inherited*, and most citizens of wealthy nations have done nothing to deserve access to it. The building that I work in was constructed long before I was born, as were the bridges and subway tunnels that I traverse on the way there. More subtly, the cumulative nature of economic growth is due to the fact that earlier generations, by producing capital goods rather than consumption goods, made it easier to produce a larger surplus in the years following, which in turn made it easier to replace those capital goods, as well as to expand the stock. Thus even my access to rapidly depreciating goods, such as the computer I am typing on, has been facilitated by the efforts of past generations, going back over a hundred years, the benefits of which I have in no way earned.

As a result, one might be inclined to think that one could run the distributive justice argument for open borders in the same way, merely substituting "capital" for "resources." There are, however, a few problems. In the resources case, a central argument for migration was that it is easier to move people to resources than resources to people. In the case of capital, however, the opposite is true. It is much easier to move capital to where people are, through foreign investment, than people to where capital is. If the central cause of inequality between rich and poor nations is that the latter have too much labour and not enough capital, relatively speaking, while the former have too much capital and not enough labour, then the problem can be solved either by moving the capital to where labour is more plentiful, or labour to where the capital is more plentiful, or some combination thereof. When an American automotive company invests millions of dollars in building a new factory in Mexico, this is analytically equivalent to allowing Mexicans to migrate to the United States and work at an American factory. Both options reduce inequality, by changing the capital-to-labour ratio in a way that puts upward pressure on wages in Mexico and downward pressure on wages in the United States. (It does not equalize wages right away, because it has only a small impact on average productivity, but the process is one that in the medium term will equalize wages in the affected labour markets.)

From this perspective, there is something perverse about the rather standard left-wing position that regards corporate "offshoring" of production to low-wage countries as perfidy, but celebrates the migration of labour from poor to wealthy countries. Given a choice between getting a better job in one's own community and having to move to another country in order to secure one, most people, whether rich or poor, vastly prefer the former. Migration is profoundly disruptive, separating people from their families and relatives, eroding social capital, creating intergenerational conflict within families, and subjecting migrants to "culture shock," including in many cases the obligation to learn and function in a second language, as well as to submit to all the disadvantages associated with belonging to a minority cultural or religious group. Migration is a distinctly second-best (if not third- or fourth-best) solution to the problem of economic underdevelopment. (This is reflected in the rather substantial "out-migration" rates in many countries. In Canada, for instance, one study of working-age male migrants showed that 35 per cent of legally admitted migrants left the country again within twenty years.[30] This is from the country that is one of the most successful in the world at integrating immigrants.)

There are, of course, many problems associated with foreign investment as well. But even without movement of capital, many economists are of the view that free trade in goods will tend to equalize payments made to factors of production, including both labour and capital. This is the upshot of Paul Samuelson's "factor price equalization theorem," which makes the rather extraordinary suggestion that even if factors are completely immobile, trade in goods will generate an outcome that is the same as if these factors were completely mobile.[31] With free trade, countries with a relative excess of capital will "export" that capital in the form of increased production of capital-intensive goods, while countries with an excess of labour will "export" it in the form of labour-intensive goods, and changes in relative prices will equalize both wages and returns to capital in both countries. From this perspective, the fact that labour is not mobile across national boundaries *is no more important than the fact that farmland is not mobile across national boundaries*. Thus proponents of open borders must explain why they prefer to see migration of people, as opposed to movement of capital, or just free trade in commodities, since all three seem to be just different ways of achieving the same desired outcome, which is the reduction of global inequality.[32]

One natural response to this is to observe that these economic models are extremely idealized, and that in the real world there are frictions that prevent the realization of these outcomes (e.g., international capital flows generate currency instability, etc.). This is, I should note, not an argument that is available to most proponents of open borders, since that view is also pitched at a very high level of idealization. It is nevertheless worthwhile to consider the reasons that existing trade and investment practices have not generated significant narrowing of certain persistent inequalities between nations. Even direct transfers (i.e., giving people money) turn out to be surprisingly ineffective at reducing inequality. Here it is essential to turn to the development literature, in order to obtain a better understanding of why foreign aid, foreign direct investment, and international trade do not automatically produce economic growth in many countries.

There is some tendency to hypostatize "capital" and to imagine it as like a pile of gold that rich countries are sitting on, that needs to be spread around more widely, in order to equalize wealth. In fact, the "capital" of a nation is a stock of productive assets that must constantly be replenished, and ideally, expanded. This process relies upon a complex set of institutional arrangements, which must be sustained over the course of generations. Most obviously, there must be a relatively secure system of savings and investment, so that individuals have some incentive to produce more than they consume, freeing up resources for renewal of the capital stock. There must be secure property rights, a transparent system of corporate law, stable lending institutions, and orderly bankruptcy procedures, all governed by perspicuous accounting standards, in order to ensure that savings actually get transformed into productive investments. This can all be disrupted in multiple ways, ranging from bank failures and confiscatory taxation to hyperinflation and currency devaluation. (Compare, for instance, the fate of Venezuela and Norway, two countries that forty years ago had approximately the same level of both national income and oil reserves. Norway now has the largest sovereign wealth fund in the world, while millions of Venezuelans are facing malnutrition and in, some cases, starvation.) The existence of a large stock of productive capital is therefore largely a by-product of a much broader *system of intergenerational cooperation*.

The large-scale failure of most Western development efforts has produced greater attention to these factors. Increasingly, the central challenge of development is seen as involving more than just shifting capital around, but rather creating systems of cooperation where previously none existed. This goes beyond just the savings and investment system of the market, but includes aspects of both the state and civil society. The quality of the law, as well as its enforcement, is an extremely important variable. The World Bank's "Doing Business" project, for instance, has documented enormous differences from one country to another in how difficult it is to accomplish the day-to-day tasks involved in carrying out complex economic activity. How long does it take to incorporate? What resources must be dedicated to tax compliance? Is it possible to secure reliable electricity supply? How many days does it take to obtain a construction permit? How costly is it to enforce contracts?[33] The differences among countries are shockingly large, and as one might expect, the upper ranks of the aggregate scoring are dominated by wealthy countries, the lower ranks by poor ones.

Thus if one wanted to ask, "What do rich countries have that poor countries lack?" it would be slightly misleading to say "capital." The existence of a large capital stock is, as Dani Rodrik, Arvind Subramanian, and Francesco Trebbi have argued, merely the "proximate cause" of national wealth.[34] What rich countries actually have is a more successful *system of cooperation*. From this perspective, the "ultimate cause" of the persistence of poverty in underdeveloped countries is institutional weakness. This is the major reason that decolonization, foreign aid, international capital flows, and free trade in commodities do not automatically rectify global inequalities. Migration, by contrast, does have the potential to redress certain inequalities, to the extent that it expands the number of people who benefit from the more successful systems of cooperation. This truth lies at the heart of the distributive justice argument for migration – every year migration offers millions of people an opportunity to vastly improve their lives. In this respect, migration has a more reliable track record at redressing poverty than foreign investment or free trade. Furthermore, because the problems in underdeveloped countries are largely institutional, the costs imposed upon the country of emigration are typically much lower than the gains achieved by the migrant. By allowing individuals to achieve something closer to their human potential, the overall process of migration becomes positive sum (and thus not "beggar thy neighbour" in relation to the country of origin).[35]

In the discussion that follows, I will treat this as the central argument in support of the contention that countries should be "open to immigration" (in the way that, for instance, countries such as Canada and Australia are). I hesitate to call it a distributive justice argument, however, because it is in certain ways dissimilar from the familiar obligations of distributive justice that arise within states. It can be defended just as easily on broadly humanitarian grounds as a duty of benevolence.[36] Furthermore, a correct understanding of the nature and causes of the wealth of nations, such as I have been recommending here, produces an important shift in perspective when thinking about this argument for migration. When migrants come to wealthy countries, hoping to improve their economic opportunities, they are not chasing after anything tangible, like a share of natural resources, or a certain quantity of capital. They are seeking to become participants in a more successful system of cooperation than the one they have left behind. If one thinks of national wealth in terms of resources or capital, then it is easy to imagine that the humanitarian aims of migration policy have been satisfied as soon as the immigrant acquires permanent residency status in the country. And of course, for migrants fleeing religious persecution, or for refugees trying to escape a civil war, there is a sense in which a state can discharge its most important obligation toward these individuals simply by letting them in. With economically motivated immigrants, by contrast, the discharge of obligations is conditional upon successful integration into the system of cooperation, which is to say, into the major social and economic institutions of the society. As a result, the broadly humanitarian aim of migration policy can fail, even after migrants have been admitted. Furthermore, there are two "directions" from which it can fail. The receiving society can exclude immigrants, either explicitly and intentionally, or by failing to make the efforts and accommodations necessary to permit successful integration. Or immigrants may fail to integrate, and thereby reproduce (often inadvertently) practices that contributed to the unsuccessful qualities of the societies that they had hoped to leave behind. Either way, integration is fraught with difficulty, even under conditions in which there is considerable goodwill on all sides.

This is, I think, the greatest problem with the open borders view – it creates the impression that states can discharge an important duty of justice simply by throwing open their borders, allowing for free movement of people. Again, the metaphor of movement is misleading. What immigrants want is not to live within the territory of another state, they want to become members of the society and to share its benefits and burdens. Making it possible for people – adults who have grown up in another culture and been socialized into different practices – to become full members of another society is an enormous challenge, one that many states have tried and failed to accomplish. And yet what is the point of a generous admissions policy that results in the creation of a marginalized (which is to say, more likely to be poor, uneducated, unemployed, incarcerated, and disaffected) ethnic minority group in the society, especially if this marginalization is reproduced intergenerationally? Apart from the impact on the immigrants themselves, such a state of affairs cultivates racism and xenophobia in the native-born population, in part because it provides what appears to be a rational basis for it. This issue, which dominates both the policy and public debates over immigration, has been sadly neglected in the normative literature. Carens, for instance, says not one word, over the course of a 300-page book on the "ethics of immigration," about the difficulties that countries have experienced at integrating immigrants (e.g., the factors that led German Chancellor Angela Merkel to describe existing immigrant integration policies as having "utterly failed."[37]) Indeed, there is a tendency to think that racism in the native-born population is the only problem that immigrants confront, and since people should not be racist, there is simply no normative issue.[38] As I will argue in the following section, a more realistic understanding of how the process of integration actually works – when it succeeds and when it fails – as well as an understanding of the burden that the obligation to integrate migrants places upon the receiving society, provides a significantly more nuanced understanding of the normative issues, as well as the key to thinking about both border control and reasonable accommodation.

2. Border Control

It may be helpful to begin by saying something about the characteristics of a "successful" system of cooperation, and by extension, a "successful" society.[39] This vocabulary may appear tendentious, or self-congratulatory, so it is important to emphasize that, in the context of migration, the relevant value judgments are the ones being made by migrants, in their decision to move to these countries. (It is also implicit in the suggestion that some objective of egalitarian justice is served by the movement of people from one country to another.) The central characteristics of successful societies, and what draws so many people to them, is not only that they have a prosperous economy, or high GDP per capita, but that they also provide their citizens with a bundle of other desirable goods: government that is relatively non-corrupt and non-authoritarian, high levels of personal security and protection of individual freedoms, quality health care and long life expectancy, a clean environment and effective consumer protection, an accessible and sophisticated education system, efficient and reliable infrastructure, and so on. Less successful societies, by contrast, fail to provide as much or as well in some or all of these dimensions. Furthermore, there is significant correlation in the level of provision of all these goods. While there are some outliers, such as Cuba, which performs very well in the areas of health and education, while doing quite poorly in GDP and quality of governance, in most cases countries that are relatively poor are also relatively corrupt, having unreliable infrastructure, high levels of crime, inadequate courts, and so on. Thus it is not an overly gross simplification to speak simply of "successful" and "unsuccessful" societies, with the understanding that the evaluation is always relative and subject to qualifications.

The fact that the traits of a successful society tend to come as a package is a reflection of the fact that these goods are all, in one way or another, the fruits of cooperation, which arise as a consequence of a core set of institutions that are able to elicit appropriate levels of cooperative effort from the population. By contrast, unsuccessful societies are marked either by institutions that are ineffective at resolving collective action problems or else exacerbate them. As a result, these societies become mired in highly dysfunctional interaction patterns, such as corruption of public officials, violent crime, shirking of work, political violence and instability, predatory taxation, insecurity of property, very high birth rates, poor public health and sanitation, low levels of interpersonal trust, widespread cheating in the education system, and poor educational outcomes. Many of these outcomes, despite being suboptimal and widely lamented, are nevertheless reproduced because they are in equilibrium. If others are treating government jobs as sinecures, either not showing up to work at all, or working far fewer hours than they are supposed to, then there is very little incentive for any individual to work much harder. If others are taking bribes, and especially if salaries are low because of the expectation that officials will be supplementing their income with bribes, then it is very difficult for one official to remain honest. If violent criminals roam the streets, and the police are unable to enforce the law, or to assure the safety of the population, then it is hard for any one individual to refrain from engaging in private uses of force, or seeking the protection of those who do.

Successful societies are also characterized by something like an equilibrium in these domains, typically one that entrenches a more efficient outcome.[40] In circumstances in which everyone shows up on time and works hard, workers themselves will tend to stigmatize or resent those who shirk. When official corruption is rare, both citizens and officials will be outraged and offended when they discover instances of corruption in their midst. When violent crime is uncommon, and the police are able to make a credible commitment to maintaining order, it is much easier for individuals to refrain from vigilantism, or to resist extortion from protection rackets.

I describe these outcomes as being "like" an equilibrium because they are, in many cases, not entirely a product of the extrinsic incentives that individuals face. Individuals will also be acting on the basis of moral or other intrinsic incentives that reinforce the pattern. In a bureaucratic environment that features very low levels of official corruption, individuals may develop a strong professional ethic that both reflects and supports this state of affairs. Decentralized enforcement of these norms may then relieve the organization of the need to provide much official deterrence against corruption. Honesty may be "self-enforcing," in this case, even though literal enforcement (i.e., through apprehension and punishment of offenders) is relatively weak. On the other hand, in an environment in which corruption is widespread, the perception that "everyone else is doing it" may provide individuals with moral licence to engage in corrupt practices, even if they recognize, at some level, that the practice is deleterious.[41] In the worst cases, an honest official may be stigmatized for having "broken ranks," or for seeking to "make trouble" for the others.[42] Thus corruption tends to be either common and systemic or rare and episodic.[43]

In other cases, it is not the culture that arises *within* organizations that either promotes or inhibits cooperation, but rather the background culture of the society. To pick just one example, it has been widely observed that cultures that cultivate very intense particularistic loyalties (e.g., to family or to clan group), face significant obstacles establishing public deference to the authority of the state.[44] This can, in turn, have a variety of dysfunctional consequences, ranging from lawlessness and violence to an incapacity to deliver certain public goods. The Christian religion has historically been quite antagonistic to particularistic loyalties, and so most states established in societies where the background culture was shaped by centuries of Christianity faced relatively few rival "poles of allegiance."[45] The situation is quite different in societies that are structured by tribal or clan loyalties, or where family and ancestral obligations are paramount. It is not just that this may pose a challenge to the capacity of the state to secure compliance with the law; it may also interfere with norms of bureaucratic behaviour, such as the need for merit-based, as opposed to nepotistic or clientelistic, appointment procedures.

Countries that get stuck in one of these complex suboptimal equilibria can have enormous difficulty extracting themselves from it. This is, in fact, the greatest challenge facing development efforts (and it is why merely "throwing money" at problems seldom does much to solve them).[46] Take, for instance, the persistent difficulty experienced by the Indian state, euphemistically referred to as "provider absence."[47] India is one of several countries in which the government is incapable of getting more than a fraction of its employees to actually do the work that they are being paid to do. In the education system, on any given day, approximately 25 per cent of teachers are absent. The health care system is worse. Despite an extensive network of public clinics, the average absenteeism rate among doctors is estimated to be 40 per cent. These teachers and doctors are all, it should be noted, still drawing their salaries. Through a combination of poor oversight, widespread collusion, and official corruption, this absenteeism goes unpunished. The problem is also quite intractable, as numerous attempts to change it have failed. An initiative undertaken by the NGO Seva Mandir, for instance, that introduced time stamp clocks for nurses, initially produced positive results, but then fell apart when local health administrators, who were supposed to be exercising oversight, conspired with nurses to undermine the system.[48] It is no surprise, therefore, that India performs very poorly in literacy, human capital development, life expectancy, and overall burden of disease. But what can be done about it? When the state apparatus itself is corrupt, it is difficult to root out state corruption.[49] The government simply does not have any lever it can pull. Furthermore, a significant fraction of elected officials are themselves corrupt, and large segments of the population are positively disposed to vote for politicians who are either facing, or have been convicted of, serious criminal charges.[50] It is no wonder then that a large number of Indians despair of ever solving these problems, and so prefer simply to leave the country.

Immigrants who move from unsuccessful to successful societies may think of themselves as merely seeking "a better life" for themselves and their children, but what they are really trying to do is break free from certain patterns of dysfunctional social behaviour. And yet they are seldom in a position to make a clean break from their society of origin or its culture. On the contrary, they will usually bring with them and attempt to reproduce various aspects of it. Furthermore, since the connection between action and consequence is seldom fully explicit, they will often bring with them some of the very same patterns of behaviour whose consequences they are trying to escape.[51] This is why it is important for the receiving society to be able to *integrate* immigrants. It must be able to draw them into the major social institutions of the society – first and foremost the economy, but also the education system and the political process – and persuade them to act in conformity with a new and different set of norms. The goal, in other words, is to switch them over to the more efficient equilibrium pattern of behaviour. In some cases this is relatively easy. An immigrant to Canada, for instance, will realize very quickly that government employees are not permitted to be absent from work without explanation, and so the habits and expectations that generate "provider absence" can be expected to disappear. In other cases, however, the process of integration will be much more difficult. A study of migrants from southern to northern Italy, for instance, showed that more subtle forms of workplace shirking, despite showing some improvement, remained persistent after many years.[52] More generally, an immigrant who observes an absence of official corruption may assume that it is just hidden, and so persist in acting in ways that suborn or encourage it.

It is important to emphasize what is *not* being said here. Societies must succeed in integrating their own citizens as well, and failures of socialization abound. Nevertheless, the task of integrating children who are born in a country, or those who immigrate at a very young age ("generation 1.5" immigrants), is relatively easy, precisely because they enter the society unsocialized. This is why the education system constitutes such an important site of contestation in debates over immigrant integration.[53] By contrast, integrating adults who grew up and were socialized into a completely different set of practices poses genuine challenges, and in many cases will only ever be partially successful. These challenges are compounded when those adults were socialized into a set of practices that are, in certain important respects, dysfunctional. And yet the self-selection that generates the immigration pool results in vast overrepresentation of precisely that group, as people seek to escape from unsuccessful societies. In the same way that tourists, seeking out pristine wilderness, or secluded beaches, risk destroying precisely what they came in search of, immigrants also risk undermining – in most cases inadvertently – the institutional foundations of the successful societies they are trying to join. This is not because they are bad people, or more antisocial by nature. It is simply because they come from unsuccessful societies and thus are likely to have habits and expectations that will need to be unlearned.

Failures of integration can take two forms. First, faced with a radically different set of expectations, not to mention hostility and inflexibility in the application of norms, immigrants may avoid joining, or may be excluded from, mainstream institutions. This is the problem of marginalization. Second, immigrants may participate in the institutions, but fail to adjust their behaviour to adapt to the prevailing set of norms. This is the problem of deviance. The most important thing to recognize is that states that are effective at integrating immigrants generally have active integration policies, that involve not just community outreach, but also forms of funding aimed at promoting second-language education, settlement, job search, and in some cases political mobilization.[54] The current situation is not like that of the nineteenth or early twentieth century, when an immigrant could simply step off a boat and find gainful employment as a manual labourer. Immigrants are seeking to join modern, complex societies, with labour markets that increasingly require not just a minimal education level, but also a range of "soft" social skills. As a result, successful immigrant integration does not happen through benign neglect, or a *laissez-faire* approach.[55] There is a difficult balancing act involved. Some states, concerned about producing "ethnic ghettos," are quite fearful of relying upon ethnic networks to deliver services, and instead want to do everything through state institutions. The evidence, however, suggests that the community partnership approach is in the long run more effective. It is important, however, to ensure that the ethnic community not provide a rival pole of attraction, allowing immigrants to opt out of integrating into the major institutions of society.

The following is a non-exhaustive list, intended to illustrate dysfunctional habits that immigrants may bring with them, which generally require active policy intervention in order to disrupt, paving the way for successful integration:

1. *Imported conflict.* Perhaps the most obvious and uncontroversially dysfunctional feature of many unsuccessful societies is the willingness of various parties to engage in political violence. One long-standing concern in receiving societies is that immigrants will remain invested in these conflicts, and may "import" forms of political violence into the country. This is not an entirely idle concern, since the single most deadly terrorist attack committed against Canadians was carried out by Sikh immigrants in British Columbia.[56] Certain state and non-state actors involved in violent conflict around the world are also quite aggressive in drawing upon diaspora communities for both resources and combatants.[57] Thus even immigrants who want to leave behind these conflicts may find themselves being drawn back in. Of course, in many cases the perception of "imported conflict" outstrips the reality, but that is in part because successful immigrant societies have in place active policies aimed at combating it. Immigrants from conflict zones typically describe their rejection of political violence, not as an instantaneous conversion, but rather as the outcome of a rather lengthy process, or "learning experience," involving extensive contact with people holding other perspectives.[58] It is perhaps unsurprising, then, that the movement away from radical or violent political ideologies is strongly associated with successful participation in the labour market, as well as the political system of the receiving society.

2. *Crime.* Fear of crime committed by immigrants is a constant refrain in nativist and xenophobic rhetoric, even though self-selection and demography are sufficient to ensure that, in most countries, immigrants commit fewer crimes on average than the native-born population. Some of the concern is due to the fact that crimes committed by immigrants are more salient, and in many cases inspire greater fear in the general population. At the same time, there are some countries in the world in which the domestic crime

rate is a major factor driving emigration. It is hardly surprising then to discover an elevated level of crime and violence within immigrant communities from those countries. While many are eager to explain this as a consequence of marginalization by the broader society, it is well known that crime has a large number of important "social determinants." It would not be surprising if many of these immigrants inadvertently brought with them practices and attitudes that are criminogenic. Beyond this, many criminals and criminal organizations remain networked with individuals in the diaspora – gangs, for instance, may set up branch operations within immigrant communities.[59] Thus certain immigrants wind up reproducing the crime problem that they were hoping to escape, and to this extent, fail to secure a major benefit of living in a successful society. They may also become victims of a vicious circle, in which crime exacerbates marginalization, and marginalization breeds more crime.

3. *Avoidance of state officials.* Many immigrants come from countries in which attitudes toward state officials, including the police, range from healthy distrust to outright fear. Successful societies, by contrast, have a more benign state apparatus – of necessity, since many items on the list of desirable goods provided by these societies are public goods, delivered by state officials. Furthermore, full integration into the society can be achieved only through interaction with state officials. Thus one of the most significant challenges of successful immigrant integration involves delivering public services to groups that seek to avoid any contact with the public sector. (This problem may be exacerbated if the immigrant community includes an "illegal" wing, who have their own reasons for wanting to avoid contact.) One challenge involved in controlling crime within certain immigrant communities, for instance, whether it be domestic assault or gang violence, is an unwillingness of witnesses to speak to the police – in some cases motivated by straightforward fear, in other cases by norms of group solidarity that condemn "snitching." Again, it is important to emphasize that these sorts of problems do not generally work themselves out, but require active integration policies. In the case of social services, for instance, successful immigrant societies generally foster the development of community groups and non-profit organizations within ethnic communities, which can either deliver the services directly, or serve as a point of contact with state agencies. Language classes, for instance, are more likely to be attended if they are not being offered directly by the state, but are instead outsourced to

local community groups. In order to achieve effective policing, such cooperation with community groups is essential as well but must generally be coupled with active recruitment and training of officers from members of the community being policed.

4. *Corruption.* Official corruption is one of the most intractable problems in unsuccessful societies, not just because of the incentive structure that it creates, but because of the occupational culture that it produces. (This is the point of the famous "New York parking ticket" study, which showed that the number of unpaid parking tickets accumulated by United Nations diplomats in New York City was highly correlated with the corruption level of their country of origin.)[60] Immigrants seldom move very quickly into positions of official authority in the receiving society, so there is little danger of corruption being reproduced directly. However, immigrants may assume that state officials are corrupt, and so offer unsolicited bribes, which may, in turn, encourage state officials to become corrupt. There are also specific areas in which cheating may be considered quite normal by immigrants and therefore requires some adjustment of attitude. Immigrants may engage in tax avoidance, for a variety of reasons: merely because they are unaccustomed to paying tax, or because they find the rates shockingly high, or because they are engaged in low-paid work where they can operate on a cash basis, or because they are working alongside illegal immigrants whose earnings are not being reported, etc. Another area in which adjustment may be required is educational cheating, which is rife in many countries, in some cases involving not just students, but extensive collusion between teachers and parents as well. The problem of educational cheating in China, for instance, is sufficiently severe that the government recently imposed a seven-year prison term on those caught cheating on state examinations. It is a criminal offence in many Indian states as well, with crackdowns sometimes leading to hundreds, or even thousands, of arrests.[61] The education systems in developed countries, by contrast, rely almost entirely on moral suasion to deter cheating.

5. *Low-trust interpersonal relations.* Many unsuccessful societies are described as suffering from a deficiency of "social capital." Typically this means that the background level of interpersonal trust is quite low, and so individuals have only a limited ability to engage in spontaneous cooperative action to address collective action problems. This may affect everything from small-business formation to local public goods provision. Studies have shown

that immigrants do not suddenly become more trusting when they arrive in high-trust societies. On the contrary, the relative trust deficit may even persist intergenerationally.[62] Furthermore, the presence of immigrants may erode social capital within the receiving society. (It is not difficult to see how, for instance, neighbours who lack a common language, and thus cannot communicate easily with one another, may have difficulty developing the systems of informal reciprocity that provide a sense of community membership and solidarity.) It is worth noting, as well, that in societies with very high rates of immigration, ethnic groups must be encouraged to develop higher levels of trust not only with members of the majority nation, but with *other* immigrant groups as well. This can be extremely challenging, in a context in which the merest cultural misunderstanding may be interpreted as a slight.[63] Essentially, a group of vulnerable people are being asked to develop trust relations with others, but without being able to rely upon any of the cues or information channels that they have traditionally used to assess trustworthiness.

6. *Patriarchy*. One common feature of successful societies is the recognition of formal equality between the sexes, typically accompanied by high rates of female labour-force participation. Unsuccessful societies are for the most part more, and in some cases extremely, patriarchal. This can generate domestic conflict within immigrant families, particularly among those who try to exercise control over their daughters' behaviour, in a legal and economic environment that offers no support for these forms of paternal authority. It may also contribute to immigrant poverty, to the extent that husbands refuse to let their wives accept paid employment.[64] These attitudes do not immediately change the moment that immigrants arrive in a new society. Female labour-force participation in immigrant groups to Canada, for example, is significantly correlated with source-country female labour-force participation.[65] More generally, many men from patriarchal societies have never had the experience of being subordinate to female authority in the workplace and so may react to it in negative or counterproductive ways. Overall, substantial adjustment may be required in order to adapt to the gender norms of the workplace in successful societies. Indeed, one suspects that an inability to navigate the complexity and shifting character of gender politics, particularly in managerial and professional roles, may be an occupational barrier for some immigrants.

Again, it is important to emphasize that the goal of this discussion is not to cast aspersions on immigrants. Many of these concerns about immigrant integration have been blown out of proportion in public discussion, and exploited by demagogues in order to fuel anti-immigrant sentiment. At the same time, it is important not to ignore or understate the difficulties involved in integrating immigrants into a society, or to allow the desire to avoid offence to limit us from a clear-eyed grasp of these problems. Immigration involves painful adjustment by migrants, and it requires active integration policies from the receiving society. Economists sometimes ignore this, because they focus so much on external incentives that they tend to assume that immigrants will just "re-optimize" as soon as they arrive in a new country and switch over to the prevailing equilibrium behaviour. Those who take social institutions and culture more seriously are likely to recognize that the task is not so simple. There is, however, a tendency in the literature to treat racism from members of the majority nation as the sole problem faced by immigrants – and to regard all other problems within these communities as a consequence of the marginalization generated by racism.[66] This diagnosis of the problem is, I believe, based on a confusion of normative and empirical claims, being driven largely by a desire to hold immigrants themselves blameless for whatever misfortunes may befall them. The issue of blame and responsibility is, in my view, entirely orthogonal to the empirical question of how immigrant integration works, what the distinctive challenges are, and the extent to which exclusion is responsible for the marginalization of certain groups. It seems clear that, even under ideal circumstances, migration has the potential to be hugely disruptive, simply because of how human culture and social institutions work, and the extent to which modern societies rely very heavily on intensive socialization practices to achieve conformity with their institutional demands. Indeed, the generalized aversion to coercion in successful societies increases the relative importance of appropriate intrinsic motivation, and thus of socialization practices, which then serves as a significant barrier to the successful integration of immigrants who have been socialized elsewhere.

Thus the central problem with the open borders position is the failure to recognize that in order to succeed on its own terms, migration must be actively managed by the state. Even if open borders did not generate an overwhelming influx of migrants, the mere fact that the process is uncontrolled would generate unpredictable migration flows, which would in turn make the planning of integration services unreasonably difficult. This would affect small countries in particular, which cannot rely upon the law of large numbers to ensure that the profile of this year's migrants much resembles that of last year's. Furthermore, because effective integration policies involve government partnership with community organizations, it is difficult for the state either to scale up or scale down its services in response to short-term fluctuations. A state bureaucracy can be expanded relatively quickly in response to increased demand for its services. If second-language education services are being delivered through a decentralized network of state-funded community organizations, by contrast, it is much more difficult to expand offerings. Thus it is important that the receiving society have foreseeable, regular immigrant flows. This is unlikely to be achieved under a policy of open borders.

Of course, one could dispense with all these difficulties if one were willing to adopt an extremely idealized specification of the conditions under which open borders would be desirable. Thus there is a sense in which the argument I am developing is merely a pragmatic one, which derives the need for border control from the empirical difficulties that arise when one brings together individuals from different cultural backgrounds. It is, however, hard to imagine how those difficulties could ever fail to arise in the real world. It is, for that reason, unclear where the gain lies in discussing norms that would prevail at a higher level of idealization. Furthermore, the discussion should be informed by the recognition that the consequences of failure in immigrant integration can be quite malign. In the worst-case scenario, it may result in the creation of a permanent underclass of marginalized, alienated, and resentful quasi-citizens. This outcome is in no one's interest. Furthermore, these problems risk becoming worse, as the accumulation of grievances and the hardening of attitudes on all sides make the possibility of successful integration increasingly remote. No plausible conception of social and distributive justice can afford to overlook these possible consequences or fail to support policies – such as immigration intake planning – that are aimed at avoiding them. Yet these policies all presuppose a system of border control.

At the same time, it is important that the policy debate not degenerate into loose talk about the "integrative capacity" of the society. There is a line of anti-immigrant argument that appeals to a vague functionalism, claiming that a "common culture" is required for social cohesion.[67] As a result, any change in the culture, such as a decline in church attendance, or a change in musical styles or modes of dress, is interpreted as a threat to social order. This type of "centre-cannot-hold" argument is problematic for several reasons, not just because many of the claims about social stability are implausible on empirical grounds, but also because it treats pluralism as a threat to social order, thereby suggesting that the domestic commitment to liberalism is as problematic as the openness to immigration. If the claim is to be made that immigrants are destabilizing certain social institutions, it is important that there be real metrics and analysis backing up that claim.[68] For instance, if government is running integration programs through community networks, providing access to language courses, job search, settlement, etc. it is important to quantify the capacity of these resources. Because most immigrants move to cities, it is also important to consider integrative capacity by tracking vacancy rates in rental and social housing, as well as effects on the school system and transportation networks. States must (and typically do) track job market integration and success among immigrants, as well as educational attainment (including the high school dropout rate, higher education participation rates, etc.). Of course, it is also important to keep an eye on the crime rate, not just in the aggregate, but within specific communities as well. And finally, it is important to pay special attention to the fortunes of second-generation immigrants, not just in the above metrics, but also through residential settlement patterns and out-group marriage rates. With first-generation immigrants, there are significant advantages to be had from residential self-segregation, as well as close participation in ethnic networks. This may create the appearance of "ethnic ghettos" within the society, but the only way to determine whether there is genuine marginalization involved requires looking at the second generation and whether they reproduce the same patterns of regional concentration. For example, Muslim immigrants to both Canada and France show lower-than-average levels of female labour-force participation.[69] However, this difference disappears when one looks at second-generation Muslim women in Canada. In France, by contrast, the difference is reduced, but there remains a significant gap. These data lend support to the widespread impression that Muslims in France are less well-integrated than in Canada.[70] Thus it is possible to have a rational, empirically informed discussion about how well a society is succeeding in integrating immigrant groups.[71] No society that is committed to equality can afford to ignore the results of such a discussion when formulating its immigration policies.

3. A Note on the "Kidnapper's Argument"

The argument for border control presented above is intended to show that successful societies are justified in controlling immigration based purely on limitations in the integrative capacity of their own institutions. Contrary to the claims of many cultural conservatives, this capacity is not zero, but neither is it unlimited, as many cosmopolitans seem to assume.[72] For instance, a country like Canada, which every year accepts a number of immigrants and migrants equal to about 1 per cent of its population, is generally thought to be pushing the limits of what is manageable.[73] (The cumulative effects of this migration rate, it should be noted, are significant. It has resulted in the population of its major cities, such as Toronto and Vancouver, being over 50 per cent foreign-born, and others, such as Brampton and Mississauga, being over 60 per cent.) There is presumably a tipping point, beyond which immigrants get so little exposure to the majority society that they have little opportunity to adjust their practices.

I have not suggested that members of these nations exercise collective ownership over the benefits of their institutions (a position defended by Ryan Pevnick[74] and Margaret Moore, among others). I also have not made any incentive argument that individuals will be less likely to construct cooperative schemes if they think that they will be opened up to outsiders. My argument has been purely immanent: to the extent that immigrants are seeking to better their own lives, they risk destroying the very thing that they are seeking if they come in too large numbers. It is important to moderate the flow of migrants into successful societies, in order to ensure that the mutually beneficial equilibria within those societies are reproduced.

There is, however, a well-known line of objection to this style of argument, which applies to my own as well as several others. The "integrative capacity" of a society is not a natural fact about the society, it is a consequence of the behaviour of the members of that society, and in particular, of their willingness to accept immigrants, or to make the adjustments necessary to facilitate immigrant integration. As a result, a society that is racist and intolerant will have more limited integrative capacity than one that is open and tolerant. It seems problematic, however, to suggest that therefore the racist society is not obliged to accept as many immigrants. For instance, Japan is a highly regimented society that is quite inflexible in the application of certain norms. But it is also generally acknowledged to be an extremely racist society (e.g., one in which even individuals born in Japan, but of Korean descent, are routinely subjected to both public abuse and private discrimination).[75] It seems wrong to suggest that Japan might be justified in being closed to immigration, or sharply limiting the intake, because large segments of the population are racist.[76]

This issue has shown up in the literature, particularly in the context of the "social trust" argument for imposing limits on migration. The latter is a somewhat peculiar and circuitous argument, which begins with the observation that the cultural pluralism that results from open migration tends to erode social capital or leads to a decline in "social trust."[77] Countries with lower levels of trust supposedly have less redistributive welfare states, because people are not willing to tolerate the same level of transfer to those who belong to an out-group. Thus it is suggested that migration may not be as effective at promoting distributive justice as its proponents would like to believe, because the presence of migrants increases the level of inequality within the receiving society, by reducing support for a robust welfare state.

Of course, even if this chain of associations were correct, it is not at all obvious that the net effect on inequality would be to increase it, simply because the movement of individuals from an extremely poor country to a rich one may increase their wealth by as much as a hundred-fold, whereas even the most generous welfare states enact transfers that seldom even double the income of their poorest members. Furthermore, the argument is strangely indirect – one would think that the major problem with a decline in social capital in the receiving society is the welfare consequences of a decline in social capital. If communities are losing their capacity for spontaneous or voluntary cooperative action, this means that they will remain mired in a broad range of collective action problems, which will in turn make everyone worse off. The fact that it may also, indirectly, reduce support for a redistributive welfare state seems, by comparison, a much more esoteric, or at least downstream, concern.

The philosophical debate, however, has focused largely on a more subtle problem with the argument. The suggestion that cultural pluralism erodes support for welfare state transfers is rendered plausible for many by the widely held conviction that animosity toward African-Americans is responsible for the relatively weak welfare state in the United States. Certainly the suggestion that black Americans benefit disproportionately from programs like food stamps, or family income support programs, is often made by domestic opponents of those programs. Most Americans also vastly overestimate the extent to which African-Americans are dependent upon government support. Thus the structure of the social trust argument for limiting immigration seems to be: "People are racist and will only support redistribution if the recipients are people who look like them. Introducing too many migrants into the society will cause a racist backlash, undermining support for redistribution, and worsening the condition of the worst-off within that society. Therefore the number of migrants should be limited." Michael Blake refers to this as the "bigot's veto."[78] The obvious concern is that it allows racists to limit migration, by threatening that, if membership is expanded, they will act in an antisocial way aimed at harming the most vulnerable members of their society, thereby undoing whatever gains in social justice might have been achieved through migration.

When put in this way, the argument is reminiscent of what G.A. Cohen referred to as "the kidnapper's argument" for wealth inequality.[79] Cohen was writing in the context of wage inequality, claiming that when the talented refuse to work unless they are paid a higher salary for their services, they are basically just threatening to act in an unjust or antisocial way if others do not give them what they want. In this respect, they are acting like a kidnapper who demands a ransom for the return of one's child. This cannot possibly serve as the basis for any constraint on our conception of justice, Cohen argues, because the demand has no legitimacy. The kidnapper has no entitlement to possession of the child, and so the threat to withhold the child cannot ground any entitlement to the ransom. The racist, according to this line of thinking, is in a comparable situation with respect to migration. Since racism is unjust, the possibility of a racist backlash to migration cannot serve as an argument for limiting the entry of migrants. Succumbing to that would be equivalent to submitting to blackmail.[80]

The core of this argument is correct – if a small group of hardcore racists were to threaten a campaign of violence against migrants, this would be a matter to be handled by the police, not something that would provide any basis for reconsidering existing migration policy. But that having been said, the argument must be handled with caution – much greater caution than is usually exercised – especially when attempting to generalize from these straightforward cases. In particular, it has become a bit too easy to dismiss all resistance to migration as merely an effect of racism or xenophobia.[81] This tendency is particularly pronounced among academics and other elites, whose job security is seldom threatened by migrants, and for whom the major welfare impact of multiculturalism is that the quality of local restaurants improves. By contrast, it is important to recognize that, beyond merely the economic effects of migration, shared culture is an important source of positive network externalities. Individuals derive real and significant benefits from living and working in proximity to others who share their culture, language and religion – this is precisely why one sees residential clustering in ethnic communities. The situation with members of the majority culture is just the same as that with a minority. The difference is that the majority culture is normally just assumed to be secure. This is, however, not necessarily the case – cities like Toronto and Vancouver have seen the dominant cultural group transform from being the overwhelming majority to being less than half of the population within a generation. Within specific residential neighbourhoods the effects are even more dramatic.

When the number of Christians in a neighbourhood declines to the point where the local churches are shuttered, this has a tangible effect on the welfare of local Christians, completely independent of whatever resentment they may feel toward the thriving new mosque or temple that is being constructed next door. Most club goods can be provided only when the number of members exceeds a certain threshold, and so if individuals want to consume them locally, they must take an interest in the consumption preference of their neighbours. There is nothing invidious about this. Ezra Klein has argued that there should be a morally neutral term, such as "demographic anxiety," to describe the concerns that individuals may have about the effects of shifting demographics (and in particular, the effect on their access to quasi-public or club goods whose provision is sensitive to local demographics).[82] Migration policy should take into consideration the legitimate concerns that individuals may have under this heading.

There are certain cases in which this demographic anxiety has been explicitly articulated and factored into migration policy. For instance, while French-Canadians are a national minority group within Canada, with respect to immigrants they form the majority group in the province of Quebec. As a minority group, their language is threatened "externally" by the English majority, and thus they are widely understood to have legitimate demographic anxieties. Large-scale immigration, however, threatens to further undermine their language "internally," because immigrants to Quebec might choose to learn the language of the national majority (English) rather than the local majority (French). Thus Canada has faced the challenge of integrating immigrants, not just into the majority society, but into the society of an internal minority, in a way that is acceptable to that minority. As a result, the only way that it has been possible to have anything resembling a national immigration policy has been to offer a set of very explicit protections for Quebec, and in particular, for the French language, in order to address these demographic anxieties. These same protections, however, have been extended to the English majority as well. So, for instance, Canada is far more explicit with immigrants about the importance of language-learning than many other countries are, in part because it has an "official languages" policy that sets out very clearly the privileged status of English and French.

In the United States, by contrast, there is enormous ambiguity about the status of Spanish – whether signs should be in Spanish, whether there should be Spanish-language public schools, when translation should be offered, and so on. Whether irrationally or not, many Americans find this ambiguity quite unsettling. Those who complain about it are typically accused of racism or xenophobia, on the grounds that no one could plausibly think that the hegemony of English is in any way threatened in America. In Canada, by contrast, there is considerably less ambiguity, because the status of English and/or French as an official language is codified in every province and by the federal government. Again, this is not because anyone thinks that English is threatened. It is because French is threatened, and so its status needs to be codified, and if one is going to codify the status of French, then one has to do English as well. As a result, as a somewhat indirect effect of the need to protect Quebec, Canada has wound up adopting integration policies that reduce the anxiety experienced by members of the majority language group as well.

Thus public opposition to migration involves a complex bundle of concerns, not all of which are illegitimate. There is a core group of people who experience an almost visceral hostility to out-group members and derive positive satisfaction from vindictiveness and cruelty toward them. Public opinion surveys in Canada show that 10–15 per cent of the population qualifies as straightforwardly racist.[83] Furthermore, many racists have learned to use the language of demographic anxiety or social integration to express their hostilities, even though this is not what is animating their concerns. This is a common state of affairs in all countries. It is very difficult to tell whether a rural voter in France, who expresses concern over the integrity of *la France profonde*, is expressing a sincere cultural attachment or is merely an Islamophobe. On the other hand, when demographic anxiety is denied any legitimate expression and silenced by accusations of racism, individuals may gravitate toward more radical or deviant expressions of the concern, such as one finds among explicitly racist political parties. Overuse of "racism" as a term of denunciation may also have the unintended effect of persuading some people that racism is more reasonable than it actually is. Denouncing expressions of rational self-interest by majority group members as racist may persuade them to subordinate their self-interest to concerns over social justice, or it may persuade them that racism is no more than an expression of their rational self-interest. This is what underlies the somewhat puzzling phenomenon that moderate voices are sometimes more racist than they initially appear, and yet self-avowed racists are sometimes more moderate.

Of course, even though not all opposition to immigration is based on racism, it can be very difficult to tell the motives apart. There is, however, little choice but to do what one can to disentangle the two.

For instance, hostility to immigration is often highest in regions that have experienced the least immigration, such as rural areas. Much of this opposition can be discounted, on the grounds that it is not based on any real experience of the successes or failures of immigrant integration. On the other hand, if survey data show increased opposition to immigration in urban areas, where immigrants are actually located, this provides more serious grounds for concern. It is absolutely pointless to insist that immigration rates remain high, as a matter of principle, if the effect of such a policy generates a backlash that both impedes successful integration, and in the extreme, empowers far-right political parties committed to actual closed borders.

Finally, while racists should not be allowed a veto over migration policy, it is important to recognize, as a fact of political sociology, that there is always likely to be a segment of the population that is racist, and that controlling this population is just one of many management problems that must be taken on by the liberal state. By "management" what I mean is that its numbers must be limited and its members regulated in such a way that they are not able to significantly affect the life chances of those who are the object of their hatred, or that they do not poison everyday relations among those who are unafflicted by the primary resentments. Racism, in other words, is a social problem that must be contained. The question that is relevant to migration policy, then, is whether this containment effort is being impeded or undermined by existing immigration rates.

4. Reasonable Accommodation

My discussion of the "integrative capacity" of societies with respect to immigration passed over one very important issue without comment. It is easy to speak as though a society had a fixed set of institutional norms, and that the integration of immigrants involved nothing more than persuading them to adjust their behaviour in order to conform to these rules. The reality is more complicated. Most of the norms governing cooperative interactions represent a compromise between competing interests and considerations. These rules are seldom gratuitously onerous or difficult to comply with. In most cases they are adapted to a particular population and its underlying constellation of interests and preferences, in such a way as to encourage, or at least remove unreasonable barriers to, compliance. As immigration changes the population, the underlying constellation of interests and preferences changes, and that may in turn make certain rules increasingly maladapted. The mismatch that develops between institutions and private preferences can generate a variety of problems, including resistance to integration on the part of immigrants. (Consider, for instance, resistance to participation in organized athletics by immigrants who are uncomfortable with the uniforms worn. This can have significant knock-on effects, since junior athletics are often just a pretext for practices aimed at increasing social capital, not least among parents.) In an open society it will also lead, quite often, to immigrants requesting changes to the rules, or else special exemptions. This is what raises the issue of *reasonable accommodation*.[84] Social integration always involves negotiation. The central question, in regard to immigrants, is when their particular demands for changes and exemptions should be granted and when they should be rejected. In other words, the question is what makes certain accommodations reasonable and others unreasonable.

This process of negotiation, it should be noted, is almost always a source of irritation for some, quite independent of whatever attitudes people may have toward immigrants. (To see this, one need only consider the fact that the renegotiation occurs intergenerationally as well, as young people enter the school system or the workforce, develop relationships, engage in child-rearing, and make what older people typically regard as unreasonable demands for changes in prevailing norms.) Often the irritation is because potentially controversial or divisive issues, that had once been considered settled, risk being reopened by the new demands. It is often impossible merely to extend a particular accommodation without putting the entire arrangement up for renegotiation. In certain cases this is exacerbated by the fact that the prevailing arrangement does not really have a principled basis, but is merely a modus vivendi, which people accept largely because they became tired of fighting over the issue. This is particularly true of religious accommodations among Christian sects, which are often more the product of exhaustion than of principled state policy. In this case, immigrants who come along and request their own accommodations may inadvertently open old wounds. To give just one example, many Canadian provinces have a secular public education system as well as a separate publicly funded Catholic school system. There is no principled basis for this arrangement. "Catholic" was just a convenient shorthand for "French," and the school system is a legacy of the terms under which the British managed the aftermath of the conquest of New France. The arrangement, despite arbitrarily privileging Catholics, is politically stable; the only force that presses for its elimination is the fact that immigrants – Hindu and Muslim in particular – have been demanding public funding for their own religious schools. This is a demand that is very unlikely to be accepted, even though rejecting it creates an obvious inequality in the treatment of religious groups. If forced to be consistent, Canadians would opt to eliminate the Catholic system, rather than permit public funding of all religious schools. Thus from the perspective of Catholics, immigrant demands for equal treatment are "rocking the boat" in a rather unhelpful way. By pointing to the precedent set by an existing, unreasonable accommodation, in order to demand a further, unreasonable accommodation, they create pressure for the elimination of all these accommodations.

This example is helpful, in that it illustrates one difficulty that specifically liberal societies encounter in immigrant integration. The reason that state funding of Catholic schools, but not other religious schools, proves awkward is that the Canadian state is not committed to the truth of the Catholic religion. It differs, in this respect, from a state like Argentina, in which Catholicism is constitutionally privileged. Similarly, states like Singapore that have a set of constitutionally entrenched "shared values" might have some grounds for exhibiting an uncompromising stance toward immigrants. Most of the countries that accept large numbers of immigrants, by contrast, are essentially liberal, which means that they are committed to state neutrality, not just toward religious conviction and practice, but also toward more general "conceptions of the good," including such questions as may arise in family structure, personal relationships, residential patterns, sexual mores, labour-force participation, education and career development, diet and health, and a vast number of other issues. Given the diversity that inevitably results from freedom of choice in these domains, the existing institutions of the society already constitute a very complex compromise with respect to competing views, while the state aspires to refrain from arbitrarily privileging any one conception, especially when dealing with measures that will be coercively imposed. Thus when immigrants arrive and begin to make demands for accommodations, they are merely suing, as it were, for something that they are already owed, under the principles that govern the prevailing arrangements. In other words, what they are asking for is usually just consistency or even-handedness in the application of principles that are already institutionalized in existing practices. Thus the demands cannot be dismissed summarily. Even if the demands are ultimately rejected, they must be taken seriously in each case. This may seem obvious, but it is worth stating explicitly, in order to explain why the sort of frankly chauvinistic response to these demands (which, for example, Michael Walzer at one point seemed willing to entertain)[85] – "if you come here, you must accept our culture" – is not only philosophically indefensible, but usually politically infeasible as well.

Another way of putting the point is to say that most demands for reasonable accommodation made by immigrants are not grounded in an appeal to the truth, correctness, or goodness of the values held by those groups. They are simply based on an appeal to the principle of equality that the liberal state is already committed to.[86] Consider, for instance, the conflict that arose in Ontario over the supposed use of "sharia law" to settle certain disputes under family law.[87] What Muslims had been using, in fact, were provisions of Ontario law that allowed the parties in certain disputes, including divorce, to opt for private arbitration (the outcome of which would subsequently be enforced by the court). This provision had been used primarily by religious Jews who do not recognize civil divorce. When Muslim immigrants began to arrive in large numbers, they naturally began to make use of these same provisions, which is what in turn provoked a backlash. (To make things more complex, the opposition was spearheaded by the "liberal" Canadian Council of Muslim Women, which objected to some of the decisions being made by conservative imams and wanted them overruled by the courts.)[88] The arrangement, however, obviously involved no endorsement of sharia principles by the Canadian state, and Muslims did not need to appeal to any aspect of their own religious doctrine to defend it. All they needed to point to, in order to defend the "accommodation," was the obvious violation of equality that would be involved in making the option of private arbitration available to Jews but not Muslims. (The province of Ontario acknowledged the obvious force of this argument, and so when it ultimately bowed to public pressure to ban "sharia" divorce, it wound up revoking the option of private arbitration for everyone, and thus for all religious groups.)

As Cécile Laborde has shown, most of the everyday demands for accommodation made by ethnic minority groups in liberal states are actually just demands for equal treatment. For instance, she argues that many of the self-declared defenders of French *laïcité*, "in their eagerness to discount many Muslim requests as moves towards the unacceptable publicization of religion, and as involving breaches of republican equality, fail to see that most religious demands are not compensatory or exemption-based, but simply require the application of the current regime of *laïcité* to Islam."[89] The creation of dedicated prayer-spaces in public buildings, or "the appointment of Muslim 'chaplains' in schools, the army, hospitals and prisons," are all just instances of Muslims suing for benefits that are already enjoyed by Jews and Christians. The changes are, in this respect, not accommodations at all.[90] This observation is what underlies the formula advanced by the Bouchard-Taylor report, which calls for "firmness" on fundamental norms, combined with "flexibility" in their application.[91]

Similarly, many "exemption-based" demands amount to little more than an appeal to the principle of equality. The impression that exemptions necessarily involve some violation of equality is, of course, encouraged by the popular view that treating people equally involves treating them all the same. Few philosophers are tempted by such a simplistic analysis. Perhaps the most sustained philosophical defence of the view that exemptions conflict with equality was put forward by Brian Barry, who developed what he called a "pincer argument" against the granting of religious-based exemptions. He claimed that, if the rule is in fact justified, then it should be applied to all. If, however, there is a good case to be made for an exemption, then that is actually an argument against having any rule at all. "Either the case for the law (or some version of it) is strong enough to rule out exemptions, or the case that can be made for exemptions is strong enough to suggest that there should be no law anyway."[92] He gives multiple examples, but perhaps the most useful is that of Sikhs requesting exemption from various safety regulations – such as the wearing of hard hats on constructions sites – in order to permit them to wear turbans. Barry's argument is that either safety is important, in which case hard hats should be mandatory, or it is not that important, in which case everyone should be free to choose.

This argument is unpersuasive for several reasons, not least because it involves an overly simplistic view of how most rules and regulations function, and how many exemptions are already built into existing arrangements (most having nothing to do with religion).[93] Consider, for instance, something as simple as the speed limit on an urban road. Like most norms, this represents a compromise between the interests of different groups. Residents and pedestrians typically would like vehicular traffic to move slowly, reducing both noise and accident risk. Drivers, on the other hand, would like to be able to move through as quickly as possible. Speed limits are set by weighing the interests of these two (primary) parties against one another. This generates the usual pattern, in which speed limits are lower in residential neighbourhoods and areas with significant pedestrian traffic (e.g., near schools), higher in low-density areas or designated thoroughfare streets. The weighing of interests is governed by a norm of equality, specifying that everyone's interests are to be given roughly equal weight – so that, for instance, the rules do not arbitrarily privilege the interests of drivers over pedestrians.[94] (And to the extent that equality is violated, opposition to the rules is typically based on precisely that point.)

At the same time, we recognize that the interest groups in question are not entirely homogeneous. Most drivers, for instance, may be commuters, who want to get home sooner rather than later, but do not have any particularly vital interest at stake. Some drivers, by contrast, may have much more important reasons for wanting to get to their destination quickly – perhaps they are bringing someone to the hospital, or rushing to put out a fire. Instead of just averaging across these different groups, in order to determine what weight to assign to the interests of drivers on the whole, what we do instead is create a rule that reflects the weight assigned to the interests of the typical driver, in this case a commuter, but then allow for certain *exceptions*. In particular, we allow a designated set of emergency vehicles the right to exceed the speed limit with impunity. Rather than averaging everything together, then raising speed limits everywhere by 2 km/h, in recognition of the fact that a small number of drivers have very urgent business, it makes more sense to keep the speed limits low, to reflect the importance of the typical driver's business, and then allow an exemption for those who happen to have urgent business.

If one considers Barry's examples, such as the issue of Sikh workers wanting exemption from hard-hat regulations, one can see that they have the same structure. Worker safety regulations always involve a compromise between a range of competing interests. The reason that workers must be forced to wear hard hats is partly that workers do not like them, since headgear can be uncomfortable, hot, and easily misplaced. If comfort were not an issue, workplace injuries could be reduced by requiring construction workers to wear Kevlar vests at all times. The question is where one should draw the line. The answer is typically determined by balancing worker interests against the prudential and paternalistic interests of the firm and the state (e.g., the worker's compensation insurance system). Thus hard hats and steel-toed boots are considered reasonable, as are safety harnesses in certain jobs, but Kevlar vests are not. Part of the reason that hard hats are imposed is that the discomfort workers experience from wearing them is not very great, and so the interest that is being overruled by the regulation is not particularly weighty. This is not true for Sikh workers, however, who have, in addition to the weak reason of comfort, a stronger reason, grounded in religious observance, not to wear hard hats. Given the exceptional nature of this group, it does not make sense to average everything together and change the rule slightly for everyone. The natural response is just to keep the rule for the typical case and to allow an exception for the one group. This is an application of, not a violation of, the principle of equality. The exemption does not mean that one person's interests are being assigned greater weight than anyone else's, it is simply a reflection of the fact that different people have significantly different interests at stake, none of which may be disregarded.

It is because so much of the debate over reasonable accommodation involves merely the extension of already-institutionalized liberal principles of equality that theorists like Will Kymlicka have been able to refrain from engaging in "grand theory," or foundational argumentation, and instead just focus on rebutting bad arguments *against* the granting of certain accommodations. Much of the difficult work of street-level multiculturalism involves simply trying to determine how strongly different people feel about the way that the rules impinge upon their particular interests. For instance, it is common for conservative or fundamentalist groups within religious communities to push for particular exemptions, not so much because members of those communities are being genuinely inconvenienced by the rules, but more as a way of advancing their own agenda – such as promoting stricter forms of religious observance – within the community. Whether the exemption is granted or not, provoking conflict over the issue is typically win-win for those groups, because it enhances the association between that practice and the identity of the group. Certain demands for accommodation also have a "me-too" quality, where groups ask for an exemption only because others have been granted one, and so want it merely as a symbolic affirmation that they are of equal status, not because any first-order interests are at stake. As a result, the simple goal of treating everyone equally quickly produces very complex hermeneutic challenges, and much of the everyday business of reasonable accommodation involves a dialogue aimed at sorting out the underlying motivation for various claims, and the importance of the interests at stake.[95]

At the same time, there are more radical demands for accommodation, as well as theoretical approaches to understanding liberalism, that reveal the limits of the straightforward egalitarian approach. While it is worth pointing out that many demands made by immigrants accept the basic framework of a liberal society, and in particular, the norm of equality, certain others do not. Where demands for accommodation become difficult is when immigrant groups request exemption *from* basic liberal norms, because this demand raises a question about where liberalism derives its authority, such that its principles can be taken to trump the non-liberal practices or principles that inform other traditions. This is where the debate over reasonable accommodation becomes a debate about what the *limits* of accommodation should be.

With the controversy over private religious arbitration in Ontario, for instance, the "sharia courts" that were set up (in particular, by the self-declared Islamic Institute for Civil Justice), which alarmed many observers, were not real courts, just private organizations offering arbitration services.[96] At the same time, the Saudi-backed Muslim World League muddied the waters quite considerably by calling for an arrangement under which Muslims would actually be exempt from Ontario family law, and subject to genuine sharia tribunals, whose substantive judgments would have legal force.[97] This proposal was never seriously entertained by the government, but it did raise a difficult theoretical question about why liberal norms should be privileged in these debates, especially when they conflict with the norms of minority cultures. The Muslim World League's demand for an exemption in this case was not defended through any internal appeal to existing liberal principles; on the contrary, it rested upon a relativization and rejection of liberalism (or at least the liberal norm of equality).

These debates strike at the heart of what Nancy Rosenblum refers to as the "liberal expectancy" – the expectation that immigrant groups will "take on liberal democracy as a moral commitment," so that "the particular roles and rules of cooperation within groups increasingly conform to liberal democratic norms."[98] Treating such an expectation normatively seems to raise theoretical difficulties, from two distinct directions. From one direction, there are "thick" conceptions of liberalism – such as various forms of "perfectionist" liberalism[99] – that regard liberalism as grounded in a set of values (such as a commitment to autonomy or freedom), or worse, that regard it as merely an outgrowth of the Christian tradition. From this perspective, liberalism looks like just one set of culturally parochial values among many, making it difficult to see why, in a pluralist society, everyone should be subject to its principles. The law governing divorce in Ontario, for instance, assumes a fundamental equality between men and women, so that both sexes enjoy equal rights in all proceedings. Both traditional Jewish and Muslim religious law, by contrast, are asymmetric, granting rights to the husband that are not enjoyed by the wife. Insisting that everything be done in accordance with secular civil law then starts to look like one group using its majority position to impose its values, or its religious ideas, upon others who do not share them. Granting this is an enormous concession by liberals to their critics, which in turn makes it difficult for them to say what is wrong with illiberal groups trying to impose *their* values on everyone else.

From the other direction, difficulties emerge for conceptions of liberalism that are overly "thin," such as the one advanced by Chandran Kukathas. Kukathas uses the image of a liberal "archipelago" in order to suggest that liberal societies should be, like islands dispersed in the sea, composed of a set of "communities" or "associations," each of which exercises authority over the individual in its own way. What makes the society "liberal" is that "individuals are at liberty to reject the authority of an association in order to place themselves under the authority of another," and more generally, "individuals are at liberty to repudiate the authority of the wider society in placing themselves under the authority of some other association."[100] For religious and cultural groups, what this means in practice is that liberalism requires no more than a "right of exit." The group need not be *internally* tolerant, much less committed to equality; on the contrary, the society could be no more than a loose conglomeration of internally illiberal communities, or worse, an incubator for illiberal social movements.

What both of these views – the "thick" and the "thin" – have in common is that they lack the resources to reject demands that seem patently unreasonable, such as the one made by the Muslim World League. This theoretical difficulty has practical correlates, often taking the form of a certain timidity or insecurity of the receiving society when responding to demands for accommodation that seem, at least on the face of it, unreasonable. What is needed is a conception of liberalism that is thicker than the minimal variants endorsed by Kukathas and others, but that can nevertheless claim to be *neutral* with respect to all of these conflicting demands, and thus cannot be dismissed as just one more set of values among others. In other words, what is wanted is some form of liberalism that redeems the promissory note issued by Rawls, that it be "freestanding" in relation to the different "comprehensive doctrines" in the society.[101] Such a doctrine would be able to distinguish "reasonable" from "unreasonable" comprehensive doctrines in a non-question-begging way, which in turn would allow it to assert the supremacy of its own principles in the face of demands stemming from unreasonable doctrines.[102] The challenge for this conception lies in the requirement that the distinction not be question-begging. In this respect, Rawls was not of much assistance, with his repeated suggestion that his conception of "political liberalism" merely articulated ideas implicit in the public political culture of democratic societies.[103] Others have tried to provide more secure foundations, but in so doing, have wound up defining what is reasonable in a way that makes it practically synonymous with what is compatible with liberal principles. Martha Nussbaum, for instance, argues that political liberalism need only tolerate reasonable comprehensive doctrines, where the latter are understood as ones that include "a serious commitment to the value of equal respect for persons as a political value," or elsewhere, that recognize "the equality of persons and the importance of equal respect."[104] These arguments all seem to be moving in a very small circle, which to the outsider can easily be mistaken for dogmatic insistence upon liberal principles.

In order to break out of the circle, it is helpful the think back to Rawls's initial presentation of his view, in which he articulated the fundamental motivation for the development of a theory of justice. The problem that he was responding to, which called for the development of a set of normative principles, was the need to establish a *system of cooperation*. In the opening pages of *A Theory of Justice*, Rawls began by observing that, despite having fundamentally different goals and interests, individuals are nevertheless capable of engaging in mutually beneficial cooperation.[105] The problem, however, is that there are various ways of organizing the cooperative scheme, and of dividing up its benefits and burdens, and seldom is any one arrangement imposed by the structure of the interaction. As a result, a set of principles is required to determine the precise modalities of cooperation. These principles form the core of a liberal theory of justice. What makes these principles neutral, in this early sense of the term, is that they are tailored to the specific task of promoting cooperation, and as such are neutral with respect to whatever first-order interests motivate the parties to engage in interaction. It is the hallmark of cooperative interactions that they leave each individual better off *by his or her own lights*.

One might easily contest this conception of neutrality on the grounds that social institutions do much more than just promote cooperation, and thus Rawls's "political ontology" remains controversial.[106] Yet these concerns are not relevant when discussing the specific terms of immigrant integration, because the distributive justice argument for immigration is based upon the obligation of successful societies *to extend their system of cooperation*, in such a way that more people can enjoy its benefits. It is helpful, at this point, to recall my earlier claim, that *immigrants are seeking to become participants in a more successful system of cooperation than the one they left behind*. Since this system of cooperation is built upon, and enabled by, the principles of liberal justice, it would be perverse for immigrants to arrive and then seek exemption from these very same principles. It would be, at very least, collectively self-defeating – like the tourists seeking pristine wilderness, or a secluded beach, destroying the very thing that they have come to enjoy. From this perspective, the reason that liberal principles of justice are privileged, and cannot be treated as merely one tradition among many, is that these principles constitute the foundation of the system of cooperation that the immigration system is trying to extend.[107]

This point has been largely overlooked in the philosophical debate, as a result of the tendency to think of liberalism as just one abstract philosophical theory in contention with others, ignoring the fact that it also represents the articulation of the set of ideas that inform existing practices in a very wide range of social institutions, including both the market economy and the welfare state.[108] The two central principles of neutralist liberalism are efficiency and equality. The principle of (Pareto) efficiency suggests that outcomes in which at least one person is better off, and no one is worse off, are to be preferred. Politically, this principle has the effect of committing liberal societies to resolving collective action problems, either directly through the state, or indirectly through market institutions and private law. The principle of equality specifies that cooperative arrangements in which no one has an incentive to switch places with anyone else are to be preferred. Politically, this has the effect of licensing the extensive system of equality rights enjoyed by citizens in modern political orders. Each of these principles promotes cooperation by eliminating a certain obvious objection to any proposed arrangement, which would automatically and inevitably arise if it were violated. Thus if the goal is to cooperate, and this can only be accomplished by achieving some agreement about the specific modalities of cooperation, then these principles naturally suggest themselves. This occurs not just theoretically, but practically as well, resulting in them becoming actually institutionalized throughout liberal societies.

The most obvious example is the market economy, which, despite the claims made by many of its advocates, is an extremely counter-intuitive institutional arrangement, one that relies very heavily upon the commitment to liberal principles. Most importantly, it depends upon the shift in juridical thinking that Max Weber described as the move from "substantive" to "formal" jurisprudence. In order to have markets, and in particular in order to have the free movement of prices that is the most important institutional feature of markets, courts must be willing to refrain from adjudicating particular private disputes in terms of substantive or first-order conceptions of the good (such as those that motivated traditional conceptions of the "just price"), and must be willing to rule on the basis of purely formal notions, such as the will of the parties as expressed in a private contract. Similarly, if one considers the rise of the welfare state in the twentieth century, much of it can be understood as a consequence of the commitment to resolving market failures, guided by the norm of efficiency.[109] The idea that it is the *state's* responsibility to ensure that individuals have adequate health insurance, or parks, or income supports, is not entirely obvious, and arises as a consequence of the commitment to liberal principles of justice, which see the state largely as a device for mediating transactions between individuals conceived of as equal citizens.

Thus it is not difficult to draw a connection between the features of successful societies that attract immigrants and the underlying commitment to liberal principles in the basic institutional structure of those societies. There are, of course, non-liberal or partially liberal societies, some of which have achieved levels of economic success approaching those of fully liberal societies. In most cases they have done so by selectively minimizing pluralism. The argument developed here does not apply in such contexts. (Most such countries, including China, are not open to immigration anyway, in part because they are non-liberal.) It applies rather to the circumstances of liberal societies, which have become successful, not by limiting pluralism, but rather by organizing their institutions around principles of justice that minimize conflict under conditions of pluralism. Precisely because the wealth, or more generally, the success of these societies depends upon the institutionalization of these principles, the commitment to respecting liberal norms is already implicit in the immigrant's own will, when he or she comes, seeking to enjoy the benefits of those institutions.

There is a close conceptual connection between this neutralist conception of liberalism and the preoccupation with immigrant integration that informs my argument regarding border control and admission policies. Indeed, the distinction between integration and assimilation tacitly presupposes an arrangement under which the basic institutional structure of the society does not simply impose a particular set of cultural practices, along with whatever conception of the good informs them. It is noteworthy, in this regard, that neither the thick nor the thin conceptions of liberalism are able to make sense of the integration/assimilation distinction. On the one hand, the thin version proposed by Kukathas does not require either – it would be perfectly acceptable in his model for immigrants to arrive in a society only to secede internally, the way that, for example, Hutterites in Western Canada have. The central problem with such an arrangement is that, in so doing, these groups would deprive themselves of the primary benefits that come from living in a successful society, and that liberals, being committed to equality, are not comfortable with the consequences. As a result, they are prone to providing these communities with benefits that can, in turn, only be fully earned through more extensive participation in mainstream society. This creates conflict in the broader society as well as pressure on these communities, both of which lead to greater integration.

Thick versions of liberalism have the opposite problem, in that they blur the distinction in unhelpful ways between integration and assimilation, generating the impression that the only way to integrate, in effect, is to assimilate. David Miller, for instance, suggests that learning the language of a society shades over into acquiring the culture, and so it is best to confront immigrants with a sort of frank parochialism about the centrality of the majority culture.[110] Although it is not stated quite so explicitly, one gets the impression that his conception of successful immigrant integration includes the development of a taste for scones, and if not church attendance, then at least an appreciation of the lyrical qualities of the Book of Common Prayer. The central problem with this view is that it underplays what is really the most important basis for the success of liberal societies over the years, which is their capacity to manage cultural pluralism, allowing individuals to set aside a great many differences, in order to work together in ways that improve everyone's condition. The strength of neutralist liberalism is that it tries to articulate the principles underlying this. While these efforts remain controversial, my central contention here has been that, in the specific case of immigrant integration, they should be less so, precisely because the focus of immigration policies is on expanding the scope, and thus diffusing the benefits of, the core system of cooperation in successful societies.

5. Conclusion

The theory that I have proposed here is intended to answer two of the most difficult questions that arise in debates over migration and multiculturalism. The first concerns the question of border control, where some liberals have had great difficulty seeing how states could be justified in excluding migrants at all. The second involves accommodations demanded by minority ethnic or religious groups who reject basic liberal norms. Again, liberals have had difficulty explaining why their tolerance for pluralism should stop as soon as it is their own principles that are being challenged. In both cases, they have risked living up to the old caricature of the liberal as one who "cannot bring himself to take his own side in a fight."

In both cases, the difficulty experienced by liberals stems from a failure to see the interconnection between liberal principles of justice and the extensive systems of cooperation that have been established in liberal societies. The best way to understand liberal principles of justice, I have suggested, is to regard them as normative principles that have been crafted with the specific aim of facilitating mutually beneficial cooperation among individuals despite first-order disagreement over fundamental questions of value. The fact that liberalism has been relatively successful at achieving these cooperative benefits is what accounts for the success of liberal societies – the fact that they are generally more prosperous, peaceful, democratic, and well-ordered than the alternatives. Liberalism has facilitated the development of more extensive and more intensive systems of cooperation than any other political ideology. It is precisely because of the benefits of these cooperative arrangements that liberal societies are the overwhelming destination of choice among prospective migrants. Because of the robustness and scalability of liberal institutions, these societies also are in a position to confer enormous benefits upon these migrants by accepting them as members. And yet they must do so in a way that is consistent with the reproduction of the basic institutional structure. This is a particular challenge in the case of migration, precisely because liberal societies rely so heavily upon intensive socialization practices, and thus internalized constraint, to maintain aspects of their liberal character, and yet have no opportunity to socialize incoming migrants. Thus a serious question arises about the capacity of these societies to successfully integrate large numbers of new members. It is this challenge, and the pragmatic imperatives imposed by the policies needed to manage it, that requires a system of controlled migration, and thus of border control.

The same basic conceptual framework can be used to explain why liberal principles are privileged when determining the extent of reasonable pluralism (i.e., why liberalism is not just one more system of values among others, all of which should be accorded equal standing). There is no need to provide a foundational philosophical justification for liberalism, showing why it is exceptional. The appropriate response is merely to observe that liberal principles are privileged because they represent an abstract articulation of the principles governing the basic institutional structure of liberal societies. One cannot reasonably expect to enjoy the benefits of a liberal society without accepting the guiding principles of the institutions that produce those benefits. Thus the acceptance of core liberal principles is an implicit consequence of the desire to become a member of a liberal society.

NOTES

1 One particularly striking poll put the number of people in the world who would like to migrate at 750 million, or 15 per cent of total population. Gallup Migration Research Center, "Number of Potential Migrants

Worldwide Tops 750 Million," *World Poll*, 10 December 2018. Of these, 47 million select Canada as their top destination, a country that at the time of writing has a population of only 37 million. Current intake of immigrants in Canada is 340,000 per year, one of the highest per capita rates in the world. Overall, more than two-thirds of global migrants go to one of only eighteen countries.

2 Here I follow Will Kymlicka in drawing the very important distinction between ethnic and national minority groups. See *Multicultural Citizenship* (Oxford: Oxford University Press, 1995).

3 The term "reasonable accommodation" has become a standard term in Canadian debates over multiculturalism, thanks to the discussion surrounding the Bouchard-Taylor commission. See Gérard Bouchard and Charles Taylor, *Building the Future: A Time for Reconciliation* (Quebec City: Gouvernement du Québec, 2008). The term "receiving society" is a somewhat awkward translation of the useful term *"societé d'acceuil"* used in Quebec. It might be translated more literally as "welcoming society," however that would be tendentious, since societies vary a great deal in how welcoming they are.

4 For my own past attempt to link them, see Joseph Heath, "Immigration, Multiculturalism, and the Social Contract," *Canadian Journal of Law and Jurisprudence* 10, no. 2 (1997): 343–61.

5 Joseph Carens, "Aliens and Citizens: The Case for Open Borders," *Review of Politics* 49, no. 2 (1987): 251–73; Carens, *The Ethics of Immigration* (Oxford: Oxford University Press, 2013); Philip Cole, *Philosophies of Exclusion* (Edinburgh: Edinburgh University Press, 2001); Arash Abizadeh, "Cooperation, Pervasive Impact, and Coercion: On the Scope (not Site) of Distributive Justice," *Philosophy and Public Affairs* 35, no. 4 (2007): 318–58.

6 Carens, *Ethics of Immigration*, 225.

7 Carens is an exponent of the former view, Abizadeh of the latter.

8 Joseph Carens, "Migration and Morality: A Liberal Egalitarian Perspective," in *Free Movement: Ethical Issues in the Transnational Migration of People and Money*, ed. Brian Barry and Robert Goodin (University Park, PA: Penn State Press, 1992), 25–47.

9 Ayelet Shachar, *The Birthright Lottery* (Cambridge, MA: Harvard University Press, 2009).

10 See Peter H. Schuck, "The Disconnect between Public Attitudes and Policy Outcomes in Immigration," in *Debating Immigration*, ed. Carol M. Swain (Cambridge: Cambridge University Press, 2007), 17–31.

11 Most importantly, David Miller, *National Responsibility and Global Justice* (Oxford: Oxford University Press, 2007); Miller, *Strangers in Our Midst* (Cambridge, MA: Harvard University Press, 2016).

12 For the non-liberal, see Michael Walzer, *Spheres of Justice* (New York: Basic Books, 1983); for the exotic, see Thomas Nagel, "The Problem of Global

Justice," *Philosophy and Public Affairs* 33, no. 2 (2005): 113–47; Michael Blake, "Distributive Justice, State Coercion and Autonomy," *Philosophy and Public Affairs* 30, no. 3 (2002): 257–96; Michael Blake, "Immigration," in *Blackwell Companion to Applied Ethics*, ed. Christopher Wellman (Oxford: Blackwell Publishers, 2003), 224–37.
13 Carens, "Migration and Morality," 28.
14 As David Miller and others have observed. See David Miller, "Immigration: The Case for Limits," in *Contemporary Debates in Applied Ethics*, ed. Andrew I. Cohen and Christopher Heath Wellman (Oxford: Blackwell, 2005), 195. Also Miller, *Strangers in Our Midst*, 50–2.
15 Margaret Moore, *A Political Theory of Territory* (Oxford: Oxford University Press, 2015); Christopher Heath Wellman, "Immigration and Freedom of Association," *Ethics* 119 (2008): 109–41; Ryan Pevnick, *Immigration and the Constraints of Justice* (Cambridge: Cambridge University Press, 2011).
16 Roger Nett, "The Civil Right We Are Not Ready For: The Right of Free Movement of People on the Face of the Earth," *Ethics* 81, no. 3 (1971): 219.
17 Moore, *Political Theory of Territory*, 203–4.
18 Cole, in *Philosophies of Exclusion*, presents the case as though it involved a negative freedom of movement.
19 Wellman, "Immigration and Freedom of Association." See also Christopher Heath Wellman and Philip Cole, *Debating Immigration* (Oxford: Oxford University Press, 2011).
20 E.g., see Moore, *Political Theory of Territory*, 34–54.
21 Carens, *Ethics of Immigration*, 225.
22 Carens, "Migration and Morality." See also Chandran Kukathas, "The Case for Open Immigration," in *Contemporary Debates in Applied Ethics*, ed. A.I. Cohen and C.H. Wellman (Oxford: Blackwell, 2005), 211.
23 Shachar, *Birthright Lottery*, 2.
24 Jeffrey D. Sachs and Andrew M. Warner, "The Big Rush, Natural Resource Booms and Growth," *Journal of Development Economics* 59, no. 1 (1999): 43–76; John Kay, *The Truth about Markets* (London: Allen Lane, 2003), 40–51.
25 Charles Beitz, *Political Theory and International Relations* (Princeton, NJ: Princeton University Press, 1979), 137.
26 OECD, "Level of GDP per Capita and Productivity," https://stats.oecd.org/Index.aspx?DataSetCode=PDB_LV.
27 World Bank, "Employment in Agriculture (% of Total Employment)," https://data.worldbank.org/indicator/SL.AGR.EMPL.ZS?end=2010&start=1997.
28 Robert Solow, "A Contribution to the Theory of Economic Growth," *Quarterly Journal of Economics* 70, no. 1 (1956): 65–94. Note the absence of any reference to resources.
29 *Economist*, "A Tightening Grip," 12 March 2015.
30 Abdurrahman Aydemir and Chris Robinson, *Return and Onward Migration among Working Age Men* (Ottawa: Statistics Canada, 2006), 21.

31 Paul A. Samuelson, "International Trade and the Equalisation of Factor Prices," *Economic Journal* 63 (1948): 163–84.
32 The philosophical debate on migration has proceeded with no mention of the fact that free movement of capital and goods is in many respects a substitute for the movement of people. This is true not only of open borders advocates. Stephen Macedo, for instance, makes the case for limiting migration to the United States from Mexico based on the impact of Mexican migrants on the wages of unskilled American labour. "The Moral Dilemma of U.S. Immigration Policy," in *Debating Immigration*, ed. Carol M. Swain (Cambridge: Cambridge University Press, 2007), 63–81. He does not mention that free trade in goods and capital (which the United States was committed to at the time) produces the same effect.
33 World Bank, "Ease of Doing Business Rankings," http://www.doingbusiness.org/rankings.
34 Dani Rodrik, Arvind Subramanian, and Francesco Trebbi, "Institutions Rule: The Primacy of Institutions over Geography and Integration in Economic Development," *Journal of Economic Growth* 9, no. 2 (2004): 131–65.
35 Paul Collier, *Exodus* (Oxford: Oxford University Press, 2013), 195–7.
36 John Rawls, *The Law of Peoples* (Cambridge, MA: Harvard University Press, 1999), 106. See also Joseph Heath, "Rawls on Global Distributive Justice: A Defence," *Canadian Journal of Philosophy Supplementary Volume*, ed. Daniel Weinstock (Lethbridge: University of Calgary Press, 2007), 197–8.
37 Matthew Weaver, "Angela Merkel: German Multiculturalism Has 'Utterly Failed,'" *Guardian*, 17 October 2010.
38 See Carens, *Ethics of Immigration*, 65–78.
39 I adopt this term from Peter A. Hall and Michèle Lamont, eds., *Successful Societies* (Cambridge: Cambridge University Press, 2009), 2.
40 Ray Fisman and Miriam A. Golden, *Corruption: What Everyone Needs to Know* (Oxford: Oxford University Press, 2017).
41 Joseph Heath, "Business Ethics and Moral Motivation: A Criminological Perspective," *Journal of Business Ethics* 83, no. 4 (2008): 595–614.
42 The classic account of this is Peter Maas, *Serpico* (New York: Viking, 1973).
43 Robert Innes and Arnab Mitra, "Is Dishonesty Contagious?," *Economic Inquiry* 51, no. 1 (2013): 722–34.
44 Francis Fukuyama, *Trust* (New York: Free Press, 1996), 84–90.
45 Fukuyama, *The Origins of Political Order* (New York: Farrar, Straus and Giroux, 2011), 229–41.
46 William Easterly, *The White Man's Burden* (New York: Penguin, 2006), 38–51.
47 Halsey Rogers and Margaret Koziol, *Provider Absence Surveys in Education and Health* (Washington, DC: World Bank, 2011); also Nazmul Chaudhury, Jeffrey Hammer, Michael Kremer, Karthik Muralidharana, and F. Halsey

Rogers, "Missing in Action: Teacher and Health Worker Absence in Developing Countries," *Journal of Economic Perspectives* 20, no. 1 (2006): 91–116.
48 Abhijit V. Banerjee, Rachel Glennerster, and Esther Duflo, "Putting a Band-Aid on a Corpse: Incentives for Nurses in the Indian Public Health Care System," *Journal of the European Economic Association* 6, nos. 2–3 (2008): 487–500. For discussion, see Daron Acemoglu and James A. Robinson, *Why Nations Fail* (New York: Crown, 2012), 449–50.
49 Fisman and Golden, *Corruption*, 234–45.
50 Milan Vaishnav, *When Crime Pays* (New Haven, CT: Yale University Press, 2017).
51 Collier, *Exodus*, 67–9.
52 Andrea Ichino and Giovanni Maggi, "Work Environment and Individual Background: Explaining Regional Shirking Differentials in a Large Italian Firm," *Quarterly Journal of Economics* 115, no. 3 (2000): 1057–90.
53 Cécile Laborde, *Critical Republicanism* (Oxford: Oxford University Press, 2008).
54 Consider the instructive comparison drawn by Irene Bloemraad between immigrant and refugee community groups in Boston and Toronto. The US government tends to fund refugee settlement, while treating immigrants with benign neglect. The Canadian government, by contrast, has active settlement programs for both groups. Bloemraad shows that levels of community organization in Vietnamese refugee groups are comparable in Boston and Toronto, but far less developed in the Boston Portuguese community (an immigrant group). See Bloemraad, *Becoming a Citizen* (Berkeley: University of California Press, 2006), 164.
55 Bloemraad, *Becoming a Citizen*, 48. On settlement programs in Canada compared to the United States, see 118–32.
56 This was the bombing of Air India flight 182 in 1985, in which 329 people, including 268 Canadians, were killed.
57 Prominent examples include, historically, the Irish Republican Army and the Tamil Tigers, and ongoing, the state of Israel.
58 John Monahan, Rima Berns-McGown, and Michael Morden, *The Perception and Reality of "Imported Conflict" in Canada* (Toronto: Mosaic Institute, 2014).
59 This also works in reverse. The US prison system, broadly construed, is one of the most criminogenic institutions in the world, and there are several instances of violent gangs having been incubated in US prisons, then exported back to poorer countries when members are deported. The MS-13 gang in El Salvador is perhaps the most significant example. The United States is, however, unique in this regard, and so the example mainly serves to illustrate the more general principle, that criminal gangs often extend their reach through migrant communities (partly

because of the economic importance of drug smuggling to many of these organizations).
60 Raymond Fisman and Edward Miguel, "Corruption, Norms and Legal Enforcement: Evidence from Diplomatic Parking Tickets," *Journal of Political Economy* 115, no. 6 (2007): 1020–48.
61 Peg Tyre, "How Sophisticated Test Scams from China Are Making Their Way in the U.S.," *Atlantic*, 21 March 2016. Shashank Bengali, "India Test Cheating Stirs Outrage – Then People Start Dying," *L.A. Times*, 17 July 2015.
62 Yann Algan and Pierre Cahuc, "Inherited Trust and Growth," *American Economic Review* 100, no. 5 (2010): 2060–92.
63 For examples of these difficulties, see Bloemraad, *Becoming a Citizen*, 145.
64 Abdolmohammad Kazemipur, *The Muslim Question in Canada* (Vancouver: UBC Press, 2014), 120–1, 139.
65 Kristyn Frank and Feng Hou, *Source-Country Female Labour Force Participation and the Wages of Immigrant Women in Canada* (Ottawa: Statistics Canada, 2015). There is significant variation: "While the female labour force participation rates for most immigrant groups are in the 60% to 80% range, some groups have rates lower than 50% (e.g., those from Pakistan, Iraq, Jordan, Saudi Arabia and Taiwan) and some groups have rates higher than 85% (e.g., those from Philippines, Belarus, Romania, Albania and Zimbabwe)," 15.
66 E.g., Teresa Hayter, *Open Borders: The Case against Immigration Controls* (London: Pluto, 2000), 21–63.
67 E.g., see Samuel Huntington, *Who Are We?* (New York: Simon and Schuster, 2004), 59–60; Richard Gwyn, *Nationalism without Walls* (Toronto: McClelland & Stewart, 1997), 240.
68 Such as one finds in OECD/EU, *Indicators of Immigrant Integration 2015* (Paris: OECD Publishing, 2015). See also Richard Alba and Nancy Foner, *Strangers No More: Immigration and the Challenge of Integration in North America and Western Europe* (Princeton, NJ: Princeton University Press, 2015).
69 Jeffrey G. Reitz, Patrick Simon, and Emily Laxer, "Muslims' Social Inclusion and Exclusion in France, Quebec and Canada: Does National Context Matter?," *Journal of Ethnic and Migration Studies* 43 (2017): 2473–498. In Canada, it should be noted, much of this is a "country of origin" effect, rather than religion per se, with immigrants from Pakistan and Iraq having particularly low rates of female labour-force participation, but not immigrants from Albania. See Frank and Hou, *Source-Country Female Labour Force Participation*.
70 This is widely thought to be, at least in part, a consequence of the hijab ban in public schools, which leads to lower levels of educational attainment

among Muslim women in France. Canada also benefits from a much higher rate of ethno-fractionalization.
71 Collier, *Exodus*, 259.
72 Bryan Caplan, *Open Borders: The Science and Ethics of Immigration* (New York: Macmillan, 2020).
73 This is, in any case, a very active concern in the federal government, which sets immigration levels. See Douglas Todd, "Canada Struggling to 'Absorb' Immigrations, Internal Report Says," *Vancouver Sun*, 11 August 2017.
74 Pevnick, *Immigration and the Constraints of Justice*, 110–14.
75 Sara Park, "Inventing Aliens: Immigration Control, 'Xenophobia' and Racism in Japan," *Race & Class* 58, no. 3 (2017): 64–80.
76 Japan is not technically closed – a very small number of individuals are able to acquire citizenship. Most of them, however, are not migrants, but rather individuals born in Japan, excluded from citizenship as a result of the country's *jus sanguinis* rule.
77 Pevnick, *Immigration and the Constraints of Justice*, 154–5. Also Stuart Soroka, Keith Banting, and Richard Johnson, "Immigration and Redistribution in a Global Era," in *Globalization and Egalitarian Redistribution*, ed. Pranab Bardhan, Samuel Bowles, and Michael Wallerstein (Princeton: Princeton University Press, 2006), 261–88. Alberto Alesina, Reza Baqir, and William Easterly, "Public Goods and Ethnic Divisions," *Quarterly Journal of Economics* 114, no. 4 (1999): 1243–84.
78 Michael Blake, *Justice, Migration and Mercy* (New York: Oxford University Press, 2020), 117.
79 G.A. Cohen, *Rescuing Justice and Equality* (Cambridge, MA: Harvard University Press, 2008), 39–40.
80 For a version of this argument in the immigration case, see Pevnick, *Immigration and the Constraints of Justice*, 158–9.
81 For an extended discussion of this issue, see Eric Kaufman, *Whiteshift* (New York: Abrams, 2019).
82 Ezra Klein, "Ezra Klein on Media, Politics, and Models of the World," *Medium*, 6 October 2016, https://medium.com/conversations-with-tyler/ezra-klein-tyler-cowen-vox-healthcare-journalism-bias-396196082c31.
83 Environics Institute, *Race Relations in Canada 2019: Final Report*, 24, https://www.environicsinstitute.org/docs/default-source/project-documents/race-relations-2019-survey/race-relations-in-canada-2019-survey---final-report-english.pdf.
84 This has become a term of art in Canadian political discourse, largely as a consequence of the Bouchard-Taylor commission in Quebec (see Bouchard and Taylor, *Building the Future*). See also Jocelyn Maclure and Charles Taylor, *Secularism and Freedom of Conscience*, trans. Jane Marie Todd (Cambridge, MA: Harvard University Press, 2011).

85 Walzer, *Spheres of Justice*, 32. David Miller as well states, "It is acceptable to give precedence to people whose cultural values are closer to those of the existing population." "Immigration: The Case for Limits," 204.
86 This point is made well by Laborde, *Critical Republicanism*.
87 Marion Boyd, *Dispute Resolution in Family Law* (Toronto: Ontario Ministry of the Attorney General, 2004). The conflict was systematically misrepresented in the international press. The UK *Guardian*, for instance, declared, "The introduction of sharia law in Ontario, Canada, was effectively recommended by a 2004 report." See James Sturcke, "Sharia Law in Canada, Almost," *Guardian*, 8 February 2008, https://www.theguardian.com/news/blog/2008/feb/08/sharialawincanadaalmost.
88 Lynda Hurst, "Ontario Sharia Tribunals Assailed: Women Fighting Use of Islamic Law, but Backers Say Rights Protected," *Toronto Star*, 1 June 2004.
89 Laborde, *Critical Republicanism*, 75.
90 For an excellent survey of the issues that arose in the Canadian context, see Bouchard and Taylor, *Building the Future*, 48–60.
91 Bouchard and Taylor, 84.
92 Brian Barry, *Culture and Equality* (Cambridge, MA: Harvard University Press, 2001), 39.
93 See Maclure and Taylor, *Secularism and Freedom of Conscience*, 68. See also Cécile Laborde, *Liberalism's Religion* (Cambridge, MA: Harvard University Press, 2017), 51–4.
94 Arthur Ripstein, *Equality, Responsibility and the Law* (Cambridge: Cambridge University Press, 1999).
95 Joseph Heath, "Culture: Choice or Circumstance?," *Constellations* 5, no. 2 (1998): 183–200.
96 Hurst, "Ontario Sharia Tribunals Assailed."
97 Lynda Clarke, "Asking Questions about Sharia: Lessons from Ontario," in *Debating Sharia*, ed. Anna C. Korteweg and Jennifer A. Selby (Toronto: University of Toronto Press, 2012), 158.
98 Nancy L. Rosenblum, *Membership and Morals* (Princeton, NJ: Princeton University Press, 1998), 57.
99 Joseph Raz, *The Morality of Freedom* (Oxford: Oxford University Press, 1986); Jeremy Waldron, "Autonomy and Perfectionism in Raz's Morality of Freedom," *Southern California Law Review* 62, nos. 3–4 (1989): 1097–1152.
100 Chandran Kukathas, *The Liberal Archipelago* (Oxford: Oxford University Press, 2003), 25.
101 John Rawls, *Political Liberalism* (New York: Columbia University Press, 1993), 12–13.
102 See Martha Nussbaum, "Perfectionist Liberalism and Political Liberalism," *Philosophy and Public Affairs* 39, no. 1 (2011): 22.
103 Rawls, *Political Liberalism*, 13–14.

104 Nussbaum, "Perfectionist Liberalism and Political Liberalism," 33, 38.
105 John Rawls, *A Theory of Justice* (Cambridge, MA: Harvard University Press, 1971), 3–4.
106 Philip Pettit, "Rawls's Political Ontology," *Politics, Philosophy and Economics* 4, no. 2 (2005): 157–74.
107 Kymlicka has advanced a similar but more restricted argument. He suggests that minority groups that wanted to defend illiberal practices enter into a sort of contradiction, because they must appeal to liberal multiculturalism policies in order to defend these practices. Will Kymlicka, *Multiculturalism: Success, Failure, and the Future* (Washington, DC: Migration Policy Institute, 2012), 10.
108 For further development of this view, see Joseph Heath, *The Machinery of Government* (New York: Oxford University Press, 2020).
109 See Joseph Heath, "Three Normative Models of the Welfare State," *Public Reason* 3, no. 2 (2011): 13–43.
110 Miller, *Strangers in Our Midst*, 145–9. What Miller says, in fact, is that immigrants "should acknowledge that expressing or strengthening the public culture is a valid reason in support of a political proposal, and … should also acknowledge that there are contexts in which it is permissible to give that culture symbolic precedence" (149).

Chapter Six

Two Dilemmas for US Race Relations

From the perspective of an outside observer, one of the most striking features of the American discourse over race relations is how insular it is. Slavery is often spoken of as though it were a uniquely "American curse," or as an "original sin," the legacy of which has been transmitted to each subsequent generation in the American republic.[1] It is surprising how seldom any attempt is made to situate the social problems related to race in America in a broader comparative perspective, by considering how other countries have dealt with such problems.[2] Similarly, when it comes to prescribing remedies, there has been very little interest in looking to see what policies have worked elsewhere. This is unfortunate, since there is a great deal to be learned from an analysis of race relations in the United States that treats it as an instance of a broader class of political and social conflicts involving minority groups, rather than as an extraordinary and unique evil. Situating the problem in this way makes it easier to understand why many policies adopted in the United States have failed, when compared to countries that have achieved greater success in resolving similar conflicts. A comparative perspective may also help us to understand why the problem in the United States has proven so intractable.

The first step toward adopting such a perspective involves seeing the problem of black-white race relations in the United States, not as a problem of race relations at all, but rather as a set of conflicts involving a minority ethnic group, viz. the descendants of the approximately half-million African slaves who were, over a period of three hundred years, brought to America involuntarily, kept in servitude for multiple generations, and subsequently subjected to both legal and social discrimination, harassment, and violence. Historically, race has been used as an effective proxy to identify members of this group, but increased non-European immigration to the United States over the past fifty years has made this proxy increasingly unreliable. As a result, the formulation of the problem as an issue of race, rather than of ethnicity, has become a major obstacle to progress. This is particularly obvious in recent debates over slavery reparations, in which it is clear that the intended beneficiaries of such a policy would be members of a particular historical community – which we can refer to, for convenience, as African-Americans – and not the larger racial group conventionally referred to as "black" (which would include, for instance, recent immigrants from Nigeria).[3] As I will attempt to show, the most important *normative* claims made by African-Americans stem from their membership in this historical community (and thus their ethnicity, in the technical sense of the term) and not their race.

The historical fixation on race, however, has encouraged Americans to see, not just the status of African-Americans, but rather *all* problems of minority integration through the "lens of race."[4] My first proposal will be to reverse this and examine American race relations through the "lens of ethnicity." This has numerous advantages, with perhaps the most important being that it allows us to situate the American problem more easily in a comparative perspective, since ethnic conflict, as well as tensions surrounding the integration of visible minority ethnic groups, is extremely common in the world today, and a fair bit is known about what constitute effective strategies for dealing with the issues that it raises.

The second major step is somewhat more abstract. It involves treating the problem of race relations in the United States as having certain features of what is referred to in the policy literature as a "wicked problem," or less dramatically, as a "stuck file."[5] Generally speaking, it is difficult to find many people in the United States who are satisfied with the amount of progress that has been made, over the past fifty years, at achieving racial harmony. During the 1960s several Western nations, including the United States, the United Kingdom, Canada, and Spain, were all facing violent internal conflict involving a minority ethnic group. While the United States experienced widespread rioting and murder, in the United Kingdom, Spain, and Canada the conflicts generated serious problems of domestic terrorism. Since that time, however, the conflicts in the United Kingdom, Spain and Canada have been, if not fully resolved, then at least pacified. Whatever tensions remain have also largely disappeared from public consciousness and discourse. In the United States, by contrast, race relations remain a source of ongoing conflict, soul-searching, and public acrimony. This naturally invites the question of why the United States has done so poorly compared to other Western nations, given that problems of this nature are not intrinsically unsolvable.

One defining feature of a wicked problem is that the different parties involved define both the problem and its solution differently. As a result, what counts as "progress" from one perspective might actually be the opposite from some other. This is a general feature of stuck files as well – they typically involve multiple objectives that are not simultaneously realizable. Progress in one dimension is possible, but it has a tendency to worsen outcomes along some other dimension. When attention shifts to that second outcome, this undoes whatever progress was made in the first. The result is often just reinforcement of the status quo. The naive tendency is to assume that social problems persist only for lack of commitment to their solution, or obstruction by "bad actors," and so the appropriate response is simply to push harder on the existing policy levers. One of the first lessons in policy analysis, when considering a particularly recalcitrant problem, is to look for contradictory imperatives, in order to determine whether the status quo is in fact the equilibrium of a set of countervailing forces. This is less intuitive, because it suggests that people of good will, who are committed to solving the problem, may nevertheless be acting in ways that contribute to the reproduction of the unsatisfactory outcome.

When examined from a broader comparative perspective, the objective of producing more harmonious race relations in the United States does not seem as though it should be too difficult. The fact that there are no major religious or linguistic differences between the African-American minority and the majority population in the United States removes two of the most common axes of ethnic conflict. Furthermore, in terms of individual attitudes, contemporary Americans are not particularly racist compared to people in other countries (although the insular quality of American public discourse on this topic has allowed the contrary belief to go largely unchallenged).[6] Far too many Americans assume, on the basis of their moral conviction that racism is a great evil, that it must be a causally significant force as well. As a result, they ignore the possibility that popular explanations for the lack of racial integration, which blame it on the prevalence of racism in American society, mistake the *explanandum* for the *explanans*. What I would like to propose instead is that the persistence of acrimonious race relations in the United States is due, at least in part, to the pursuit of contradictory objectives in the quest for a solution. I will draw attention to two sets of these in the discussion that follows.

First, with respect to social integration, it has become conventional in the philosophical literature to distinguish two axes of internal diversity, which can be referred to, following Will Kymlicka, as polyethnic and multinational pluralism.[7] Both have corresponding models of social integration that have been reasonably successful in ethnically plural states, with the former being most appropriate for the accommodation of immigrants, the latter for "internal minorities." As descendants of slaves, African-Americans are of course not immigrants, and yet they lack certain characteristics of a national minority group. As a result, Americans have adopted an approach to integration that attempts to combine elements from both the polyethnic and multinational models. The problem, as I will attempt to show, is that the two approaches in many ways push in opposite directions, leading not to successful integration but rather to marginalization (or to the reinforcement of an existing dynamic of marginalization). This is, incidentally, an observation that Kymlicka made of the American case many years ago, but the point has not received sufficient uptake, and so I hope to elaborate on his analysis.[8]

The second dilemma arises when one considers what should count as successful polyethnic integration, and in particular, how one ascertains the level of ambient discrimination. Here there are two coherent alternatives, the first of which focuses on the process level, of how people behave when they interact with one another, the second of which focuses on the outcome level, of whether a representative mix of individuals wind up occupying various social positions. It is not difficult to show that attempts to achieve integration in one sense may preclude achieving it in the other. As a result, successful models of multicultural integration tend to pick just one. Stylizing only somewhat, it is possible to distinguish the "Singapore model" of inclusion, which focuses almost exclusively on outcomes, from the "Canadian model," which focuses on process neutrality. Once these two ideal types have been described, it is not difficult to see that there is no agreement in the United States about which one provides the appropriate criterion of success, as a result of which policy has tended to pursue both models simultaneously, resulting in a failure to achieve satisfactory outcomes in either dimension.

The presence of these two different models of integration, and two different ways of understanding multiculturalism, is what generates the dilemmas for US race relations. My use of the term "dilemma" is intended to be somewhat stricter than that made famous by Gunnar Myrdal.[9] With respect to both integration and multicultural inclusion there are two very different approaches, which generate incompatible sets of policy options. A choice must be made, and yet there are serious arguments to be made against both approaches. Thus African-Americans as a group find themselves in a situation in which there is no way to advance that does not involve serious compromise, and yet the prima facie unreasonableness of the options generates paralysis and internal division. I will try to illustrate this, in more concrete terms, by showing how these two dilemmas translate into paralysis in specific policy domains, the first in policing, the second in residential integration. My objective, it should be noted, is merely to describe these dilemmas, not to offer any (no doubt unwelcome) suggestions on how they should be resolved.

1. Preliminary Clarifications

Several peculiarities of American discourse about race and ethnicity can be confusing for outside observers and therefore merit clarification prior to any sustained discussion. Most importantly, there is the enormous impact that US Federal Government Census categories have on the more informal categorizations used in public discourse. The US federal government recognizes five official "races": (1) White, (2) Black or African-American, (3) American Indian or Alaska Native, (4) Asian American, and (5) Native Hawaiian or Other Pacific Islander. Apart from this (and confusingly) it recognizes a single "ethnicity": Hispanic.[10] Obviously there is a great deal of arbitrariness in these divisions, and they make sense only when seen in the context of the historical processes that gave rise to them. Since the US Census predates the American Civil War, the original purpose of the "White" and "Black" categories was to differentiate the free European settler population from slaves. In a quite separate development, the 1848 Treaty of Guadalupe Hidalgo (through which the United States annexed more than half the territory of Mexico) extended full citizenship to all Mexican citizens who wished to remain in the conquered territories. It was the desire to keep track of this group, along with more recent migrants from Mexico, that gave rise to the "Hispanic" category. The decision to treat it as an ethnicity, and not a race, emerged over time for essentially political reasons, motivated by the desire to maintain good relations with Mexico. The various Indigenous categories were introduced for obvious reasons. The final category, Asian American, was the only one intended to identify a minority immigrant group – in this case, the Japanese and Chinese who arrived on the West Coast in large numbers during the nineteenth century.

The important point is that the US Census categories did not arise through an attempt to classify world population into racial groups. (This is most obvious in the "Asian" category, which fails to distinguish the population of the Indian subcontinent from that of China and the surrounding region.) The categories were created in order to track internal pluralism, to identify the major domestic ethnic groups as they emerged over the course of the nineteenth century. Furthermore, the language of "race" was used quite loosely in the vernacular until well into the twentieth century (e.g., it was common to distinguish the "Irish race" from the "German race," etc.).[11] As a result, a set of census categories that was intended to identify what we would now be inclined to describe as ethnic groups became entrenched as a system of racial classification. And with the de facto prohibition on non-European immigration for the better part of the twentieth century, there was initially little reason to change these categories. They became bureaucratically entrenched, and so despite dramatic changes in the population profile with the development of non-white immigration after the 1965 Immigration and Nationality Act was passed, the nineteenth-century classification system remains in place and essentially unchanged.

One important factor contributing to the bureaucratic entrenchment is that, after the abolition of slavery, the Jim Crow laws in the American South used the census categories of "Black" (or "Negro") and "White" (along with "Colored") as the basis for discrimination. When these laws were struck down by the courts, or overridden by the US federal government, the remedies adopted typically used the same language and categories. A particularly influential instance of this is the *Brown v Board of Education* decision, which found that segregation of children of the "Negro race" from "white" children violated the Equal Protection Clause of the Fourteenth Amendment. In 1954, there was no confusion over who the beneficiaries of this decision were. Over time, however, things became more confusing, as America became the destination of many immigrants from both Africa and the Caribbean who would be classified racially as black, and yet are not part of the historical community of African-Americans. This produced an unhelpful ambiguity, especially because the formulation of the remedies in terms of race, rather than ethnicity, has expanded eligibility for certain benefits to include a large number of people who would not appear to have any claim to them.

For a useful comparison, consider the case of the Métis in Canada, another group categorization that is ambiguous between being a racial and an ethnic identifier. For more than a century prior to the British colonization of western Canada, French fur traders travelling by canoe had a significant presence in the territory and had set up numerous trading posts and small settlements. Since almost no women travelled with them, many of these *voyageurs* settled down and married Indian women. The result was a relatively large population of mixed-race individuals – known as Métis – in the region of the Red River Valley west of the Great Lakes, in what is now the Province of Manitoba. They did not identify as Indian, in part because they were largely French-speaking and Catholic, nor were they accepted as members by any Indian band. When the British arrived in force, it was this Métis population that put up the most significant military resistance to colonization, with major armed rebellions in both Manitoba and Saskatchewan. As a result, the British found themselves engaged in parallel negotiations with two quite distinct groups – Indians, with whom they signed treaties, and the Métis, with whom they made largely religious accommodations (most notably, Catholic public schooling). In this way, the Métis became one of the three recognized Indigenous groups in Canada, alongside Indians (or "First Nations") and the Inuit.

Traditionally, the term Métis was used in a racial sense, to designate someone of mixed Indian and European heritage. For instance, no one thought it unusual that the Métis writer Maria Campbell gave her memoirs the title *Half-Breed* – the latter was seen as just a pejorative term for the former.[12] Over time, however, this racial definition came under strain, because the Métis were recognized as a national minority group, as a result of which they enjoy certain entitlements that members of other groups do not (such as hunting rights on traditional lands). This creates a problem, because there are an enormous number of Canadians who have no connection to the historical community of the Red River Valley, and yet have some Indian ancestry, which according to the racial definition of the term allows them to claim to be Métis. Indeed, since the French colony in North America suffered a chronic shortage of European women, most of the francophone population of Quebec (*de souche*) has some Indian ancestry. Over time, mixed-race individuals outside the traditional Métis group began demanding their rights as Indigenous peoples. Specifically, two men charged with hunting out of season in Sault Ste. Marie, Ontario, defended themselves by claiming that they were exercising their Aboriginal rights.[13] This generated pushback from members of the traditional Métis community, who began to argue that the term should be used in the narrower, ethnic sense, to refer only to mixed-race individuals possessing ancestral ties to the Red River Valley population.[14]

A similar state of affairs prevails in use of the term "black" in the United States, and one can see the development of similar pushback. For certain purposes it does not matter whether the term is used in the broad, racial sense, or in the narrower, ethnic sense. Many African-Americans, from the standpoint of personal identity, conceive of themselves as members of a racial group, and so, for example, strongly identify with the struggles of blacks in South Africa. Even with regard to certain normative entitlements that African-Americans have against the American state, such as the non-discrimination rights enshrined in civil rights legislation, it does not particularly matter whether they are conceived of as a racial or an ethnic group (the 1964 Civil Rights Act prohibits discrimination on the basis of "race, color, or national origin," effectively treating the three as equivalent). There is, however, a certain set of issues that are central to race relations in America in which the distinction does matter. These are issues in which the claims made by African-Americans, and the remedial policies that have been adopted, are justifiable only with reference to the legacy of the injustices perpetrated against this specific historic community.

This is obvious in the case of slavery reparations, but it applies equally to the case of affirmative action and school integration. For example, there are many minority groups in America with poor levels of educational attainment, who could benefit from special consideration in university admissions. Vietnamese-Americans, for instance, have poor test scores on average and relatively low levels of high-school graduation.[15] Given the deep involvement of the American government and military in the creation of the Vietnamese diaspora, one might even think that the United States has some special obligations to this group. Yet it would be difficult to find anyone in America who has worried even for a moment about the tragic under-representation of people of Vietnamese origin in American higher education. (On the contrary, Vietnamese-Americans are lumped together with all other Asians, which in turn reduces their chances of admission to competitive universities.) It is understood implicitly that affirmative action policies are not intended to benefit all disadvantaged minority groups in American society, but are intended to benefit blacks (and to a lesser extent Hispanics). Since it is difficult to make the case for this as a response to present discrimination alone, such policies are typically seen as a response to the legacy of past discrimination against this specific group.

Unfortunately, the formulation of these policies in terms of the census categories, and thus in racial terms with respect to African-Americans, has meant that the benefits are flowing increasingly to individuals who have either no claim or else a dubious claim to membership in the group that actually suffered the past discrimination. A disturbingly large percentage of the beneficiaries of affirmative action in competitive American universities are in fact recent immigrants or foreigners.[16] The same is true of minority "set-asides" in government contracting, where preference is given to "minority business enterprises," many of which are owned by immigrants. Given how extremely divisive these programs are in American society, even when they serve the intended beneficiaries, the practice of giving preference to immigrants with no plausible claim to such benefits, over native-born Americans, puts what many would regard as unnecessary strain on the American body politic.[17] Beyond this, however, African-Americans find themselves in a situation analogous to that of the Métis, where programs that were put in place in response to the claims of their specific group are generating benefits for individuals who are outside that group, because race is used as the group identifier. In the same way that Métis groups have begun to push for a narrower definition of the term, organizations such as American Descendants of Slavery have argued that the benefits of affirmative action should be limited to members of that particular historical community (which is to say, to African-Americans as an ethnic group).[18] In order to avoid confusion, in the discussion that follows I will use the term "African-American" when I want to refer to members of the specific ethnic group, and use the term "black" ambiguously, to refer both to this group and to the (much larger) racial group. I will, in this respect, be breaking with the American practice of using the two terms interchangeably.

A second peculiarity of US discourse is also worth noting. Given the emotionally fraught nature of relations between African-Americans and the white majority, along with the central importance of this conflict in American history, there is a tendency for black-white race relations to occlude all other divisions and conflicts. Indeed, the term "race relations" is often used to refer only to relations involving the African-American minority. (Thus an American, reading the title of this chapter, would automatically infer – correctly as it turns out – that the topic is black-white race relations, even though this is not stated explicitly.) Similarly, the term "racism" is often used as a short-hand to refer to anti-black racism. For the most part this is just harmless shorthand. What is more confusing is the habit that Americans have of using the term "white" to refer, in some cases, to individuals of European ancestry, but in other cases, to anyone who is not black. Thus when speaking of "black-white race relations," there is a tendency to use the term "white" to refer to all non-black Americans, as though the world contained only black people and white people. As a result, Jews almost always, but often Asians and Arabs as well, find themselves classified as "white" in American public discourse.[19] For example, Elizabeth Anderson registers her objections to black residential self-segregation by saying that "when blacks self-segregate, whites are of necessity racially isolated."[20] This is, of course, only a conceptual necessity if the word "white" is being used to mean "not-black."

In some cases this way of speaking helps to avoid unnecessary complications, but in other cases it can become an important source of confusion, not least because it tends to downplay significant cleavages within the non-black population (e.g., the attitude of Asian immigrants toward residential integration may be quite different from that of native-born Americans of European ancestry). Similar confusion used to prevail in Canada in the ethno-national conflict involving the French-speaking minority. It was common to describe this as a conflict between "French" and "English" (and within Quebec, between "Catholic" and "Protestant").[21] This generated certain peculiarities, such as the fact that the Jewish minority in Quebec often wound up being referred to as "Protestants" in public discourse. Nevertheless, for the most part, people knew what was meant. Immigration, however, wound up making this vocabulary increasingly tenuous, and Quebecers began to realize that there was no longer any such thing as a hegemonic "English" Canada opposed to their interests. Thus the term "English" was gradually replaced by the acronym ROC (for "rest of Canada" – *le ROC* in French). This has one important benefit. Among members of minority groups, it is common for this group membership to form an important element of individuals' personal identity (in part just because they are constantly being reminded of it). There is a complementary tendency to imagine that members of the majority group must self-identify in the same way. There is often a failure to realize that, precisely because they are in the majority, members of that group often lack a cohesive, oppositional group identity. For example, the greatest privilege of being in a majority linguistic group is that one's language need *not* form part of one's identity, precisely because one is so seldom obliged to think about it. (For example, it is doubtful that many African-Americans take special pride in being native speakers of English, the hegemonic language of global science and commerce.[22]) Personal identity tends to crystallize around differentiating traits, which means that majority characteristics are much less salient in the formation of identity. Thus there is an enormous asymmetry in the role that group membership plays in the personal identity of minority and majority groups. The use of a slightly awkward acronym such as "the ROC," rather than "the

English," serves as a useful reminder, since no one could imagine that Canadians outside Quebec go around thinking of themselves as proud members of an explicitly residual category.

In the United States, the term "white" is often used to refer to what is, from the perspective of African-Americans, the ROA (rest of America).[23] It might be salutary for Americans to adopt this way of speaking, rather than the racializing vocabulary currently in use, since it would draw attention to an important asymmetry in what far too many Americans persist in regarding as symmetric racial polarization. This is not likely to happen, and so for now I will settle with a warning that when Americans use the term "white," they are not always using the term in the literal sense, but rather in the ROA sense.[24] When it is convenient to do so and will not cause confusion, I will adhere to this US convention of using white as a residual category, rather than as a racial designator.

2. Race Relations as a Stuck File

When dealing with any persistent or longstanding social problem, especially one that is widely acknowledged and yet remains unresolved, there is a natural tendency to attribute the lack of progress to others' failure of commitment. In some cases, the frustration of progressive plans is most naturally seen as the product of widespread indifference (e.g., the persistence of homelessness is seen as a consequence of the broader public simply not caring enough about the problem to want to solve it). In other cases, it is seen as a consequence of bad actors who have blocked efforts of those seeking a solution (e.g., the lack of progress on mitigating climate change is seen as a consequence of disinformation spread by the fossil fuel industry). These explanations are often intended, not as empirical claims, but rather as rallying cries, aimed at motivating those who are on the right side of the issue to greater exertions. As a result, those who respond to them as ordinary empirical claims and question whether the evidence actually supports them are often chastised for undermining solidarity among those committed to change (and are often accused of being sympathetic to or siding with the bad actors). This impulse can easily become problematic, because there are many instances in which it genuinely does matter what the aetiology of a particular social problem is, because the only way to resolve it is to address its *actual* causes. If bad actors are actually causing the problem, then that is important to know, but if bad actors are not causing the problem – if they are merely a symptom, rather than the cause – then it is important not to be distracted by them. One can waste much time and energy in symbolic confrontation with groups who are not actually important or efficacious social actors.

In order to avoid these difficulties, one of the first lessons in academic policy analysis is that, when confronting a persistent social problem (or a so-called stuck file), one be attentive to the possibility of conflicting policy imperatives. The status quo on any particular issue is typically an equilibrium of social forces pushing in different directions. Not all good things necessarily go together, and so a bad outcome in one particular dimension can easily be the result of someone pursuing a good outcome in some other. Classic examples of this sort of analysis can be found in the work of Michael Lipsky or James Q. Wilson on bureaucracy.[25] As Wilson notes, there is widespread acknowledgment, from left to right to centre, that there is a "problem" with bureaucracy in the US government. The surprising thing is that, even though "everybody seems to agree that we ought to do something about the problem of bureaucracy," nothing ever gets fixed.[26] The naive tendency is to think that this is because bad actors within these bureaucracies successfully resist reform. One imagines that these dysfunctional organizations must be staffed by individuals who exhibit the same dysfunctions – faceless, impersonal bureaucrats, "men without qualities" who enjoy enforcing meaningless rules, etc. And yet this view seldom corresponds to anyone's lived experience.[27] The majority of bureaucrats are ordinary people who experience the usual range of human emotions and have the usual level of sensitivity to the needs of others.

The reason that the problem never gets solved, Wilson claims, is that "there is not one bureaucracy problem, there are several, and the solution to each is in some degree incompatible with the solution to every other."[28] The pathological features of bureaucracy are caused by the fact that it is subject to multiple demands. As Herbert Kaufman famously observed, one person's "red tape" is just someone else's "due process."[29] One is tempted to say that the demands are contradictory, but it is not so simple. The demands pull in different directions, as a result of which making progress toward one worthy objective makes it harder to make progress toward some other, often in unobserved ways. Wilson identifies five distinct objectives to which government bureaucracies are subject: accountability, equity, efficiency, responsiveness, and fiscal integrity. Each is supported by a distinct constituency, which for wholly understandable reasons assigns priority to one of these objectives over the others. The characteristic set of bureaucratic pathologies (legalism, officiousness, lethargy, risk-aversion, etc.), as well as the impossibility of eliminating these pathologies, arises as the net effect of all these groups pursuing their reasonable interests. This is why, when one looks for bad actors who are resisting change, it proves so difficult to find them, or to find enough of them to account for the problem. What one finds instead is a preponderance of reasonable actors pursuing incompatible objectives. Of course, this is not to say that one cannot find some bad actors, or people who meet the stereotype of an obstructionist bureaucrat. It is just that blaming the entire problem on them winds up vastly overestimating their causal powers.

The relevance of this analysis to the problem of race in America should be obvious. The ongoing drama of black-white race relations has all the hallmarks of a stuck file.[30] Acknowledgment that there is a problem is widespread, considerable effort has been made to resolve it, and yet nothing ever seems to improve. (Indeed, "Afro-pessimism" is a growing trend among African-American intellectuals, who claim that it will *never* be resolved.)[31] Again, there is a temptation to assume that, because the problem has not been solved, not enough effort can have been made to resolve it. But this is precisely the view that needs to be interrogated. The first step involves asking what a "solution" would look like. Here, one is immediately struck by the long-standing division within the African-American community between "integrationist" and "nationalist" thinking – two approaches that obviously push in opposite directions and that generate often conflicting demands on American society.[32] Yet there remains a stubborn insistence that the problem must be explained by the persistence of bad actors. In other words, racism and racial discrimination are posited as the key factors that explain the persistence of racial disparities in America. This finds expression in the popularity of the view that African-Americans are living under a "new Jim Crow," which differs not in kind from the old, but has merely become more indirect.[33] There is, of course, a surfeit of anecdotal evidence that supports this hypothesis – it is not difficult to find racism, both implicit and explicit, in America. There are, however, ample social-scientific grounds to suspect that these high-profile instances of racial animosity are a distraction from the deeper forces at work. (The unending series of provocations emanating from US President Donald Trump for a long time robbed a large segment of the American left of any capacity for impartial assessment of the evidence on this front.)

First, there is the simple fact that the level of attitudinal racism among Americans is not that high compared to that of people in other countries. Americans think that other Americans are quite racist and are constantly accusing one another of being racist, but that is primarily because they take the persistence of the race problem, or lack of support for preferred policy responses, as evidence of racism.[34] They generally fail to realize just how racist people are in other countries. If one were to look at a scatterplot of liberal-democratic countries on racial and ethnic tolerance, the United States would not be an outlier.[35] On the other hand, there are other social, economic, and political issues affecting the population as a whole on which the United States is a clear outlier. These include lack of class mobility, inadequacy of the social safety net, poor quality of diet, extreme inequalities in primary education funding, artificial scarcity in elite post-secondary education, high levels of crime, especially violent crime, astronomical incarceration levels, high levels of police violence, widespread gun ownership and gun crime, sclerotic political parties, and governance failure in the democratic system. Set against these problems, traditional racial discrimination does not seem like the most pressing issue facing disadvantaged minorities in America.

The other reason for suspicion of the bad actor theory is that racism – at least of the overt, attitudinal variety – has declined quite precipitously in the United States since the 1960s, and yet many problems have persisted. To take just one example, condemnation of interracial marriage has collapsed almost entirely, and yet the rate of out-group marriage among African-Americans remains quite low. According to a 2013 study, "among young married or cohabiting couples aged twenty-five to thirty-four who are either native-born or childhood immigrants, about 16% of black men and 7% of black women have a white partner in the USA." By comparison, the rates in Canada are 62 per cent and 49 per cent respectively.[36] The fact that only 77 per cent of Americans have a favourable view of black-white interracial marriage, versus 92 per cent of Canadians, does not indicate a profound enough difference to account for these numbers.[37] Since African-Americans make up only 12 per cent of the US population, it would take less than 14 per cent of the white (i.e., ROA) population being open to the idea in order for every African-American in the country to intermarry. Similarly, it would take only the participation of a small minority of white Americans to achieve integration of residential areas and schools.[38] Thus attitudinal racism would have to be extremely widespread in order to function as a genuine causal explanation of the observed patterns in cases of decentralized social choice.

Yet despite difficulties with the hypothesis, many Americans remain resistant to the suggestion that the persistence of racial inequality could be due to anything other than racism. The initial response was to suggest that the racism was still present, but that it had merely become hidden. According to this view, since social norms changed in such a way as to stigmatize the expression of racist attitudes, many Americans simply ceased to report their true beliefs to pollsters. As a result, the racism was still there. It had merely become invisible to social scientists who study the question. But this claim merely invited the development of more sophisticated social-scientific techniques, which tended to confirm the decline-of-racism story.[39] As a result, the explanation shifted to the notion of "implicit bias." According to this view, the racism is hidden not just from pollsters, but also from the racists themselves, because it is subconscious.[40] Again, empirical support for this hypothesis is less than overwhelming. It is not difficult to discover evidence of subconscious bias. The problem lies in showing that it has a significant effect on behaviour.[41] The primary evidence that it does, in most cases, is just the persistence of the race problem, combined with the assumption that it must be caused by discriminatory attitudes. As a result, implicit bias winds up functioning in these theories in much the same way that dark matter does in our understanding of the physical universe. We are not able to actually detect or measure it, but we know it must be there, because it is the only way that we can account for the behaviour of the matter that we can see. The question is whether bias is actually the only way or even the best way of accounting for observed patterns of racial inequality.

Recognition of the problems with these bad actor explanations is implicit in the movement away from an analysis based on attitudinal racism (the conventional sort of racism that involves the psychological states of social actors) toward one based on "structural" or "systemic" racism (which is produced as an effect of social institutions or systems of interaction, in some cases completely independent of the racial attitudes of individuals). This type of institutional analysis raises a number of complex issues, but for now it may suffice to observe that the shift to the vocabulary of systemic racism usually involves a shift to agnosticism on the question of causation. Systemic racism cannot serve as an *explanation* of racial disparities in outcome, because it is typically just another way of describing those disparities. For example, if the over-incarceration of African-Americans serves as the primary evidence of systemic racism in the criminal justice system, then these disparities obviously cannot be *explained* by systemic racism, on pain of circularity. Thus the over-representation of African-Americans must be explained by something else, such as attitudinal racism, along with some complex combination of social determinants. Of course, the diagnosis of systemic racism is often made in a way that is intended to suggest that attitudinal discrimination is widespread in a particular domain.[42] Strictly speaking, however, it is neutral on the question of causation and in this respect winds up serving as a diplomatic way of abandoning the assumption that the persistence of racial disparities must be due to traditional attitudinal racism.

As a result, my analysis of racial inequality in America as a stuck file could be described as a way of specifying the notion of "systemic racism." My inclination, however, is to avoid that term, because once the pretence at causal explanation has been abandoned, use of the term "racism" – a term that in my mind always implies moral condemnation – winds up being tendentious, since one cannot condemn a racially disparate outcome without knowing what caused it. As long as there are cultural differences between white and black Americans, there will be differences in modes of behaviour, which will generate disparities in certain outcomes, many of which will be perfectly innocent, the aggregate effect of choices that no one has any desire to interfere with. Thus if one wants to affirm the moral proposition that racism is always wrong, it is best to use the term only in its traditional sense, to denote attitudinal racism.[43] And when one focuses on racism in this sense of the term, it seems very doubtful that America's ongoing race problems are being caused, first and foremost, by racists (as opposed to being merely *exacerbated* by racists). The primary reason for this suspicion is that, across the American population as a whole, there are simply not enough racists, their social status and economic power are too low, and they are too geographically isolated to be able to block the efforts of those Americans who act with good will. This is bolstered by the first lesson of policy analysis, which is to resist our natural tendency to assume that bad outcomes must be caused by bad actors. The hypothesis that I would like to explore, in the discussion that follows, is that America's race problems persist at least in part because of reasonable disagreement about how they should be resolved.[44] Again, I take inspiration from Wilson, who argued that, in the context of bureaucracy, "The only point at which very much leverage can be gained on the problem *is when we decide what it is we are trying to accomplish.*"[45] With respect to race, the problem is not just that progressive Americans, both white and black, have not agreed upon any clear conception of what would constitute success in addressing racial inequality (and animosity), the problem is that they are pursuing incompatible models of ethnic integration. Part of that is because these disagreements involve responding to genuine dilemmas – choices in which both options involve real sacrifice.

The proof, of course, will lie in the persuasiveness of the argument that follows. My goal so far has merely been to explain the methodological intuition that informs it. It is perhaps worth clarifying as well that, by refraining from any discussion of attitudinal racism as a causal factor, my goal is not to excuse or exonerate racists, but rather to grapple with the full complexity of the race problem in America. Only then can we begin to combat the perception, widespread in political philosophy, that race in America does not pose any interesting or difficult questions. As Charles Mills has noted, it is surprising how little has been said about race by major American political philosophers (i.e., outside the specialized sub-field of "philosophy of race").[46] Yet while Mills sees this as just another example of white supremacy in action, my inclination is to attribute it to the widespread perception that American racism is a "no-brainer" – that the injustices are self-evident, and the institutional imperatives are clear. Mills takes John Rawls to task for writing a 500-page book called *A Theory of Justice* that makes no mention of the legacy of slavery.[47] And yet Rawls's book makes no mention of murder either, which does not mean he was participating in a conspiracy of silence aimed at condoning murder. It means that he saw the injustice of murder as self-evident, and thus not in need of any specifically philosophical treatment. So while I agree with Mills – there is, indeed, something rather preposterous about Rawls having published a book with that title, in 1971, in America, that barely mentioned race – my reasons are somewhat different. Redressing racial inequality in America is a task that raises genuine philosophical difficulties. The illusion of self-evidence, I believe, is rooted in the insistence that racism is what underlies it all, and since racism is self-evidently wrong, there is nothing philosophically interesting to be said on the question.

3. Two Models of Integration

The major challenge to modern societies posed by ethnic pluralism is due to the difficulties it creates for *social integration*. Every social interaction is governed by rules, or norms, which provide scripts, or instructions on how to act, but serve also as the basis for the legitimate expectations of others. These norms produce uniformities of behaviour, which provide benefits ranging from the essential to the trivial. A shared language, for instance, produces enormous benefits. People derive similar, non-trivial benefits from having shared procedures for the allocation of scarce resources (e.g., forming a queue), for resolving disputes, managing conversation, negotiating exchanges, partitioning physical space, initiating courtship, sharing information, discharging bodily functions, expressing grief, and so on. Thus human cultures are characterized by a very thick set of norms, which people rely upon for guidance on how to carry out virtually every aspect of social, and indeed often personal, life. Social integration is achieved when most people largely share the same set of norms, in the sense that they usually conform to them, they expect others to conform to them, and these expectations are mostly fulfilled. This radically reduces both the cognitive and emotional demandingness of social interaction. In a well-integrated society, individuals seldom experience "nasty surprises" when going about their daily affairs.[48]

It is because of these structural features of social interaction, which underlie all human culture, that intercultural contact, communication, and interaction have always been fraught with difficulty. When people subscribe to entirely different norms, they tend naturally to disappoint one another's expectations, which in turn elicits a punitive impulse. Orderly and cooperative interaction therefore requires ongoing suppression of this impulse. Behaviour that would ordinarily be classified as deviant must be explicitly reclassified as due to differences in expectation, and thus as innocent. And because deviance is punished, misunderstanding on this point can easily give rise to resentment, distrust, "friction," and even violence. Except, of course, it is important not to be naive, because people will sometimes try to take advantage of these situations and act in ways that are in fact deviant, under cover of cultural disagreement. Following this line of reasoning a bit further, it is not difficult to see why mature *intercultural* competence is exponentially more demanding than mature cultural competence and for that reason is also a great deal more aversive.

So far I have been discussing only social norms, and the informal order that they support. But exactly the same dynamic, and many of the same dilemmas, arises in the political and legal sphere. There is much to be said for having a uniform system of law that imposes the same demands on everyone and generates a shared set of expectations. Beyond this, the modern state, with its expansive administrative system and economic reach, relies heavily upon standardization for a great many of its organizational achievements. As Ernest Gellner has observed, this creates the need for an official language for the conduct of public affairs, as well as a uniform set of social expectations.[49] The creation of a universal public education system reinforces this demand. Thus the rise of modern nation states has generated enormous pressure toward linguistic and institutional homogeneity. Elements of the capitalist economy also push toward uniformity and shared norms. Major corporations, for example, go to great lengths to standardize the "customer experience," so that clients always know what to expect when interacting with the firm. Many give front-line employees scripts, which they are obliged to follow word-for-word in all customer interactions.[50] Thus both bureaucratic and commercial culture tend to push in the direction of, and to reward, uniformity of social behaviour. And from the individual's perspective, *access* to these institutional systems and their benefits requires a certain facility in managing and conforming to these expectations.

In a culturally plural society these institutional imperatives have the potential to generate significant conflict. For instance, there is often a great deal at stake for different linguistic groups when determining what the official language of the state, or of the education system, will be. Again, as Gellner has observed, there are powerful reasons to select just one language, and yet selecting one language will generate significant benefits for those who are native speakers of that language. This is why, in the postcolonial period, many newly liberated states decided to keep the language of the former colonial power as the official language of government. The goal was to avoid fomenting ethnic conflict, in cases where there was more than one linguistic group in the country, because promoting any one indigenous language to the status of official language would generate enormous advantages for members of that one group, and resistance from all the others. This was aimed in many cases at reducing the risk of civil war, or to stave off the threat of secession. Any group that finds itself disadvantaged as an ethno-linguistic minority within a larger state has an obvious temptation to resolve the issue by breaking away and forming a smaller state, in which it constitutes the demographic majority and therefore can enjoy the benefits of designating its own language as the official language.

States that have been able to resolve this problem internally in a non-repressive way typically do so by adopting what Kymlicka refers to as the "multinational" model of cultural pluralism. The centrepiece of this approach involves the devolution of powers to subsidiary political units within the society, in such a way as to allow *institutional pluralism* to develop. This in turn frees members of the minority group from having to integrate into a homogeneous set of national institutions. The standard approach involves the federalist strategy of dividing up the state into smaller territorial units, with a corresponding order of government, in such a way as to create "minority-majority" jurisdictions. It is then possible to devolve certain powers to that level of government. For example, while in France both language policy and education are administered nationally, in Canada these are provincial responsibilities, which means that the French-speaking minority is able to administer its own French-language school system in the province of Quebec, as well as institute French as the official language for the conduct of all provincial business. Thanks to this arrangement Quebecers are not forced to share institutions in certain domains with the ROC and are thus able to avoid many of the disadvantages that would arise from being minority-language speakers. Social and political integration at the national level is then achieved by limiting the set of laws and institutions imposed at that level to those where the benefits to be had from uniformity across the entire country are large enough to outweigh the disadvantages that this uniformity creates for internal minorities.

This approach to social integration, Kymlicka notes, is typically appropriate only for dealing with what he refers to as *national minority groups,* by which he means "a historical community, more or less institutionally complete, occupying a given territory or homeland, sharing a distinct language and culture."[51] This internal pluralism in states typically arises only through "the incorporation of previously self-governing, territorially concentrated cultures into a larger state."[52] Most often this is a consequence of colonialism or conquest, and thus involves states that were founded through force, but are now seeking to reorganize their internal affairs in order to satisfy the demands of justice. Territorial concentration of the minority group is a particularly important feature, not just because it allows for the devolution of state powers. Quebec, for example, is not just a province of Canada. It is a province that encompasses most of the former colony of New France (ceded to the British in 1763) and thus exercises political authority over an entire society that functions in French. This society is "institutionally complete," in the sense that there is an education system, newspapers and television stations, an entire entertainment industry, a university system, an economy that includes many large corporations, a court system, a public bureaucracy, state-owned enterprises, and an entire third sector, including churches, clubs, and community associations, that function entirely in French. Thus it is possible to grow up and live one's life as a unilingual French speaker in Quebec, without suffering any major disadvantage – social, economic, or political. Most importantly, the society is able to provide a first-world standard of living to its members, by sustaining a modern economy with a high level of labour productivity, several universities, major global corporations in several sectors, a technologically advanced health care system, and a robust welfare state. As a result, the lack of integration of the francophone minority into the institutions of the majority population is compatible with the goal of securing equality of life chances among all citizens of Canada.

Thus the multinational model solves the problem of social integration by not requiring social integration, or more specifically, by being more selective about when and where social integration is required. Instead of just imposing a uniform set of rules on everyone – an arrangement that typically benefits members of the majority culture – it allows different rules to prevail within different groups, whenever the costs of doing so are not too high. Of course, in order for these costs to be low, members of the different groups must not interact with one another very often, or very much. For example, even though there are very high levels of bilingualism within the Canadian Armed Forces, army units are still divided up linguistically, with a major regiment in Quebec functioning under francophone command.[53] In the air force, by contrast, national integration is unavoidable, and so francophones are simply obliged to learn English. The level of pluralism that is compatible with operational efficacy is very much determined by the amount of interaction that occurs – army bases are much more self-contained than air force squadrons – which is why multinational arrangements are most feasible where minority groups are geographically concentrated.

One can see where the model works less well by considering First Nations in Canada. There are multiple problems, starting with the fact that less than half of the status Indian population lives "on reserve," while the rest is dispersed across the country, primarily in urban areas. There is no way to meet the needs of the latter group through devolution of political powers. By contrast, it is possible to address a great number of issues on reserves through a strategy of "Indigenous self-government," which is to say, turning reserves into an order of government, with their own jurisdiction and powers. Unfortunately, the size and geography of reserves vary enormously and dramatically affect their capacity to provide an institutionally complete society for their members. This in turn makes a uniform devolution of powers impossible. "Self-government" means one thing on the Kahnawake Mohawk reserve, which has a population of over 8,000 and is situated next door to a major metropolitan centre. This reserve has both the means and the capacity to run a primary school system that functions entirely in Mohawk. Compare that the Red Pheasant reserve, population 600, in rural Saskatchewan. Even if there were the capacity to deliver primary-language Cree education, there is practically no economic opportunity on reserve, and no obvious way of creating it. A self-governing minority nation in this case would refrain from providing members with the skills required for successful integration into the majority culture, but fail to provide a viable alternative set of institutions that would allow for a comparable level of economic opportunity, political influence, and social satisfaction. Thus the multinational model of cultural pluralism in this case becomes a recipe for marginalization. It allows members of the group to opt out of majority institutions, relieving them on the one hand from having to integrate into a culturally alien set of practices, but on the other hand denying them access to the considerable benefits of these mainstream institutions (in particular, white-collar work in the modern economy). If the institutions of the minority nation are unable to compensate for the loss of those mainstream benefits, the result will be the emergence of significant inequality between members of the minority and majority groups.

It should be noted that these issues – involving the feasibility of constructing parallel institutional systems – are not what most people have in mind when they think of cultural pluralism. The more familiar form of pluralism, and the form that is addressed through official multiculturalism policies, is that produced through immigration. As Kymlicka observed, the expectations that immigrants bring with them are radically different from those of national (or non-immigrant) minority groups. In particular, while immigrants inevitably retain some elements of their background culture, including their language and religion, they do not in general expect to retain their major social institutions or to recreate them in their new land. This is in fact the major difference between immigrants and settlers or colonists. Immigrants expect to integrate into the basic institutional structure of the receiving society. Furthermore, immigrants are not in a strong position to demand much more. Unlike national minority groups, who were almost all involuntarily incorporated into the society, immigrants chose to come, and most retain citizenship in their country of origin, which leaves them free to return if they develop second thoughts (as a surprisingly large number do).[54]

Liberal societies are particularly attractive destinations for immigrants, not just because these societies are wealthy, but because of a pair of commitments that are central to the liberal political tradition. The first is the commitment to limited government, which generates an unusually large private sphere, in which individuals are free to reproduce a certain range of traditional practices. Thus, for example, in liberal societies immigrants can expect to practise their own religion, and not just in the privacy of their own home; they expect to be able to create associations of co-religionists, build places of worship, and so on. They also expect the freedom to found social clubs, open restaurants and music venues, print newspapers in the language of their choosing, and create facilities to cater to traditional marriage or other rituals.[55] As a result, they expect that integration into a liberal society will require much less participation in majority institutions than would be required in a non-liberal society. This is, however, closely tied to a second commitment, which is central to the political culture of liberal societies. This is the commitment to liberal neutrality, which requires that where a uniform system of rules must be imposed on all, individuals should be able to participate in them on roughly equal footing. This implies that the distribution of the burdens and the benefits of integration should not be too unequal or be arranged in such a way as to arbitrarily privilege one group. In principle, this is supposed to reconcile the preservation of pluralism in the private sphere with rough equality of life chances among members of different ethnic groups.

It is the second of these commitments that proves to be the most difficult to uphold and that forms the core of what Kymlicka refers to as the "polyethnic" model of integration. The centrepiece of this model is a set of anti-discrimination rights and policies, intended to prevent the exclusion of minority-group members from mainstream institutions. This is often coupled with a set of benevolent policies aimed at providing modest sponsorship and support for pluralism in private life (e.g., funding local cultural associations or social clubs). These two strategies alone, however, are seldom sufficient, because there are inevitably a great number of barriers to participation in mainstream institutions for minorities that do not involve explicit discrimination, or discriminatory intent. Institutional arrangements that were thought to be neutral with respect to ethnicity often turn out to be not-so-neutral as the range of ethnic variation increases. Thus the third component of the polyethnic model of integration is a strategy of "reasonable accommodation," which involves adjusting institutional rules in such a way as to eliminate barriers to the full and equal participation of minorities in mainstream social institutions. To take just one example, many police services in Canada used to have a minimum height requirement for officers – often 175 centimetres or more. This proved to be a significant impediment to the recruitment of Asian officers, and so with the growth of non-European immigration such restrictions were either lowered or abandoned.

The "reasonable" qualifier is important, because many of these rules were imposed for a reason, and so deciding whether to change them necessarily involves balancing considerations that push in different directions. For example, the old height restrictions on police recruits disqualified a significant fraction of the European-stock population as well. This was nevertheless thought to be acceptable, particularly at a time when police were more averse to the use of weapons, because it was thought that officers should have an imposing physical presence. The benefits of increased police effectiveness were obviously felt to outweigh the cost associated with the exclusionary effect of the rule. Increased Asian immigration, however, increased the cost, in terms of the fraction of the population excluded by the rule, while also reducing police effectiveness (by making it more difficult to police Asian communities). Thus it was not difficult to make the case for this accommodation, and since it went largely unnoticed by much of the population, it did not generate any particular controversy. In many other cases, however, these accommodations have become the flashpoint for significant social conflict. Often this was because members of the majority population enjoyed the benefits of the existing arrangement, while the costs of exclusion were born entirely by the minority group. As a result, the balancing of reasons required a standpoint of strict impartiality, which neither side had any particular motivation to adopt.

These two different models of integration – multinational and polyethnic – are often able to operate side-by-side quite happily, as long as they are applied to different population groups. As Kymlicka observes, countries such as Canada, Australia, and the United States contain both ethnic and national minority groups.[56] The failure to draw a clear distinction between the two models of integration has been the source of much unnecessary friction. In Canada, for example, the introduction of the multiculturalism policy in 1971 (which put in place the key features of the polyethnic model) was met with fervent opposition in Quebec, where it was regarded by many as an attempt to demote French-Canadians to the status of just one ethnic group among many. Meanwhile, in constitutional debates much of the public opposition in the ROC to the granting of "special status" to Quebec was based on the concern that, if special arrangements were made for the French, a long queue would form of minority linguistic groups seeking the same arrangements. (This difficulty was exacerbated by the tendency among Quebec sovereigntists to avoid formulating their claims in terms of shared culture, in order to avoid the suggestion that theirs is a form of ethnic nationalism.[57] And yet, by insisting that the issue is strictly about language and not the historic community, they made it difficult to explain why every other linguistic group in Canada should not be granted the same status.) The solution, in both cases, lay in recognizing that French-Canadians, as well as Indigenous peoples, are national groups, so their claims are very different from those of immigrants. As a result, there is no inconsistency in according a certain special status to French, as a form of national accommodation, while not granting the same status to Ukrainian or Chinese.

Of course, there would be no pressing reason to oppose the conflation of multinational and polyethnic claims were it not for the fact that the two models of integration, while compatible when pursued by *different* ethnic groups, cannot both be applied to the *same* group. This is implicit in Kymlicka's discussion, but he does not draw out the implications as clearly as one might like. While the polyethnic model is intended to encourage integration into mainstream institutions, by removing all unreasonable impediments to equal participation, the multinational model is intended to allow individuals to opt out of integration without suffering undue cost. In some cases the multinational model even involves some discouragement of integration. Indeed, the type of welcoming accommodation that is expected in the polyethnic model is routinely condemned as assimilationism in the multinational model. If too many people from a national minority group defect, by deciding to participate in majority institutions, this makes it more difficult for the minority group to maintain an institutionally complete social structure, and thus to guarantee equal life chances for those who do opt out. So while subsidizing English-language education for immigrants is one of the more enlightened policies of the Canadian federal government, if it were to be caught subsidizing English-language education in Quebec this would generate a national crisis. Instead, the federal government allows Quebec to pursue language education policies that tacitly discourage the learning of English.

Conflict of this form arose in dramatic fashion in 1969, when the Government of Canada issued a White Paper on Indian affairs, proposing to abolish the Indian Act, phase out the reserve system (on the grounds that the policy of "separation" and "different status" "has led to a blind alley of deprivation and frustration"), and integrate Indians into Canadian society as "equal" members. This proposal was emphatically rejected by Indigenous leaders, not just as bad policy, but as a "betrayal."[58] The entire episode is now looked back upon as a dark period in Crown-Indigenous relations, and the White Paper is routinely condemned as a template for "cultural genocide."[59] The mistake lay in the federal government having laid out a road map for integration with a population group that instead favoured, and was entitled to demand, self-government.

Since that time Indigenous policy in Canada has remained very much caught in a bind. Many reserves are not economically self-sufficient and have no credible prospect of providing an institutionally complete society. Yet neither are they able to equip their members with the capabilities required to achieve success in mainstream Canadian institutions (the education system, the labour market, etc.). The government cannot make up for the latter set of deficits too assertively, or pursue the standard set of polyethnic policies to integrate First Nations peoples, because that might be seen as encouraging members to live off reserve (and thus as promoting cultural genocide). The result is huge inequality of opportunity (typically characterized in terms of the "third world" living conditions that prevail on many reserves), which the government then attempts to blunt by intervening in the administration of reserves in ways that are an affront to their sovereignty. The result is a classic stuck file, with self-government, integration, and equality standing in relations of mutual antagonism.

4. Integration and the African-American Experience

It is not difficult to see how, with respect to these two models of integration, African-Americans fall through the cracks. As Kymlicka noted, their situation is highly unusual, in that they do not form part of a group whose members immigrated voluntarily to America. At the same time, they do not possess the central characteristics of a national group, in part because of the lack of territorial concentration, but also because slaves were subject to intentional disruption of their language and culture, which resulted in African-Americans both speaking English as a native language and becoming overwhelmingly Christian.[60] As a result, their situation is quite different from that of recent immigrants from Africa or the Caribbean, whose legitimate demands can be met through standard application of the polyethnic model, aimed at facilitating integration into the mainstream institutions of American society. There is, by contrast, strong *anti-integrationist* sentiment within African-American communities (often phrased more positively, as a desire to affirm a distinct black identity, or to preserve "race consciousness").[61] And yet there is practically no appetite for the creation of a distinct society within America, on the model of Puerto Rico (or Quebec in Canada), in which African-Americans would form a governing majority. This is seen as an "apartheid" solution.[62] Since the decline of black nationalism from the sixties, no major constituency of African-Americans has made the *political* demands traditionally associated with minority nationalism, which the multinational model of pluralism aims to accommodate.[63] The standard political claim is therefore that African-Americans want "integration" into American society. This is, however, potentially misleading, since there is still widespread nationalist sentiment, which leads most African-Americans to reject integration on the terms that immigrants routinely accept. As a result, neither the multinational nor the polyethnic model of integration can be applied to the African-American case.[64]

Because African-Americans are in many ways "omni-American" and have been so influential in the development of American culture, there is a tendency to underestimate the degree to which they possess the characteristics of a national group.[65] Ironically, the development of a "parallel society" for blacks in America was not a consequence of slavery per se, but began rather in the Reconstruction era, with the near-total exclusion of former slaves and their descendants from all institutions of mainstream American society.[66] The existence of black churches has been widely noted, but less commonly recognized is the development of an entire network of black magazines, newspapers, schools (including universities), sports leagues, entertainment venues, businesses, and in some cases towns. Many of these were reproduced with the "Great Migration" northward, leading to the creation of important African-American institutions in cities like Chicago, Detroit, and especially New York. This period also saw the emergence of a distinctive dialect of English, whose status remains an object of intense controversy. Currently referred to as African-American Vernacular English (AAVE), it is not merely an accent, since it involves systematic grammatical departures from Standard American English (SAE), as well as a distinctive lexicon.[67]

Some of these parallel institutions – such as the sports leagues – collapsed with the abolition of formal discrimination, but others persisted, in part because they were valued independently by African-Americans, who saw them as a providing a space for the reproduction of their own distinctive culture and traditions. As a result, the dynamic of integration has been met with, at very least, profound ambivalence.[68] One can see this in the characterization and frequent ridicule of African-Americans who adopt mainstream behaviour patterns as "acting white." This is most obvious in the case of English grammar and pronunciation, where SAE is often regarded as pretentious or haughty.[69] By contrast, many immigrants carefully monitor the media exposure of their children, in order to ensure that they grow up speaking standard English with a neutral accent. In America, by contrast, these issues are all racialized. Because the behaviour of the majority is characterized as "white," conformity to mainstream norms is seen as exhibiting, in many cases, a lack of racial solidarity. At worst, excessive solicitude toward the sensibilities of white people can earn the stinging rebuke of being an "Uncle Tom" or a "house Negro."

Consider, for example, the question that many minorities face when naming their children. The common dilemma faced by immigrants involves the choice of giving the child a name that is traditional in their own family or culture, but that would clearly mark the child as being from a non-majority background, or giving the child a name that would make her indistinguishable from the majority. The latter option reduces the probability of being subject to discrimination in many contexts. There is ample evidence, for instance, that Algerians in France with names that identify them as Muslim suffer from discrimination by employers when applying for work (whereas those with names that are clearly African, and yet Christian, suffer no such discrimination).[70] As a result, there is some pressure for Muslim Algerians to give their children traditional Christian or French names (or at least to steer clear of obvious giveaways like "Mohammed"). The goal is not just to avoid discrimination but also to signal that "this particular Muslim is coming from a family that is committed to integration into France."[71]

African-Americans, of course, face no such difficulty, because not only are they almost uniformly Christian, but also the stable of traditional African-American names is quintessentially American. Upon emancipation, most slaves were faced with the task of choosing a family name. Many chose the name of an American president or founding father, which is what led to so many African-Americans having names like Washington, Hamilton, Jackson, Baldwin, and Johnson. During the Jim Crow period, most African-Americans therefore had names that, thrown into a hat, made them indistinguishable from the white population. After the civil rights movement, however, and the push toward greater integration, many African-Americans reacted in a way that is the exact opposite to that of most immigrants. Given that traditional African-American names failed to set their children apart from the majority, they began to invent new names (sometime referred to as "neo-African," on the grounds that they sound African to the American ear) or else to adopt Muslim ones. Common sense suggests that these naming conventions result in labour-market discrimination, although there is some controversy over this.[72] However, it is clear that it constitutes a symbolic rejection of integration. (One can see a similar impulse with the invention of the specifically African-American holiday of Kwanzaa, which parallels the Jewish Hanukkah. It is, in a sense, superfluous, since African-Americans are overwhelmingly Christian and so celebrate Christmas just like most white Americans.)

These examples are all symbolic, but they reflect a very consistent pattern in American public life. With any mainstream behaviour, the majority of people who do it are going to be white, simply by virtue of the demographics of American society. Thus it is easy to characterize that behaviour, not as mainstream, but as specifically "white." For example, Christian Lander, author of the popular *Stuff White People Like*, declares that white Americans "love nothing better than sipping free-trade gourmet coffee, leafing through the Sunday *New York Times*."[73] Most of the book is like this, just a long list of bourgeois American culture and practices. It is bizarre to think of this behaviour in *racial*, as opposed to class-specific terms, yet both white and black Americans are constantly doing it. Unfortunately, characterizing the behaviour as white subtly pressures African-Americans to avoid all the usual forms of upper-middle-class status signalling, or indeed, practising any sort of majoritarian behaviour. The fact that white Americans offer up these characterizations in a self-deprecatory tone does nothing to change the fact that, if reading the Sunday *New York Times* comes to be seen as a specifically white affectation, this discourages blacks from reading the Sunday *New York Times*. Thus integration – participating in any of the practices and institutions of mainstream American culture or society – comes to be characterized as acting white.

Of course, the integrationist ideal most often pursued by white Americans is one in which every neighbourhood, every business, and every school and college has a level of "diversity" that reflects the composition of America on the whole. The implication is that African-Americans should be immersed in social environments in which they are constantly outnumbered nine to one by white people. Unsurprisingly, this is an ideal that has much greater appeal to whites than to blacks. For whites, it allows them to feel good about themselves for embracing diversity while still remaining the overwhelming majority in every interaction. In democratic politics, for instance, it means always being the demographic majority in every jurisdiction. For blacks, it means being completely swamped and outnumbered by whites. This is why Stokely Carmichael and Charles Hamilton complained that "integration, as traditionally conceived, would abolish the black community."[74] Children of immigrants are often happy to disappear into the general population in this way. Among African-Americans, by contrast, not only would integration on these terms generate a cultural loss, it would also represent for many a capitulation to whiteness, and to white America, that would constitute a betrayal of the historical community to which they belong. Indeed, if African-Americans were a national minority in the traditional mould, the integrationist vision would seem like an obvious instance of what is routinely denounced as cultural genocide in other contexts.[75]

Some proponents of integration, such as Elizabeth Anderson, avoid this difficulty by arguing that African-Americans do not possess a distinctive culture. She dismisses claims that they do as "folk anthropological."[76] This is, in a sense, to miss the point, since what matters is not whether African-Americans possess a distinct culture in the social-scientific sense, but whether they *perceive* themselves as having a distinct culture that they feel obliged to preserve. Mainstream perception within the community is clearly that they do. Consider Ta-Nehisi Coates's rapturous description of "The Mecca" at Howard University. It was the experience of attending an all-black college that led him to feel that "*we were* something, that we were a tribe – on one hand, invented, and on the other, no less real. The reality was out there on the Yard, on the first warm day of spring when it seemed that every sector, borough, affiliation, county, and corner of the broad diaspora had sent a delegation to the great world party."⁷⁷ This is easily recognizable as nationalist *sentiment*, which can be very powerful, even when it does not translate into a traditional nationalist politics.⁷⁸

African-Americans are not immigrants to America. Most have no desire to act like immigrants, and many bristle at the suggestion that there are even any parallels between their situation and that of immigrants. A substantial number are committed to preserving a distinct identity and a distinct historical community within America. They are in this respect like a national minority group. And yet, despite being six times more numerous than francophone Canadians, they are not able to sustain an institutionally complete society, largely as a result of geographic dispersion. Traditional black nationalism attempted to square the circle in this regard by demanding "community control" of institutions such as schools, local governments, and business associations.⁷⁹ The problem is that control over a partial set of institutions is not a recipe for autonomy, but rather marginalization. Multinational arrangements work only with nations that are able to internally provide opportunities equivalent to the ones being foregone by the decision not to integrate into the institutions of the larger society.⁸⁰

Consider, for example, the question that arises in nationalist discussions of how AAVE should be treated in schools. The relationship between AAVE and SAE is actually quite similar to that of Québécois and Standard French. Again, Québécois French is not just an accent but a dialect, which is considered both improper and absurd by "France French" standards (and is routinely mocked in France, in very much the same way that AAVE was in early-twentieth-century America). For example, academic publishers in France refuse to publish books written in Québécois French, and trade barriers prevent the direct sale of most books published in Quebec. Thus many Québécois with global ambitions learn to "code-switch" to Standard French. At the same time, one of the most important effects of the Québécois nationalist movement in Canada was a rebellion against the national school curriculum imported from France and its replacement by a domestically produced French-Canadian curriculum. This had the effect of dramatically reducing exposure to Standard French for several generations of French-Canadian students.⁸¹

One can see a similar nationalist impulse in the United States with AAVE. There is, on the one hand, extreme discomfort with the idea that

SAE should be treated as normative for all students – and that teachers should correct students who use characteristic AAVE grammatical constructions. At the same time, there is little appetite for the development of a parallel AAVE curriculum for black students, which would elevate AAVE to the status of a recognized variant of English. The primary reason is that it would disadvantage black students too much in the broader American society. A Québécois lawyer can write up a contract or plead a case in court in Québécois French, because there is an entire legal system that functions in that dialect. An African-American lawyer, by contrast, has no choice but to switch to SAE in order to work in the American legal system. Thus a primary education system that reduced exposure to SAE for black students would disadvantage them. So even though, from a normative point of view, AAVE deserves to be treated as a legitimate dialect of English, it is not economically or socially viable. Furthermore, unlike the Québécois, who actively promote the learning of Québécois French among immigrants, AAVE speakers do not try to expand use of the dialect, and in many cases strongly discourage others (especially white Americans) from speaking it. As a result, AAVE winds up persisting in an ambiguous and marginal state. The American education system teaches SAE, but there is widespread hesitancy to stamp out AAVE, just as there is resistance among African-Americans to adopting SAE. Thus African-American students in many regions of the United States perform worse on standardized English-language proficiency exams than immigrant groups – including many immigrants from Africa – for whom English is a learned language.[82] Thus the benefits of being a native English speaker – a massive source of competitive advantage in the global economy – are effectively negated for many African-Americans.

Examples such as these lend support to Kymlicka's view that "we should not expect policies which are appropriate for either voluntary immigrants or national minorities to be appropriate for African-Americans, or vice versa."[83] His suggestion, however, is that "some new model of integration will have to be worked out."[84] It is not clear, however, what this new model of integration is supposed to look like, or why one would think that a third model was feasible. In one sense at least, opting out of mainstream institutions is easy in a liberal society. The problem is that doing so increases inequality, because it involves foregoing many of the very significant advantages that come from participation in these institutions, most obviously those that are obtained from access to the upper end of the modern labour market. The key to the multinational solution is that it provides a feasible alternative locus of integration, which allows the minority to opt out of majority institutions without significant penalty. Anything in between these two options, however, is likely to generate inequality and marginalization.

This is not to say that Americans have not tried to work out a third way. Roy Brooks's concept of "limited separation" is probably the most well-developed theoretical effort.[85] And in practice, one way of understanding the unique set of policies that have featured centrally in the American response to racial inequality is to see them as attempting to square the circle between these two models of integration. The most obvious is the racial gerrymandering of electoral districts, in order to ensure that a certain number of African-American representatives are elected. The creation of "minority-majority" political jurisdictions is a hallmark policy of *national* minority accommodation. Gerrymandering represents a somewhat inelegant way of dealing with the problem that can be handled more forthrightly with territorially concentrated groups. Many minority set-asides and affirmative action programs can be understood in the same way.[86] They create, in effect, a "parallel track" for African-Americans, so that they are not obliged to compete directly against members of the majority. This allows for integration into a common set of institutions without actually forcing the application of common norms and standards on all members.

All of these policies, however, are extremely unstable. Partly this is because American courts have been unwilling to accept a system of racially differentiated rights, which has led them to outlaw certain of the more explicit race-based schemes. Thus many of these practices, such as gerrymandering or set-asides, have been restructured or redescribed in ways intended to make them immune to being overturned by the courts (specifically, racial gerrymandering is now done under the guise of partisan gerrymandering). Partly they are unstable because they are in tension with the widespread commitment to integration (and the fact that many of these policies were initially defended as transitional, aimed at promoting integration). If electoral districts are gerrymandered in order to ensure black representation, this means that blacks who move out of these neighbourhoods will often forego political representation for themselves, as well as weaken the basis of representation for others. By contrast, status Indians in Canada who live off reserve still retain the right to vote in band elections.[87] This is feasible only because they are given a legally verified identity card that confirms their status as members of a national minority group – an arrangement that is far too evocative of apartheid to ever be accepted in the United States for African-Americans.[88]

5. Example: Policing

Because African-Americans share some characteristics of a national minority group (involuntary incorporation into the state, distinctive culture and institutions), and some characteristics of an immigrant group (geographic dispersal, demand for accommodations aimed at greater inclusion), neither of the two established models of pluralistic integration can be applied directly to their case. However, rather than developing a new model of integration, tailored to the special circumstances of African-Americans, what Americans have instead produced is an inconsistent hybrid, caused by partial implementation of elements drawn from both models. The question is whether this is inevitable – or whether a third way has been overlooked. The success of American efforts so far provides no reason for optimism in this regard.

Consider, for example, the issue of policing, which remains an enormous source of anguish. The first step to understanding the challenges posed by cultural pluralism to the practice of policing involves recognizing that the enforcement of statutory law represents a relatively small fraction of what the police actually do. Most of the activities of patrol officers involves discharging a social function that is variously described as "peacekeeping," "order-maintenance," or imposing norms of "respectability."[89] This role, it should be noted, is traditionally devalued by police; it persists primarily because there is significant public demand for these services. In a sense, the police act as a backstop for the order that is maintained through informal sanctions within the community, using the discretionary application of statutory law as a way of bringing the organized coercive power of the state to bear upon situations in which the informal order proves inadequate. Effective policing must therefore always meet society halfway, with the police involved in maintaining social order and society involved in maintaining the legal order.[90]

As a result, it is extremely important for police officers to have an intimate understanding of the society that they are involved in policing. (This point is often obscured by the persistent tendency to overstate the importance of statutory enforcement.) The most effective way to achieve this is by having officers drawn from, and retaining close ties to, the community that they are expected to police. This often produces problems for minority communities who, even when they are not being targeted by explicit discrimination, wind up being subjected to majority norms and majority conceptions of respectability. Thus it is extremely common throughout the world for policing to become a flashpoint for conflict involving minority groups.[91] As a result, any successful model of minority integration must offer some remedy for these problems. There is, however, a considerable difference between the approach recommended by the polyethnic and the multinational model. As Kymlicka observes, one can see this quite clearly in two major debates that occurred in Canada involving policing of minorities.[92]

The first controversy involved a proposal to modify the uniform of the national police force (the Royal Canadian Mounted Police, or RCMP), in order to allow Sikh officers to wear a turban instead of the traditional Stetson. This was strongly resisted in certain parts of the country, and in certain social circles, because of the iconic character of the RCMP uniform. The change, however, was a standard example of the type of reasonable accommodation recommended by the polyethnic model. The central demand being made by Sikhs was for inclusion in a shared institution, and so the basic orientation of the demand for accommodation was integrationist. Sikhs *wanted* to join the national police force. They were, however, facing an inadvertent barrier. It is highly unlikely that the RCMP would have adopted a uniform that conflicted with a Christian religious observance.[93] Thus the violation of religious neutrality was unintended. Sikhs were merely asking for correction of this oversight, so that they could participate as equals.

To see the integrationist orientation of this request, it is helpful to contrast it with a movement that developed at about the same time to reform policing on many First Nations reserves. The RCMP, along with two provincial counterparts (the Ontario Provincial Police and the Sûreté de Québec) are responsible for policing small communities and rural regions throughout Canada, which includes most reserves. In 1992, under the First Nations Policing Program, initiatives were undertaken to create First Nations administered (FNA) police forces, staffed entirely by Indigenous officers, that could replace the RCMP.[94] This was motivated primarily by ongoing tension and complaints about the RCMP, and in particular the "cultural insensitivity" of officers.[95] The FNA arrangements could be described as an accommodation for a minority group, except that the valence of the accommodation is exactly the opposite from that of the Sikh case. Far from wanting to join the RCMP, these First Nations wanted absolutely nothing to do with the RCMP. (Indeed, the creation of many of these forces led to arrangements under which the RCMP, and more pointedly the Sûreté du Québec, were not allowed even to set foot on the reserve. In the case of an arrest for a serious crime, the suspect would be brought to the border of the reserve and handed over to provincial or federal authorities.) Thus the demand is fundamentally anti-integrationist, combined with the creation of a parallel, minority-majority institution.

For African-Americans, however, neither of these two solutions is feasible. The situation of many African-American neighbourhoods bears a certain resemblance to that of First Nations reserves in Canada. There is a high rate of criminal victimization within the community, especially murder, which generates heavy demand for policing.[96] The policing that is provided, however, has historically been delivered by officers who are, at best, out of touch with the community, and at worst, racist and violent. Combined with the legacy of overtly repressive policing throughout most of American history, this produces widespread distrust of the police among African-Americans, which in turn makes policing less effective, as well as encouraging more coercive techniques of social control. The result is the seemingly paradoxical situation of African-Americans being both "over-policed" and "under-policed."[97] The community as a whole is subject to an often overbearing police presence, which does not actually succeed very well in protecting anyone from crime. As a result, it becomes easy to draw the conclusion that harassment of the community is in fact the objective that police are pursuing.

The most straightforward way to break out of this spiral would be through self-policing on the FNA model, except that this is not practicable in most jurisdictions in the United States. While the administration of policing in America is often quite small-scale and local, the unstable dynamics of neighbourhood racial composition make self-policing impossible to implement. Where there is a serious mismatch between the racial composition of the police force and that of the population, with a predominantly white police force in a predominantly black area, it is often because the composition of the community has changed dramatically over a short period of time.[98] Police officers in America enjoy considerable employment security, and so white officers cannot simply be fired when the racial composition of the neighbourhood changes, and neither can they be reassigned, precisely because the administration (and often financing) of policing is so small-scale and local. It is the enormous urban police forces (like the NYPD or LAPD) that are in a position to achieve better "matching" between officers and citizens, simply through a large numbers effect, but they of course are beyond black community control, since they serve a majority-white population. Thus the demand for self-policing (i.e., black officers policing black citizens) and local control often pull in opposite directions.

As a result, Americans have historically pursued a predominantly integrationist approach to police reform, by seeking to recruit minority officers and being very proactive in promoting African-Americans to leadership positions. Unfortunately this appears to have made a lot less difference to the practice of policing than many had hoped. And perhaps just as importantly, it has done very little to change public perception or the perceived legitimacy of the police.[99] Furthermore, the fact that black officers were involved in some of the high-profile police killings that became a flashpoint for conflict in the past decade does not seem to have done much to allay suspicion that the killings were racially motivated.[100] Black officers are often perceived as having merely been co-opted into a larger "system" that they are powerless to change.

So when it comes to African-Americans and policing, integration is inadequate, but self-government is unobtainable. One can see the tensions that this generates in the difficulties faced by the Black Lives Matter (BLM) movement, which formed in response to a number of highly publicized police killings of unarmed African-Americans. Initially coalescing around expressions of spontaneous outrage, the movement became a conduit not just for opposition to police racism, but also for the expression of anger toward police in general. This posed a challenge when it came time to formulate specific demands for reform. With a standard national group, an anti-police movement is able to generate actionable policy demands, since it is possible to deny the majority-dominated police force its jurisdiction over members of the minority group, so long as a self-policing arrangement can be put in place. But this is precisely what cannot be done in the case of African-Americans, for the same reason that they cannot execute the vast majority of self-government strategies. And yet the alternative, of demanding greater inclusion, presupposes a positive desire of minority-group members to join the police force. The two demands have opposite valences. Going to a demonstration at which the police are denounced as little more than a branch of the KKK is unlikely to encourage many African-Americans to want to become a police officer.

As a result, despite encouraging considerable anti-police sentiment, the BLM movement initially put forward a policy agenda that was integrationist. This inevitably came across as a climb-down from its more radical rhetoric. The *Vision for Black Lives* document, released by the Movement for Black Lives in 2016, demanded only "direct democratic community control of local, state and federal law enforcement agencies."[101] Although the phrase "community control" is a nod to black nationalist rhetoric, the fact that it is applied to federal and state police suggests that the demand is ultimately integrationist, since at this level whites form the majority. In any case, it is difficult to see how this form of control could be implemented. In part as a result of the perceived inadequacy of this agenda, the second major round of protests, after the killing of George Floyd, featured the more radical demand to "defund the police." Although this slogan was highly effective in capturing the attention of police chiefs, it did not really constitute an actionable demand. Indeed, its defenders spent a great deal of time explaining how the slogan did not mean what a literal interpretation of the words would lead one to conclude. They failed, however, to come to any agreement on what it did mean. The most commonly articulated demand was for an increase in funding for social services that would, in turn, reduce the need for policing.[102] Unfortunately, the protests over the summer of 2020 coincided with a sharp increase in the murder rate, concentrated in predominantly African-American neighbourhoods, which was enough to cause legislators in practically every jurisdiction to abandon any ambitious defunding plans.[103] In addition, the declaration of a "police-free zone" in Seattle quickly led to occupation of the neighbourhood by rival armed militias, resulting in several shootings, two of which were fatal.[104] Thus the major effect of the defund slogan was simply to solidify BLM as an anti-police movement, signalling abandonment of the integrationist agenda. And yet without a viable alternative model of crime control on offer, it is difficult to see where the next move lies. If one considers the set of policy objectives advanced under the "defund" rubric, it is not difficult to see why police reform in America is a stuck file.

6. Two Models of Inclusion

As a non-immigrant minority group, African-Americans are entitled to demand arrangements of the sort that are normally made available to national minority groups. And yet for essentially practical reasons, these arrangements cannot be effectively institutionalized, or cannot be institutionalized in a way that offers anything close to equality of life chances between members of the minority and majority group. As a result, African-Americans have largely had to settle for the type of accommodations offered to immigrant groups, aimed at facilitating greater inclusion. Even here, however, difficulties loom, because there are two quite different ways of understanding what successful inclusion would amount to. Again, the best way to see the issue is to show how other countries – specifically Singapore and Canada – have implemented pure versions of either model. In both countries these are described as "multiculturalism" policies, although I will be sparing in my use of that term because it is sometimes interpreted as diminishing the national claims of African-Americans. The question at stake involves determining how to ensure that, when members of both majority and minority groups are obliged to share a common set of institutions, they are able to do so on equal terms. I will use the somewhat vague but currently popular term "inclusion" to describe a state in which equal participation has been achieved.

Many large-scale formal institutions can be represented as input-output systems. They take a given social state as input, perform certain operations that change it in largely designated ways, producing an altered social state as output. Consider, for example, a welfare bureaucracy that is charged with administering a means-tested social assistance program, aimed at addressing a particular need. The bureaucracy cannot act directly upon that need. The social state must first be transformed into a set of actionable inputs. This will normally involve the development of a set of eligibility criteria, which will require individuals to demonstrate that they are in the targeted condition and have no other resources to remedy the situation. Decisions will subsequently be made about how to identify these individuals (e.g., should they be expected to apply to the program? should the bureaucracy seek them out?), how to prioritize their claims, etc. Once these inputs are ordered, the bureaucracy will then act upon them to transform the social state. This may involve something as simple as a cash transfer, or a more complex and long-term entanglement. The bureaucracy will not necessarily stage the same intervention or perform the same operation upon each individual, because there may be substantial judgment involved in the management of each case. The resulting social state can be regarded as the output of the institution.

When institutions of this sort govern a heterogeneous population, there is often a reasonable concern among different population groups, distinguished along different dimensions, that they not be disadvantaged in the way they are being treated, or their claims are being processed, by the institution. For example, if the eligibility criteria are relatively coarse, designed to pick out the typical case, this may work to the disadvantage of minority groups members, whose cases may be typical within their group but atypical from the standpoint of the population as a whole. When done properly, the value of "intersectional" analysis lies in the way that it can expose the sometimes unanticipated ways that individuals can be disadvantaged, or advantaged, when there are multiple dimensions of difference. The more basic problem, however, is that even in simple cases, such as trying to determine whether blacks and whites are treated fairly by a particular institution, there are very different approaches to answering that question.

The obvious place to begin, when assessing an institution, is to look at its outputs, in order to see whether members of different groups are benefiting equally (or being harmed equally) by its operations. This can never be more than the beginning of the analysis, however, because the outputs can be assessed only relative to the inputs, and beyond that, to the baseline distribution of targeted factors in the population. For example, when one examines the prison system in America, it is easy to see enormous disparities among different population groups in rates of incarceration, the most obvious being that over 90 per cent of inmates are male. It is difficult to know how much to make of this, however, because the penal system in America is not intended to impose prison sentences on a randomly selected sample of the population. Rather, it is intended to punish those who commit crimes. The propensity to commit crime differs greatly among members of different population groups and is much more elevated among men than among women. At the same time – and partially *because* of this fact – there is also evidence of pervasive bias against men in the criminal justice system.[105] Men are more likely than women to be arrested, more likely to be charged, and if convicted, more likely to be assigned a longer prison sentence. It is, however, difficult to determine how much of the over-incarceration of men (or the under-incarceration of women) is due to gender-based discrimination in the criminal justice system, because it is necessary to factor out whatever differences are due to the elevated crime rate among men. Thus the *mere* fact that more men than women are incarcerated tells us absolutely nothing about whether they are being treated equally by that institution. It serves only as a source of research hypotheses.

Two factors further complicate the exercise. First, one cannot look at just the relationship between the inputs and outputs of the system in order to detect bias, because the inputs are typically constructed by the system and therefore cannot be taken at face value. It is, for instance, difficult to know how much more crime is committed by men than by women, because the criminal justice system takes "arrests" as its basic input. Policing is highly discretionary, and police are in general more likely to arrest a man than a women for the same offence. (Victim complaints in some ways provide a more reliable picture, except that the victim is more likely to be able to describe the offender in the case of certain crimes, such as those that involve violence or direct physical intimidation. If men are more likely to commit these crimes, this may again lead to an overstatement of the male crime rate.) Second, even if institutions should not treat individuals differently on the basis of some trait, such as gender, that trait may well be correlated with traits that do serve as a basis of legitimate differences in treatment. For instance, female offenders may be more likely to be single parents with dependent children, which may prompt the courts to seek alternatives to incarceration in sentencing. Thus it is also necessary to distinguish legitimate from illegitimate differential treatment.[106]

Given these difficulties, many consider it wise to give up on outcome-based approaches to the assessment of institutions and to focus instead on process neutrality. Since it may be hard to tell if the institution as a whole is treating all citizens equally, a better strategy may be to identify and test important decision points, in order to ensure that decision-making is unbiased. For example, if some trait of the individual is not supposed to play a role in the decision-maker's judgment, then there is no reason to provide the decision-maker with information about that trait. Eliminating bias entirely is not as easy as it sounds, because of the problem of correlated traits, but there is nevertheless a wide range of different techniques that can be applied to analyse decision-making procedures for their neutrality, and then reform them as necessary.

These two different approaches generate a very different set of policies when applied to the issue of polyethnic integration (or inclusion). Consider first the case of Singapore, which has pursued a set of resolutely outcome-oriented policies to manage internal ethnic diversity. Like Canada and South Africa, and to a lesser extent the United States, the Singaporean system has its origins in British colonial administration. The majority population is Chinese, with a large minority population of Malays and Indians (i.e., South Asians), a division that became entrenched through the census, which created what is known as the CMIO (Chinese, Malay, Indian, and Other) classification system.[107] Residency was originally quite segregated, with four distinct "quarters" of the city. After the departure of the British in the 1960s, racial unrest and rioting broke out, primarily involving a backlash by Malays against the preferential treatment the Chinese had received under British rule. Singaporean multiculturalism policy was introduced in an attempt to resolve these conflicts.

Under the multiculturalism system, all citizens are assigned a race, which is registered on their birth certificate and printed on their identity card. In the case of mixed marriages, children traditionally inherited their father's race, although parents have recently acquired the right to decide what race to assign to mixed children. Children's race determines a wide range of different entitlements, starting with the second language they are taught in school. More ambitiously, the Singaporean state has eliminated residential segregation through its "ethnic integration policy," which requires that each neighbourhood contain a population that is no more than 84 per cent Chinese, 22 per cent Malay, and 10 per cent Indian and Other. Apartments in high-rise buildings within the public housing system are divided up in accordance with the same strict racial quotas. Since 85 per cent of Singaporeans live in public housing, this means that not only is almost every neighbourhood racially integrated, but every building within every neighbourhood is also integrated.

The government has also been quite proactive in ensuring that each racial group has appropriate political representation. The "group representation constituency" system requires that each political party field a minimum number of candidates from each racial group. The presidency of the country also now alternates among racial groups, so that each gets its turn (e.g., in 2017 only Malays were allowed to run for president). National holidays are divided up equally, with two assigned to each of the three major groups. Finally, civic harmony is achieved by making it a punishable crime to "utter words, etc. with deliberate intent to wound the religious or racial feelings of any person."[108]

Compare this to the case of Canada, which has been almost entirely process-oriented in its approach to multiculturalism. This is centred upon a core set of anti-discrimination policies, the most important of which emanate from the 1982 Constitution, which prohibits "discrimination based on race, national or ethnic origin, colour, religion, sex, age or mental or physical disability," with further specification that these rights "shall be interpreted in a manner consistent with the preservation and enhancement of the multicultural heritage of Canadians." A similar schedules of rights is reproduced in human rights legislation enacted in each province, enforced by a set of tribunals that provides greater access and expedited adjudication of complaints.[109] Despite the mention of race as a prohibited ground for discrimination, the federal government does not engage in race-based classification of citizens. The census does not impose racial categories, but instead asks only about "ethnic origins." This is a write-in question on the long-form census (i.e., it does not ask respondents to choose from among a set of categories), and up to six responses per person are accepted. For major social institutions, such as the criminal justice system or the universities, there has traditionally been no collection of either race-based or ethnic data.

As a result of this relative paucity of data, the sort of outcome-based policies adopted in Singapore cannot be implemented in Canada. For example, Canadian universities practise no affirmative action in admissions. Indeed, they could not do so even if they wanted to, since applications are in many cases administered centrally by the government, which does not collect this information. Applicants to university in Ontario, for instance, may opt to declare official Indigenous status and are asked to specify their first language, but are otherwise not invited to provide information about their race or ethnic origins. As a result, most universities have very little information about the ethnic composition of their student body, unless they choose to collect it themselves. Similarly, there is no attempt made to integrate primary schools along racial or ethnic lines, or to assign quotas. Equality is achieved by equalizing funding across school districts, so that even though education is funded primarily through local property taxes, per pupil spending is the same in every district.

It is important to observe that this process-based approach is not strictly incompatible with an outcome-based approach. Under conditions of perfect information, examining the outputs of an institution, then comparing them to the baseline, and seeing whether any deviations can be attributed to permissible forms of discrimination in the treatment of cases, is an excellent way of determining whether processes are in fact neutral. The problem is that in many cases the baseline is unknown, and so institutional inputs must be used as a proxy. This approach is often unsatisfactory, however, because of the suspicion that the inputs do not actually reflect baseline rates. This becomes particularly problematic when the major determinant of the baseline is individual preference, which will often be the case, since most institutions in a liberal society are designed to be highly preference-sensitive. For example, it is conventional to defend against charges of discrimination in a competitive admissions or hiring process by comparing the success rate of individuals belonging to different groups to the composition of the applicant pool. Thus an engineering program that admits more men than women will point to the fact that few women apply, in order to defend its admissions procedures. This seldom settles the argument, however, because critics will claim that various features of the program, including the fact that its students are predominantly male, discourage women from applying, and so the inputs do not fully capture the appropriate baseline (which is the number of women who have a preference for studying engineering). Much public polemic about these situations involves speculation about whether the disparities among groups represent differences in preference or more subtle forms of discrimination.

There is, however, one slight modification of the outcome-based approach, which many of its proponents are tempted by, that makes it irreconcilable with the process model. It is very difficult to judge equality and inequality in institutions by looking at outcomes, because every outcome must be judged against some baseline, and the correct baseline is often unknown. This generates a temptation to engage in *normative* specification of the baseline – taking people as they should be, rather than as they are. For example, it is tempting to judge the acceptability of gender imbalance in an engineering program against one's sense of the number of women who *would have* applied, had they not been subjected to pervasive bias throughout their primary schooling. Or it is tempting to judge the performance of the criminal justice system against what the crime rate *would have been* under more just social conditions. One can then demand that the institution produce the outcome that would be equal with respect to this normatively specified baseline, on the grounds that doing so moves society toward greater justice. Unfortunately, under conditions in which the real baseline deviates from the ideal, such an outcome can be achieved only by violating process neutrality in the institution. At this point the two models become genuinely incompatible.

This is what accounts for the most striking feature of the Singaporean system, which is that it interferes with personal freedom to an extent that is almost comical by Western standards. For example, it solves the problem of local rioting by ethnic Malays by dispersing them, so that they cannot form more than 22 per cent of the population of any neighbourhood. This undoubtedly violates the preferences of many Malays, who might like to live in a neighbourhood that is not overwhelmingly Chinese. Similarly, under conditions of perfect freedom and equality, it is doubtful that each apartment building in Singapore would contain the exact same fraction of Chinese, Malay, and Indian/Other residents.

The Canadian system exhibits much greater preference-sensitivity, but at the expense of tolerating greater disparities in outcome. The need for such tolerance is attenuated somewhat by the fact that the two major minority groups, francophones and Indigenous peoples, are subject to multinational arrangements that can incorporate consideration of outcomes in different ways. Nevertheless, by focusing so much on process neutrality in its approach to multicultural integration, the Canadian approach requires much greater forbearance. This includes a willingness to wait to see if certain inequalities are due to preference. In the case of immigrants, it also requires a willingness to worry less about integration of the first generation and to focus on outcomes for the second or third. To a certain degree this is facilitated by an absence of data about outcomes, which discourages hand-wringing over disparities where it is difficult to know whether they are due to discrimination or differences in baseline preference.

Americans are, both by political tradition and temperament, far more disposed toward accepting the Canadian model than the Singaporean. Furthermore, unlike the Singaporean constitution, which entrenches a set of shared values, the United States has a rights-based constitution. This favours a process-based approach in several ways. It gives individuals standing to demand equal treatment, and it protects various spheres of personal choice from social control. It also blocks implementation of outcome-based schemes that violate process neutrality too egregiously. Thus the courts have played an important role in pushing Americans in the direction of the process-based model. At the same time, a large number of Americans lack the forbearance to sit by while process neutrality does its work. And African-Americans are, for obvious reasons, tired of waiting for justice and equality. Given the background racial inequalities in American society, many perfectly neutral institutions are guaranteed to produce radically unequal outcomes. For example, the race-blind application of admissions criteria at many ultra-competitive American universities would result in many classes in which almost no African-American applicants were accepted. The optics of this is one that many Americans consider intolerable.[110] As a result, the practice of adjusting admissions procedures to ensure more equal outcomes has become widespread.

Complicating the discursive landscape is the fact that the issue has become polarized along partisan lines, with conservative courts attempting to impose constitutional constraints on any departure from process neutrality.[111] This has pushed Democrats in the direction of a more outcome-based way of thinking about equality, in part as a way of avoiding adverse court judgments. For example, affirmative action programs in university admissions that apply very different standards to individuals in different census categories have been successfully defended against charges of unconstitutionality by insisting that they are not about screening applicants, but rather about crafting an incoming class that will maximize the quality of the educational experience. Achievement of the pedagogical objectives of the program is said to be enhanced if a certain level of "diversity" is present in the incoming class, and so race becomes a relevant consideration in assessing applications (rather than a prohibited ground of discrimination). Although adopted primarily for legal reasons, this defence of affirmative action has increasingly influenced the way that Americans think about the moral aspect of these programs as well, pushing them in the direction of more consequentialist forms of reasoning and outcome-based measures.

Ibram X. Kendi, for example, defines racial inequality in purely outcome-based terms, as any division of advantages that does not result in members of each racial group receiving the same amount on average.[112] He then defines as "racist" any policy or institutional process that promotes, generates, or preserves racial inequality. Predictably, he then has no use for process-neutrality. In his view, "racial discrimination" will be bad only if it promotes racially unequal outcomes, but good if it promotes equal outcomes.[113] This approach is consonant with many discussions of systemic or structural racism, which assume that merely observing inequalities of outcome is sufficient to convict an institution of an objectionable form of racism. This outcome-based thinking has also trickled into popular discourse, so that racial representation is increasingly not construed in terms of non-discrimination, but rather in terms of the outcome-based language of "diversity" (or in the current parlance, of creating institutions that "look like America").[114] All of this thinking takes the US population as a baseline and then tries to arrange institutions to produce outcomes that precisely mirror this baseline.

As a result, the best way to describe the current American approach to racial inclusion would to be say that it is attempting to achieve Singaporean outcomes using Canadian methods. Part of the unwillingness to use Singaporean methods is due to different factions within American society endorsing different approaches, but part of it involves a genuine case of willing the end but not the means. Americans are, after all, perfectly capable of achieving Singaporean outcomes, under circumstances in which they are willing to use Singaporean methods. The most clear-cut example is the US military, which is widely regarded as the most successfully integrated institution in American society. That is because the military is not obliged to care about the preferences of its soldiers on such questions as lodgings, dress, or diet. When the decision was made to desegregate, the US Army integrated its barracks in basically the same way that the government of Singapore integrates an apartment building. If the United States were willing to desegregate residential apartment buildings in the same way, the problem of segregation would have disappeared a long time ago.

Unfortunately, instead of sticking to a process-based approach, which is more in keeping with its national traditions, the United States has instead adopted an inconsistent hybrid of wanting outcomes that perfectly reflect the demographics of American society, but then leaving individuals free to make choices that will significantly affect those outcomes. One can see this most clearly in the policies that have been adopted to integrate its primary and secondary school system. Instead of equalizing student funding across school districts, which would have eliminated a major incentive that drives residential sorting, American courts opted instead for the more overtly coercive option of race-based quotas in schools, combined with busing, and the almost complete elimination of school choice within the public system. This is all consistent with a Singaporean approach. And yet, in a uniquely American touch, this was combined with a "back door" that allowed people to escape from it – either by putting their children in private school, or moving to suburban neighbourhoods outside the busing zone. As a result, the coercive features of the American system wound up falling only on the lower and working classes (who, if white, where then accused of racism when they complained about it). Because complaints about the program were interpreted as racist, they were treated as just more evidence of the need for the program. The resulting spiral of protest and coercion generated class resentments among white Americans that still have not subsided.[115]

Because African-Americans are a national minority group, with a shared culture and traditions, there is no reason to expect their preferences to be the same as those of the majority population. Despite being distinguished by arbitrary characteristics, they are not a random sample of the population. And yet there is a constant expectation that institutions will produce outcomes that exactly mirror the racial profile of American society – so that 12 per cent of the cast of every television show will be black, 12 per cent of the musicians in every symphony orchestra will be black, 12 per cent of the faculty at any university department will be black, and so on.[116] These outcomes would be expected only if there were uniformity of preference between the white and black population, but uniformity of preference implies cultural homogeneity. This leads Americans to adopt commitments that are ultimately not compatible – to respect individual preferences and yet to achieve institutional outcomes that mirror the population. For example, the United States has over 100 "historically black colleges and universities" (HBCUs), such as Howard University, which enrol a significant fraction of African-American undergraduate students.[117] There is a commitment to respecting the choice of African-Americans who attend such institutions, as well as faculty who teach there. At the same time, there is the expectation that the rest of the university system will be integrated, where integration is understood to mean a fraction of black students and faculty that roughly matches that of the population.[118] It is no surprise that American universities find themselves importing foreigners in order to achieve these objectives (and why they have switched to the outcome-based language of "diversity" to justify their practices).

7. Example: Residential Integration

Few issues have produced greater recrimination, hand-wringing, and self-criticism among whites in the United States than that of residential integration. Popular perception seems to have been that, once formal discrimination ended in property purchase and rental, an influx of African-Americans into white neighbourhoods should have begun that would have gradually transformed every neighbourhood into a microcosm of America as a whole. The reality has been quite different. Of course, the phenomenon of residential "clustering" is hardly unique to African-Americans. In Canadian cities, for example, one can find neighbourhoods in which the population is almost entirely Chinese or Indian. The suspicion, however, is that African-American residential clustering is significantly less voluntary. Indeed, there is ample evidence of discrimination against African-Americans by lending institutions, landlords, and real estate agents, as well as their prospective white neighbours.[119] What makes the issue of residential segregation so intractable, however, is the fact that it is impossible to disaggregate the effects of past discrimination, present discrimination, and the exercise of preference.

It is important to observe that the mechanism through which populations are distributed across residential districts is extremely decentralized. With an apartment building full of rental units, there is usually a single person who decides who is to be accepted as a tenant and who is to be rejected. Thus if a building is entirely white, in the midst of a heterogeneous society, there is good reason to suspect the landlord of discrimination. With owner-occupied housing, on the other hand, there is no central gatekeeper; the racial composition of a neighbourhood is the product of hundreds of uncoordinated individual decisions. As a result, it is impossible to ascertain the preferences of individuals by looking at the composition of neighbourhoods. To take a highly stylized example, if both whites and blacks prefer to live in integrated neighbourhoods, but members of each group would also prefer to live in a neighbourhood in which their own race is in the majority, then the only way this preference can be satisfied is through a system of complete segregation.[120] The resulting spatial distribution does not actually correspond to anyone's actual preference, but no one controls the spatial distribution. People control only their own choices. As a result, everyone will complain about segregation, but no one will actually move.

When white Americans think about residential integration, they tend to imagine a situation in which the composition of each neighbourhood roughly reflects the fraction of each minority group in the population as a whole. In order to achieve this distribution, there would have to be no discrimination in housing. But it would also have to be the case that no one took any account of the racial composition of the neighbourhood in deciding where to live. The latter is perhaps a plausible account of how whites expect that other whites should make such decisions, but whites also tend to recognize that minorities suffer disadvantages living in majority-white neighbourhoods. As a result, most consider it permissible (i.e., not racist) for minorities to have reasonably strong own-race preferences. It is also not difficult to imagine circumstances in which it would be permissible for whites to have modest own-race preferences (e.g., many white and black Americans belong to Christian denominations that are not particularly integrated, and so wanting to live in a neighbourhood in which one can attend a local church generates a certain amount of residential clustering).

But once it is allowed that individuals can take the racial composition of the neighbourhood into account as a legitimate consideration when deciding whether to live there, it becomes impossible to say anything about the relative levels of discrimination or tolerance merely from observing the spatial distribution of individuals of different races. This is the upshot of Thomas Schelling's models of neighbourhood sorting, which show how counterintuitive the results can be of even modest own-race preferences for one's immediate neighbours. (As Schelling put it, racial assortment in housing is "a complex system with collective results that bear no close relation to individual intent.")[121] It is extremely easy to construct models in which permissible racial preferences generate very extreme clustering. The natural conclusion to draw from this would be that it does not make any sense to focus on outcomes. One cannot realistically infer anything about discrimination by looking at the spatial distribution, especially if one does not know what the underlying preferences are. It certainly does not make sense to call neighbourhoods "segregated" – which always implies moral condemnation – when one has no idea whether there is any actual exclusion at work. Policy therefore should be process-based, focused on eradicating discrimination in lending, rental, and real estate markets.

Many Americans, however, subscribe to an inconsistent triad of views, in which they want to achieve certain outcomes (such as neighbourhoods that "look like America"), but also want to respect process-neutrality and tolerate minority own-race preferences. This is an example of wanting to achieve Singaporean outcomes using Canadian methods. Consider Anderson, who articulates a traditional pro-integrationist position. Her argument for integration is primarily consequentialist, in that she thinks it generates benefits for all Americans. These benefits arise only if the spatial distribution actually puts whites and blacks in contact with one another. Thus the "imperative of integration" flows from a normative commitment to the neighbourhoods-that-look-like-America outcome.[122] And yet at the same time, she acknowledges that many African-Americans want to live in majority-black neighbourhoods and grants that this preference is legitimate.¹²³ Assuming that a range of such sentiment is permissible, it follows that the only way to achieve the outcome she considers imperative would be by violating process-neutrality. In other words, there would have to be a system of racial quotas in different neighbourhoods (or perhaps race-based surtaxes to discourage excessive clustering). And yet while she endorses racial "selection" and "goals" in certain institutional contexts, her recommendations in housing all focus on eliminating discrimination and reducing attitudinal racism among whites.¹²⁴ These are both good, but they are not actually means to the realization of the ends she favours.

Some American progressives go even further than Anderson, wanting both to integrate predominantly white neighbourhoods *and* to preserve the character of historically black neighbourhoods. Thus they find themselves in the position of applauding when African-Americans move into white neighbourhoods, but condemning (as "gentrification") the complementary process of whites moving into black neighbourhoods.¹²⁵ (Structurally, this is identical to those who would like to integrate US higher education *and* promote flourishing HBCUs.) One might find this comical, were it not for the fact that it has the capacity to gridlock property development, municipal planning, and even neighbourhood improvement in American cities, by motivating activists to impose demands that in principle can never be satisfied.

Many Americans believe that they can judge the level of discrimination and racial hostility in a community just by looking at its demographics. They are, in this respect, profoundly mistaken; it is practically impossible to infer underlying preferences from observed patterns. Furthermore, because African-Americans are a relatively small fraction of the US population, residential preferences within that group have an outsized impact on the integration of majority-white neighbourhoods. Thus the fact that enthusiasm for integration has cooled quite significantly within the African-American community is a factor that must be taken seriously.¹²⁶ It is noteworthy, for instance, that the most prominent African-American philosopher writing on issues of racial justice, Tommie Shelby, treats residential integration as essentially a non-issue.¹²⁷ Increasingly, whites care much more about residential integration than blacks. This may have something to do with the fact that, in many social circles, whites suffer a status injury from living in "lily-white suburbs," precisely because of the common view that this homogeneity is a symptom of underlying racism, and thus lack of urbanity or sophistication.

When it comes to residential patterns, Americans are united in the conviction that the current state of affairs is a reflection of societal racism, if not attitudinal then structural. The proposed remedy is "integration." And yet there is no consensus on what integration amounts to, nor is there any willingness to force integration on those who do not want it. Furthermore, any solution to the problem would have to be implemented via a hugely decentralized system (i.e., an overwhelmingly private, owner-occupied residential housing market), in which individuals are left free to act upon a wide range of permissible preferences. Thus it is hardly a surprise that the problem is never solved. Not only is there no coherent policy in place, there is not even a coherent vision of what the imperative of integration actually requires.

8. Conclusion

As an involuntarily incorporated minority group, African-Americans have little interest in following the immigrant route to integration, and neither can they be obliged to do so. And yet they are also not, to use the felicitous French term, *étatisable*, largely as the result of geographical dispersion, which effectively blocks the standard set of multinational arrangements. Stylizing somewhat, we can think of the polyethnic and multinational models of social integration as the "all-in" or the "all-out" approaches to institutional pluralism. For African-Americans, partly as a result of the distinctiveness of their normative claims, the United States has pursued an approach that blends elements of both, what might be thought of as a "half-in" model (or perhaps a "sometimes-in, sometimes-out" model). The question is whether there actually is a stable and coherent model to be found that is consistent with equality. Such a new model of integration has so far proven elusive.

In conclusion, I would like to suggest one reason for pessimism about the possibility of developing such a model. A great deal of group conflict is driven by an underlying feature of human psychology, sometimes referred to as "groupishness," which causes us to exhibit greater solidarity with individuals whom we perceive as "in-group" members, combined with antagonism toward those who are classified as "out-group."[128] While this cognitive bias is both powerful and pervasive, it is also (thankfully) subject to manipulation, because there is no innate specification of the basis for the distinction between in-group and out-group. Thus it is possible to change the group identification of individuals by increasing the salience of different social cues, causing them to distinguish in-group from out-group members in different ways. For certain differences, such as spoken language, such redirection can be extremely difficult, because mutual incomprehension will always be highly salient in any interaction between members of different linguistic groups. But for other differences, such as physiological variations in hair, eye, and skin colour, it is much less difficult to reduce their salience, so that they no longer serve as a basis for group identification.[129]

Out-group hostility contributes the visceral component to a substantial portion of xenophobia and attitudinal racism. It is also extremely difficult to overcome, once triggered, through straightforward reasoning and inhibition. As a result, successful polyethnic integration is normally achieved through measures that reduce the salience of those differences between individuals that are the most common axes of conflict, so that they do not become the focus of in-group bias and division.[130] Rather than allowing for the formation of strong ethnic identities, then suppressing any conflict that may develop, successful polyethnic integration is typically achieved by encouraging the formation of identities that cross-cut ethnic divisions. Minority group members who integrate typically collaborate in this effort, by diverting attention away from certain differentiating traits or limiting their public display.

National minority groups, by contrast, do the exact opposite. In part because of the challenges involved in sustaining an institutionally complete society, these groups are often under pressure to cultivate high levels of social solidarity, which can often be achieved by promoting in-group identification along ethnic lines, combined with antagonism toward out-group members. Because the multinational model of integration limits interaction between in-group and out-group members, the benefits of heightened solidarity within the group easily outweigh the frictions caused by greater antagonism toward outsiders. As a result, national minority groups will often seize upon small differences and amplify them, promoting them as central features of group identity and sources of ethnic pride.

The predominant tendency among African-Americans since the late 1960s has been to act in the way that national minority groups act, by promoting group identification or "race consciousness" (and by condemning "colour blindness" as involving a failure of recognition). This has the effect of increasing the salience of race in everyday interactions. Again, this cultural politics would be unexceptional if pursued in tandem with a political strategy that promotes institutional independence. But it fits very poorly with integrationist goals, since it blocks a major strategy used in successful models of polyethnic integration. (The recent American trend of seeking to promote "uncomfortable" conversations about race in everyday interaction represents an extreme form of this tendency. Successful multicultural societies have traditionally done the opposite, encouraging people of different ethnicities to become *more*

Table 1. Approaches to integration

	Institutions	
Group differences	Parallel	Shared
High salience	Minority nationalism	?
Low salience	Federalism	Multiculturalism

comfortable interacting with one another.) Again, one cannot say that there is no workable solution to be found here, only that it is very difficult to think of an instance in which the approach has been successful (see table 1). At very least, much more theoretically informed comparative analysis would be useful – to see whether there is any society in which a structure of shared institutions, combined with commitments that heighten the salience of group differences in everyday interaction, has resulted in a stable model of integration.

The integrationist ideal that is associated with Martin Luther King Jr. and the civil rights movement has conditioned Americans to expect social integration of African-Americans on the polyethnic model, with outcome-based measures of successful inclusion. But in neither case have Americans, either white or black, been willing to accept the means necessary to achieve these ends. This is what generates the two dilemmas that I have been trying to describe. The commitment to preservation of a distinct African-American culture and identity, on the one hand, and the aversion to compulsory forms of inclusion, on the other, have clearly worked at cross-purposes with the objectives specified by the integrationist ideal. Unwilling to decide which option to pursue, or more often, deeply divided over which option to pursue, African-Americans have been unable to formulate a unified set of demands. Lack of direction from the black community has, in turn, generated almost complete paralysis on the issue among progressive whites. As Gary Peller has observed, "While conservatives in America have articulated a substantive and existentially evocative vision of how the world should be, liberals and progressives have instead struggled over whether it is acceptable to have a position at all."[131] Absent any coherent policy agenda, white Americans have turned increasingly inward, toward extreme forms of confessional self-criticism.[132]

Although it may seem very far removed from the issue, Wilson's analysis of the bureaucracy problem provides a helpful way of thinking about the ongoing drama of race in America. Because the policy imperatives are contradictory, Wilson claims, there is no such thing as "solving" the bureaucracy problem. The most that we can do is choose which bureaucracy problem we are willing to live with.[133] Similarly, if the analysis that I have provided is correct, then Americans cannot solve the race problem. The most that they can do is choose which race problem they are willing to live with. Neither the multinational nor the polyethnic model of integration is fully adequate to the claims of African-Americans, and neither is the Singaporean nor Canadian model of inclusion. Unfortunately, these are the only models that are conceptually coherent and enjoy some record of practical success. Adopting just one approach to either dilemma would involve some compromise at the level of principle, but would have the advantage of generating a set of policy prescriptions that could actually be implemented in practice.

NOTES

1 E.g., Jim Wallis, *America's Original Sin* (Grand Rapids, MI: Brazos, 2016).
2 For two striking examples, see Ibram X. Kendi, *How to Be an Anti-Racist* (New York: Random House, 2019); Roy L. Brooks, *Integration or Separation?* (Cambridge, MA: Harvard University Press, 1999). Two recent examples from the philosophical literature are Elizabeth Anderson, *The Imperative of Integration* (Princeton, NJ: Princeton University Press, 2010); and Tommie Shelby, *Dark Ghettos* (Cambridge, MA: Harvard University Press, 2018). None of these books contain any reference to the experience of any nation other than the United States.
3 See Roy L. Brooks, *Atonement and Forgiveness: A New Model for Black Reparations* (Berkeley: University of California Press, 2004), who refers to it as "slave redress." See also William A. Darity and A. Kirsten Mullen, *From Here to Equality* (Chapel Hill: University of North Carolina Press, 2020). For a misleading presentation of the claim as centred on race, see Randall Robinson, *The Debt: What America Owes to Blacks* (New York: Penguin, 2000).
4 To pick just one rather extreme but not atypical example, consider "American Immigrants and the Dilemma of 'White-Sounding' Names," *Atlantic*, 3 January 2019. The Chinese student interviewed describes his dilemma of whether to adopt an "Anglo" name, such as Mark, Daniel, or Jason. The American writer, however, redescribes the choice in racial terms, thereby turning Mark into a white name, rather than an English or a Christian one.
5 B. Guy Peters, "What Is so Wicked about Wicked Problems? A Conceptual Analysis and a Research Program," *Policy and Society* 36, no. 3 (2017): 385–96.
6 See Max Fisher, "A Fascinating Map of the World's Most and Least Racially Tolerant Countries," *Washington Post*, 15 May 2013.

7 Will Kymlicka, *Multicultural Citizenship* (Oxford: Oxford University Press, 1996).
8 One exception is Andrew Valls, "A Liberal Defense of Black Nationalism," *American Political Science Review* 104, no. 3 (2010): 467–81. For modest elaboration of the view, see Will Kymlicka, "American Multiculturalism in the International Arena," *Dissent* (Fall 1998): 73–9.
9 Gunnar Myrdal, *An American Dilemma*, 2 vols. (New York: Harper & Brothers, 1944).
10 Americans often ignore this distinction and treat Hispanic as another race, e.g., Kendi, *How to Be an Antiracist*, 38. The distinction matters because Hispanic Americans are often subdivided into Black and white Hispanics. Note that Kendi uses the term "Latinx" instead of Hispanic. I will not use the former term because it does not correspond to either the official category or the preferred self-description of the majority of American Hispanics.
11 Harold Abramson, "Assimilation and Pluralism," in *Harvard Encyclopedia of American Ethnic Groups*, ed. Stephen Thernstrom (Cambridge, MA: Harvard University Press, 1980), 151.
12 Maria Campbell, *Half-Breed* (Toronto: McClelland & Stewart, 1973).
13 This formed the basis of the Canadian Supreme Court decision *R v Powley* (2003) SCC 43.
14 See Chris Andersen, *"Métis"* (Vancouver: UBC Press, 2014), 65–90. Note that large segments of the Métis population do not constitute a "visible minority," because they are indistinguishable from the majority white population. Indeed, the most celebrated Métis leader and rebel, Louis Riel, was only one-eighth Indian.
15 See Irene Bloemraad, *Becoming a Citizen* (Berkeley: University of California Press, 2006), 76–7. A comparable story can be told of Filipino Americans. See Paul Ong and Kate Viernes, "Filipino Americans and Educational Downward Mobility," *Asian American Policy Review* 23 (2012–13): 21–39.
16 While universities are not keen to publicize these numbers, it would appear that around 40 per cent of black students at competitive US universities are foreign. See Cord Jefferson, "Ivy League Fooled: How America's Top Colleges Avoid Real Diversity," *Good*, 2 September 2011, https://www.good.is/articles/ivy-league-fooled-how-america-s-top-colleges-avoid-real-diversity. See also Eghosa Asemota, "When Affirmative Action Becomes Diversity Only," *Cornell Policy Review*, 14 January 2018, https://web.archive.org/web/20201111212437/http://www.cornellpolicyreview.com/affirmative-action-becomes-diversity/. A surprisingly large fraction of the diversity in American institutions with public-facing roles, such as journalism or television, is achieved by importing Canadians, who are able to "pass" quite easily as American.

17 Arlie Hochschild, *Strangers in Their Own Land* (New York: New Press, 2017) has shown what a powerful fount of resentment these policies are. She analyses what she refers to as the "deep story" that underlies the Southern white politics of resentment. This involves the image of a queue, with many patiently waiting in line while others cut in front of them. She describes this narrative as one that "feels true" to many, but never takes seriously the possibility that it might actually *be* true (or if she does, she never explains to the reader why she thinks it is false).
18 Farah Stockman, "'We're Self-Interested': The Growing Identity Debate in Black America," *New York Times*, 8 November 2019. Note that this demand gets coded, within American partisan discourse, as "anti-immigrant," which then leads to its pre-emptory dismissal by most progressive Americans.
19 This is true of philosophical discourse as well. Reading Charles W. Mills, *The Racial Contract* (Ithaca, NY: Cornell University Press, 1997), it is easy to lose track of who is white (e.g., 44–5, 127).
20 Anderson, *Imperative of Integration*, 186.
21 See Norman Lester, *Le livre noir du Canada anglais*, tome 1 (Montreal: Intouchables, 2001).
22 Alan Patten, "Liberal Neutrality and Language Policy," *Philosophy and Public Affairs* 31, no. 4 (2003): 361–2; Philippe Van Parijs, "Linguistic Justice," in *Language Rights and Political Theory*, ed. Will Kymlicka and Alan Patten (Oxford: Oxford University Press 2003), 153–68.
23 Consider Mills's declaration that "whiteness is not a color at all, but rather a set of power relations," *Racial Contract*, 127.
24 Eric Kaufman, in *Whiteshift* (New York: Abrams Press, 2019), argues that the "white" designator is extremely flexible, shifting to include formerly non-white groups, and Asians in the process of becoming white, while Persians are for the most part already considered white. What Kaufman does not explain is why he embraces the racializing language, instead of advocating its termination.
25 Michael Lipksy, *Street-Level Bureaucracy*, 30th anniversary ed. (New York: Russell Sage, 2010), 45–8; James Q. Wilson, *Bureaucracy* (New York: Basic Books, 1989); see also James Q. Wilson, "The Bureaucracy Problem," *Public Interest* 6 (1967): 3–9.
26 Wilson, "Bureaucracy Problem," 4.
27 This is why "bad actor" explanations are always more popular with the young, who lack the relevant lived experience.
28 Wilson, "Bureaucracy Problem," 4.
29 Herbert Kaufman, *Red Tape* (Washington, DC: Brookings, 1977), 35.
30 Or as President Barack Obama put it, a "racial stalemate." Quoted in Edmund Fong, *American Exceptionalism and the Remains of Race* (New York: Routledge, 2015), 5.

31 Frank B. Wilderson III, *Afropessimism* (New York: W.W. Norton, 2020); Ta-Nehisi Coates, *We Were Eight Years in Power* (New York: Random House, 2017).
32 Brooks, *Integration or Separation?*
33 Michelle Alexander, *The New Jim Crow* (New York: New Press, 2012).
34 J. Micah Roos, Michael Hughes, and Ashley V. Reichelmann, "A Puzzle of Racial Attitudes: A Measurement Analysis of Racial Attitudes and Policy Indicators," *Socius* 5, no. 1 (2019): 1–14.
35 E.g., Kaufman, *Whiteshift*, 380. The United States is an outlier here for having the highest fraction of the population who say it is racist to want to reduce immigration in order to preserve majority demographic share. Note also that the level of discrimination experienced by African-Americans in the US housing market is extremely mild in comparison with minority groups in many European countries. Kaufman, *Whiteshift*, 391.
36 Feng Hou, Zheng Wu, Christoph Schimmele, and John Myles, "Cross-Country Variation in Interracial Marriage: A USA-Canada Comparison of Metropolitan Areas," *Ethnic and Racial Studies* 38, no. 9 (2015): 1591. The first step to understanding the difference in outgroup marriage rates is to observe that Blacks constitute a much smaller fraction of the Canadian population (0.1 per cent in 1951, although since then significantly increased as the result of immigration), which means many have no choice but to "marry out." The structure of social networks also has an enormous impact, as witnessed by the rather significant "Tinder bump" experienced in rates of interracial marriage in the United States. The widespread use of dating apps makes it much easier for individuals to meet others outside their real-life social networks. The fact that this led to a large-scale increase in interracial dating and marriage shows that the previous low levels were not due entirely to attitudinal racism, but rather were significantly limited by opportunity. See Philipp Hergovich and Josué Ortega, "The Strength of Absent Ties: Social Integration via Online Dating," SSRN working paper (14 September 2018), https://doi.org/10.2139/ssrn.3044766.
37 Hou et al., "Cross-Country Variation in Interracial Marriage," 1592. Note that American approval for Asian-white intermarriage is *lower* than for black-white intermarriage, even though rates of Asian-white intermarriage are higher in the United States than in Canada.
38 Richard L. Morrill, "School Busing and Demographic Change," *Urban Geography* 10, no. 4 (1989): 348. The fact that court-ordered busing schemes were often so inefficient meant that they bused far more children than necessary, which in turn caused many Americans to overestimate the magnitude of the problem.
39 John B. McConahay, Betty B. Hardee, and Valerie Batts, "Has Racism Declined in America? It Depends on Who Is Asking and What Is Asked," *Journal of Conflict Resolution* 25, no. 4 (1981): 563–79.

40 Anthony G. Greenwald and Linda Hamilton Krieger, "Implicit Bias: Scientific Foundations," *California Law Review* 94, no. 4 (2006): 945–67. Brooks describes white racism not as an attitude but a "state of being," in *Integration or Separation?*, 107.

41 Frederick L. Oswald, Gregory Mitchell, Hart Blanton, James Jaccard, and Philip E. Tetlock, "Predicting Ethnic and Racial Discrimination: A Meta-Analysis of IAT Criterion Studies," *Journal of Personality and Social Psychology* 105, no. 2 (2013): 171–92. For discussion, see Olivia Goldhill, "The World Is Relying on a Flawed Psychological Test to Fight Racism," *Quartz*, 3 December 2017, https://qz.com/1144504/the-world-is-relying-on-a-flawed-psychological-test-to-fight-racism/.

42 E.g., Jane H. Hill, *The Everyday Language of White Racism* (Chichester, UK: Wiley-Blackwell, 2008), 2–3.

43 Michael Hardimon, "Should We Narrow the Scope of 'Racism' to Accommodate White Sensitivities?," *Critical Philosophy of Race* 7, no. 2 (2019): 223–46, has defended the "broader" use of the term "racism," on the grounds that the level of moral condemnation that is implicit in the use of the term can admit of degrees. His argument, however, does not deal with the issue that concerns me, which is that many contemporary uses of the term "systemic racism" do not provide the basis for *any* condemnation. Tommie Shelby, "Racism, Moralism, and Social Criticism," *Du Bois Review* 11, no. 1 (2014): 57–74, has defended a more subtle position, according to which "racism" need not imply *moral* condemnation, only that the arrangement is unjust. Again, the problem is that theorists like Ibram Kendi, who use the term "racist" to describe any institution that generates racial disparities in outcome, are using it to describe states of affairs that Shelby would not recognize as unjust either.

44 The problem is exacerbated, I believe, by the fact that the issue is so emotionally fraught among Americans that most are unable to debate it dispassionately. The fact that accusations of racism are made so freely, even in response to very slight disagreements, does not help. For an extreme example, see Ibram X. Kendi, *Stamped from the Beginning* (New York: Nation Books, 2016); also Kendi, *How to Be an Anti-Racist*.

45 Wilson, "Bureaucracy Problem," 8.

46 Mills, *Racial Contract*, 77.

47 Mills, 77.

48 Trudy Govier, *Social Trust and Human Communities* (Montreal and Kingston: McGill-Queen's University Press, 1997), 108.

49 Ernest Gellner, *Nations and Nationalism* (Ithaca, NY: Cornell University Press, 1983).

50 Arlie Russell Hochschild, *The Managed Heart* (Berkeley: University of California Press, 2012). Although this is not Hochschild's point, her

discussion makes it easy to see how the consumer economy creates problems in contexts of cultural pluralism.
51 Kymlicka, *Multicultural Citizenship*, 11.
52 Kymlicka, 10.
53 This is the Royal 22nd Regiment, known colloquially as the "Van Doos," which is the English pronunciation of the French pronunciation of the number 22.
54 Abdurrahman Aydemir and Chris Robinson, *Return and Onward Migration among Working Age Men* (Ottawa: Statistics Canada, 2006). Note that refugees pose a different set of issues. Here, as elsewhere, when I refer to "migrants" I am referring to immigrants, not displaced persons.
55 See the concept of an "open access" order in Douglass C. North, John Joseph Wallis, and Barry R. Weingast, *Violence and Social Orders* (Cambridge: Cambridge University Press, 2009).
56 Kymlicka, *Multicultural Citizenship*, 17.
57 See Joseph H. Carens, ed., *Is Quebec Nationalism Just?* (Montreal and Kingston: McGill-Queen's University Press, 1995).
58 Alan Cairns, *Citizens Plus* (Vancouver: UBC Press, 2001), 52.
59 Harold Cardinal, *The Unjust Society* (Vancouver: Douglas & McIntyre, 1969), 139.
60 Kymlicka, *Multicultural Citizenship*, 24. For discussion, see Fong, *American Exceptionalism and the Remains of Race*, 36–8.
61 Brooks, *Integration or Separation?*; Gary Peller, *Critical Race Consciousness* (New York: Taylor & Francis, 2012).
62 For an example of the checkmate this can generate, see Harold Cruse, *The Crisis of the Negro Intellectual* (New York: NYRB books, 2005). The fact that this would be a "win" for white supremacists is, for many, sufficient to discredit the option.
63 Kymlicka, "American Multiculturalism in the International Arena," 76. See also Valls, "Liberal Defense of Black Nationalism," 468–70.
64 Brooks, *Integration or Separation?*, 189.
65 On the American qualities of African-Americans, see Albert Murray, *The Omni-Americans* (New York: Plenum, 1970).
66 Kymlicka, I believe, underestimates the national character of African-Americans because he focuses too much on the lack of shared culture and institutions at the point of incorporation into American society, and pays too little attention to the subsequent history.
67 J.L. Dillard, *Black English* (New York: Random House, 1972).
68 Andrew Valls, "The Broken Promise of Racial Integration," in *NOMOS XLIII: Moral and Political Education*, ed. Stephen Macedo and Yael Tamir (New York: NYU Press, 2001), 462.
69 John U. Ogbu, "Beyond Language: Ebonics, Proper English, and Identity in a Black-American Speech Community," *American Educational Research*

Association 36, no. 2 (1999): 147–84. In a more popular vein, much of the comedy in the TV show *The Fresh Prince of Bel Air* arose from the tension between Will, who is presented as authentically black ("west Philadelphia born and raised") and his "stuck-up" Californian cousin, Carlton, who is mocked for his inability to dance, seriousness about school, and standard English diction.

70 Claire L. Adida, David D. Laitin, and Marie-Anne Valfort, *Why Muslim Integration Fails in Christian-Heritage Societies* (Cambridge, MA: Harvard University Press, 2016), 152.

71 Adida et al., *Why Muslim Integration Fails*, 153.

72 The classic study that found discrimination is Marianne Bertrand and Sendhil Mullainathan, "Are Emily and Greg More Employable than Lakisha and Jamal? A Field Experiment on Labor Market Discrimination," *American Economic Review* 94, no. 4 (2004): 991–1013. For a null result, see Rajeev Darolia, Cory Koedel, Paco Martorell, Katie Wilson, and Francisco Perez-Arce, "Race and Gender Effects on Employer Interest in Job Applicants: New Evidence from a Resume Field Experiment," *Applied Economics Letters* 23, no. 12 (2015): 1–4.

73 Christian Lander, *Stuff White People Like* (New York: Random House, 2008).

74 Stokely Carmichael and Charles V. Hamilton, *Black Power* (New York: Vintage, 1967), 55.

75 Robert Browne describes it "as a sort of painless genocide." Robert S. Browne, "A Case for Separation," in *Separatism or Integration?*, ed. Robert S. Browne and Bayard Rustin (New York: A. Philip Randolph Educational Fund, 1968), 7.

76 Anderson, *Imperative of Integration*, 76–7.

77 Ta-Nehisi Coates, *Between the World and Me* (New York: Spiegel and Grau, 2015), 56.

78 Note that in American academic and public discourse, Black nationalism is traditionally construed as opposed to liberalism, where as liberalism is simply identified with integrationist policies.

79 Carmichael and Hamilton, *Black Power*, 164–77.

80 They also work for groups that do not care about the inequalities that may develop. The old-order Amish in America or the Hutterites in Canada are perfectly happy to secede from mainstream institutions, even though their own society provides only a limited set of compensations. The fact that they are untroubled by the inequalities in standard of living that result from this arrangement is what makes it stable.

81 As a student at a French Catholic school, I studied the French national curriculum until grade 3, in 1974, at which point the school system switched to the domestic curriculum.

82 Ogbu, "Beyond Language," 147. See also an excellent summary of the difference in attitude toward SAE between immigrants and "non-immigrant minorities," 154–5.
83 Kymlicka, *Multicultural Citizenship*, 25.
84 Kymlicka, 25.
85 Brooks, *Integration or Separation?*
86 For a nationalist interpretation of affirmative action, see Gary Peller, "Race Consciousness," *Duke Law Journal* 39, no. 4 (1990): 776–7.
87 *Corbiere v Canada (Minister of Indian and Northern Affairs)* 1999 2 SCR 203.
88 It is, in fact, not just a little bit like apartheid – both are the product of the same system of British colonial administration. The difference is that in South Africa it was applied to a group that formed the demographic majority.
89 For the "peacekeeper" characterization, see John van Maanen, "The Asshole," in *Policing*, ed. P.K. Manning and J. Van Maanen (Santa Monica: CA Goodyear, 1978), 227–38. On "respectability," see P.A.J. Waddington, *Policing Citizens* (London: Routledge, 1999), 62.
90 Jane Jacobs, *Death and Life of Great American Cities* (New York: Vintage, 1961), 35–8.
91 Waddington, *Policing Citizens*, 49–55.
92 Kymlicka, *Multicultural Citizenship*, 236.
93 Kymlicka, 115.
94 Savvas Lithopoulos, *Lifecycle of First Nation Administered Police Services in Canada* (Ottawa: Public Safety Canada, 2018). Note that similar arrangements already prevailed provincially. Quebec has its own provincial police force in part because no one ever imagined that the RCMP – in its origins essentially a cavalry division of the British army – could have policed the former French colony.
95 Lithopoulos, *Lifecycle of First Nation Administered Police Services in Canada*.
96 Nathaniel J. Pallone and James J. Hennessy, "Blacks and Whites as Victims and Offenders in Aggressive Crime in the U.S.," *Journal of Offender Rehabilitation* 30, nos. 1–2 (2000): 1–33. On demand for policing, see James Forman Jr., *Locking Up Our Own* (New York: Farrar, Straus and Giroux, 2017).
97 Anthony A. Braga and Rod K. Brunson, "The Police and Public Discourse on 'Black-on-Black' Violence," *New Perspectives in Policing*, May 2015, 1–21; Anderson, *Imperative of Integration*, 41–3.
98 Jeremy Ashkenas and Haeyoun Park, "The Race Gap in America's Police Departments," *New York Times*, 8 April 2015. The prime example is Ferguson, MO, where Michael Brown was killed in 2014.
99 Kendi, *How to Be an Anti-Racist*, 147–8.

100 Three of the six Baltimore police officers charged in the killing of Freddie Grey in 2015 were Black or minority, just as one of the three officers who failed to prevent the killing of George Floyd in 2020 was Black. Coates expresses what I suspect is a widespread view when discussing the 2000 police shooting of Prince Jones, *Between the World and Me*, 83. The fact that the officer was Black makes no particular difference, since "I knew that Prince was not killed by a single officer so much as he was murdered by his country and all the fears that have marked it from birth" (78).

101 Movement for Black Lives, *A Vision for Black Lives*, 14, http://whitesforracialequity.org/wp-content/uploads/2017/07/BLM-vision-booklet.pdf.

102 Aaron Ross Coleman, "Police Reform, Defunding, and Abolition, Explained," *Vox*, 16 July 2020, https://www.vox.com/21312191/police-reform-defunding-abolition-black-lives-matter-protests. Note that most European welfare states, which provide more generous funding for social services, *also* have a significantly higher number of police officers per capita than the United States.

103 John D. Harden and Justin Jouvenal, "Crime Rose Unevenly When Stay-at-Home Orders Lifted: The Racial Disparity Is the Widest in Years," *Washington Post*, 9 October 2020, https://www.washingtonpost.com/graphics/2020/local/public-safety/crime-rate-coronavirus/.

104 Elle Reeve and Samantha Guff, "They Envisioned a World without Police: Inside Seattle's CHOP Zone, Protestors Struggled to Make It Real," *CNN*, 6 July 2020, https://www.cnn.com/2020/07/05/us/chop-seattle-police-protesters-public-safety. As Americans like to say, "This is why we can't have nice things."

105 Sonja B. Starr, "Estimating Gender Disparities in Federal Criminal Cases," *American Law and Economics Review* 17, no. 1 (2015): 127–59.

106 This is what the US Supreme Court has tried to get at with its distinction between "disparate impact" and "disparate treatment." See Joseph A. Seiner, "Disentangling Disparate Impact and Disparate Treatment: Adapting the Canadian Approach," *Yale Law and Policy Review* 25, no. 1 (2006–7): 95–142.

107 For an overview, see Geetha Reddy, "Race Rules in Singapore," in *Singapore: Negotiating State and Society, 1965–2015*, ed. Jason Lim and Terence Lee (New York: Routledge, 2016), 54–75.

108 *Statutes of the Republic of Singapore: Penal Code*, rev. ed. (Singapore: Law Revision Commission, 2008), 155 (chap. 15, §298).

109 For an American perspective on this tribunal system, see Mark Hemingway, "Idiot's Guide to Completely Idiotic Canadian 'Human Rights' Tribunals," *National Review*, 5 June 2008.

110 At the time of writing, the City of New York is considering closing down its competitive-admission public secondary schools, because of the declining number of African-American students who are being accepted. See Eliza Shapiro, "Only 7 Black Students Got into Stuyvesant, N.Y.'s Most Selective High School, out of 895 Spots," *New York Times*, 18 March 2019.

111 Chief Justice of the Supreme Court John Roberts's line, that "the way to stop discrimination on the basis of race is to stop discriminating on the basis of race," is often quoted as a way of dismissing the approach, not because there is anything intrinsically wrong with the claim, but merely because John Roberts said it. *Parents Involved in Community Schools v Seattle School District*, No. 1, 551 U.S. 701 (2007).

112 Kendi, *How to Be an Antiracist*, 18.

113 Kendi, 19. It is important to emphasize how radically consequentialist these claims are. On Kendi's view, a system of race-based taxation, in which white Americans were charged higher income taxes than Black Americas, based solely on their race, would be "anti-racist."

114 E.g., see Katherine C. Naff, *To Look Like America* (New York: Taylor & Francis, 2001).

115 For a good account of how acrimonious this became, see David Frum, *How We Got Here* (New York: Basic Books, 2000).

116 For a striking example of the recent shift in American thinking, away from a concern over discrimination and toward an outcome-based conception of diversity, see Anthony Tommasini, "To Make Orchestras More Diverse, End Blind Auditions," *New York Times*, 16 July 2020.

117 Brooks, *Integration or Separation?*, 33–4.

118 Valls writes, "If predominantly black schools have a legitimate place in our education system, the same cannot be said of schools that are all, or nearly all white.... Majority-white schools should do everything they can to attract and retain black students, and the existence of privileged, lily-white schools is certainly to be lamented." "Broken Promise of Racial Integration," 471–2.

119 Brooks, *Integration or Separation?*, 58–68; Richard Rothstein, *The Color of Law* (New York: Liveright, 2017).

120 Thomas Schelling, *Micromotives and Macrobehavior* (New York: W.W. Norton, 1978). His example is that of a party, in which there are two rooms, but partygoers prefer to be in the room that has the most people (187). As a result, everyone winds up in one room, and no one in the other. This is not the outcome that anyone wants, and everyone will complain about how crowded it is, but no one will move to the other room. Their desire is for *others* to move.

121 Thomas Schelling, "Models of Segregation," *American Economic Review* 59, no. 2 (1969): 488.
122 Anderson, *Imperative of Integration*, 25–6.
123 Anderson, 113.
124 Anderson, 177. The only exception is her support for a housing voucher scheme "to promote black entry into non-black middle-class neighbourhoods" (177). It is doubtful, however, that she would support a program that would provide vouchers only to Blacks, who would be required to use them in white neighbourhoods.
125 A striking example can be found in the *New York Times*, 22 August 2021, which contained one article lamenting the difficulties experienced by owners in historically Black neighbourhoods finding buyers who are *not* white (see Jacquelynn Kerubo, "What Gentrification Means for Black Homeowners," *New York Times*, 22 August 2021), while a second article focused on the difficulties experienced by Blacks wanting to move into non-Black neighbourhoods (*New York Times*, "In New York, No Shelter from the Ills of Racial Bias," 22 August 2021), comparing the situation to that of "South Africa apartheid."
126 Brooks, *Integration or Separation?*, 189.
127 Shelby, *Dark Ghettos*, 62.
128 Jonathan Haidt, *The Righteous Mind* (New York: Vintage, 2012), 221.
129 Joseph Heath, *Enlightenment 2.0* (Toronto: HarperCollins, 2014), 332–3.
130 For an interesting study of "practices of toleration" in the context of religious conflict, see Benjamin J. Kaplan, *Divided by Faith* (Cambridge, MA: Harvard University Press, 2007).
131 Peller, *Critical Race Consciousness*, 102.
132 E.g., Robin DeAngelo, *White Fragility* (Boston: Beacon, 2018).
133 Wilson, "Bureaucracy Problem," 8.

Bibliography

Abizadeh, Arash. "Cooperation, Pervasive Impact, and Coercion: On the Scope (Not Site) of Distributive Justice." *Philosophy and Public Affairs* 35, no. 4 (2007): 318–58.

Abramson, Harold. "Assimilation and Pluralism." In *Harvard Encyclopedia of American Ethnic Groups*, edited by Stephen Thernstrom, 150–60. Cambridge, MA: Harvard University Press, 1980.

Acemoglu, Daron, and James Robinson. *Why Nations Fail*. New York: Random House, 2012.

Adida, Claire L., David D. Laitin, and Marie-Anne Valfort. *Why Muslim Integration Fails in Christian-Heritage Societies*. Cambridge, MA: Harvard University Press, 2016.

Adler, Matthew D. "The Pigou-Dalton Principle and the Structure of Distributive Justice." SSRN working paper, 2013. https://ssrn.com/abstract=2263536.

Ainslie, George. *Picoeconomics*. Cambridge: Cambridge University Press, 1992.

Alba, Richard, and Nancy Foner. *Strangers No More: Immigration and the Challenge of Integration in North America and Western Europe*. Princeton, NJ: Princeton University Press, 2015.

Alesina, Alberto, Reza Baqir, and William Easterly. "Public Goods and Ethnic Divisions." *Quarterly Journal of Economics* 114, no. 4 (1999): 1243–84.

Alexander, Michelle. *The New Jim Crow*. New York: New Press, 2012.

Algan, Yann, and Pierre Cahuc. "Inherited Trust and Growth." *American Economic Review* 100, no. 5 (2010): 2060–92.

Allee, W.C. "Dominance and Hierarchy in Societies of Vertebrates." In *Structure et physiologie des sociétées animales : colloques internationaux*, edited by P.P. Grasse, 157–81. Paris: CNRS, 1952.

Allen, David. *Getting Things Done*. London: Penguin, 2001.

Allen, Nick. "Nigel Farage Says Donald Trump Was 'Like a Silverback Gorilla' in US Presidential Debate." *Telegraph*, 10 October 2016. https://

www.telegraph.co.uk/news/2016/10/10/nigel-farage-says-donald-trump-was-like-a-silverback-gorilla-in/.
Allen, Robert. *Farm to Factory*. Princeton, NJ: Princeton University Press, 2003.
American Psychiatric Association. *Diagnostic and Statistical Manual of Mental Disorders*, 5th ed. Washington, DC: American Psychiatric Publishing, 2013.
Anderson, Cameron, Michael W. Kraus, Adam D. Galinsky, and Dacher Keltner. "The Local-Ladder Effect: Social Status and Subjective Well-Being." *Psychological Science* 23, no. 7 (2012): 764–71.
Andersen, Chris. *"Métis."* Vancouver: UBC Press, 2014.
Anderson, Elijah. "The Code of the Streets." *Atlantic*, 1 May 1994.
Anderson, Elizabeth. *The Imperative of Integration*. Princeton, NJ: Princeton University Press, 2010.
– "What Is the Point of Equality?" *Ethics* 109, no. 2 (1990): 287–337.
Anderson, Joel. "Structured Nonprocrastination: Scaffolding Efforts to Resist the Temptation to Reconstrue Unwarranted Delay." In *Procrastination, Health, and Well-Being*, edited by Fuschia M. Sirois and Timothy A. Pychyl, 43–63. Amsterdam: Elsevier, 2016.
Arluke, Arnold, Louanne Kennedy, and Ronald C. Kessler. "Reexamining the Sick-Role Concept: An Empirical Assessment." *Journal of Health and Social Behavior* 20, no. 1 (1979): 30–6.
Arneson, Richard J. "'Equality of What?' Revisited." SSRN, 5 August 2010. https://ssrn.com/abstract=1653981.
Arnsperger, Christian. "Envy-Freeness and Distributive Justice." *Journal of Economic Surveys* 8, no. 2 (1994): 155–86.
Asemota, Eghosa. "When Affirmative Action Becomes Diversity Only." *Cornell Policy Review*, 14 January 2018. https://web.archive.org/web/20201111212437/http://www.cornellpolicyreview.com/affirmative-action-becomes-diversity/.
Ashkenas, Jeremy, and Haeyoun Park. "The Race Gap in America's Police Departments." *New York Times*, 8 April 2015.
Aydemir, Abdurrahman, and Chris Robinson. *Return and Onward Migration among Working Age Men*. Ottawa: Statistics Canada, 2006.
Ayres, Ian, and John Braithwaite. *Responsive Regulation*. New York: Oxford University Press, 1992.
Bains, Camille. "Illicit Drug Users Try to Shed Stigma of Being Called Addicts." *Toronto Star*, 28 January 2017.
Bakan, Joel. *The Corporation: The Pathological Pursuit of Profit and Power*. Toronto: Penguin, 2004.
Bandura, Albert. "Self-Efficacy: Toward a Unifying Theory of Behavioral Change." *Psychological Review* 84, no. 2 (1977): 191–215.
Banerjee, Abhijit V., Rachel Glennerster, and Esther Duflo. "Putting a Band-Aid on a Corpse: Incentives for Nurses in the Indian Public Health Care

System." *Journal of the European Economic Association* 6, nos. 2–3 (2008): 487–500.

Barkow, Jerome H., Leda Cosmides, and John Tooby, eds. *The Adapted Mind*. Oxford: Oxford University Press, 2003.

Baron, Marcia. "Justifications and Excuses." *Ohio State Journal of Criminal Law* 2, no. 2 (2005): 387–406.

Barry, Brian. *Culture and Equality*. Cambridge, MA: Harvard University Press, 2001.

Bascom, William R. "Ponapean Prestige Economy." *Southwestern Journal of Anthropology* 4, no. 2 (1948): 211–21.

Baumgartner, Mary P. "The Myth of Discretion." In *The Uses of Discretion*, edited by Keith Hawkins, 129–62. Oxford: Clarendon, 1992.

Bebchuk, Lucian, and Jesse Fried. *Pay without Performance*. Cambridge, MA: Harvard University Press, 2009.

Becker, Gary. *The Economics of Discrimination*. Chicago: University of Chicago Press, 1957.

Beitz, Charles. *Political Theory and International Relations*. Princeton, NJ: Princeton University Press, 1979.

Bengali, Shashank. "India Test Cheating Stirs Outrage – Then People Start Dying." *Los Angeles Times*, 17 July 2015.

Bermúdez, José Luis. "Defining 'Harm' in the Tuvel Affair." *Inside Higher Ed*, 5 May 2017.

Bernstein, Irwin S. "Dominance: The Baby and the Bathwater." *Behavioral and Brain Sciences* 4, no. 3 (1981): 419–29.

Bertrand, Mariann, and Sendhil Mullainathan. "Are Emily and Greg More Employable than Lakisha and Jamal? A Field Experiment on Labor Market Discrimination." *American Economic Review* 94, no. 4 (2004): 991–1013.

Bishop, Bill. *The Big Sort*. New York: Houghton Mifflin, 2008.

Blair, Margaret M. "Firm-Specific Human Capital and the Theories of the Firm." In *Employees and Corporate Governance*, edited by Margaret M. Blair and Mark J. Roe, 58–91. Washington, DC: Brookings, 2000.

Blake, Michael. "Distributive Justice, State Coercion and Autonomy." *Philosophy and Public Affairs* 30, no. 3 (2002): 257–96.

– "Immigration." In *Blackwell Companion to Applied Ethics*, edited by Christopher Heath Wellman, 224–37. Oxford: Blackwell Publishers, 2003.

– *Justice, Migration and Mercy*. New York: Oxford University Press, 2020.

Bloemraad, Irene. *Becoming a Citizen*. Berkeley: University of California Press, 2006.

Boehm, Christopher. *Hierarchy in the Forest*. Cambridge, MA: Harvard University Press, 1999.

– *Moral Origins*. New York: Basic Books, 2012.

Bonabeau, Eric, Guy Theraulaz, and Jean-Louis Deneubourg. "Mathematical Model of Self-Organizing Hierarchies in Animal Societies." *Bulletin of Mathematical Biology* 58, no. 4 (1996): 661–717.
Bouchard, Gérard, and Charles Taylor. *Building the Future: A Time for Reconciliation*. Quebec City: Gouvernement du Québec, 2008.
Bowles, Samuel, and Herbert Gintis. *A Cooperative Species*. Princeton, NJ: Princeton University Press, 2011.
Boyce, Christopher J., Gordon D.A. Brown, and Simon C. Moore. "Money and Happiness: Rank of Income, Not Income, Affects Life Satisfaction." *Psychological Science* 21, no. 4 (2010): 471–5.
Boyd, Marion. *Dispute Resolution in Family Law*. Toronto: Ontario Ministry of the Attorney General, 2004.
Boyd, Robert, and Peter Richerson. "The Evolution of Reciprocity in Sizable Groups." *Journal of Theoretical Biology* 132, no. 3 (1988): 337–56.
– *Not by Genes Alone*. Chicago: University of Chicago Press, 2005.
– "Solving the Puzzle of Human Cooperation." In *Evolution and Culture*, edited by S. Levinson, 105–32. Cambridge, MA: MIT Press, 2005.
Braga, Anthony A., and Rod K. Brunson. "The Police and Public Discourse on 'Black-on-Black' Violence." *New Perspectives in Policing*, May 2015, 1–21.
Braithwaite, John. *Crime, Shame and Reintegration*. Cambridge: Cambridge University Press, 1989.
Bratman, Michael. "Time, Rationality, and Self-Governance." *Philosophical Issues* 22, no. 1 (2012): 73–88.
Brennan, Geoffrey, and Philip Pettit. *The Economy of Esteem*. Oxford: Oxford University Press, 2006.
Brennan, Jason. *Why Not Capitalism?* Oxford: Routledge, 2014.
Briggs, Jean. *Never in Anger*. Cambridge, MA: Harvard University Press, 1971.
Brighouse, Harry, and Adam Swift. "Equality, Priority, and Positional Goods." *Ethics* 116, no. 3 (2006): 471–97.
Brooks, David. *Bobos in Paradise*. New York: Simon and Schuster, 2000.
Brooks, Roy L. *Atonement and Forgiveness: A New Model for Black Reparations*. Berkeley: University of California Press, 2004.
– *Integration or Separation?* Cambridge, MA: Harvard University Press, 1999.
Browne, Robert S. "A Case for Separation." In *Separatism or Integration?*, edited by Robert S. Browne and Bayard Rustin, 7–15. New York: A. Philip Randolph Educational Fund, 1968.
Buchanan, Allen. "Perfecting Imperfect Duties: Collective Action to Create Moral Obligations." *Business Ethics Quarterly* 6, no. 1 (1996): 27–42.
Burnham, Terence C., and Brian Hare. "Engineering Human Cooperation." *Human Nature* 18, no. 2 (2007): 88–108.
Cairns, Alan. *Citizens Plus*. Vancouver: UBC Press, 2001.
Campbell, Maria. *Half-Breed*. Toronto: McClelland & Stewart, 1973.

Caplan, Bryan. *Open Borders: The Science and Ethics of Immigration.* New York: Macmillan, 2020.
Cardinal, Harold. *The Unjust Society.* Vancouver: Douglas & McIntyre, 1969.
Carens, Joseph. "Aliens and Citizens: The Case for Open Borders." *Review of Politics* 49, no. 2 (1987): 251–73.
– *The Ethics of Immigration.* Oxford: Oxford University Press, 2013.
–, ed. *Is Quebec Nationalism Just?* Montreal and Kingston: McGill-Queen's University Press, 1995.
– "Migration and Morality: A Liberal Egalitarian Perspective." In *Free Movement: Ethical Issues in the Transnational Migration of People and Money*, edited by Brian Barry and Robert Goodin, 25–47. University Park, PA: Penn State Press, 1992.
Carmichael, Stokely, and Charles V. Hamilton. *Black Power.* New York: Vintage, 1967.
Center for Humane Technology. "App Ratings." https://www.humanetech.com/app-ratings.
Chaudhury, Nazmul, Jeffrey Hammer, Michael Kremer, Karthik Muralidharana, and F. Halsey Rogers. "Missing in Action: Teacher and Health Worker Absence in Developing Countries." *Journal of Economic Perspectives* 20, no. 1 (2006): 91–116.
Chen, Stefanos. "In New York, No Shelter from the Ills of Racial Bias." *New York Times*, 22 August 2021.
Chiao, Joan Y. "Neural Basis of Social Status Hierarchy across Species." *Current Opinion in Neurobiology* 20, no. 6 (2010): 803–9.
Clark, Andy. *Being There.* Cambridge, MA: MIT Press, 1998.
Clarke, Lynda. "Asking Questions about Sharia: Lessons from Ontario." In *Debating Sharia*, edited by Anna C. Korteweg and Jennifer A. Selby, 153–91. Toronto: University of Toronto Press, 2012.
Clinard, Marshall B., and Peter C. Yeager. *Corporate Crime.* New York: Free Press, 1980.
Coates, Ta-Nehisi. *Between the World and Me.* New York: Spiegel and Grau, 2015.
– *We Were Eight Years in Power.* New York: Random House, 2017.
Cohen, Albert K. *Delinquent Boys.* Glencoe, IL: Free Press, 1955.
Cohen, G.A. "On the Currency of Egalitarian Justice." *Ethics* 99, no. 4 (1989): 906–44.
– *If You're an Egalitarian, How Come You're So Rich?* Cambridge, MA: Harvard University Press, 2001.
– *Rescuing Justice and Equality.* Cambridge, MA: Harvard University Press, 2008.
– *Why Not Socialism?* Princeton, NJ: Princeton University Press, 2009.
Cole, Philip. *Philosophies of Exclusion.* Edinburgh: Edinburgh University Press, 2001.

Coleman, Aaron Ross. "Police Reform, Defunding, and Abolition, Explained." *Vox*, 16 July 2020. https://www.vox.com/21312191/police-reform-defunding-abolition-black-lives-matter-protests.

Collier, Paul. *Exodus*. Oxford: Oxford University Press, 2013.

Congleton, Roger D. "Efficient Status Seeking: Externalities and the Evolution of Status Games." *Journal of Economic Behavior and Organizations* 11, no. 2 (1989): 175–90.

Cosmides, Leda, John Tooby, and Robert Kurzban. "Perceptions of Race." *Trends in Cognitive Science* 7, no. 4 (2003): 173–9.

Cressy, Donald R. *Other People's Money*. Glencoe, IL: Free Press, 1953.

Cross, Patricia. "Not Can But Will College Teaching Be Improved?" *New Directions for Higher Education* 17 (1977): 1–15.

Cruse, Harold. *The Crisis of the Negro Intellectual*. New York: NYRB Books, 2005.

Dahl, Robert A. *A Preface to Economic Democracy*. Berkeley: University of California Press, 1985.

Dalrymple, Theodore. *Life at the Bottom*. Chicago: Ivan R. Dee, 2001.

– *Our Culture, What's Left of It*. Chicago: Ivan R. Dee, 2005.

Dana, Jason, Robyn Dawes, and Nathaniel Peterson. "Belief in the Unstructured Interview: The Persistence of an Illusion." *Judgment and Decision Making* 8, no. 5 (2013): 512–20.

Darity, William A., and A. Kirsten Mullen. *From Here to Equality*. Chapel Hill: University of North Carolina Press, 2020.

Darolia, Rajeev, Cory Koedel, Paco Martorell, Katie Wilson, and Francisco Perez-Arce. "Race and Gender Effects on Employer Interest in Job Applicants: New Evidence from a Resume Field Experiment." *Applied Economics Letters* 23, no. 12 (2015): 1–4.

Darwall, Stephen L. "Two Kinds of Respect." *Ethics* 88, no. 1 (1977): 36–49.

Davies, Robert William, Mark Harrison, and S.G. Wheatcroft. *The Economic Transformation of the Soviet Union, 1913–1945*. Cambridge: Cambridge University Press, 1994.

Deri, Sebastian, Shai Davidai, and Thomas Gilovich. "Home Alone: Why People Believe Others' Social Lives Are Richer than Their Own." *Journal of Personality and Social Psychology* 113, no. 6 (2017): 858–77.

de Soto, Hernando. *The Mystery of Capital*. New York: Basic Books, 2000.

de Waal, Frans B.W. *Good Natured: The Origins of Right and Wrong in Humans and Other Animals*. Cambridge, MA: Harvard University Press, 1997.

– "Natural Normativity: The 'Is' and 'Ought' of Animal Behavior." In *Evolved Morality*, edited by Frans B.W. de Waal, Patricia Smith Churchland, Telmo Pievani, and Stefano Parmigiani, 49–68. Leiden: Brill, 2014.

Diamond, Jared. *The World until Yesterday*. New York: Viking, 2012.

DiAngelo, Robin. *White Fragility*. Boston: Beacon, 2018.

Dillard, J.L. *Black English*. New York: Random House, 1972.
Dow, Gregory K. *Governing the Firm: Workers' Control in Theory and Practice*. New York: Cambridge University Press, 2003.
Dunbar, Robin. "Neocortex Size as a Constraint on Group Size in Primates." *Journal of Human Evolution* 22, no. 6 (1992): 469–93.
Durkheim, Émile. *The Division of Labor in Society*, translated by W.D. Halls. New York: Free Press, 1997.
– *Professional Ethics and Civic Morals*, translated by Cornelia Brookfield. London: Routledge, 2003.
Dworkin, Ronald. *Sovereign Virtue*. Cambridge, MA: Harvard University Press, 2000.
Easterbrook, Frank H., and Daniel R. Fischel. *The Economic Structure of Corporate Law*. Cambridge, MA: Harvard University Press, 1991.
Easterly, William. *The White Man's Burden*. New York: Penguin, 2006.
Economist. "The Link between Polygamy and War," 19 December 2017.
– "A Tightening Grip," 12 March 2015.
Edwards, Donald H., and Edward A. Kravitz. "Serotonin, Social Status and Aggression." *Current Opinion in Neurobiology* 7, no. 6 (1997): 812–19.
Eller, Jack Deavid. *Cruel Creeds, Virtuous Violence*. Amherst, NY: Prometheus, 2010.
Ellis-Sloan, Kyla. "Teenage Mothers, Stigma and Their 'Presentation of Self.'" *Sociological Research Online* 19, no. 1 (2014): 1–13.
Environics Institute. *Race Relations in Canada 2019: Final Report*, 2019. https://www.environicsinstitute.org/docs/default-source/project-documents/race-relations-2019-survey/race-relations-in-canada-2019-survey---final-report-english.pdf.
Estrin, Saul, and Virginie Pérotin. "Does Ownership Always Matter?" *International Journal of Industrial Organization* 9, no. 1 (1991): 55–72.
Exline, Julie J., and Anne L. Zell. "Antidotes to Envy: A Conceptual Framework." In *Envy: Theory and Research*, edited by Richard H. Smith, 315–31. Oxford: Oxford University Press, 2008.
Falk, Gerhard. *Stigma*. Amherst, NY: Prometheus, 2001.
Feigenbaum, Harvey B. "Public Enterprise in Comparative Perspective." *Comparative Politics* 15, no. 1 (1982): 101–22.
Festinger, Leon. "A Theory of Social Comparison Processes." *Human Relations* 7, no. 2 (1954): 117–40.
Finkelstein, Claire. "*Duress*: A Philosophical Account of the Defense in Law." *Arizona Law Review* 37 (1995): 251–83.
Fisher, Mark. "Exiting the Vampire Castle." *OpenDemocracy*, 24 November 2013.
– "A Fascinating Map of the World's Most and Least Racially Tolerant Countries." *Washington Post*, 15 May 2013.
Fiske, Susan T. *Envy Up, Scorn Down*. New York: Russell Sage, 2011.

Fisman, Raymond, and Edward Miguel. "Corruption, Norms and Legal Enforcement: Evidence from Diplomatic Parking Tickets." *Journal of Political Economy* 115, no. 6 (2007): 1020–48.
Flannery, Kent, and Joyce Marcus. *The Creation of Inequality.* Cambridge, MA: Harvard University Press, 2014.
Flew, Anthony. "The Profit Motive." *Ethics* 86, no. 4 (1976): 312–22.
Fong, Edmund. *American Exceptionalism and the Remains of Race.* New York: Routledge, 2015.
Forman, James Jr. *Locking Up Our Own.* New York: Farrar, Straus and Giroux, 2017.
Fourie, Carina. "To Praise and to Scorn." In *Social Equality*, edited by Carina Fourie, Fabian Schuppert, and Ivo Wallimann-Helmer, 88–106. Oxford: Oxford University Press, 2015.
– "What Is Social Equality? An Analysis of Status Equality as a Strongly Egalitarian Ideal." *Res Publica* 18, no. 2 (2012): 107–26.
Fourie, Carina, Fabian Schuppert, and Ivo Wallimann-Helmer, eds. *Social Equality.* Oxford: Oxford University Press, 2015.
Frank, Kristyn, and Feng Hou. *Source-Country Female Labour Force Participation and the Wages of Immigrant Women in Canada.* Ottawa: Statistics Canada, 2015.
Frank, Robert H. *Choosing the Right Pond.* Oxford: Oxford University Press, 1999.
– *Luxury Fever.* Princeton, NJ: Princeton University Press, 1999.
Frank, Robert H., and Philip J. Cook. *The Winner-Take-All Society.* New York: Penguin, 1995.
Frankfurt, Harry. "Alternate Possibilities and Moral Responsibility." *Journal of Philosophy* 66, no. 23 (1969): 829–39.
Fraser, Nancy. *Adding Insult to Injury.* Edited by Kevin Olson. London: Verso, 2008.
– "Recognition without Ethics?" *Theory, Culture and Society* 18, nos. 2–3 (2001): 21–42.
– "From Redistribution to Recognition? Dilemmas of Justice in a Post-Socialist Age." *New Left Review* 222 (1995): 68–93.
– "Rethinking Recognition." *New Left Review* 3 (2000): 107–20.
Freeman, Jo. "The Tyranny of Structurelessness." *Berkeley Journal of Sociology* 17 (1972–3): 151–64.
Freiman, Christopher. "Priority and Position." *Philosophical Studies* 167, no. 2 (2014): 341–60.
Freud, Sigmund. *Civilization and Its Discontents.* Translated by James Strachey. New York: W.W. Norton, 2010.
– *The Psychopathology of Everyday Life.* Edited by A.A. Brill. New York: MacMillan, 1914.

Fried, Morton H. *The Evolution of Political Society*. New York: Random House, 1967.
Friedersdorf, Conor. "The Destructiveness of Call-Out Culture on Campus." *Atlantic*, 8 May 2017.
Friedman, Benjamin. *The Moral Consequences of Economic Growth*. New York: Penguin, 2006.
Frum, David. *How We Got Here*. New York: Basic Books, 2000.
Fukuyama, Francis. *The End of History and the Last Man*. New York: Free Press, 1992.
– *Origins of Political Order*. New York: Farrar, Straus and Giroux, 2011.
– *Trust*. London: Penguin, 1996.
Fulford, Robert. "Calling Alcoholism a Disease Lets Rob Ford off the Hook." *National Post*, 5 July 2014.
Gallup Migration Research Center. "Number of Potential Migrants Worldwide Tops 750 Million." *World Poll*, 10 December 2018.
Garfinkel, Harold. "Studies of the Routine Grounds of Everyday Activities." In *Studies in Ethnomethodology*, 35–75. Cambridge: Policy, 1984.
Gat, Azar. *War in Human Civilization*. Oxford: Oxford University Press, 2006.
Gellner, Ernest. *Nations and Nationalism*. Ithaca, NY: Cornell University Press, 1983.
Gilovich, Thomas. *How We Know What Isn't So*. New York: Free Press, 1991.
Gini, Al, and Alexei Marcoux. *The Ethics of Business*. Lanham, MD: Rowman & Littlefield, 2012.
Goffman, Erving. *Stigma*. New York: Simon and Schuster, 1963.
Goldhill, Olivia. "The World Is Relying on a Flawed Psychological Test to Fight Racism." *Quartz*, 3 December 2017. https://qz.com/1144504/the-world-is-relying-on-a-flawed-psychological-test-to-fight-racism/.
Govier, Trudy. *Social Trust and Human Communities*. Montreal and Kingston: McGill-Queen's University Press, 1997.
Granovetter, Mark. "Economic Action and Social Structure: The Problem of Embeddedness." *American Journal of Sociology* 91, no. 3 (1985): 481–510.
Greenfield, Kent. "The Puzzle of Short-Termism." *Wake Forest Law Review* 46, no. 3 (2011): 627–40.
Greenwald, Anthony G., and Linda Hamilton Krieger. "Implicit Bias: Scientific Foundations." *California Law Review* 94, no. 4 (2006): 945–67.
Groupe de travail du comité interministériel des entreprises publiques. *Rapport sur les entreprises publiques*. Paris: La Documentation française, Éditions de Secrétariat Général du Gouvernement, 1967.
Gwyn, Richard. *Nationalism without Walls*. Toronto: McClelland & Stewart, 1997.
H.M. Treasury. *Nationalised Industries: A Review of Financial and Economic Objectives*. Command 3437. London: HMSO, 1967.

Habermas, Jürgen. *The Philosophical Discourse of Modernity*, translated by Frederick Lawrence. Cambridge, MA: MIT Press, 1987.
- *The Theory of Communicative Action*, vol. 2., translated by Thomas McCarthy. Boston: Beacon, 1987.
Haidt, Jonathan. *The Righteous Mind*. New York: Vintage, 2012.
Haidt, Jonathan, and Jesse Graham. "When Morality Opposes Justice: Conservatives Have Moral Intuitions That Liberals May Not Recognize." *Social Justice Research* 20, no. 1 (2007): 98–116.
Hall, Brian J., and Kevin J. Murphy. "The Trouble with Stock Options." *Journal of Economic Perspectives* 17, no. 3 (2003): 49–70.
Hall, Michael H., Cathy W. Barr, M. Easwaramoorthy, S. Wojciech Sokolowski, and Lester M. Salamon. *The Canadian Nonprofit and Voluntary Sector in Comparative Perspective*. Toronto: Imagine Canada, 2005.
Hall, Peter A., and Michèle Lamont, eds. *Successful Societies*. Cambridge: Cambridge University Press, 2009.
Hansen, Pelle Guldborg. "The Definition of Nudge and Libertarian Paternalism: Does the Hand Fit the Glove?" *European Journal of Risk Regulation* 7, no. 1 (2016): 155–74.
Hansmann, Henry. *The Ownership of Enterprise*. Cambridge, MA: Harvard University Press, 2000.
- "The Role of Nonprofit Enterprise." *Yale Law Journal* 89, no. 5 (1980): 835–901.
Harden, John D., and Justin Jouvenal. "Crime Rose Unevenly When Stay-at-Home Orders Lifted: The Racial Disparity Is the Widest in Years." *Washington Post*, 9 October 2020. https://www.washingtonpost.com/graphics/2020/local/public-safety/crime-rate-coronavirus/.
Hardimon, Michael. "Should We Narrow the Scope of 'Racism' to Accommodate White Sensitivities?" *Critical Philosophy of Race* 7, no. 2 (2019): 223–46.
Hardin, Russell. *Collective Action*. Baltimore, MD: Johns Hopkins University Press, 1982.
Hayek, Friedrich A. "The Moral Imperative of the Market." In *The Unfinished Agenda*, edited by Martin J. Anderson, 56–89. London: Institute of Economic Affairs, 1986.
Hayter, Teresa. *Open Borders: The Case against Immigration Controls*. London: Pluto, 2000.
Heath, Joseph. "An Adversarial Ethic for Business: or When Sun-Tzu Met the Stakeholder." *Journal of Business Ethics* 72, no. 4 (2007): 359–74.
- "Business Ethics and Moral Motivation: A Criminological Perspective." *Journal of Business Ethics* 83, no. 4 (2008): 595–614.
- "Contractualism: Micro and Macro." In *Morality, Competition and the Firm*, 145–72. New York: Oxford University Press, 2014.
- "Culture: Choice or Circumstance?" *Constellations* 5, no. 2 (1998): 183–200.

- *Enlightenment 2.0.* Toronto: HarperCollins, 2014.
- *Filthy Lucre.* Toronto: HarperCollins, 2008.
- *Following the Rules.* New York: Oxford University Press, 2008.
- "Immigration, Multiculturalism, and the Social Contract." *Canadian Journal of Law and Jurisprudence* 10, no. 2 (1997): 343–61.
- *The Machinery of Government.* New York: Oxford University Press, 2020.
- *Morality, Competition and the Firm.* New York: Oxford University Press, 2014.
- "Rawls on Global Distributive Justice: A Defence." *Canadian Journal of Philosophy Supplementary Volume,* edited by Daniel Weinstock, 193–226. Lethbridge, AB: University of Calgary Press, 2007.
- "Thorstein Veblen and American Social Criticism." In *Oxford Handbook of American Philosophy,* edited by Cheryl Misak, 235–53. Oxford: Oxford University Press, 2008.
- "Three Normative Models of the Welfare State." *Public Reason* 3, no. 2 (2011): 13–43.

Heath, Joseph, and Joel Anderson. "Procrastination and the Extended Will." In *The Thief of Time,* edited by Chrisoula Andreou and Mark White, 233–53. New York: Oxford University Press, 2010.

Heath, Joseph, and Wayne Norman. "Stakeholder Theory, Corporate Governance and Public Management: What Can the History of State-Run Enterprises Teach Us in the Post-Enron Era?" *Journal of Business Ethics* 53, no. 3 (2004): 247–65.

Heath, Joseph, and Andrew Potter. *The Rebel Sell.* Toronto: HarperCollins, 2004.

Hegel, G.W.F. *The Phenomenology of Spirit,* translated by A.V. Miller. Oxford: Oxford University Press, 1977.

Hemingway, Mark. "Idiot's Guide to Completely Idiotic Canadian 'Human Rights' Tribunals." *National Review,* 5 June 2008.

Hergovich, Philipp, and Josué Ortega. "The Strength of Absent Ties: Social Integration via Online Dating." SSRN working paper, 14 September 2018. https://doi.org/10.2139/ssrn.3044766.

Hill, Jane H. *The Everyday Language of White Racism.* Chichester, UK: Wiley-Blackwell, 2008.

Hirsch, Fred. *The Social Limits to Growth.* London: Routledge and Kegan Paul, 1977.

Hochschild, Arlie Russell. *The Managed Heart.* Berkeley: University of California Press, 2012.
- *Strangers in Their Own Land.* New York: New Press, 2017.

Hollingshead, August de Belmont. *Two Factor Index of Social Position.* New Haven, CT: Hollingshead, 1957.

Honneth, Axel. *The Struggle for Recognition.* Translated by Joel Anderson. Cambridge, MA: MIT Press, 1992.

Honneth, Axel, and Nancy Fraser. *Redistribution or Recognition?* London: Verso, 2003.
Hood, Christopher, Oliver James, George Jones, Colin Scott, and Tony Travers. *Regulation inside Government*. Oxford: Oxford University Press, 1999.
Hou, Feng, Zheng Wu, Christoph Schimmele, and John Myles. "Cross-Country Variation in Interracial Marriage: A USA-Canada Comparison of Metropolitan Areas." *Ethnic and Racial Studies* 38, no. 9 (2015): 1591–1609.
Huntington, Samuel. *Who Are We?* New York: Simon and Schuster, 2004.
Hurst, Lynda. "Ontario Sharia Tribunals Assailed: Women Fighting Use of Islamic Law, but Backers Say Rights Protected." *Toronto Star*, 1 June 2004.
Husak, Douglas. "'Already Punished Enough.'" *Philosophical Topics* 18, no. 1 (1990): 79–99.
Hussain, Waheed. "Why Should We Care about Competition?" *Critical Review of International Social and Political Philosophy* 21, no. 5 (2018): 570–85.
Ichino, Andrea, and Giovanni Maggi. "Work Environment and Individual Background: Explaining Regional Shirking Differentials in a Large Italian Firm." *Quarterly Journal of Economics* 115, no. 3 (2000): 1057–90.
Innes, Robert, and Arnab Mitra. "Is Dishonesty Contagious?" *Economic Inquiry* 51, no. 1 (2013): 722–34.
International Cooperative Alliance. *The Capital Conundrum for Co-operatives*. https://ica.coop/en/media/news/new-report-capital-conundrum-co-operatives.
– *Guidance Notes to the Cooperative Principles*. https://www.ica.coop/sites/default/files/2021-11/ICA%20Guidance%20Notes%20EN.pdf.
Isherwood, Baron, and Mary Douglas. *The World of Goods: Towards an Anthropology of Consumption*. London: Routledge, 1979.
Jacobs, Jane. *Death and Life of Great American Cities*. New York: Vintage, 1961.
Jefferson, Cord. "Ivy League Fooled: How America's Top Colleges Avoid Real Diversity." *Good*, 2 September 2011. https://www.good.is/articles/ivy-league-fooled-how-america-s-top-colleges-avoid-real-diversity.
Jensen, Michael. "Value Maximization, Stakeholder Theory, and the Corporate Objective Function." *Journal of Applied Corporate Finance* 14, no. 3 (2001): 8–21.
Kahneman, Daniel, Jack L. Knetsch, and Richard Thaler. "Fairness as a Constraint on Profit Seeking: Entitlements in the Market." *American Economic Review* 76, no. 4 (1986): 728–41.
Kaplan, Benjamin J. *Divided by Faith*. Cambridge, MA: Harvard University Press, 2007.
Kaufman, Eric. *Whiteshift*. New York: Abrams, 2019.
Kaufman, Herbert. *Red Tape*. Washington, DC: Brookings, 1977.
Kay, John. *The Truth about Markets*. London: Allen Lane, 2003.

Kazemipur, Abdolmohammad. *The Muslim Question in Canada*. Vancouver: UBC Press, 2014.
Kendi, Ibram X. *How to Be an Anti-Racist*. New York: Random House, 2019.
– *Stamped from the Beginning*. New York: Nation Books, 2016.
Kerubo, Jacquelynn. "What Gentrification Means for Black Homeowners." *New York Times*, 22 August 2012.
King of Kensington. Aired 1975–80 on CBC. Title sequence, 12 April 2008. YouTube video, 1:00. https://youtu.be/NrP8mjsmy8U.
Kiser, Dominik, Ben Steemers, Igor Branchi, and Judith R. Homberg. "The Reciprocal Interaction between Serotonin and Social Behavior." *Neuroscience and Biobehavioral Reviews* 36, no. 2 (2011): 786–98.
Klein, Ezra. "Ezra Klein on Media, Politics, and Models of the World." *Medium*, 6 October 2016. https://medium.com/conversations-with-tyler/ezra-klein-tyler-cowen-vox-healthcare-journalism-bias-396196082c31.
Kojève, Alexandre. *Introduction to the Reading of Hegel: Lectures on the Phenomenology of Spirit*. Ithaca, NY: Cornell University Press, 1980.
Kraakman, Reiner, John Armour, Paul Davies, Luca Enriques, Henry Hansmann, Gerard Hertig, Klaus Hopt, Hideki Kanda, Mariana Pargendler, Wolf-Georg Ringe, and Edward Rock. *The Anatomy of Corporate Law*. 2nd ed. Oxford: Oxford University Press, 2009.
Kramer, Roderick M., and Marilyn B. Brewer. "Effects of Group Identity on Resource Use in a Simulated Commons Dilemma." *Journal of Personality and Social Psychology* 46, no. 5 (1984): 1044–57.
Kukathas, Chandran. "The Case for Open Immigration." In *Contemporary Debates in Applied Ethics*, edited by Andrew I. Cohen and Christopher Heath Wellman, 376–90. Oxford: Blackwell, 2005.
– *The Liberal Archipelago*. Oxford: Oxford University Press, 2003.
Kymlicka, Will. "American Multiculturalism in the International Arena." *Dissent* (Fall 1998): 73–9.
– *Multicultural Citizenship*. Oxford: Oxford University Press, 1995.
– *Multiculturalism: Success, Failure, and the Future*. Washington, DC: Migration Policy Institute, 2012.
Laborde, Cécile. *Critical Republicanism*. Oxford: Oxford University Press, 2008.
– *Liberalism's Religion*. Cambridge, MA: Harvard University Press, 2017.
Lander, Christian. *Stuff White People Like*. New York: Random House, 2008.
Landsheer, Johannes A., Harm 't Hart, and Willem Kox. "Delinquent Values and Victim Damage." *British Journal of Criminology* 34, no. 1 (1994): 44–53.
Langford, John. "Air Canada." In *Public Corporations and Public Policy in Canada*, edited by Allan Tupper and G. Bruce Doern, 251–84. Montreal: Institute for Research on Public Policy, 1981.

Langford, John, and Ken Huffman. "Air Canada." In *Privatization, Public Policy and Public Corporations in Canada*, edited by Allan Tupper and G. Bruce Doern, 93–150. Montreal: Institute for Research on Public Policy, 1988.

Lee, Richard B. *The !Kung San: Men, Women, and Work in a Foraging Society*. Cambridge: Cambridge University Press, 1979.

Leovy, Jill. *Ghettoside*. New York: Penguin Random House, 2015.

Lester, Norman. *Le livre noir du Canada anglais*. Tome 1. Montreal: Intouchables, 2001.

Leviten-Reid, Catherine, and Brett Fairbairn. "Multi-Stakeholder Governance in Cooperative Organizations: Toward a New Framework for Research?" *Canadian Journal of Nonprofit and Social Economy Research* 2, no. 2 (2011): 25–36.

Link, Bruce, and Jo Phelan. "Conceptualizing Stigma." *Annual Review of Sociology* 27, no. 6 (2001): 363–85.

Lipksy, Michael. *Street-Level Bureaucracy*. 30th anniversary edition. New York: Russell Sage, 2010.

Lippert-Rasmussen, Kasper. *Relational Egalitarianism*. Cambridge: Cambridge University Press, 2018.

Lithopoulos, Savvas. *Lifecycle of First Nation Administered Police Services in Canada*. Ottawa: Public Safety Canada, 2018.

Ljungqvist, Olle, Michael Scott, and Kennet C. Fearon, "Enhanced Recovery after Surgery." *JAMA Surgery* 152, no. 3 (2017): 292–8.

Louis Vuitton. "Backpacks." https://us.louisvuitton.com/eng-us/men/bags/backpacks/ (page discontinued).

Lucas, Robert. "The Industrial Revolution: Past and Future." 2003 Annual Report Essay. Minneapolis: Federal Reserve Bank of Minneapolis, 2004.

Maas, Peter. *Serpico*. New York: Viking, 1973.

Macedo, Stephen. "The Moral Dilemma of U.S. Immigration Policy." In *Debating Immigration* edited by Carol M. Swain, 63–81. Cambridge: Cambridge University Press, 2007.

Maclure, Jocelyn, and Charles Taylor. *Secularism and Freedom of Conscience*. Translated by Jane Marie Todd. Cambridge, MA: Harvard University Press, 2011.

Majer, John M., Leonard A. Jason, and Bradley D. Olson. "Optimism, Abstinence Self-Efficacy, and Self-Mastery: A Comparative Analysis of Cognitive Resources." *Assessment* 11, no. 1 (2004): 57–63.

Mann, Michael. *The Sources of Social Power*. Vol. 1, 2nd ed. Cambridge: Cambridge University Press, 2012.

Marmot, Michael. *The Status Syndrome*. New York: Henry Holt, 2004.

Masiero, Marianna, Claudio Lucchiari, and Gabriella Pravettoni. "Personal Fable: Optimistic Bias in Cigarette Smokers." *International Journal of High Risk Behavior and Addiction* 4, no. 1 (2015): e20939.

McClendon, Gwyneth H. *Envy in Politics*. Princeton, NJ: Princeton University Press, 2018.

McClennen, Edward F. "Pragmatic Rationality and Rules." *Philosophy and Public Affairs* 26, no. 3 (1997): 210–58.

McCloskey, Deirdre. *The Bourgeois Virtues*. Chicago: University of Chicago Press, 2006.

McCloskey, Michael. "Intuitive Physics." *Scientific American* 248, no. 4 (1983): 122–30.

McConahay, John B., Betty B. Hardee, and Valerie Batts. "Has Racism Declined in America? It Depends on Who Is Asking and What Is Asked." *Journal of Conflict Resolution* 25, no. 4 (1981): 563–79.

McLean, Bethany, and Peter Elkind. *The Smartest Guys in the Room*. New York: Penguin, 2003.

Mears, Ashley. *Very Important People*. Princeton, NJ: Princeton University Press, 2020.

Milgram, Stanley. *The Individual in a Social World*. New York: McGraw Hill, 1992.

Mill, John Stuart. *On Liberty*. Edited by Elizabeth Rapaport. Indianapolis: Hackett, 1978.

– *Socialism*. Chicago: Belfords, Clarke, 1879.

Miller, David. "Equality and Justice." *Ratio* 10, no. 3 (1997): 222–37.

– "Immigration: The Case for Limits." In *Contemporary Debates in Applied Ethics*, edited by Andrew I. Cohen and Christopher Heath Wellman, 193–206. Oxford: Blackwell, 2005.

– *National Responsibility and Global Justice*. Oxford: Oxford University Press, 2007.

– *Strangers in Our Midst*. Cambridge, MA: Harvard University Press, 2016.

Miller, Timothy. *The 60s Communes*. Syracuse, NY: Syracuse University Press, 1999.

Mills, Charles W. *The Racial Contract*. Ithaca, NY: Cornell University Press, 1997.

Milward, Robert. *Private and Public Enterprise in Europe*. Cambridge: Cambridge University Press, 2005.

Mischel, Walter, Oziem Ayduk, Marc G. Berman, B.J. Casey, Ian H. Gotlib, John Jonides, Ethan Kross, Theresa Teslovich, Nicole L. Wilson, Vivian Zayas, and Yuichi Shoda. "'Willpower' over the Life Span: Decomposing Self-Regulation." *Social Cognitive and Affective Neuroscience* 6, no. 2 (2011): 252–6.

Monahan, John, Rima Berns-McGown, and Michael Morden. *The Perception and Reality of "Imported Conflict" in Canada*. Toronto: Mosaic Institute, 2014.

Monterosso, John, and George Ainslie. "The Behavioral Economics of Will in Recovery from Addiction." Supplement, *Drug & Alcohol Dependence* 90, no. S1 (2007): S100–11.

Moore, Margaret. *A Political Theory of Territory*. Oxford: Oxford University Press, 2015.
Morrill, Richard L. "School Busing and Demographic Change." *Urban Geography* 10, no. 4 (1989): 336–54.
Mounk, Yascha. "Americans Strongly Dislike PC Culture." *Atlantic*, 10 October 2018.
Movement for Black Lives. *A Vision for Black Lives*, 1 August 2016. https://neweconomy.net/a-vision-for-black-lives-policy-demands-for-black-power-freedom-and-justice/.
– *A Vision for Black Lives*. http://whitesforracialequity.org/wp-content/uploads/2017/07/BLM-vision-booklet.pdf.
Murray, Albert. *The Omni-Americans*. New York: Plenum, 1970.
Myrdal, Gunnar. *An American Dilemma*. 2 vols. New York: Harper & Brothers, 1944.
Naff, Katherine C. *To Look Like America*. New York: Taylor & Francis, 2001.
Nagle, Angela. *Kill All Normies*. Winchester, UK: Zero Books, 2017.
– "A Tragedy of Manners." *Baffler*, 5 September 2017.
Nagel, Thomas. "The Problem of Global Justice." *Philosophy and Public Affairs* 33, no. 2 (2005): 113–47.
National Commission on the BP Deepwater Horizon Spill. *Deep Water: The Gulf Oil Disaster and the Future of Offshore Drilling*. Washington, DC: U.S. Government Printing Office, 2011.
Nett, Roger. "The Civil Right We Are Not Ready For: The Right of Free Movement of People on the Face of the Earth." *Ethics* 81, no. 3 (1971): 212–27.
Neumann, Christof, Julie Buboscq, Constance Dubuc, Andri Ginting, Ade Maulana Irwan, Muhammad Agil, Anja Widdig, and Antje Engelhardt. "Assessing Dominance Hierarchies: Validation and Advantages of Progressive Evaluation with Elo-Rating." *Animal Behavior* 82, no. 4 (2011): 911–21.
Norman, Donald A., and Tim Shallice. "Attention to Action: Willed and Automatic Control of Behavior." In *Consciousness and Self-Regulation*, edited by Richard J. Davidson, Gary E. Schwartz, and David Shapiro, 4:1–18. New York: Plenum, 1986.
Norman, Wayne. "Business Ethics as Self-Regulation: Why Principles That Ground Regulations Should Be Used to Ground Beyond-Compliance Norms as Well." *Journal of Business Ethics* 102, no. 1 (2011): 43–57.
Norman, Wayne, and Chris Macdonald. "Getting to the Bottom of the 'Triple Bottom Line.'" *Business Ethics Quarterly* 14, no. 2 (2004): 243–62.
North, Douglass C., John Joseph Wallis, and Barry R. Weingast. "A Conceptual Framework for Interpreting Recorded Human History." NBER working paper 12795, 2006.
– *Violence and Social Orders*. Cambridge: Cambridge University Press, 2009.

Nove, Alec. *The Economics of a Feasible Socialism Revisited*. New York: Taylor & Francis, 1991.
Nozick, Robert. *Anarchy, State and Utopia*. New York: Basic Books, 1974.
Nussbaum, Martha. *The Fragility of Goodness*. Cambridge: Cambridge University Press, 1986.
- "Inscribing the Face: Shame, Stigma, and Punishment." In *Political Exclusion and Domination: Nomos XLVI*, edited by Stephen Macedo and Melissa Williams, 259–302. New York: New York University Press, 2005.
- "Perfectionist Liberalism and Political Liberalism." *Philosophy and Public Affairs* 39, no. 1 (2011): 3–45.
O'Barr, William M. *Linguistic Evidence: Language, Power and Strategy in the Courtroom*. New York: Academic, 1982.
OECD/EU. *Indicators of Immigrant Integration 2015*. Paris: OECD Publishing, 2015.
OECD. "Level of GDP per Capita and Productivity." https://stats.oecd.org/Index.aspx?DataSetCode=PDB_LV.
Ogbu, John U. "Beyond Language: Ebonics, Proper English, and Identity in a Black-American Speech Community." *American Educational Research Association* 36, no. 2 (1999): 147–84.
Ogien, Ruwen. *L'éthique aujourd'hui*. Paris: Gallimard, 2007.
Okun, Arthur. *Equality and Efficiency: The Big Trade-off*. Washington, DC: Brookings, 1975.
O'Neill, Martin. "What Should Egalitarians Believe?" *Philosophy and Public Affairs* 36, no. 2 (2008): 119–56.
Ong, Paul, and Kate Viernes. "Filipino Americans and Educational Downward Mobility." *Asian American Policy Review* 23 (2012–13): 21–39.
Oswald, Frederick L., Gregory Mitchell, Hart Blanton, James Jaccard, and Philip E. Tetlock. "Predicting Ethnic and Racial Discrimination: A Meta-Analysis of IAT Criterion Studies." *Journal of Personality and Social Psychology* 105, no. 2 (2013): 171–92.
Pallone, Nathaniel J., and James J. Hennessy. "Blacks and Whites as Victims and Offenders in Aggressive Crime in the U.S." *Journal of Offender Rehabilitation* 30, nos. 1–2 (2000): 1–33.
Park, Sara. "Inventing Aliens: Immigration Control, 'Xenophobia' and Racism in Japan." *Race & Class* 58, no. 3 (2017): 64–80.
Parsons, Talcott. *The Social System*. New York: Free Press, 1951.
Patten, Alan. "Liberal Neutrality and Language Policy." *Philosophy and Public Affairs* 31, no. 4 (2003): 356–86.
Peller, Gary. *Critical Race Consciousness*. New York: Taylor & Francis, 2012.
- "Race Consciousness." *Duke Law Journal* 39, no. 4 (1990): 758–847.
Peters, B. Guy. "What Is so Wicked about Wicked Problems? A Conceptual Analysis and a Research Program." *Policy and Society* 36, no. 3 (2017): 385–96.

Pettit, Philip. "Rawls's Political Ontology." *Politics, Philosophy and Economics* 4, no. 2 (2005): 157–74.
Pevnick, Ryan. "Democratizing the Nonprofit Sector." *Journal of Political Philosophy* 21, no. 3 (2013): 260–82.
– *Immigration and the Constraints of Justice*. Cambridge: Cambridge University Press, 2011.
Pinker, Steven. *The Better Angels of Our Nature*. New York: Penguin, 2011.
– *Enlightenment Now*. New York: Penguin Random House, 2018.
Pinsker, Joe. "American Immigrants and the Dilemma of 'White-Sounding' Names." *Atlantic*, 3 January 2019.
Pires, Roberto R.C. "Beyond the Fear of Discretion: Flexibility, Performance, and Accountability in the Management of Regulatory Bureaucracies." *Regulation and Governance* 5, no. 1 (2011): 43–69.
Polanyi, Karl. *The Great Transformation*. Boston: Beacon, 1957.
Ravitch, Diane. "When Public Goes Private, as Trump Wants: What Happens?" *New York Review of Books*, 8 December 2016.
Rawls, John. "Justice as Fairness." In *Collected Papers*, edited by Samuel Freeman 47–72. Cambridge, MA: Harvard University Press, 1999.
– *Justice as Fairness: A Restatement*, edited by Erin Kelly. Cambridge, MA: Harvard University Press, 2001.
– *The Law of Peoples*. Cambridge, MA: Harvard University Press, 1999.
– *Political Liberalism*. New York: Columbia University Press, 1993.
– *A Theory of Justice*. Cambridge, MA: Harvard University Press, 1971.
– *A Theory of Justice*. Rev. ed. Cambridge, MA: Harvard University Press, 1999.
Raymond Fisman, and Miriam A. Golden, *Corruption: What Everyone Needs to Know*. Oxford: Oxford University Press, 2017.
Raz, Joseph. *The Morality of Freedom*. Oxford: Oxford University Press, 1986.
Reddit. "People of Walmart." https://www.reddit.com/r/peopleofwalmart/.
– "All Things Trashy!" https://www.reddit.com/r/trashy/.
Reddy, Geetha. "Race Rules in Singapore." In *Singapore: Negotiating State and Society, 1965–2015*, edited by Jason Lim and Terence Lee, 54–75. New York: Routledge, 2016.
Reeve, Elle, and Samantha Guff. "They Envisioned a World without Police: Inside Seattle's CHOP Zone, Protestors Struggled to Make It Real." *CNN*, 6 July 2020. https://www.cnn.com/2020/07/05/us/chop-seattle-police-protesters-public-safety.
Reitz, Jeffrey G., Patrick Simon, and Emily Laxer. "Muslims' Social Inclusion and Exclusion in France, Quebec and Canada: Does National Context Matter?" *Journal of Ethnic and Migration Studies* 43, no. 15 (2017): 2473–98.
Richerson, Peter J., and Robert Boyd. "The Evolution of Human Ultra-Sociality." In *Indoctrinability, Ideology, and Warfare*, edited by Irenäus Eibl-Eibesfeldt and Frank Kemp Salter, 71–95. New York: Berghan Books, 1998.
– *Not by Genes Alone*. Chicago: University of Chicago Press, 2005.

Ridgeway, Cecilia L. "Why Status Matters for Inequality." *American Sociological Review* 79, no. 1 (2014): 1–16.
Ripstein, Arthur. *Equality, Responsibility and the Law*. Cambridge: Cambridge University Press, 1999.
Robinson, Paul H. "Why Does the Criminal Law Care What the Layperson Thinks Is Just? Coercive versus Normative Crime Control." *Virginia Law Review* 86, no. 8 (2000): 1839–69.
Robinson, Randall. *The Debt: What America Owes to Blacks*. New York: Penguin, 2000.
Rodrik, Dani, Arvind Subramanian, and Francesco Trebbi. "Institutions Rule: The Primacy of Institutions over Geography and Integration in Economic Development." *Journal of Economic Growth* 9, no. 2 (2004): 131–65.
Roemer, John E. "Equality and Responsibility." *Boston Review* 20 (1995): 3–16.
Rogers, Halsey, and Margaret Koziol. *Provider Absence Surveys in Education and Health*. Washington, DC: World Bank, 2011.
Ronzoni, Miriam. "Life Is Not a Camping Trip: On the Desirability of Cohenite Socialism." *Politics, Philosophy and Economics* 11, no. 2 (2011): 171–85.
Roos, J. Micah, Michael Hughes, and Ashley V. Reichelmann. "A Puzzle of Racial Attitudes: A Measurement Analysis of Racial Attitudes and Policy Indicators." *Socius* 5, no. 1 (2019): 1–14.
Rosen, Sherwin. "The Economics of Superstars." *American Economic Review* 71, no. 5 (1981): 845–58.
Rosenblum, Nancy L. *Membership and Morals*. Princeton, NJ: Princeton University Press, 1998.
Ross, Don, Harold Kincaid, David Spurrett, and Peter Collins. *What Is Addiction?* Cambridge, MA: MIT Press, 2010.
Ross, Marc Howard. *The Culture of Conflict*. New Haven, CT: Yale University Press, 1993.
Roszell, Patricia, David Kennedy, and Edward Grabb. "Physical Attractiveness and Income Attainment among Canadians." *Journal of Psychology* 123, no. 6 (1989): 547–59.
Rothblum, Esther D. "'I'll Die for the Revolution, but Don't Ask Me Not to Diet': Feminism and the Continuing Stigmatization of Obesity." In *Feminist Perspectives on Eating Disorders*, edited by Patricia Fallon, Melanie A. Katzman, and Susan C. Wooley, 53–76. New York: Guildford, 1994.
Rothstein, Richard. *The Color of Law*. New York: Liveright, 2017.
Rousset, Marion. "La sociologie, une profession incomprise." *Le Monde*, 6 October 2016.
Rozin, Paul. "The Process of Moralization." *Psychological Science* 10, no. 3 (1999): 218–21.
Runciman, W.G. "'Social' Equality." *Philosophical Quarterly* 17, no. 68 (1967): 221–30.

Sachs, David. "How to Distinguish Self-Respect from Self-Esteem." *Philosophy and Public Affairs* 10, no. 4 (1981): 346–60.
Sachs, Jeffrey D., and Andrew M. Warner. "The Big Rush, Natural Resource Booms and Growth." *Journal of Development Economics* 59, no. 1 (1999): 43–76.
Samuelson, Paul A. "International Trade and the Equalisation of Factor Prices." *Economic Journal* 58 (1948): 163–84.
Scanlon, T.M. *Why Does Inequality Matter?* Oxford: Oxford University Press, 2018.
Schelling, Thomas. *Micromotives and Macrobehavior.* New York: W.W. Norton, 1978.
– "Models of Segregation." *American Economic Review* 59, no. 2 (1969): 488–93.
Schuck, Peter H. "The Disconnect between Public Attitudes and Policy Outcomes in Immigration." In *Debating Immigration*, edited by Carol M. Swain, 17–31. Cambridge: Cambridge University Press, 2007.
Schwartz, Richard D., and Jerome H. Skolnick. "Two Studies of Legal Stigma." *Social Problems* 10, no. 2 (1962): 133–43.
Schweickart, David. *After Capitalism.* Oxford: Rowman and Littlefield, 2002.
– *Capitalism or Worker Control?* New York: Praeger Publishing, 1980.
Scott, James C. *Against the Grain.* New Haven, CT: Yale University Press, 2017.
Seabright, Paul. *The Company of Strangers.* Princeton, NJ: Princeton University Press, 2004.
Sedikides, Constantine, Rosie Meek, Mark D. Alicke, and Sarah Taylor. "Behind Bars but above the Bar: Prisoners Consider Themselves More Prosocial than Non-Prisoners." *British Journal of Social Psychology* 53, no. 2 (2014): 396–403.
Seiner, Joseph A. "Disentangling Disparate Impact and Disparate Treatment: Adapting the Canadian Approach." *Yale Law and Policy Review* 25, no. 1 (2006–7): 95–142.
Sen, Amartya. *The Idea of Justice.* Cambridge, MA: Harvard University Press, 2009.
Shachar, Ayelet. *The Birthright Lottery.* Cambridge, MA: Harvard University Press, 2009.
Shapiro, Eliza. "Only 7 Black Students Got into Stuyvesant, N.Y.'s Most Selective High School, out of 895 Spots." *New York Times*, 18 March 2019.
Shelby, Tommie. *Dark Ghettos.* Cambridge, MA: Harvard University Press, 2018.
– "Racism, Moralism, and Social Criticism." *Du Bois Review* 11, no. 1 (2014): 57–74.
Shipman, Alan. *The Market Revolution and Its Limits.* London: Routledge, 1999.
Silverman, David. *Harvey Sacks: Social Science and Conversation Analysis.* Oxford: Oxford University Press, 1998.
Simpson, Sally. *Corporate Crime, Law and Social Control.* Cambridge: Cambridge University Press, 2002.
Singal, Jesse. "This Is What a Modern-Day Witch Hunt Looks Like." *New York Magazine*, 2 May 2017.

Singer, Abraham. *The Form of the Firm*. New York: Oxford University Press, 2019.

Slovic, Paul. "Cigarette Smokers: Rational Actors or Rational Fools?" In *Smoking: Risk, Perception and Policy*, edited by Paul Slovic, 97–124. Thousand Oaks, CA; Sage, 2001.

Smith, Adam. *An Inquiry into the Nature and Causes of the Wealth of Nations*. Edited by R.H. Campbell and A.S. Skinner. Oxford: Oxford University Press, 1976.

Snyder-Mackler, Noah, Jordan N. Kohn, Luis B. Barreiro, Zachary P. Johnson, Mark E. Wilson, and Jenny Tung. "Social Status Drives Social Relationships in Groups of Unrelated Female Rhesus Macaques." *Animal Behavior* 111 (2016): 307–17.

Solow, Robert. "A Contribution to the Theory of Economic Growth." *Quarterly Journal of Economics* 70, no. 1 (1956): 65–94.

Soroka, Stuart, Keith Banting, and Richard Johnson. "Immigration and Redistribution in a Global Era." In *Globalization and Egalitarian Redistribution*, edited by Pranab Bardhan, Samuel Bowles, and Michael Wallerstein, 261–88. Princeton, NJ: Princeton University Press, 2006.

Sreenivasan, Gopal. "Health Care and Equality of Opportunity." *Hastings Center Report* 37, no. 2 (2007): 21–31.

Stanovich, Keith. *The Robot's Rebellion*. Chicago: University of Chicago Press, 2005.

Starr, Sonja B. "Estimating Gender Disparities in Federal Criminal Cases." *American Law and Economics Review* 17, no. 1 (2015): 127–59.

Statutes of the Republic of Singapore: Penal Code. Rev. ed. Singapore: Law Revision Commission, 2008.

Stiglitz, Joseph. *Whither Socialism?* Cambridge, MA: MIT Press, 1994.

Stockman, Farah. "'We're Self-Interested': The Growing Identity Debate in Black America." *New York Times*, 8 November 2019.

Stout, Lynn A. "Why We Should Stop Teaching *Dodge v. Ford*." *Virginia Law and Business Review* 3, no. 1 (2008): 164–76.

Strawson, Peter. "Freedom and Resentment." *Proceedings of the British Academy* 48 (1962): 1–25.

Sturcke, James. "Sharia Law in Canada, Almost." *Guardian* (UK edition), 8 February 2008. https://www.theguardian.com/news/blog/2008/feb/08/sharialawincanadaalmost.

Surowiecki, James, ed. *Best Business Crime Writing of the Year*. New York: Random House, 2002.

Sutherland, Edwin H. "Is 'White Collar Crime' Crime?" *American Sociological Review* 10, no. 2 (1944): 132–9.

– *Principles of Criminology*. 4th ed. Chicago: Lippincott, 1947.

Sykes, Gresham M., and David Matza. "Techniques of Neutralization: A Theory of Delinquency." *American Sociological Review* 22, no. 6 (1957): 664–70.

Tainter, Joseph A. *The Collapse of Complex Societies*. Cambridge: Cambridge University Press, 1988.
Tajfel, Henri. "Social Psychology of Intergroup Relations." *Annual Review of Psychology* 33 (1982): 1–39.
Tajfel, Henri, Michael Billig, R.P. Bundy, and Claude Flament. "Social Categorization and Intergroup Behavior." *European Journal of Social Psychology* 1, no. 2 (1971): 149–77.
Tamir, Yael. *Liberal Nationalism*. Princeton, NJ: Princeton University Press, 1993.
Taylor, Charles. "The Politics of Recognition." In *Multiculturalism: Examining the Politics of Recognition,* edited by Amy Gutmann, 25–73. Princeton, NJ: Princeton University Press, 1992.
Thaler, Richard, and Cass Sunstein. *Nudge*. New Haven, CT: Yale University Press, 2008.
Todd, Douglas. "Canada Struggling to 'Absorb' Immigrations, Internal Report Says." *Vancouver Sun*, 11 August 2017.
Tomasello, Michael. *A Natural History of Human Morality*. Cambridge, MA: Harvard University Press, 2016.
Tomasi, John. *Free Market Fairness*. Princeton, NJ: Princeton University Press, 2012.
Tommasini, Anthony. "To Make Orchestras More Diverse, End Blind Auditions." *New York Times*, 16 July 2020.
Turiel, Elliot. *The Development of Social Knowledge*. Cambridge: Cambridge University Press, 1983.
Turnbull, Colin M. *The Forest People*. New York: Simon and Schuster, 1963.
Tyre, Peg. "How Sophisticated Test Scams from China Are Making Their Way in the U.S." *Atlantic*, 21 March 2016.
Vaishnav, Milan. *When Crime Pays*. New Haven, CT: Yale University Press, 2017.
Valls, Andrew. "The Broken Promise of Racial Integration." In *NOMOS XLIII: Moral and Political Education*, edited by Stephen Macedo and Yael Tamir, 456–74. New York: New York University Press, 2001.
– "A Liberal Defense of Black Nationalism." *American Political Science Review* 104, no. 3 (2010): 467–81.
Van Berkel, Laura, Chris Crandall, Scott Eidelman, and John Blanchar. "Hierarchy, Dominance, and Deliberation: Egalitarian Values Require Mental Effort." *Personality & Social Psychology Bulletin* 41, no. 9 (2015): 1207–22.
Van Maanen, John. "The Asshole." In *Policing*, edited by Peter K. Manning and John Van Maanen, 227–38. Santa Monica, CA: CA Goodyear, 1978.
Van Parijs, Philippe. "Equal Endowments and Undominated Diversity." *Recherches économiques de Louvain* 56, nos. 3–4 (1990): 327–55.
– "Linguistic Justice." In *Language Rights and Political Theory*, edited by Will Kymlicka and Alan Patten, 153–68. Oxford: Oxford University Press, 2003.

Veblen, Thorstein. *The Theory of the Leisure Class*. Oxford: Oxford University Press, 2007.
Waddington, P.A.J. *Policing Citizens*. London: Routledge, 1999.
Waldron, Jeremy. "Autonomy and Perfectionism in Raz's Morality of Freedom." *Southern California Law Review* 62, nos. 3–4 (1989): 1097–1152.
Wallis, Jim. *America's Original Sin*. Grand Rapids, MI: Brazos, 2016.
Walzer, Michael. *Spheres of Justice*. New York: Basic Books, 1983.
Ward, Benjamin. "The Firm in Illyria: Market Syndicalism." *American Economic Review* 48, no. 4 (1958): 566–89.
Weaver, Matthew. "Angela Merkel: German Multiculturalism Has 'Utterly Failed.'" *Guardian*, 17 October 2010.
Weber, Max. *Economy and Society*. Edited by Claus Wittich and Guenther Ross. Berkeley: University of California Press, 1978.
Webster, Murray Jr., and James E. Driskell Jr. "Beauty as Status." *American Journal of Sociology* 89, no. 1 (1983): 140–65.
– "Status Generalization: A Review and Some New Data." *American Sociological Review* 43, no. 2 (1978): 220–36.
Wellman, Christopher Heath. "Immigration and Freedom of Association." *Ethics* 119, no. 1 (2008): 109–41.
Wellman, Christopher Heath, and Philip Cole. *Debating Immigration*. Oxford: Oxford University Press, 2011.
White, Mark. *The Manipulation of Choice*. New York: Palgrave Macmillan, 2013.
Wilderson, Frank B. III. *Afropessimism*. New York: W.W. Norton, 2020.
Wilkinson, Richard, and Kate Pickett. *The Spirit Level*. London: Penguin, 2009.
Wilson, James Q. *Bureaucracy*. New York: Basic Books, 1989.
– "The Bureaucracy Problem." *Public Interest* 6 (1967): 3–9.
Wilson, Timothy. *Strangers to Ourselves*. Cambridge, MA: Harvard University Press, 2004.
World Bank. "Ease of Doing Business Rankings." http://www.doingbusiness.org/rankings.
– "Employment in Agriculture (% of Total Employment)." https://data.worldbank.org/indicator/SL.AGR.EMPL.ZS?end=2010&start=1997.
Wrangham, Richard. *The Goodness Paradox*. New York: Pantheon, 2019.
Yang, Lawrence Hsin, Arthur Kleinman, Bruce G. Link, Jo C. Phelan, Sing Lee, and Byron Good. "Culture and Stigma: Adding Moral Experience to Stigma Theory." *Social Science and Medicine* 64, no. 7 (2007): 1524–35.
Young, Iris Marion. *Justice and the Politics of Difference*. Princeton, NJ: Princeton University Press, 1990.
Zurn, Christopher. "Identity or Status? Struggles over 'Recognition' in Fraser, Honneth and Taylor." *Constellations* 10, no. 4 (2003): 519–37.

Index

addiction: nature of, 181, 189, 193, 196n23; social media, 145; substance, 164, 169, 170, 174, 175, 178, 181, 191, 196n23, 198n61; treatment, 178–9, 182, 183, 191, 198n61
affirmative action, 259–60, 283, 292, 295
Africa, 125, 252, 257, 277
African-Americans: vs "black," 253, 256–7, 259, 260, 262; group characteristics, 254, 255, 256, 261–2, 277–9, 281, 288, 309n66; integration of, 256, 264, 277–83, 284, 286–8, 297, 298–301, 302–4; social issues, 121, 194n3, 226, 266, 286–8, 295, 307n35, 313n110
African-American Vernacular English (AAVE), 278, 281–2
agency problems, 79, 85–6, 87, 89
agricultural societies, 35
Air Canada (formerly, Trans-Canada Airlines), 89–90
akrasia. *See* weakness of will
alcoholism, 169, 178, 191, 198n61
Algerians, 278–9
Alle, Warder Clyde, 109
altruism, 12, 17, 86, 112, 150

Amabosu (member of Mbuti band), 28
America. *See* United States (US)
American Descendants of Slavery, 260
Amish, 310n80
Anderson, Elizabeth, 261, 280, 299–300
Anderson, Joel, 182, 186–7
animal kingdom, 12, 109, 111. *See also* ants; chimpanzees; dogs; primates
Annual Review of Sociology, 163
anthropology, 26, 34, 108, 124; folk, 280
antisocial behaviours: causes of, 14, 23, 33, 40–2, 217, 227; corporate (*see* corporate misconduct); in the market, 74; prevention of, 44; and stigmatization, 164, 176, 183
ants, 48, 109
apartheid, 277, 283, 311n88, 314n125
arbitration, 233, 236–7
Aristotle, 3, 112, 177, 182
Arneson, Richard, 16, 22, 25
Arrow, Kenneth, 158n85
Asians, 261, 274–5, 306n24, 307n37; Asian American, 256–7, 259; South, 291
Atkinson, Anthony, 131

Australia, 211, 275
autarky, 26, 40, 50
authority: in businesses, 78, 89, 97; emergence of, 34–5; female, 221; political, 35, 201, 215, 220, 271; structures, 36–7, 41, 47, 56, 221, 238
autonomy: actions, 30; in business context, 88, 104n58; individual, 164, 166, 191, 194; liberalism and, 237; nationalism and, 281; "scaffolded autonomy," 187; self-control and, 183, 189–90

Baby Jessica, 19
Bakan, Joel, 66
Baltimore (US), 312n100
bankruptcy, 69, 70, 84; and SOEs, 85, 86, 88
Barry, Brian, 234–5
Baumgartner, Mary Pat, 149
Becker, Gary, 98
Beitz, Charles, 206
"beta" culture, 145
"big fish in small pond," 118, 140, 142, 144
big-man, 34, 152n7
Black Lives Matter (BLM), 287–8
blacks (racial group): definitions, 253, 256–7, 259, 260–1; nationalism (*see* nationalism: black); people and community, 277, 283, 286, 287, 303, 307n36, 309–10n69, 312n100; social policies, 226, 259; vs whites, 267, 279–80, 289, 297, 298–300, 313n113, 313n118, 314n125
Blair, Margaret, 84
Bloemraad, Irene, 247n54
blood feud, 29, 34
Boehm, Christopher, 109, 112
Book of Common Prayer, 242
border control, 202–5, 213–24, 241–3
Boston (US), 247

Bouchard-Taylor report, 233–4, 244n3, 249n84
Boyd, Robert, 14, 39, 44
BP (formerly British Petroleum), 65, 73
Brennan, Geoffrey, 112, 155n38
Brennan, Jason, 58
Brighouse, Harry, 128, 157n72
Britain. *See* United Kingdom (UK)
British Columbia (Canada), 218
Brooks, David, 125
Brooks, Roy, 283
Brown, Michael, 311n98
Brown v Board of Education (decision), 257
business ethics, 97
business judgment rule, 71, 98
business organizational forms, 66–7, 74, 96. *See also* cooperatives; corporations; non-profit organizations; state-owned enterprises (SOEs)
buyback (corporate mechanism), 71

California (US), 86, 206, 309–10n69
Callas, Maria, 128
call-out culture, 134
Campbell, Maria, 258
camping trip: Cohen on, 15, 19, 20, 26, 58, 131; extension to larger groups, 21–2, 25, 47–8, 51, 54, 56
Canada: businesses, 78, 89–91; history, 35, 253, 257–8; immigration issues, 209, 211, 216, 221, 224, 225, 229, 243–4n1, 247n54, 248n69, 249n84; multiculturalism in, 10, 228–9, 231–2, 233, 244n3, 255, 257–8, 265, 275, 277, 288, 291, 292, 294; public entities and officials, 89, 196n24, 272, 274, 285–6; public policies, 175, 228–9, 270–2, 276; racial and ethnic groups, 40, 241,

248–9n70, 250n87, 253, 257–8, 261–2, 275, 281, 283, 305n16, 307n36, 307n37
Canadian Council of Muslim Women, 233
capital goods, 52, 55
capitalism: features of, 74, 94, 269; history of, 127; objections to, 8, 71, 74, 99; vs socialism, 48, 51–6, 58–9
capitalist firms, 67–8, 94, 100, 100n9; vs cooperatives, 74–80, 102n26; non-capitalist organizational forms, 95–6; vs SOEs, 85–91
capital stock, 207–8, 210, 211
Carens, Joseph, 203, 205, 212
Caribbean, 257, 277
Carlisle, Sir Richard (TV character), 158n91
Carlton (TV character), 309–10n69
Carmichael, Stokely, 280
cash economy, 125
Catholics, 231–2, 258, 261, 310n81
central planning, 54, 74, 94
Cephu (member of Mbuti band), 28–9
"Chapters on Socialism" (Mill), 16
charity auction, 150
chief, 34–5. *See also* tribal chieftainships
chimpanzees, 13, 109
China: culture and society, 45, 49, 220, 241, 257; economy, 207; imperial, 40
Chinese (people), 256, 291, 294, 298, 304n4
Christianity: Christian names, 279, 304n4; history and tradition 177, 215, 237, 285; pluralism and 200, 228, 231; Protestant, 261; structure, 38; in the United States, 277, 279, 299. *See also* Catholics.
church: community, 223, 228, 242, 299; social role of, 94, 271, 278
Civil Rights Act (US), 259

civil rights movement, 135, 279, 303
Clark, Andy, 183, 189
Clinard, Marshall, 99
Clinton, Hillary, 111
club goods, 228
Coates, Ta-Nehisi, 280, 312n100
cognitive bias, 161n126, 183, 185, 301
cognitive dissonance, 184
Cohen, G.A.: on inequality 227; philosophical methods, 30, 131–2; on socialism, 8, 14–22, 25–6, 47–56, 58–9
collective action problems, 5, 120, 214; solutions to 57, 220, 226
Communism, 48–9
competition: consumption and lifestyle, 121, 133, 145; fixed-sum, 120–1; within institutions, 87–8, 96; market, 8, 14, 15, 54, 57, 59, 74, 78, 85–6, 93, 94, 97–9, 206, 207; status, 108, 111–3, 116, 117, 119–21, 124–5, 133–6, 143–6, 150, 159n102, 160–1n125, 161n126
"Conceptualizing Stigma" (Link and Phelan), 163
Congo, 28, 205
conservativism: on agent responsibility, 172, 173, 178–9, 187; on immigration, 224–5, 236; on race relations, 295, 303; on stigmatization, 170, 172, 173, 175–9, 196n29
Constitution (Canada), 292
consumerism, 121, 123, 145
coordination, 19, 20–1, 34, 56, 97; market as mechanism for, 48; of punishment, 33
cooperatives, 67, 74–80, 94–7, 102n26; vs capitalist firms, 99; customer, 75, 76, 77, 79, 82, 96; dairy, 75–6, 78, 79; insurance, 76; membership fees, 82; multi-stakeholder, 102n24; pseudo,

cooperatives (*continued*)
  82, 104n58; in raising capital, 80–5; self-financing, 83, 85; social status within, 133–4; vs SOEs, 85, 87; supply, 75, 77, 82; worker, 75–80, 81–5, 93, 100n9, 104n58, 108
corporate culture, 73, 99
"corporate greed," 66, 73, 86
corporate malfeasance. *See* corporate misconduct
corporate misconduct: causes of 66–8; managerial, 73, 86; solutions to, 74, 95, 97–100, 101n10, 102n26
corporate objectives. *See* organizational objectives
corporations: activities and objectives, 5, 66, 68, 70–2, 80, 87, 97–9, 100n7, 101n19, 208 (*see also* corporate misconduct; organizational objectives); culture and norms, 73, 86, 99, 269–70; formation and development, 25, 38, 73, 88, 128, 271; forms and structures, 56, 66, 73, 74–5, 92, 94–6. *See also* capitalist firms; investor-owned firms; profit-oriented firms; standard business corporations
corporatization, 67, 89, 91
corruption, 65, 213–6, 220
cost of capital, 67, 83, 88, 93
Crawley, Mary (TV character), 158n91
credit union, 75, 82
Cressey, Donald, 184
criminology, 4, 184, 186, 188
Cultural Revolution (China), 49

Dabhol power plant (India), 87
Dalrymple, Theodore, 173, 176–9, 188
day-care centres, 77, 92, 94
debt, 55, 69–70, 81, 86, 103n32
Deepwater Horizon oil spill, 65–6, 68, 99

democracy: in business entities, 79–80; in modern states and societies, 136, 238, 243, 280, 287. *See also* liberal democracies
de-responsibilization argument, 175, 188
Descartes, René, 174
de-stigmatization, 169, 193, 195n10; of divorce, 169, 187; of illness, 192; left-wing on, 170, 172, 174–5, 178, 188; of obesity, 171–2; and self-control, 9, 164, 179, 187, 189, 190
de Waal, Frans B.W., 111
Diagnostic and Statistical Manual of Mental Disorders, 5th Edition (DSM-V), 179
diminishing marginal returns: of material goods, 123; of social organizations, 39; of social status, 114–6, 121
discrimination, 163, 225, 255, 278–9, 284; disability, 165–6; homophobia, 134, 135, 165–6; Islamophobia, 229; policies, 274, 292–4, 295; racism (*see* racism); sexism, 116, 134, 135, 149, 290; social status and, 114, 135, 149–50; transphobia, 134; in the United States, 194n3, 252, 257, 259–60, 264–8, 298, 307n35; xenophobia, 212, 218, 227, 229, 302
distributive justice, 6, 8, 117; business firm structures and, 101n10; economic growth and, 125–6; Fraser on, 138; immigration and, 202, 205, 207–8, 211, 223, 226, 239; Marxist, 135–6; Rawls on, 118, 147; social status and, 151, 156n56
division of labour: conditions for, 36, 40, 51–6; division of moral labour, 20, 47; large-scale, 8, 14, 16, 44, 56; small-scale, 152n7; in socialist economy, 50

Dodge v. Ford (decision), 71
dogs, 109
"Doing Business" project (World Bank), 210
dominance: behaviours and displays, 110–1, 135; in communes, 45; disposition (*see under* human psychology); in early society, 34; Hegel on, 136; hierarchies (*see* hierarchies: dominance); human vs animals, 108–12; informal, 106, 152n7; institutionalized, 152n7; male, 120, 152n7; ranking, 110, 111–2; recognition and, 137
"Dominance and Hierarchy in Societies of Vertebrates" (Allee), 109
Downton Abbey (TV show), 158n91
Dunbar, Robin, 31
Durkheim, Émile, 4, 14, 33
Dworkin, Ronald, 139
dyadic social structures, 61–2n36, 109, 110

early societies. *See* agricultural societies; foraging societies; hunter-gatherers; sedentary societies; solidary groups; tribal societies
Easterbrook, Frank, 72
economies of scale, 16, 22
education: cheating in, 214, 220; impacts and effects, 49, 170, 189, 248; integration and, 216, 217, 224, 231, 232, 248n70; language and, 223, 270, 271, 272, 276, 282; race relations and, 259, 293, 295, 300, 313n118; social role and structure, 157n72, 213, 265, 271, 276; social status and, 4, 106, 122, 129, 133, 147–8, 149; systems, 215, 231, 269–70, 272, 282, 296, 313n118
egalitarianism, 7, 213; compensation and, 138–9; discrimination and, 135–6; distributive, 117, 151 (*see also* distributive justice); in early or small-scale societies, 30–1, 108–9, 152n7; limits of, 236; luck, 147, 154n34, 202; positional economy and, 128–9; relational, 116, 131, 154n34, 154n36; social status and, 8–9, 107–8, 112–3, 116, 124–34, 138, 149, 150–1, 155n44; welfare, 140. See also *equalisandum*; equality; liberal egalitarianism
eliminativism, 108, 133, 136
elitism, 4
Elo rating system, 137
El Salvador, 247n59
Employee Stock Ownership Plan (ESOP), 82, 84
English (language): in Canada, 228–9, 261, 272, 276; in the United States, 277, 278, 282, 304n4. *See also* African-American Vernacular English (AAVE); Standard American English (SAE)
Enron corporation, 86–7
environment of evolutionary adaptation (EEA), 30, 42, 43, 58
envy-freeness, 139–40
equalisandum, 18, 139, 151
equality, 6, 134, 301; conceptions of, 19, 127, 139–40, 144, 147, 151, 152n5; gender, 221, 237; immigration and, 224, 233, 234–6, 241; institutionalization of, 130–1, 293–4; integration and, 271, 277, 295; liberalism and, 236–8, 240–1, 274; of living standards, 127, 129–30, 288; mutual recognition and, 136–8; of positional goods, 126–7; socialism and, 8, 15; social status and, 107, 108, 116, 119, 127–9, 146, 149. *See also* egalitarianism
Equal Protection Clause, 257

equity: capital, 76, 81; cushion, 76; vs debt, 69–70, 81, 103n32; holders, 72, 73, 84, 95; organizational form, 95; payment, 73
Ethics of Business, The (Gini and Marcoux), 98
Europe: civilization, 45; Europeans in North America, 35, 256, 258, 260–1, 274; social issues, 307n35; southern, 115, 205; states, 312n102
eusocial species, 12
evils of profit, 8, 66, 68
experiments in living, 45
explanatory inversions, 3–6, 7–8
extended mind, 182–3
extended will, 179, 182–3
externalities, 78, 97, 227

Falk, Gerhard, 165, 192
familism, 40–1
Farage, Nigel, 111
feminism, 135, 171
Ferguson (US), 311n98
First Nations, 258, 272, 276, 283, 285–6
First Nations Policing Program, 285
Fischel, Daniel, 72
Fisher, Mark, 134
Floyd, George, 288, 312n100
food stamps, 141, 226
foraging societies, 35, 40
Ford, Rob (Toronto Mayor), 198–9n61
Ford Motor Corporation, 71
Fortune 500 US business corporations, 128
Fourie, Carina, 116, 161n126
Fourteenth Amendment (US), 257
France: colony, 258, 311n94; corporatization, 89, 90; foreign policies, 281; government officials, 196n24; immigration and integration issues, 224, 229, 233, 248–9n70, 270, 278–9
Frank, Robert, 140
Frankfurt, Harry, 196n25
Fraser, Nancy, 137–8
freedom: of choice, 232; of movement, 203–4, 212; negative, 245n18; of the will, 165, 172–4, 184, 193, 196n29
free-riding, 17, 22, 32
French (language), 228–9, 231, 261, 270–1, 281–2, 310n81; Québécois, 281–2
French-Canadians, 228, 258, 261, 270–1, 275, 281
Fresh Prince of Bel Air, The (TV show) 309–10n69
Freud, Sigmund, 179; Freudian, 133
Fukuyama, Francis, 25, 40, 57, 159n102

game theory, 5, 27, 41
Garfinkel, Harold, 26
Gat, Azar, 40
Gellner, Ernest, 269–70
gerrymandering, 283
Gini, Al, 98
GINI coefficients, 129
Goffman, Erving, 136, 163, 164, 165–6
golf, 115, 157n72
Greenfield, Kent, 97
Grey, Freddie, 312n100
"groupishness," 113, 301
Guardian (UK), 250n87

Habermas, Jürgen, 56
Haidt, Johnathan, 62n39
Half-Breed (Campbell), 258
Hamilton, Charles, 280
Hansmann, Henry, 84

hard-hat regulations, 235
harm: Dalrymple on, 177; harmful actions and behaviours, 27, 28, 101n19, 164, 166–8, 175, 193, 227; inequality and, 130, 136, 290; Mill on, 168–70; perceptions of, 42; to self vs to others, 168, 177, 193
Harper, Stephen (Prime Minister, Canada), 196
Harvard (university), 116, 158n85
Hayek, Friedrich, 16
Hegel, G.W.F., 136–7; Hegelian, 108
heuristics, 42–3
hierarchies, 36–9, 44–5, 116; administrative, 56; dominance, 108–12, 113, 118, 137; early forms of, 40; informal, 107, 152n7, 158n87; organizational, 36; status (see status hierarchy); of values, 178
Hirsch, Fred, 121–3, 124, 126
Hispanic, 135, 256, 259, 305n10
Hobbes, Thomas, 5, 12, 30; left Hobbesian, 7
homosexuality, 135, 165, 166, 168, 169, 189
Honneth, Axel, 137
honour, 112, 124, 138
hospitals, 92, 93
Howard University, 280, 297
"How Criminologists Foster Crime" (Dalrymple), 178
Howe, C.D., 89
human psychology: adapted evolved and innate, 14, 26, 30, 33, 39–44, 47, 58–9, 113, 116, 133, 301; dominance disposition, 109–12, 133; limits to, 131, 174; pro-social dispositions, 12, 14, 33, 39; punitive dispositions, 32, 41–2; visual processing, 42, 43
Hume, David, 174
hunter-gatherers, 26, 29, 30–1, 35, 37

Hutterites, 241, 310n80
hyperbolic discounting model, 180–1, 187

identity politics, 137–8, 154–155n36
"'I'll Die for the Revolution, but Don't Ask Me Not to Diet': Feminism and the Continuing Stigmatization of Obesity" (Rothblum), 171
immigration: accommodations for, 200–1, 230–42, 255, 260, 284, 288; economic inequality and, 205–211; expectations of immigrants, 209, 211–2, 213, 216, 239, 273; integration and, 202, 212–3, 216–8, 230, 241–2, 253, 261, 277–9, 282, 294, 301; integration problems, 217, 218–21, 222, 232; level of, 200–2, 224–30, 242–3, 243–4n1, 307n35; liberalism and (see liberalism: on immigration and integration); open borders argument, 202–12, 222–3, 246n32; oppositions to, 229–30, 306n18; standard positions on, 202–4, 205, 242
Immigration and Nationality Act (US), 257
implicit bias, 266
incentives: in business context, 66, 67, 73, 77–8, 86, 93–4, 97, 99, 101n20; collective action problems and, 5, 214, 225; culture and, 220; extrinsic, 18, 21–2, 25, 32, 97, 214, 222 (see also sanctions); human dispositions and biases and, 112, 185; institutionalization and, 17–8; intrinsic, 18, 21, 32, 38, 99, 214, 222; perverse, 49; stigmatization as, 190, 193
India, 215–6, 220, 257

346   Index

Indian Act (Canada), 276
Indians: in Canada, 298; immigrants in UK, 173; in Singapore, 291, 294
Indians (Canada). See First Nations.
Indigenous groups (Canada), 272, 275, 276–7, 285, 292, 294. See also First Nations, Inuit, Métis
inequality: causes of, 8, 189, 294; economic, 128, 129, 131, 150, 154n34, 205; of health outcomes, 129–30; immigration and, 226, 231–2; income and wealth, 66, 129, 227; between majority and minority, 273, 276, 282–3, 293, 310n80; between nations, 205–10; natural, 147; positional good, 126; racial, 265–6, 267, 268, 283, 295; of social status, 9, 106–8, 113, 116, 117, 119, 129–30, 130–4, 136–8, 141, 143, 146–9, 150–1, 153n17, 154n36. See also equality
Inequality: What Can Be Done? (Atkinson), 131
information: and institutionalization 18, 50, 53; private, 20
in-group bias, 41, 113–4, 301–2
institutionalization: constrains and limitations, 6, 7, 8, 30, 45, 50, 54, 288; effects and purposes of, 4, 17, 96, 152n7; immigration and, 203, 232; of normative principles, 130–1, 138, 236, 240–1; toolkits and strategies for, 26, 32, 33, 44, 46, 49
institutions: corporate (*see* business organizational forms); development and progress, 21–2, 24–5, 37, 39, 45, 46, 48, 57f; functions and roles of, 164, 188, 193, 211, 214, 218, 225, 239–41, 266, 272–3, 289–91, 302; human dispositions and, 43, 109, 112; integration into, 212, 216, 217,

222–3, 230–1, 276–8, 280–5, 296, 303t, 310n80; large-scale, 36–8, 43, 48, 56, 243, 289; scalability profiles of 23f, 24f, 38f, 46f, 57f; small-scale, 37, 38, 58; social status and, 107, 108, 118, 130, 132, 135, 149; structure and arrangements, 14, 22, 28, 31, 35, 41, 43, 58, 210, 241, 268, 269–71, 272–4, 276, 289, 292–4, 295–7, 300, 301, 305n16, 309n66. See also market (economic system); solidary groups; states (as institutions); tribal chieftainship
insurance, 81; cooperatives, 75, 76; Dworkin's hypothetical insurance market, 139; health, 129, 240; industry, 81; worker's compensation, 235
intergenerational conflict, 83–4, 209
International Cooperative Alliance (ICA), 79
Internationale (song), 133
intraspecies violence, 13
Inuit, 40, 258
investor-owned firms, 68, 95, 97; vs cooperatives, 74–80; insurance, 76; vs state-owned enterprises (SOEs), 85–91
Islam, 38, 233
Islamic Institution for Civil Justice, 237
Italy, 216

Japan, 206, 225, 249; Japanese, 256
Jenner, Caitlyn, 135
Jensen, Michael, 87
Jews, 200, 233, 237, 261, 279
Jim Crow laws (US), 257, 264, 279
Jones, Prince, 312n100

Kahnawake Mohawk reserve (Canada), 272
Kant, Immanuel, 12

Kaufman, Herbert, 263
Kendi, Ibram X., 295, 308n43
kidnapper's argument, 227
King, Martin Luther, Jr., 303
kin-recognition, 44
Klein, Ezra, 228
Kojève, Alexandre, 136
Kukathas, Chandran, 237, 238, 241
!Kung band, 29
Kwanzaa, 279
Kymlicka, Will, 236; on integration, 255, 270–1, 274, 275, 277, 282, 285, 309n66; on minority groups, 244n2, 251n107, 271, 273

Laborde, Cécile, 233
labour productivity, 121, 125, 207, 208
Lander, Christian, 279
Latinx, 135, 159n95, 305n10
laws: business related, 71–2, 84, 86, 95, 210; compliance, 4, 97, 184, 198n52, 204, 215; emergence of, 36; enforcement of, 148–9, 202, 210, 214, 284, 287; and race relations, 257, 271, 282; and religion, 233–4, 237; role and function, 17, 45, 66, 86, 97, 148, 200, 202, 210, 240, 269, 284; and social status, 123, 149, 164
liberal democracies, 200, 237, 265
liberal egalitarianism, 7, 154n36, 189. *See also* egalitarianism
liberalism: conceptions and principles, 201, 202–3, 236–43 (*see also* neutrality: liberal); on discrimination, 135, 230, 264, 293; on immigration and integration, 173, 200, 202–4, 208, 223–4, 232–3, 236, 273, 282, 303, 310n78; norms in liberal society, 62n39; on stigmatization (*see* stigmatization: liberals on). *See also* liberal egalitarianism

Link, Bruce, 163
Lippert-Rasmussen, Kasper, 154n34
Lipsky, Michael, 263
Locke, John, 174
loyalties: in businesses, 77; in early societies 40, 47; particularistic, 38, 40, 215
Lucas, Robert, 127
luxury brand, 119

MacDonald, Scott, 196n23
Macedo, Stephen, 246
Malays, 291–2, 294
Mann, Michael, 36, 46
Mao, Zedong, 49
Marcoux, Alexei, 98
marginalization: causes of, 212, 217, 219, 222, 255, 272, 281, 283; consequences of, 219, 222, 224; marginalized groups, 137, 223
market (economic system): actors, 74, 94, 97; failure, 101n10, 240; invisible hand, 48, 54–6, 59; as mechanism for cooperation, 48, 54; principles and processes, 68, 74, 85, 86, 93, 94, 96, 97–100, 240; relations, 77, 78, 81
market (specific): "blue chip," 71; conditions, 75, 76, 81, 85; electricity, 86; global, 206; housing, 301; insurance, 76; labour, 83, 84, 204, 207–8, 217, 218, 279, 282; milk, 75–6; secondary, 82, 83; share price, 70; stock, 83
market socialism, 48, 68, 74, 94
Marmot, Michael, 129
marshmallow test, 189
Marx, Karl, 69, 125, 132, 136, 150; anti-Marxian, 115; Marxism, 135; Marxist definition of "profit," 56, 69, 103n32; Marxists, 136
materialism, 173

348 Index

Matza, David, 184
Mbuti band, 28
McCloskey, Deirdre, 58
Merkel, Angela (Chancellor, Germany), 212
Mesoamerican civilization, 45
Métis, 257–8, 260, 305n14
Mexico, 205, 206, 207–8, 246, 256
Microsoft Corporation, 71
Milgram, Stanley, 26
military: class, 45; conflicts, 37; leadership, 107; organization, 38, 63n61, 296; social status within, 113; strength, 37, 45
Mill, John Stuart, 16, 168–70, 175, 189; Millian, 190
Miller, David, 116, 242, 250n85
Mills, Charles, 268
minorities, 189, 251n107, 252; African-Americans (*see* African-Americans); cultural and religious, 166, 209, 227, 237, 242; ethnic, 166, 212, 233, 242, 244n2, 252, 253, 254, 270, 275; integration and inclusion of, 253, 278, 284–7, 289, 298–9, 301–2 (*see also* multinational integration model; polyethnic integration model); internal, 228, 270–1; membership, 261; national, 228, 244n2, 255, 258, 270–3, 275–7, 280–4, 288, 294, 297, 302; owned businesses, 72, 260; racial, 114, 256, 259, 265, 298–9, 312n100; sexual (*see* homosexuality); visible, 135, 253, 305n14
Mondragon cooperative network, 82
Moore, Margaret, 225
moral intuitions, 47, 58, 131
mortgage, 69, 84
motivation. *See* incentives
Movement for Black Lives, 287

MS-13 gang, 247n59
multiculturalism, 9, 10, 244n3; difficulties, 236, 242; effects of, 227; integration, 255, 303t (*see also* multinational integration model; polyethnic integration model); policies, 251n107, 273, 275, 288, 291, 292, 302; reactions to, 203
multinational integration model, 255, 270–2, 275–6, 277, 285, 301–4
Munchausen syndrome, 192
Muslims, 224, 231, 233, 237, 248–9n70, 279
Muslim World League, 237, 238
mutual recognition model, 136–8, 159n102. *See also* status model
Myrdal, Gunnar, 255

Nagle, Angela, 135
Nationalised Industries: A Review of Financial and Economic Objectives (UK), 89
nationalism, 113, 132, 133; black, 264, 277, 281, 287, 310n78; ethnic, 275; minority, 277, 281, 303t
natural resources, 205–6, 208, 211
Netherlands, 206
Nett, Roger, 204
neutrality: legal, 95; liberal, 238–9, 240, 241–2, 273–4; moral, 163; process, 255, 291, 293–5, 299–300; religious, 285; state, 232
neutralizations (of norms), 184–5, 186, 188
New France, 231, 271
Newton, Isaac, 3
New York City (US), 220, 313n110
"New York parking ticket" study, 220
New York Times, 279–80, 314n125
New York Times Corporation, 72

Nile delta, 36
non-fungibility, 117–9, 139–40
non-governmental organizations (NGOs), 92
non-profit organizations, 67, 74, 92–4, 95, 97, 219
Nora report (France), 89–90
normativland, 17, 25
norms, 175; business, 77, 99, 101n10; changes to, 202, 217, 221, 223, 230–7; conflicting, 237; conformity to, 18, 28, 35, 47, 112, 216, 219; enforcement of, 18, 26–8, 33–4, 41, 167, 214, 215, 225; informal, 15–6, 26, 47–8; institutions and, 47, 50; liberal, 236, 237, 241, 242; social, 26, 34, 138, 167, 184, 265, 268–9; violations, 27, 28, 30, 42, 167–8, 174, 183–4, 186, 188
North, Douglass, 57
Norway, 210
Nozick, Robert, 133
Nussbaum, Martha, 194n4, 238

Obama, Barack (US President), 306n30
O'Barr, William, 148
obesity: causes of, 171–2, 174; and harm 168, 169, 175; and self-control, 170, 189–90
obsessive-compulsive disorder (OCD), 179
"Okun's leaky bucket," 155n45
onboard resources, 185; cognitive, 14, 30, 50, 58–9, 182; motivational, 190; psychological, 183; volitional, 187, 189
online communities, 144–5. See also Reddit
Ontario (Canada), 233, 237, 258, 292
open access order, 57–8, 57f, 309n55

optimism bias, 142–3, 146
organizational objectives, 67, 68, 70–3, 86–7, 93; multiple, 88; profit as (see profit: as organizational objective); social, 88–9, 91.
ostracism, 27, 117, 187
overcapitalization, 88, 93
Oxford University, 132

Pareto: efficiency, 101n10, 240; improvement, 58, 101n10
Parsons, Talcott, 134, 191
paternalism, 168–9, 190, 221, 235
pathology: bureaucratic, 93, 96, 263; psychopathology, 179, 192; social, 121, 178, 180, 188, 193
patriarchy, 120, 221
pecking order, 109
Peller, Gary, 303
Pettit, Philip, 112, 155n38
Pevnick, Ryan, 225
Phelan, Jo, 163
physical attractiveness, 106, 133, 145, 152n6
Pickett, Kate, 100n9, 130
Pigou-Dalton transfer principle, 129
Pinker, Steven, 62n46
Plato, 12
pluralism: cultural, 226, 242, 270–3, 284, 308–9n50; ethnic, 200, 257, 268, 274; institutional, 270, 301; Kymlicka on, 255, 270–1, 273, 274; and liberalism, 223, 237, 241–3; multinational, 271, 272, 277, 301; in social ranking, 143–4
police: discretion, 149, 284, 290; expenditure, 88, 312n102; law enforcement, 148, 214, 227; minorities and, 219, 256, 274, 285–8, 312n100; social role of, 20, 284–5; violence, 265

policy intervention. *See* social intervention.
political correctness, 134, 166
polyethnic integration model, 274, 291; African-Americans and, 277; vs multinational model, 255, 275–6, 285, 301–4
polygyny, 120
Ponapaens of Micronesia, 124
population viscosity, 142
positional economy, 121–4, 127–8
positional goods, 121–4, 126, 157n72
poverty, 114, 127; global, 66; immigrant, 205, 221; in the UK, 173, 176; in underdeveloped countries, 211; in the United States, 126–7
prestige economy, 124–5
price system, 53, 68, 74, 85, 94, 101n10
priests, 45
primates, 12, 108–9, 111–2
primitive economy, 26
principle of community, 47–51
principles of justice: approach to, 17; equality (*see* equality); liberal, 239, 240–1, 242; Rawls on, 147
Prisoner's Dilemma, 5
privatizations, 67, 91, 100n7
profit: definitions of, 56, 68–9, 71, 72, 76, 81, 98, 103n32; disbursements and retainment of, 67, 70–1, 75, 76, 81, 83, 85, 92, 96; earning of, 73, 76, 87, 89, 93; maximization of, 66–8, 80, 86, 94, 98, 99; as organizational objective, 8, 66–8, 70, 71–4, 77, 80, 85–7, 90–1, 94, 96–8, 100, 100n7; as standard of measure, 70, 87, 88
profit-oriented firms, 66, 67, 73, 97, 100; vs non-profit organizations, 92–4
public corporation, 75

public goods, 5, 96, 215, 219
public ownership. *See* state-owned enterprises (SOEs)
public shaming, 27
Puerto Rico, 277
punishments: costly, 27, 32; effectiveness of, 29, 31, 187–8; enforcement of 28, 32, 33–4, 35–6, 41–2, 214; exemptions from, 34, 269; justifications for, 168; as motivation, 18, 21; self-binding, 185, 187, 190; stigmatization as, 165, 175, 176–8; symbolic, 27–8, 29, 31; zero-tolerance, 41–2. *See also* incentives; sanctions; withdrawal of cooperation

Quebec (Canada): history, 258, 271; as national minority, 228–9, 261–2, 270–2, 275, 276, 277; policies in, 244n3, 249n84, 281, 311n94

racism: attitudinal, 264–7, 300, 301, 302; definitions of, 266–7, 295, 308n43; immigration and, 212–3, 222, 225, 226–7, 229–30; on social media, 135; social status and, 113–4, 116, 134, 149, 165–6, 173; stigma and, 165–6; structural, 296, 301; in the United States, 254, 264–8, 286–7, 297, 300–1, 307n36, 308n44, 313n111
Rawls, John, 17, 118, 130, 143, 146, 238; *Theory of Justice, A*, 7, 158n85, 239, 268
real estate, 122, 298, 299; investment trusts, 94
recidivism, 167
reciprocity, 12, 25, 47–51, 51–5; indirect, 31; strict, 52; strong, 27, 32; weak, 27, 52
Reddit, 144

Index   351

redistribution, 6; under central authority, 47; distributive justice and (*see* distributive justice); of income and wealth, 100–1n9, 119, 127; positional economy and, 127–30, 160n118; social status and, 108, 117, 118, 126, 132, 140
Red Pheasant reserve (Canada), 272
Red River Valley (Canada), 258
refugees, 212, 247n54, 309n54
REI Co-op (US outdoor leisure retailer), 76
rent seeking, 86
residential integration, 261, 297–301
residual claim (on earnings): homeowner, 69; in cooperatives, 75, 76, 79, 81, 82, 83, 85; the lack of, 92; in non-profit organizations, 93
residuum, 68, 76, 81, 92, 130n32
retained earnings, 72, 83
reverse dominance hierarchy, 109
Richerson, Peter, 14, 39, 44
Ridgeway, Cecilia, 149, 153n17
Riel Louis, 305n14
risk premium, 81
rituals, 33, 109, 110, 134, 273
Roberts, John (US Supreme Court Chief Justice), 313n111
Rochdale principles, 79
Rodrik, Dani, 211
Ronzoni, Miriam, 60n16
Rosenblum, Nancy, 237
Rothblum, Esther, 171, 189
Rousseau, Jean-Jacques, 17
Royal Canadian Mounted Police (RCMP), 285, 311n94
rural communities, 144, 230, 272, 285

Samuelson, Paul, 209
sanctions, 21; enforcement of, 34; informal and social, 26, 29, 192, 284; justifications for, 169, 171, 174–5, 177; as self-control, 185, 187; in small groups, 27–9; as social control, 18, 23, 25, 167; symbolic, 27–9. *See also* punishments
Saskatchewan (Canada), 258, 272
savings, 55
scaffolding: "scaffolded autonomy," 187; social, 164, 183, 188, 190; stigmatization as, 187; volitional, 192
scalability: of computer systems, 13; limitations, 17, 31–2, 33; profiles, 23, 23f, 24f, 37, 38f, 46f, 57f; of systems of cooperation, 13–4, 22–4, 56–9
Scanlon, T.M., 116
Schelling, Thomas, 5, 299
Seattle (US), 288
sedentary societies, 35
self-control: effective, 183, 185–6, 192; failure, 169, 170, 177, 179, 183–5, 185–90, 190–1, 193; nature of, 9, 181–2; stigmatization and, 9, 164, 185–90
self-esteem: definitions of, 112, 152n5, 155n38, 155n43; social status and, 106, 107, 138, 143; recognition and, 136
self-respect, 108, 118–9, 152n5, 155n41, 155n43
Sen, Amartya, 158n85
serotonin, 111
Shachar, Ayelet, 205
shareholder value, 68, 71, 72, 74, 96
sharia courts, 236–7
Shelby, Tommie, 300, 308n43
sick role, 191–3
signalling (of status), non-physical forms of, 124, 132, 134, 141, 149–50, 158n85; online, 144; physical forms of, 110, 111
Sikhs, 218, 234–5, 285

Singapore, 232, 255, 288, 291–2, 294
Singer, Peter, 62n46
situationism, 174
slavery, 268; history of, 252, 256, 277; laws and policies on, 257, 259, 278
Smith, Adam, 48, 54, 73, 116
smoking, 170, 175, 188
SNCF (Société nationale des chemins de fer français, French national railway operator), 90
social capital, 23, 209, 220–1, 226, 231
social censure, 167, 168, 169, 189, 193
social collapse, 39, 46
social control, 192, 286, 295; informal mechanisms of, 25; in small groups, 25–9, 31–2; stigmatization as, 167
social housing, 119, 141, 224
social intervention, 117, 119, 121, 132–3, 190, 218
socialism, 8, 16; Cohen on, 15, 21–2, 48–51, 58, 59, 132; on cooperatives, 82; feasibility of, 14; objections to, 16; utopian, 47, 58
socialization, 18; failures of 217; limitations, 21, 23; social structure and, 36, 133, 222, 243
Social Limits to Growth, The (Hirsch), 121
social media, 134–5, 145–6, 180
social ranking: health and, 129–30; online, 145; physiological effects on, 111; social equality and, 107, 112–3, 116, 127–30, 157n72, 160n118; systems of, 106, 109–10, 113, 118, 120, 142, 143, 153n19
social welfare, 120, 124
social status. *See* socioeconomic status (SES)
socioeconomic status (SES), 106, 156n56; assessment of, 130; comparisons and differences, 114–7, 119, 123, 132, 140–1, 166; competition (*see* competition: status); consumption and, 124–6; Fraser on, 138; high-SES, 107, 115, 117, 123, 134, 148, 149; injury, 114, 118, 134, 151, 300; low-SES, 107, 111, 114, 115, 121, 132, 139, 140, 141, 173, 176–7; multidimensional basis, 137, 141–3; mutual recognition and, 136–8; non-fungibility of, 117–9; as positional goods, 121–4; stigmatization and, 164, 167–8, 190, 194n5. *See also* equality: social status and; inequality: of social status
sociology, 149, 163, 172, 196n24, 230; microsociology, 25
solidary groups, 25–33; developments of, 37; and human psychology, 39, 58; norms, 47; reciprocity in, 47–8; vs tribal chieftainships, 35–6
Solow growth model, 207
South Africa, 259, 291, 311n88
Soviet Union, 16
Spain, 253
Spanish (language), 228–9
speed limit, 234
Spirit Level, The (Wilkinson and Pickett), 130
Sreenivasan, Gopal, 129
SSRIs (selective serotonin reuptake inhibitors), 111
Stalin, Joseph, 49
Standard American English (SAE), 278, 281–2
standard business corporations, 67, 72, 74; vs cooperatives, 77, 79, 81–5, 99; vs non-profit organizations, 93; vs SOEs, 91
Stanovich, Keith, 58
state-owned enterprises (SOEs), 67, 74, 85–91, 271; reforms of 88–9; self-financing, 88

states (as institutions), 36, 56, 57;
  actors and officials, 218, 219, 284;
  authority and role, 169, 201, 202–4,
  206, 215, 219, 240–1; formation
  of, 37, 40, 45, 206; policies on
  immigration and integration, 201,
  202–3, 222–3, 231–3, 217–8, 224,
  255, 270–1; policies on social status,
  117, 136, 140–1; structures, 40, 44,
  120, 269; territory, 203, 206
status hierarchy: difficulties for
  egalitarianism, 114, 116, 121,
  124–31; egalitarian movements and,
  107–8, 113–4; eliminating, 132–3;
  equality and, 116, 138, 140; global
  vs local, 142–5; human dispositions
  and, 111–2, 118; insulation and, 146;
  mutual recognition and, 136–8;
  neutralization of, 143–4
status model, 137–8. *See also* mutual
  recognition model
sterile castes, 40
Stiglitz, Joseph, 78
Stigma (Goffman), 163
stigmatization: achieved vs
  existential, 164, 165–6, 169–71,
  172–3, 192–3; conservative views
  on, 175, 176–9; definitions of, 164,
  194n5; effects of, 165, 171; of illness,
  192; liberals on, 170–5, 178–9, 188;
  as punishment, 165, 166–9, 214,
  215; racism and, 265; self-control
  and, 9, 164, 170, 185–90, 193; and
  social status, 114, 117, 118–9, 165;
  standard views on, 163–4, 194n3,
  194n4; vocabulary, 166, 195n10,
  196n23. *See also* de-stigmatization
stock options, 73, 101n20
Stout, Lynn, 71
Strawson, Peter, 174
stuck file, 253, 262–4, 267, 277, 288
Stuff White People Like (Lander), 279

Subramanian, Arvind, 211
sufficientarianism, 126, 138
Supplemental Nutrition Assistance
  Program (SNAP), 141
Supreme Court (US), 312n106,
  313n111
Sûreté du Québec, 285
Swift, Adam, 128, 157n72
Sykes, Gresham, 184
symbolic marking, 44
systems of cooperation:
  egalitarianism and, 148;
  intergenerational, 210; large-scale,
  7, 8, 13, 43, 46, 58–9 (*see also under*
  institutions); market economy
  as, 10, 48, 56–8; principles and
  conditions, 6–7, 12, 148, 239,
  242–3; scalability of, 13–4, 22–4;
  successful, 211–2, 213–6, 239, 242

Tainter, Joseph, 39
taxation: compliance, 210, 220;
  deductions and reductions, 71, 96;
  effect on market, 54, 210; equality
  and, 127–8, 155n44, 293; predatory,
  214; race-based, 300, 313n113
taxi industry, 75, 77, 78, 80
Taylor, Charles, 137
terrorism, 196n24, 203, 218, 253
theory of criminality, 186
Theory of Justice, A (Rawls), 7, 158n85,
  239, 268
Theory of the Leisure Class, The
  (Veblen), 115
theory of mind, 12
tit-for-tat retaliation, 13
Tomasi, John, 58
Toronto (Canada), 198n61, 225, 227,
  247n54
totalitarianism, 50
Trans-Canada Airlines (subsequently,
  Air Canada), 89–90

Treaty of Guadalupe Hidalgo (1848), 256
Trebbi, Francesco, 211
tribal chieftainships, 35, 39, 152n7; developments of, 37; limitations, 36; reciprocity in, 47; vs solidary groups, 35–7; vs states, 36
tribal marking, 44
tribal social instincts, 14
tribal societies, 35, 44, 45
Trudeau, Pierre, 90
Trump, Donald (US President), 111, 264
Turiel, Elliot, 175
Turnball, Colin, 28
Tuvel affair, 159n95
/Twi (member of !Kung band), 29
Twitter, 159n95

ultrasocial species, 48
Ulysses, 182
undifferentiated citizenship, 136
undominated diversity, 108, 143–4, 146
uniforms (school), 133
United Kingdom (UK): civil servants, 129; criminals, 198; entities, 73, 75, 129; in foreign territories, 231, 257–8, 271, 291, 311n88, 311n94; immigration and integration, 173, 253; politicians, 111; public policies, 89; social class, 148, 158n91, 176, 178
United Nations, 220
United States (US): business and private entities, 45, 128, 152n4, 205, 207–8; government and public entities, 65, 71, 92, 93, 256–7, 263, 312n106; laws regulations and policies, 71, 72, 141, 228–9, 247n54, 310n78, 312n102, 313n113; politics, 120, 154–5n36, 295–6, 304n4, 306n17–18; prison system, 247n59, 290; race relations, 10, 113, 166, 194n3, 252–7, 259–62, 264–8, 275, 277–84, 286–8, 291, 294–304, 305n10, 305n16, 307nn35–7, 308n44, 309n66; social issues, 121, 126, 168, 226, 246; territories, 206, 256, 257
universalistic ideology, 38, 41
universities, 92–3, 94, 155n44, 271; campus, 115; donations, 118; minorities and, 260, 292, 295, 297, 305n16; professors, 114–5, 142, 160–1n125. See also Harvard (university); Howard University; Oxford University
"unsocial sociability," 12, 14, 33, 39, 59
U.S. Federal Government Census, 256–7
utilitarian approach, 18, 188
utopia: egalitarian, 125; experiments, 133; failures, 45; socialism, 47, 58; utopian views, 7, 17, 203

Valls, Francois (Prime Minister, France), 196n24
Van Parijs, Philippe, 143
Vancouver (Canada), 225, 227
Veblen, Thorstein, 115–6, 120, 121, 124–6, 141, 153n21
Venezuela, 210
Vietnamese: Americans, 259; refugee, 247n54
virtue theory, 112, 177
Vision for Black Lives, 287
Volkswagen, 99
voting rights: in business enterprises, 79–80

Wallis, John, 57
Walmart, 106, 152n4
Walrasian auction, 54

Walzer, Michael, 232, 156n56, 244n12
warfare, 13, 35, 45
watching eyes effect, 42
weakness of will, 179, 180–2, 186, 190
Weber, Max, 113, 115, 138, 240; Weberian, 137–8
Weingast, Barry, 57
welfare policies, 118
welfare states: policies, 67, 95, 118, 271; principles, 240; structure, 57, 226, 271, 312n102
welfarism, 147
white collar crime, 99, 168, 184
Whitehall study (Marmot), 129
Wilkinson, Richard, 100n9, 130
Will (TV character), 309–10n69
Wilson, James Q., 263, 267, 303

withdrawal of cooperation, 27, 28, 31, 32
Why Does Inequality Matter? (Scanlon), 116
Why Not Socialism? (Cohen), 14–25, 131
"Why We Should Stop Teaching *Dodge v. Ford*" (Stout), 71
woke culture, 134
World Bank, 210

yams, 124
Yeager, Peter, 99

zero-sum interactions, 112, 117, 119–21, 122, 135
Zurn, Christopher, 138

www.ingramcontent.com/pod-product-compliance
Lightning Source LLC
Chambersburg PA
CBHW020240030426
42336CB00010B/556